W9-CCZ-497

Taste *of* Home®
ALL-TIME
BEST RECIPES

TASTE OF HOME BOOKS • RDA ENTHUSIAST BRANDS, LLC • MILWAUKEE, WI

TASTE OF HOME
TEST
KITCHEN
RECIPE OF THE YEAR
★ ★ ★ ★ ★

Taste *of* Home
ALL-TIME
BEST RECIPES

FAVORITE RECIPES FROM OUR KITCHEN TO YOURS

Taste of Home®

©2021 RDA Enthusiast Brands, LLC. 1610 N. 2nd St., Suite 102 Milwaukee, WI 53212-3906
All rights reserved. Taste of Home is a registered trademark of RDA Enthusiast Brands, LLC.
Visit us at tasteofhome.com for other Taste of Home books and products.

Trade ISBN: 978-1-62145-700-8
DTC ISBN: 978-1-62145-707-7
Trade Component Number: 115702753S
DTC Component Number: 115800580S
LOCC: 2021931569

Executive Editor: Mark Hagen
Senior Art Director: Raeann Thompson
Designer: Arielle Anttonen
Deputy Editor, Copy Desk: Dulcie Shoener
Copy Editor: Amy Rabideau Silvers

Cover
Photographer: Mark Derse
Food Stylist: Shannon Norris
Set Stylist: Stephanie Marchese

Pictured on front cover:
That Good Salad, p. 97
Raspberry Swirl Cheesecake Pie, p. 314
Garlic Herbed Beef Tenderloin, p. 179
Best Ever Crescent Rolls, p. 82

Pictured on spine:
Crunchy Chili Cilantro Lime Roasted Shrimp, p. 134

Pictured on title page:
Loaded Huevos Rancheros with Roasted Poblano Peppers, p. 68

Pictured on back cover:
Buffalo Wing Enchiladas, p. 156
Oreo Cupcakes with Cookies & Cream Frosting, p. 289
Curry-Rubbed Roast Chicken, p. 171
Green Onion Rolls, p. 77
Key Lime Blondie Bars, p. 248
Frozen Brandy Old-Fashioneds, p. 37

Printed in USA
1 3 5 7 9 10 8 6 4 2

More ways to connect with us:

Welcome to Our Kitchen

Let me take a quick moment to introduce myself. I'm Sarah, and I'm the executive culinary director at *Taste of Home*. Over the years, I've developed, tested and tasted thousand of recipes in our Test Kitchen, so it's probably no surprise that I have hundreds of favorites. That's why I was excited to share my most-loved dishes in *Taste of Home All-Time Best Recipes*.

Inside, you'll discover 417 recipes the staff and I believe are tops. These are the weeknight dishes we serve our own families, add to holiday menus and prepare when friends visit. We truly believe they'll be hits in your home, too.

My most-used recipes are those that fall in the "comfort" zone—warm, cozy and hearty. Nearest and dearest to my heart is The Best Ever Chili on page 13. I developed this recipe using fresh chili powder I brought back from my honeymoon in Santa Fe. It's rich and beefy with layers of savory flavors that add depth and dimension.

DISHING WITH

Sarah Farmer
Taste of Home
Executive Culinary Director

Our Test Kitchen team members rave about their personal faves as well. Some of these recipes were created by our staff, but most were shared by home cooks across the country. We even added the top contenders from our Recipe of the Year contest, including the grand prizewinner, Loaded Huevos Rancheros with Roasted Poblano Peppers, found on page 68. We've marked these extra-special recipes to help you find our best-of-the-best.

TASTE OF HOME TEST KITCHEN RECIPE OF THE YEAR

What other types of recipes do we crave most? We all cherish luscious desserts along with all the gooey, cheesy classics *Taste of Home* is famous for. But we also love fresh, healthy, and quick and easy dishes as well as recipes that are global-inspired. You'll find all of these must-try delights and more in *All-Time Best Recipes*.

Whether it's meaty or meatless, decadent or dairy-free, air-fried or country-fried, our Test Kitchen touches all kinds of fantastic recipes that feed the soul, connect us to family and friends, and make us smile! I just know you'll find several new favorites in this exciting collection, resulting in smiles all around your kitchen table.

Happy cooking,

Take a Peek Inside Our Test Kitchen

Family cooks sharing their all-time best recipes—that's long been the hallmark of *Taste of Home.* And while we couldn't do what we do without these gracious home cooks, it's our Test Kitchen team that makes sure each recipe we share will turn out perfect. Here's a peek into some of what goes on behind the scenes.

What kind of education or professional credentials do the Taste of Home *Test Kitchen staffers have?*

Our Test Kitchen professionals are trained and trusted experts. We have earned degrees in varied fields that relate to food or publishing: food science, culinary arts, nutrition and wellness, art and design, and dietetics. We have more than 200 years of combined professional culinary experience.

What do you look for in new recipes submissions?

We embrace recipes that have a little something extra to offer—a classic recipe with a new flavor spin, for example, or something slightly different from what is already in our extensive collection. The recipe must also have easy-to-follow instructions.

What three ingredients does the kitchen use most?

We have 229,000 recipes in our database from all kinds of cooking styles and cuisines. Our top-rated recipes are consistently down-home comfort dishes that warm the soul. It's no surprise that cheese, with a total of 13,000 ounces, takes the lead as the most-used ingredient in the past year. Flour weighs in at 7,200 pounds. Butter is right up there with 382 pounds. We also use mass quantities of milk, eggs, olive oil and everyone's favorite ingredient—bacon!

What about all the groceries?

Over the course of a year, we process more than 400 grocery orders and prep 24,000 ingredients. Our grocery inventory, ordering and shopping process is significant and requires hours of dedicated work each week from Test Kitchen team members. We rely on our recipe management database to help. This remarkable tool keeps multiple grocery lists organized, collating every ingredient for every recipe scheduled for testing, photography or video, by grocery departments like fresh produce, meats, staples, canned and packaged, dairy, deli, frozen, etc.

From there, our prep kitchen team produces shoppable lists and schedules them on different shopping days. (We don't want to buy perishable produce on Monday if it's not needed until Friday.) Some orders are placed online through a local grocery store that makes weekly deliveries. Others are picked up at stores throughout the week by our prep kitchen staff. We even have a shopping van with our *Taste of Home* logo on it!

Who washes all the dishes?

In the blink of an eye, towering stacks of dirty dishes pile up in the Test Kitchen, prep kitchens and even our photo studio. We are so thankful to have a team of two fabulous full-time employees responsible for keeping our pots, pans, measuring cups and all sorts of cooking tools and equipment cleaned and organized. The dishwashers loop around the kitchens and studios throughout the day, loading up their carts with bins of dirty dishes for cleaning at the wash station. We couldn't keep up the pace without them!

CONTENTS

ALL-TIME BEST

THE BEST EVER CHILI
PAGE 13

ALL-TIME BEST

Staff Favorites

At *Taste of Home*, we're all about authentic family-pleasing meals. Here are some of our very own recipes—the dishes we've tasted, tested and perfected in our own home kitchens. Whether you're feeding a crowd or just your own hungry crew, dig in to these staff creations that we think truly capture the essence of home cooking.

MEXICAN STREET
CORN CHOWDER

DISHING WITH

Rashanda Cobbins
Food Editor

Summer corn is one of my favorite vegetables, so when it's in season I make this easy soup in the slow cooker.

MEXICAN STREET CORN CHOWDER
—Rashanda Cobbins, Food Editor

- -

Prep: 35 min. • **Cook:** 3½ hrs.
Makes: 8 servings (2¼ qt.)

- 10 ears fresh corn (about 5½ cups)
- 1¼ to 2 cups water
- 6 bacon strips, chopped
- 2 small onions, chopped
- 2 small green peppers, chopped
- 1 jalapeno pepper, seeded and finely chopped
- 1 tsp. ground chipotle pepper
- 2 tsp. salt
- ¾ tsp. ground cumin
- ¼ tsp. pepper
- 1 cup heavy whipping cream
- 1 medium lime, zested and juiced
  Optional: Fresh cilantro, lime wedges, sliced jalapeno, chopped bell pepper and crumbled cotija cheese

1. Cut corn off cobs. Rub the edge of a knife over each cob to "milk" it; add enough water to cob juice to equal 2 cups. Add corn and liquid to a 5-qt. slow cooker.
2. In a large skillet, cook bacon over medium heat until crisp, 5-7 minutes. Remove with a slotted spoon; drain bacon on paper towels. Discard drippings, reserving 2 Tbsp. in pan. Add the onion, green pepper and jalapeno to skillet; cook and stir over medium-high heat until soft, 3-4 minutes. Add seasonings and cook 1 minute more; transfer to slow cooker. Cook on low 3½-4 hours, until corn is tender and mixture has thickened slightly.
3. Stir in cream and lime zest and juice. Puree mixture with an immersion blender to desired consistency. Garnish with reserved bacon. If desired, top with cilantro and serve with lime wedges, jalapeno, bell pepper and cojita cheese.
1 cup: 287 cal., 18g fat (9g sat. fat), 43mg chol., 743mg sod., 29g carb. (10g sugars, 4g fiber), 8g pro.

SLOW-COOKER DOUGHNUT BREAKFAST BAKE

This extravagant dish will be the star of the brunch table. Try serving it with sausage, fresh berries and yogurt.
—Rashanda Cobbins, Food Editor

- -

Prep: 15 min. • **Cook:** 4 hours + standing
Makes: 12 servings

24   cake doughnuts, cut into bite-sized pieces
2   apples, peeled and chopped
1   cup heavy whipping cream
4   large eggs
1   Tbsp. vanilla extract
½   cup packed brown sugar
1   tsp. ground cinnamon
     Optional: Whipped cream and fresh berries

1. Line inside of 5-qt. slow cooker with a double layer of heavy duty foil; spray insert and foil with cooking spray. Layer half the doughnut pieces in slow cooker; top with half the apples. Repeat with remaining doughnuts and apples. In large bowl, whisk together cream, eggs and vanilla; pour over doughnut pieces and apples. In a small bowl, mix the brown sugar and cinnamon; sprinkle over doughnut mixture.
2. Cook, covered, on low 4-5 hours or until set. Remove insert. Let stand, uncovered, for 20 minutes. If desired, serve with whipped cream and fresh berries.
1 serving: 609 cal., 36g fat (17g sat. fat), 95mg chol., 547mg sod., 64g carb. (32g sugars, 2g fiber), 8g pro.

TEST KITCHEN TIP
This recipe is similar to bread pudding, but has an even more sticky and rich consistency.

PORK & CHEESY MACARONI SLIDERS

PORK & CHEESY MACARONI SLIDERS

I love sliders! This sweet and savory recipe was created out of leftover ingredients that I had in my fridge. They're perfect for both weeknight meals and special occasions.
—Rashanda Cobbins, Food Editor

- -

Prep: 30 min. • **Bake:** 10 min.
Makes: 12 servings

1   cup uncooked cavatappi pasta
1   Tbsp. butter
1½   tsp. all-purpose flour
¼   tsp. pepper
½   cup 2% milk
¾   cup shredded sharp cheddar cheese
1   pkg. (18 oz.) Hawaiian sweet rolls
1   carton (16 oz.) refrigerated fully cooked barbecue shredded pork, warmed
2   Tbsp. melted butter
1   Tbsp. honey
½   tsp. ground mustard
1   jalapeno pepper, sliced, optional

1. Preheat oven to 375°. Cook the pasta according to package directions.
2. Meanwhile, in a small saucepan, melt butter over medium heat. Stir in flour and pepper until smooth; gradually whisk in milk. Bring to a boil, stirring constantly; cook and stir until thickened, 3-5 minutes. Stir in the cheese until melted. Drain pasta; stir into cheese sauce. Set aside.
3. Place roll bottoms in a greased 13x9-in. baking dish. Layer with pork, pasta mixture and roll tops. Combine melted butter, honey and mustard. Brush over roll tops.
4. Bake until tops are golden brown and filling is hot, 10-12 minutes. If desired, top with jalapeno pepper slices.
1 slider: 305 cal., 10g fat (6g sat. fat), 48mg chol., 466mg sod., 39g carb. (17g sugars, 2g fiber), 14g pro.

CRUNCHY HONEY-GLAZED BUTTERNUT SQUASH

I'm now required to bring this to every family gathering during the holidays because it's so awesome!
—Sarah Farmer, Executive Culinary Director

- -

Prep: 20 min. • **Bake:** 45 min.
Makes: 10 servings

- ½ cup honey
- 1 tsp. dried thyme, divided
- 1 large butternut squash (about 5 lbs.), peeled, halved, seeded and thinly sliced
- 3 Tbsp. water
- ¼ cup plus 2 Tbsp. olive oil, divided
- 1½ tsp. salt, divided
- 1½ tsp. pepper, divided
- ½ cup panko bread crumbs

1. Preheat oven to 375°. In a large saucepan, heat the honey and ½ tsp. thyme, stirring occasionally, over low heat until fragrant, 3-4 minutes.

2. Meanwhile, in a large microwave-safe dish, combine the squash and water; microwave, covered, on high until the squash is tender, 6-8 minutes. Drain. Add ¼ cup olive oil, 1 tsp. salt and 1 tsp. pepper; toss to coat.

3. On a flat surface, stack the squash slices. Arrange stacks on their sides in a greased 9-in. square baking dish. (To make stacking easier, set baking dish on end; fill with squash stacks as seen on page 8. When the dish is full, return to original position.) Drizzle 3 Tbsp. honey mixture over the squash.

4. Bake until squash is tender, 45-50 minutes. In a small skillet, heat the remaining oil over medium heat. Add bread crumbs; toss with remaining thyme and remaining salt and pepper. Cook and stir until golden brown, about 5 minutes. Sprinkle over the baked squash; if desired, drizzle with additional honey mixture.

1 serving: 237 cal., 8g fat (1g sat. fat), 0 chol., 373mg sod., 43g carb. (20g sugars, 8g fiber), 3g pro.

CRUNCHY HONEY-GLAZED BUTTERNUT SQUASH

EASY CHOCOLATE SOUFFLES

Try these simple souffles for your next dinner party. The miniature servings have a maximum portion of deliciousness.
—Sarah Farmer, Executive Culinary Director

- -

Prep: 20 min. • **Bake:** 15 min.
Makes: 6 servings

- 4 large eggs
- 6 tsp. plus 1 Tbsp. sugar, divided
- 1 cup light corn syrup
- ½ cup baking cocoa
- 1 tsp. vanilla extract
  Confectioners' sugar

1. Separate the eggs; let stand at room temperature for 30 minutes. Coat six 6-oz. souffle dishes with cooking spray. Sprinkle 1 tsp. of sugar into each dish, tilting to cover the bottom and sides; set aside.

2. Preheat oven to 375°. In a large bowl, whisk corn syrup, cocoa, egg yolks and vanilla until blended; set aside. In a large bowl with clean beaters, beat egg whites on medium speed until soft peaks form. Gradually beat in remaining sugar on high until stiff peaks form. Gently fold a fourth of the egg white mixture into chocolate mixture; fold in remaining egg white mixture.

3. Spoon batter into prepared dishes. Bake 15-20 minutes or until a toothpick inserted in the center comes out clean. Dust with confectioners' sugar. Serve warm.

1 serving: 250 cal., 4g fat (1g sat. fat), 142mg chol., 108mg sod., 53g carb. (34g sugars, 1g fiber), 5g pro.

THE BEST EVER CHILI
—Sarah Farmer, Executive Culinary Director

Prep: 20 min. • **Cook:** 1 hour 20 min.
Makes: 8 servings

- 3 dried ancho or guajillo chiles
- 1 to 2 cups boiling water
- 2 Tbsp. tomato paste
- 3 garlic cloves
- ¼ cup chili powder
- 1½ tsp. smoked paprika
- 2 tsp. ground cumin
- 1 lb. ground beef
- 1½ tsp. Montreal steak seasoning
- 2 lbs. beef tri-tip roast, cut into ½-in. cubes
- 2 tsp. salt, divided
- 2 tsp. coarsely ground pepper, divided
- 2 Tbsp. canola oil, divided
- 1 large onion, chopped (about 2 cups)
- 1 poblano pepper, seeded and chopped
- 1 tsp. dried oregano
- 1½ tsp. crushed red pepper flakes
- 3 cups beef stock
- 1 bottle (12 oz.) beer
- 2 cans (14½ oz. each) fire-roasted diced tomatoes, undrained
- 1 can (16 oz.) kidney beans, drained
- 3 Tbsp. masa harina
  Optional: American cheese slices, sour cream, shredded cheddar cheese, diced red onion and corn chips

1. Combine the chiles and enough boiling water to cover; let stand until chiles are softened, about 15 minutes. Drain, reserving ⅓ cup of the soaking liquid. Discard the stems and seeds. Process the chiles, tomato paste, garlic and reserved liquid until mixture is smooth.

2. In a small skillet, toast chili powder, paprika and cumin over medium heat until aromatic, 3-4 minutes; remove and set aside. In a Dutch oven, cook and stir ground beef and steak seasoning over medium-high heat until beef is no longer pink, about 5 minutes; remove and drain.

3. Sprinkle steak cubes with 1 tsp. each salt and pepper. In same Dutch oven, brown beef in batches in 1 Tbsp. oil over medium-high heat; remove and set aside. Saute onion and poblano pepper in the remaining 1 Tbsp. oil until tender, about 5 minutes. Stir in toasted spices, oregano and pepper flakes. Add the cooked meats along with beef stock, beer, tomatoes, beans, remaining salt and pepper, and chile paste mixture. Cook over medium heat 20 minutes; reduce heat to low. Stir in masa harina and simmer 30-45 minutes longer. Serve with desired toppings.

Freeze option: Freeze the cooled chili in freezer containers. To use, partially thaw in refrigerator overnight. Heat through in a saucepan, stirring occasionally; add a little broth or water if necessary.

1¾ cups: 473 cal., 20g fat (6g sat. fat), 103mg chol., 1554mg sod., 29g carb. (8g sugars, 7g fiber), 41g pro.

THE BEST EVER CHILI

DISHING WITH

Sarah Farmer
Executive Culinary Director

My dad and my father-in-law are the gurus in our chili-loving clan. But after my honeymoon to New Mexico, inspired by the fresh and fragrant chile peppers at the Santa Fe farmers market, I felt it was time to introduce them to my spicy, meaty version with a touch of masa harina.

DISHING WITH

Peggy Woodward
Senior Food Editor

I love how a hint of heat with a touch of sweetness from the Gustus Vitae spicy chocolate cinnamon cane sugar adds a layer of flavor to this contest-winning chili recipe originally from Jeanne Larson of Rancho Santa Margarita, California.

SPICED BUTTERNUT SQUASH CHILI

SPICED BUTTERNUT
SQUASH CHILI
—Peggy Woodward, Senior Food Editor

Prep: 20 min. • **Cook:** 30 min.
Makes: 8 servings (2 qt.)

- 1 lb. ground beef or turkey
- ¾ cup chopped red onion
- 5 garlic cloves, minced
- 3 Tbsp. tomato paste
- 1 Tbsp. chili powder
- 1 tsp. ground cumin
- ½ to 1 tsp. salt
- 1¾ to 2 cups water
- 1 can (15 oz.) black beans, rinsed and drained
- 1 can (15 oz.) pinto beans, rinsed and drained
- 1 can (14½ oz.) diced tomatoes
- 1 can (14½ to 15 oz.) tomato sauce
- 1 Tbsp. Gustus Vitae spicy chocolate cinnamon cane sugar
- 3 cups peeled butternut squash, cut into ½-in. cubes
- 2 Tbsp. cider vinegar
  Optional: Chopped avocado, plain Greek yogurt and shredded mozzarella cheese

1. In a Dutch oven over medium heat, cook beef and onion, crumbling meat, until the beef is no longer pink and onion is tender, 6-8 minutes.
2. Add next 5 ingredients; cook 1 minute longer. Stir in water, both types of beans, diced tomatoes, tomato sauce and spicy chocolate cinnamon sugar. Bring to a boil; reduce heat. Stir in squash; simmer, covered, until squash is tender, 20-25 minutes. Stir in the vinegar.
3. If desired, serve with avocado, Greek yogurt and shredded mozzarella cheese.
1 cup: 261 cal., 8g fat (3g sat. fat), 35mg chol., 704mg sod., 32g carb. (6g sugars, 8g fiber), 18g pro.

VEGAN PEANUT BUTTER COOKIES

Even without butter or eggs, these peanut butter cookies are soft and chewy. No one will be able to tell they're vegan! If you want a little extra texture, feel free to use chunky peanut butter or add a quarter-cup crushed peanuts to the dough.
—Katie Bandurski, Associate Digital Editor

- -

Prep: 15 min. • **Bake:** 10 min. + cooling
Makes: 3 dozen

- 1 cup creamy peanut butter
- ½ cup sugar
- ½ cup packed brown sugar
- 1 Tbsp. vanilla extract
- ⅓ cup unsweetened almond milk
- 1 cup all-purpose flour
- 1 tsp. baking soda
- ½ tsp. baking powder
- ½ tsp. salt

1. Preheat oven to 350°. In a large bowl, cream the peanut butter, sugars and vanilla until light and fluffy, about 4 minutes. Beat in the almond milk. In another bowl, whisk flour, baking soda, baking powder and salt; gradually beat into creamed mixture.
2. Shape level tablespoonfuls into balls. Place 2 in. apart on parchment-lined baking sheets; flatten with a fork. Bake until set, 8-10 minutes. Cool on pan 5 minutes before removing to wire racks to cool completely.
1 cookie: 79 cal., 4g fat (1g sat. fat), 0 chol., 107mg sod., 10g carb. (7g sugars, 0 fiber), 2g pro.

TEST KITCHEN TIP
Letting the cookies rest once they're out of the oven is very important. Since they contain no butter or eggs, they need a little time to firm up. If you remove them from the pan too early, they'll crumble.

DUTCH-OVEN BREAD

Warm homemade bread makes an average day extraordinary. Enjoy this beautiful crusty loaf as is, or stir in a few extras like cheese, garlic, herbs or dried fruits.
—Catherine Ward, Prep Kitchen Manager

- -

Prep: 15 min. + rising
Bake: 45 min. + cooling
Makes: 1 loaf (16 slices)

- 3 to 3½ cups (125 grams per cup) all-purpose flour
- 1 tsp. active dry yeast
- 1 tsp. salt
- 1½ cups water (70° to 75°)

1. In a large bowl, whisk 3 cups flour, yeast and salt. Stir in water and enough remaining flour to form a moist, shaggy dough. Do not knead. Cover and let rise in a cool place until doubled, 7-8 hours. Preheat oven to 450°; place a Dutch oven with lid onto center rack and heat for at least 30 minutes. Once Dutch oven is heated, turn dough onto a generously floured surface. Using a metal scraper or spatula, quickly shape into a round loaf. Gently place on top of a piece of parchment.
2. Using a sharp knife, make a slash (¼ in. deep) across the top of the loaf. Using the parchment, immediately lower bread into heated Dutch oven. Cover; bake 30 minutes. Uncover and bake until loaf is deep golden brown and sounds hollow when tapped, about 15-20 minutes longer, partially covering if browning too much. Remove loaf from pan and cool completely on wire rack.
1 slice: 86 cal., 0 fat (0 sat. fat), 0 chol., 148mg sod., 18g carb. (0 sugars, 1g fiber), 3g pro.

DUTCH-OVEN BREAD

CHICKEN WITH PEACH-AVOCADO SALSA

This fresh dinner is pure summer—juicy peaches, creamy avocado, grilled chicken and a kick of hot sauce and lime. Make the salsa ahead to get it on the table even faster.
—Shannon Norris, Senior Food Stylist

Takes: 30 min. • **Makes:** 4 servings

- 1 medium peach, peeled and chopped
- 1 medium ripe avocado, peeled and cubed
- ½ cup chopped sweet red pepper
- 3 Tbsp. finely chopped red onion
- 1 Tbsp. minced fresh basil
- 1 Tbsp. lime juice
- 1 tsp. hot pepper sauce
- ½ tsp. grated lime zest
- ¾ tsp. salt, divided
- ½ tsp. pepper, divided
- 4 boneless skinless chicken breast halves (6 oz. each)

1. For salsa, in a small bowl, combine the peaches, avocado, red pepper, onion, basil, lime juice, hot sauce, lime zest, ¼ tsp. salt and ¼ tsp. pepper.

2. Sprinkle chicken with remaining salt and pepper. On a lightly greased grill rack, grill the chicken, covered, over medium heat for 5 minutes. Turn; grill until a thermometer reads 165°, about 7-9 minutes longer. Serve with salsa.

1 chicken breast half with ½ cup salsa: 265 cal., 9g fat (2g sat. fat), 94mg chol., 536mg sod., 9g carb. (4g sugars, 3g fiber), 36g pro. **Diabetic exchanges:** 5 lean meat, 1 fat, ½ starch.

THE BEST SWEET POTATO PIE

—Shannon Norris, Senior Food Stylist

Prep: 1½ hours + chilling
Bake: 35 min. + cooling • **Makes:** 8 servings

CRUST:
- 1 large egg yolk
- ¼ to ½ cup ice water, divided
- 2½ cups all-purpose flour
- 3 Tbsp. sugar
- ½ tsp. salt
- ½ cup cold shortening, cubed
- ½ cup cold butter, cubed

FILLING:
- 2½ lbs. sweet potatoes
- ⅔ cup packed brown sugar
- ½ cup sour cream
- 3 large eggs, lightly beaten
- ⅓ cup butter, melted
- 1 Tbsp. bourbon
- 2 tsp. vanilla extract
- 1½ tsp. ground cinnamon
- ½ tsp. ground nutmeg
- ½ tsp. salt
  Optional toppings: Whipped cream and sugared cranberries

1. In a small bowl, mix egg yolk with ¼ cup ice water; set aside. Place the flour, sugar and salt in a food processor; pulse until blended. Add the shortening and butter; pulse until shortening and butter are the size of peas. While pulsing, add egg yolk mixture. Add just enough of remaining ice water to form moist crumbs. Divide dough in half. Shape each into a disk; wrap and refrigerate dough for 1 hour or overnight.

2. Preheat oven to 400°. Scrub sweet potatoes; place in a 13x9-in. baking pan with 1½ cups water. Bake until tender, 45-50 minutes. Meanwhile, on a lightly floured surface, roll 1 disk of dough to a ⅛-in.-thick circle; transfer to a 9-in. deep-dish pie plate. Trim pastry to ½ in. beyond rim of plate; flute edge. Roll remaining disk to ⅛-in. thickness; cut into desired shapes with floured 1-in. cookie cutters. Place on a parchment-lined baking sheet. Refrigerate crust and cutouts for at least 30 minutes.

3. Peel potatoes when they are cool enough to handle; place in a food processor. Pulse to coarsely mash. Add brown sugar and the next 8 ingredients; blend until smooth. Pour filling into chilled crust. Bake on lowest oven rack 15 minutes. Reduce oven setting to 350°; bake until the center is just set, 20-25 minutes. Bake pastry cutouts on an upper oven rack until golden brown, 10-12 minutes. Cool on a wire rack; decorate pie with crust cutouts and toppings as desired.

1 piece: 726 cal., 37g fat (18g sat. fat), 147mg chol., 500mg sod., 88g carb. (38g sugars, 6g fiber), 10g pro.

CHICKEN WITH PEACH-AVOCADO SALSA

DISHING WITH

Shannon Norris
Senior Food Stylist

I love this recipe's rich sweet potato flavor and irresistibly buttery crust. Sour cream makes the filling super smooth, and the brown sugar and spices make it extra cozy. There's no doubt that this is the best sweet potato pie!

FREEZER BREAKFAST
SANDWICHES

FREEZER BREAKFAST SANDWICHES
—Christine Rukavena, Editor

Prep: 25 min. • **Cook:** 15 min.
Makes: 12 sandwiches

- 12 **large eggs**
- ⅔ **cup 2% milk**
- ½ **tsp. salt**
- ¼ **tsp. pepper**

SANDWICHES

- 12 **English muffins, split**
- 4 **Tbsp. butter, softened**
- 12 **slices Colby-Monterey Jack cheese**
- 12 **slices Canadian bacon**

1. Preheat oven to 325°. In a large bowl, whisk eggs, milk, salt and pepper until blended. Pour into a 13x9-in. baking pan coated with cooking spray. Bake until set, 15-18 minutes. Cool on a wire rack.
2. Meanwhile, toast the English muffins (or bake at 325° until lightly browned, 12-15 minutes). Spread 1 tsp. butter on each muffin bottoms.
3. Cut eggs into 12 portions. Layer muffin bottoms with an egg portion, a cheese slice (tearing cheese to fit) and Canadian bacon. Replace muffin tops. Wrap the sandwiches in foil; freeze in a freezer container or bag.
4. To use frozen sandwiches: Remove foil. Wrap the sandwich in a paper towel and microwave at 50% power until thawed, 1-2 minutes. Turn sandwich over; microwave at 100% power until hot and a thermometer reads at least 160°, 30-60 seconds. Let stand 2 minutes before serving.
1 sandwich: 334 cal., 17g fat (9g sat. fat), 219mg chol., 759mg sod., 26g carb. (3g sugars, 2g fiber), 19g pro.

DISHING WITH

Christine Rukavena
Editor

On busy mornings, these freezer breakfast sandwiches save the day. A hearty combo of eggs, Canadian bacon and cheese will keep you fueled through lunchtime and beyond.

TEST KITCHEN TIP
Cooked eggs can be frozen for up to 1 year, but we find they taste best within 3 to 6 months of the freezing date.

BACON-WRAPPED AVOCADO WEDGES

We all know almost everything is improved with bacon, and avocado is no exception. Since it's made in an air fryer, this appetizer is one to remember. It will definitely impress your friends!
—James Schend, Deputy Editor, Culinary

Takes: 30 min. • **Makes:** 1 dozen

- 2 medium ripe avocados
- 12 bacon strips

SAUCE
- ½ cup mayonnaise
- 2 to 3 Tbsp. Sriracha chili sauce
- 1 to 2 Tbsp. lime juice
- 1 tsp. grated lime zest

1. Preheat air fryer to 400°. Cut each avocado in half; remove pit and peel. Cut each half into thirds. Wrap 1 bacon slice around each avocado wedge. Working in batches if needed, place wedges in a single layer in the fryer basket and cook until bacon is cooked through, 10-15 minutes.
2. Meanwhile, in a small bowl, stir together mayonnaise, sriracha sauce, lime juice and zest. Serve wedges with sauce.
1 wedge: 142 cal., 13g fat (3g sat. fat), 9mg chol., 274mg sod., 3g carb. (1g sugars, 2g fiber), 3g pro.

THE BEST HUMMUS

THE BEST HUMMUS

Hummus is my go-to appetizer when I need something quick, easy and impressive. Over the years I've picked up a number of tricks that helped make this the best hummus you'll ever try.
—James Schend, Deputy Editor, Culinary

Prep: 25 min. • **Cook:** 20 min. + chilling
Makes: 1½ cups

- 1 can (15 oz.) garbanzo beans or chickpeas, rinsed and drained
- ½ tsp. baking soda
- ¼ cup fresh lemon juice
- 1 Tbsp. minced garlic
- ½ tsp. kosher salt
- ½ tsp. ground cumin
- ½ cup tahini
- 2 Tbsp. extra virgin olive oil
- ¼ cup cold water
  Optional: Olive oil, roasted chickpeas, toasted sesame seeds, ground sumac

1. Place garbanzo beans in a large saucepan; add water to cover by 1 in. Gently rub beans together to loosen outer skin. Pour off the water and any skins that are floating. Repeat 2-3 times until no skins float to the surface; drain. Return to saucepan; add baking soda and enough water to cover by 1 in. Bring to a boil; reduce heat. Simmer, uncovered, until beans are very tender and just starting to fall apart, 20-25 minutes.
2. Meanwhile, in a blender, process lemon juice, garlic and salt until almost a paste. Let stand 10 minutes; strain, discarding solids. Stir in cumin. In a small bowl, stir together tahini and olive oil.
3. Add garbanzo beans to blender; add cold water. Loosely cover and process until completely smooth. Add lemon mixture and process. With blender running, slowly add tahini mixture, scraping sides of blender as needed. Adjust seasoning with additional salt and cumin if desired.
4. Transfer mixture to a serving bowl; cover and refrigerate for at least 30 minutes. If desired, top with additional olive oil and assorted toppings.
¼ cup: 250 cal., 19g fat (3g sat. fat), 0 chol., 361mg sod., 15g carb. (2g sugars, 5g fiber), 7g pro.

CHOCOLATE BABKA

—Lisa Kaminski, Associate Digital Editor

Prep: 20 min. + chilling
Bake: 35 min. + cooling
Makes: 2 loaves (16 slices each)

- 4¼ to 4¾ cups all-purpose flour
- ½ cup sugar
- 2½ tsp. quick-rise yeast
- ¾ tsp. salt
- ⅔ cup butter
- ½ cup water
- 3 large eggs plus 1 large egg yolk, room temperature, beaten
- 2 Tbsp. grated orange zest

FILLING
- ½ cup butter, cubed
- 5 oz. dark chocolate chips
- ½ cup confectioners' sugar
- ⅓ cup baking cocoa
- ¼ tsp. salt

GLAZE
- ¼ cup sugar
- ¼ cup water

CHOCOLATE BABKA

1. In a large bowl, mix 2 cups flour, sugar, yeast and salt. Cut in butter until crumbly. In a small saucepan, heat water to 120°-130°; stir into dry ingredients. Stir in eggs and yolk, orange zest and enough remaining flour to form a soft dough (dough will be sticky).
2. Turn dough onto a floured surface; knead until smooth and elastic, 6-8 minutes. Place in a greased bowl, turning once to grease the top. Cover dough and refrigerate 8 hours or overnight.
3. Turn out dough onto a lightly floured surface; divide in half. Roll each half into a 12x10-in. rectangle. For the filling, in a microwave, melt butter and chocolate chips; stir until smooth. Stir in confectioners' sugar, cocoa and salt. Spread filling to within ½ in. of edges. Roll up jelly-roll style, starting with a long side; pinch seam and ends to seal.

4. Using a sharp knife, cut each roll in half lengthwise; carefully turn each half cut side up. Loosely twist strips around each other, keeping cut surfaces facing up; pinch ends together to seal. Place in 2 greased 9x5-in. loaf pans, cut side up. Cover with kitchen towels; let rise in a warm place until almost doubled, about 1 hour. Preheat oven to 375°.
5. Bake until golden brown, 35-45 minutes, tenting with foil halfway through baking. Meanwhile, in a saucepan, combine sugar and water; bring to a boil. Reduce heat; simmer, uncovered, 10 minutes. Brush over warm babka. Cool for 10 minutes before removing from pans to wire racks.

1 slice: 181 cal., 9g fat (5g sat. fat), 41mg chol., 136mg sod., 23g carb. (10g sugars, 1g fiber), 3g pro.

DISHING WITH

Lisa Kaminski
Associate Digital Editor

I love this chocolate babka. It's a rewarding recipe for taking the next step in your bread baking. Even if it's slightly imperfect going into the oven, it turns out gorgeous. Look at those swirls!

MAKEOVER CHEDDAR BISCUITS

These biscuits have a cheesy richness that everyone will love. I serve them with bowls of steaming chili or a hearty beef soup.
—Alicia Rooker, Recipe Editor/Tester

Takes: 30 min. • **Makes:** 15 biscuits

- 1 cup all-purpose flour
- 1 cup cake flour
- 1½ tsp. baking powder
- ¾ tsp. salt
- ½ tsp. garlic powder, divided
- ¼ tsp. baking soda
- 4 Tbsp. cold butter, divided
- ⅓ cup finely shredded cheddar cheese
- 1 cup buttermilk
- ½ tsp. dried parsley flakes

1. In a large bowl, combine the flours, baking powder, salt, ¼ tsp. garlic powder and baking soda. Cut in 3 Tbsp. butter until the mixture resembles coarse crumbs; add cheese. Stir in buttermilk just until moistened.
2. Drop by 2 tablespoonfuls 2 in. apart onto baking sheets coated with cooking spray. Bake at 425° until golden brown, 10-12 minutes. Melt remaining butter; stir in parsley and remaining garlic powder. Brush over biscuits. Serve warm.
1 biscuit: 106 cal., 4g fat (3g sat. fat), 11mg chol., 233mg sod., 14g carb. (1g sugars, 0 fiber), 3g pro.

BEST VANILLA BUTTERCREAM

With its powerfully decadent vanilla bean flavor and delightfully creamy texture, your family and friends will scrape every last bit of this frosting off their plates.
—Margaret Knoebel, Culinary Assistant

Prep: 30 min. + cooling • **Makes:** 5 cups

- 6 oz. white baking chips
- ¼ cup heavy whipping cream
- 1 Tbsp. vanilla bean paste
- 1 Tbsp. vanilla extract
- 6 large egg whites, room temperature
- 1½ cups sugar
- ½ tsp. cream of tartar
- ½ tsp. salt
- 2 cups unsalted butter, cubed

1. In a microwave, melt white baking chips with cream until smooth, stirring every 30 seconds. Stir in the vanilla bean paste and extract. Set aside to cool slightly. Meanwhile, in a heatproof bowl of a stand mixer, whisk egg whites, sugar, cream of tartar and salt until blended. Place over simmering water in a large saucepan over medium heat. Whisking constantly, heat mixture until a thermometer reads 160°, 8-10 minutes.
2. Remove from the heat. With whisk attachment of stand mixer, beat on high speed until cooled to 90°, about 7 minutes. Gradually beat in butter, a few tablespoons at a time, on medium speed until smooth. Beat in the cooled baking chip mixture until blended.
2 Tbsp.: 144 cal., 11g fat (7g sat. fat), 27mg chol., 43mg sod., 10g carb. (10g sugars, 0 fiber), 1g pro.

BEST VANILLA BUTTERCREAM

DISHING WITH

Josh Rink

Food Stylist

What makes this recipe so unique is the slow overnight fermentation of the dough. The flour has time to hydrate and relax, which makes the dough so much easier to roll out.

THE BEST SAUSAGE PIZZAS
—Josh Rink, Food Stylist

Prep: 30 min. • **Bake:** 15 min.
Makes: 2 pizzas (8 slices each)

- 1 batch The Best Pizza Dough (recipe at right)
- 1 lb. bulk Italian sausage
- 1 cup pizza sauce
- 4 cups shredded part-skim mozzarella cheese
- 1 medium red onion, sliced
- 1 medium green pepper, chopped
- 2 cups sliced fresh mushrooms
  Optional: Grated Parmesan cheese, crushed red pepper flakes and fresh oregano leaves

1. Divide dough in half. With greased fingers, pat each half onto an ungreased 12-in. pizza pan. Prick dough thoroughly with a fork. Bake at 400° until crust is lightly browned, 10-12 minutes. Meanwhile, in a large skillet, cook the sausage over medium heat until no longer pink; drain.
2. Spread pizza sauce over crusts. Top with cheese, onion, green pepper, mushrooms and sausage. Bake at 400° until top is golden brown and cheese is bubbly, 12-15 minutes. If desired, top pizzas with grated Parmesan cheese, crushed red pepper flakes and fresh oregano leaves.
Freeze option: Wrap unbaked pizzas and freeze for up to 2 months. To use, unwrap and place on pizza pans; thaw in the refrigerator. Bake at 400° until crust is golden brown, 18-22 minutes.
1 slice: 344 cal., 20g fat (7g sat. fat), 41mg chol., 651mg sod., 26g carb. (2g sugars, 1g fiber), 15g pro.

TEST KITCHEN TIP
You should still be able to see dough after spreading on the sauce. We also recommend not using more than 2 cups cheese.

THE BEST PIZZA DOUGH

THE BEST PIZZA DOUGH
This dough is the key to an extraordinary homemade pizza. Using double zero flour—ultra refined flour—will take your crust to the next level. It can be hard to find, but you can usually score it at Italian grocery stores or online. If you're not able to find it, all-purpose flour works fine, too. Either way, you won't be disappointed with the results!
—Josh Rink, Food Stylist

Prep: 30 min. + chilling
Makes: 2 crusts (8 servings each)

- 1¼ cups warm water (110° to 115°)
- 2 tsp. sugar, divided
- 1 pkg. (¼ oz.) active dry yeast
- 3½ to 4 cups all-purpose or 00 flour
- 1 tsp. sea salt
- 1 tsp. each dried basil, oregano and marjoram, optional
- ⅓ cup vegetable or olive oil

1. In a small bowl, mix warm water and 1 tsp. sugar; add yeast and whisk until dissolved. Let stand until bubbles form on surface. In a large bowl, whisk 3 cups flour, salt, remaining 1 tsp. sugar and, if desired, dried herbs. Make a well in center; add yeast mixture and oil. Stir until smooth. Add enough remaining flour to form a soft dough.
2. Turn onto a floured surface; knead, adding more flour to surface as needed until no longer sticky and dough is smooth and elastic, 6-8 minutes. Place in a large greased bowl; turn once to grease top. Cover and let rise in a warm place for 30 minutes; transfer bowl to refrigerator and chill overnight. Allow dough to come to room temperature, about 30 minutes, before rolling.
1 piece: 144 cal., 5g fat (1g sat. fat), 0 chol., 121mg sod., 22g carb. (1g sugars, 1g fiber), 3g pro.

DOUBLE CHOCOLATE
ESPRESSO POUND CAKE

DISHING WITH

Rachel Bernhard Seis
Senior Editor

Two of my biggest loves in life—
chocolate and coffee—come
together in this velvety pound
cake. Grate some extra chocolate
on top. You'll thank me later!

DOUBLE CHOCOLATE
ESPRESSO POUND CAKE
—Rachel Bernhard Seis, Senior Editor

Prep: 20 min. • **Bake:** 80 min. + cooling
Makes: 16 servings

    5   oz. milk chocolate, chopped
    ¼   cup brewed espresso
    1   cup butter, softened
    3   cups sugar
    5   large eggs, room temperature
    2   tsp. vanilla extract
    3   cups all-purpose flour
    1½ tsp. baking powder
    ½   tsp. salt
    ⅔   cup 2% milk
    1   cup (6 oz.) dark chocolate chips
FROSTING
    ¼   cup butter, softened
    3   cups confectioners' sugar
    3   Tbsp. 2% milk
    3   tsp. vanilla extract
    ½   tsp. salt

1. In a double boiler or metal bowl over hot water, melt milk chocolate in espresso; stir until smooth. Remove from the heat.
2. In a large bowl, beat butter and sugar until crumbly, about 2 minutes. Add eggs, 1 at a time, beating well after each addition. Beat in vanilla. Combine flour, baking powder and salt; add to the creamed mixture alternately with milk, beating well after each addition. Stir in dark chocolate chips and melted chocolate mixture.
3. Transfer to a greased and floured 10-in. fluted tube pan. Bake at 325° until a toothpick inserted near the center comes out clean, 80-90 minutes. Cool 10 minutes before removing from pan to a wire rack to cool completely.
4. In a large bowl, beat butter until light and fluffy. Beat in the confectioners' sugar, milk, vanilla and salt; frost cake.
1 slice: 573 cal., 22g fat (14g sat. fat), 100mg chol., 344mg sod., 91g carb. (71g sugars, 2g fiber), 6g pro.

PULLED PORK PARFAIT

I tried a version of this meaty parfait at Miller Park, home of my favorite baseball team, the Milwaukee Brewers. I take it up a notch by layering in corn and creamy mac and cheese, so it truly is a full barbecue meal that you can easily take on the go.
—Rachel Bernhard Seis, Senior Editor

Takes: 15 min. • **Makes:** 4 servings

- 1 pkg. (16 oz.) refrigerated fully cooked barbecued shredded pork
- 1 cup frozen corn
- 2 cups refrigerated mashed potatoes
- 2 cups prepared macaroni and cheese

In each of four 1-pint wide-mouth canning jars, divide and layer ingredients in the following order: pulled pork, corn, mashed potatoes, and macaroni and cheese. Cover and freeze or refrigerate until ready to serve. When ready to serve, remove jar lids and microwave until heated through. To serve from freezer, partially thaw in refrigerator overnight before microwaving.

1 serving: 349 cal., 8g fat (4g sat. fat), 45mg chol., 1116mg sod., 41g carb. (20g sugars, 1g fiber), 17g pro.

EASY MEXICAN BROWNIES

EASY MEXICAN BROWNIES

I was hosting a fun Mexican-themed cocktail party and needed a quick dessert. Dressing up an ordinary box brownie mix made life easy and delicious!
—Susan Stetzel, Field Editor Coordinator

Takes: 30 min. • **Makes:** 2 dozen

- 1 pkg. fudge brownie mix (13x9-in. pan size)
- 2 tsp. ground cinnamon
- 1 tsp. ground ancho chili pepper
- ¾ cup dark chocolate chips

ADDITIONAL INGREDIENTS
- 2 large eggs, room temperature
- ½ cup canola oil
- ¼ cup water

1. Whisk together brownie mix and spices. Transfer mixture to a 1-qt. glass jar. Top with chocolate chips. Cover and store in a cool dry place up to 3 months.
2. To prepare brownies: Preheat oven to 350°. Whisk eggs, canola oil and water until blended. Gradually add chocolate chips and brownie mix, mixing well. Spread into a greased 13x9-in. baking pan.
3. Bake brownies until a toothpick inserted in center comes out clean (do not overbake), 20-25 minutes. Cool completely in pan on a wire rack.

1 brownie: 173 cal., 10g fat (3g sat. fat), 16mg chol., 92mg sod., 21g carb. (15g sugars, 1g fiber), 2g pro.

DISHING WITH

Ellie Martin Cliffe
Executive Editor

This crimson sauce has just the right amount of tartness to complement poultry, pork and game.

PORT WINE CRANBERRY SAUCE
—Ellie Martin Cliffe, Executive Editor

Takes: 20 min. • **Makes:** 2 cups

1 pkg. (12 oz.) fresh or
  frozen cranberries
1¼ cups sugar
¼ cup port wine or grape juice
2 tsp. cornstarch
2 Tbsp. cold water

In a small saucepan, cook cranberries, sugar and wine over medium heat just until berries begin to pop, 10-12 minutes. Combine the cornstarch and water until smooth; stir into cranberry mixture. Bring to a boil; cook and stir until berries pop and sauce is thickened, about 2 minutes. Serve warm or cold. Refrigerate leftovers.

¼ cup: 146 cal., 0 fat (0 sat. fat), 0 chol., 1mg sod., 38g carb. (34g sugars, 2g fiber), 0 pro.

PORT WINE CRANBERRY SAUCE

MOM'S SUPER STUPENDOUS POTATO SALAD

In college, my best friend and I debated whose mom made the best potato salad. Turns out they were almost identical! Even though I've since tweaked our recipe, it still takes me home again.
—Ellie Martin Cliffe, Executive Editor

- -

Prep: 20 min. • **Cook:** 15 min. + chilling
Makes: 12 servings

- 1 garlic clove, peeled
- 3 lbs. small red potatoes, quartered
- 2 Tbsp. cider vinegar, divided
- 1½ tsp. salt, divided
- 6 hard-boiled large eggs, divided
- 1 cup mayonnaise
- ½ cup sour cream
- 1 Tbsp. Dijon mustard
- ½ tsp. paprika, plus extra for garnish, optional
- ¼ tsp. pepper
- 1 medium sweet onion, finely chopped
- 2 celery ribs, finely chopped
- 2 Tbsp. minced fresh parsley

1. Skewer garlic with a toothpick (to make it easy to find after cooking). Place potatoes, 1 Tbsp. vinegar, 1 tsp. salt and skewered garlic in a Dutch oven; add water to cover. Bring to a boil. Reduce heat; simmer until tender, 10-12 minutes. Drain potatoes, reserving garlic; remove the skewer and crush the garlic.
2. Meanwhile, chop 5 eggs. Whisk together mayonnaise, sour cream, mustard, paprika, pepper, garlic and remaining vinegar and salt. Stir in potatoes, chopped eggs, onion and celery. Refrigerate 4 hours or until cold.
3. Just before serving, slice remaining egg. Top salad with egg; sprinkle with parsley and, if desired, additional paprika.
¾ cup: 281 cal., 19g fat (4g sat. fat), 107mg chol., 472mg sod., 20g carb. (2g sugars, 2g fiber), 6g pro.

MOM'S SUPER STUPENDOUS POTATO SALAD

**HOT SHRIMP DIP
PAGE 34**

Snacks

At the *Taste of Home* Test Kitchen, we enjoy our share of snack attacks. From dips and sliders to meatballs and other tasty bites, the awesome appetizers and finger foods found here always hit the spot.

FRESH SHRIMP
& AVOCADO NACHOS

FRESH SHRIMP & AVOCADO NACHOS

I'm a fan of shrimp, and my family loves nachos. When I combined those favorites and added fresh avocado, the result was a cool yet satisfying snack.
—Teri Rasey, Cadillac, MI

Prep: 30 min. + chilling • **Makes:** 10 servings

- 4 plum tomatoes, chopped
- 3 tomatillos, husked and chopped
- 4 jalapeno peppers, seeded and finely chopped
- 1 small onion, chopped
- 2 garlic cloves, minced
- ¼ cup minced fresh cilantro
- 3 Tbsp. olive oil
- 2 Tbsp. seasoned rice vinegar
- 3 Tbsp. lime juice, divided
- 1½ tsp. sea salt
- ½ tsp. dried oregano
- 1 lb. peeled and deveined cooked shrimp (31-40 per lb.), coarsely chopped
- 2 medium ripe avocados, peeled and pitted, divided
- ½ cup sour cream
- 8 cups tortilla chips
- 1 cup shredded lettuce

1. In a large bowl, combine the first 11 ingredients. Cover and refrigerate until chilled, at least 30 minutes. Stir in shrimp.
2. For avocado cream, mash 1 avocado with sour cream and 1 Tbsp. remaining lime juice until smooth. Cube remaining avocado and toss with remaining 1 Tbsp. lime juice.
3. To serve, arrange tortilla chips on a large platter. Top with shrimp mixture, cubed avocado, shredded lettuce and avocado cream; serve immediately.
1 serving: 264 cal., 16g fat (3g sat. fat), 72mg chol., 542mg sod., 20g carb. (3g sugars, 3g fiber), 12g pro.

SALTY DOG SANGRIA

SALTY DOG SANGRIA

Mix up grapefruit vodka, ginger ale, grapefruit juice, a little wine and simple syrup and what do you get? A perfectly refreshing and beautiful sipper fit for any holiday or special gathering.
—Becky Hardin, St. Peters, MO

Prep: 30 min. + chilling
Makes: 16 servings (3 qt.)

- 1 cup sugar
- 1 cup water
- 2 bottles (750 ml each) rosé wine
- 2 cups ruby red grapefruit juice
- 1 can (12 oz.) ginger ale
- 1 cup ruby red grapefruit-flavored vodka
  Grapefruit slices
  Coarse sea salt and grated grapefruit zest

1. In a small saucepan, bring sugar and water to a boil. Reduce heat; simmer 10 minutes. Cool completely. Transfer to a large pitcher. Stir in the wine, juice, ginger ale, vodka and grapefruit slices. Refrigerate at least 2 hours.
2. Using water, moisten the rims of 16 wine glasses. Mix salt and grapefruit zest on a plate; hold each glass upside down and dip rim into salt mixture. Set aside. Discard remaining salt mixture. Serve sangria in prepared glasses over ice.
¾ cup: 186 cal., 0 fat (0 sat. fat), 0 chol., 2mg sod., 24g carb. (15g sugars, 0 fiber), 0 pro.

TEST KITCHEN TIP
Use simple syrup—sugar-infused water—to sweeten iced tea and lemonade as well as cocktails.

SLIM BLOODY MARY DEVILED EGGS

Jazz up your appetizer buffet with these tasty change-of-pace bites. The sinfully delicious treats take things to a new level without a lot of extra sodium or fat. Try them at your next brunch!
—*Taste of Home* Test Kitchen

Takes: 20 min. • **Makes:** 1 dozen

- 6 hard-boiled large eggs
- 3 Tbsp. reduced-fat mayonnaise
- 1 Tbsp. reduced-sodium tomato juice
- ¾ tsp. prepared horseradish
- ¼ tsp. hot pepper sauce
- ⅛ tsp. salt
- ⅛ tsp. pepper
  Crumbled cooked bacon, optional

1. Cut eggs in half lengthwise. Remove yolks; set aside egg whites and 4 yolks (discard remaining yolks or save for another use).
2. In a large bowl, mash reserved yolks. Stir in mayonnaise, tomato juice, horseradish, pepper sauce, salt and pepper. Stuff or pipe into egg whites. If desired, garnish with bacon. Chill until serving.
1 stuffed egg half: 39 cal., 3g fat (1g sat. fat), 70mg chol., 87mg sod., 1g carb. (0 sugars, 0 fiber), 3g pro.

CRANBERRY & BACON SWISS CHEESE DIP

CRANBERRY & BACON SWISS CHEESE DIP

This warm, rich and creamy cheese dip is guaranteed to please family and friends alike. Served with thin, crunchy slices of French bread, it makes an ideal appetizer. Best of all, you can prepare it ahead, put it in the fridge, and then bake it just before you want to serve it.
—Jeanne Holt, Mendota Heights, MN

Prep: 20 min. • **Bake:** 25 min. • **Makes:** 3 cups

- ⅔ cup mayonnaise
- ⅓ cup spreadable chive and onion cream cheese
- 1 Tbsp. stone-ground mustard
- ¼ tsp. garlic pepper blend
- 3 cups shredded Swiss cheese
- 1 pkg. (10 oz.) frozen chopped onions, thawed and patted dry
- 8 pieces ready-to-serve fully cooked bacon, chopped
- ½ cup sliced almonds, divided
- ⅓ cup dried cranberries, chopped
  Slices French bread baguette (¼ in. thick), toasted

1. Preheat oven to 325°. In a large bowl, combine the mayonnaise, cream cheese, mustard and garlic pepper blend. Add the Swiss cheese; mix well. Stir in onions, bacon, ¼ cup almonds and cranberries. Spread into a greased 3-cup baking dish. Sprinkle with the remaining ¼ cup almonds. Place on a baking sheet.
2. Bake, uncovered 25-30 minutes or until bubbly. Serve warm with baguette slices.
¼ cup dip: 266 cal., 22g fat (8g sat. fat), 30mg chol., 222mg sod., 8g carb. (5g sugars, 1g fiber), 10g pro.

LAYERED HUMMUS DIP

My love for Greece inspired this fast-to-fix Mediterranean dip. It's great for parties and is a delicious way to include garden-fresh veggies on your menu.
—Cheryl Snavely, Hagerstown, MD

Takes: 15 min. • **Makes:** 12 servings

- 1   carton (10 oz.) hummus
- ¼   cup finely chopped red onion
- ½   cup Greek olives, chopped
- 2   medium tomatoes, seeded and chopped
- 1   large English cucumber, chopped
- 1   cup crumbled feta cheese
      Baked pita chips

Spread hummus into a shallow 10-in. round dish. Layer with onion, olives, tomatoes, cucumber and cheese. Refrigerate until serving. Serve with pita chips.

1 serving: 88 cal., 5g fat (2g sat. fat), 5mg chol., 275mg sod., 6g carb. (1g sugars, 2g fiber), 4g pro.

> I love this dip and always have the ingredients on hand. It's my go-to snack or dinner when my kids and husband are busy, and I have the house to myself.
>
> —RAEANN THOMPSON, SENIOR ART DIRECTOR

LAYERED HUMMUS DIP

FRIED CHICKEN & PULLED PORK CORNBREAD POPPERS

These fun little apps are an instant conversation starter wherever they're served. We love them on game day, but they'd be a hit at brunch, too.
—Crystal Schlueter, Northglenn, CO

Takes: 25 min. • **Makes:** 2 dozen

- 2   oz. frozen popcorn chicken
- 1   pkg. (8½ oz.) cornbread/muffin mix
- 4   seeded jalapeno peppers or pickled jalapeno peppers, cut into 6 slices each
- ¼   cup refrigerated fully cooked barbecued pulled pork
- ½   cup maple syrup or honey
- 1   tsp. Sriracha chili sauce, optional

1. Preheat oven to 400°. Bake popcorn chicken according to package directions. When cool enough to handle, cut chicken into 12 pieces.

2. Meanwhile, prepare cornbread mix according to package directions. Place a jalapeno slice in each of 24 foil-lined mini muffin cups. Fill each cup with 1 Tbsp. cornbread batter. Gently press a piece of popcorn chicken into the centers of half the cups. Spoon 1 tsp. pulled pork into the centers of remaining cups.

3. Bake until poppers are golden brown, about 12 minutes. Serve with maple syrup; if desired, whisk chili sauce into syrup.

1 mini muffin: 74 cal., 2g fat (1g sat. fat), 10mg chol., 120mg sod., 13g carb. (7g sugars, 1g fiber), 2g pro.

MINI CHEESE BALLS

HOT SHRIMP DIP

I came across a similar recipe that called for crawfish, and it sounded delicious. We don't have a lot of crawfish available in my area and I'm a big fan of shrimp, so I used that instead. It's become a family favorite and I can guarantee there will be no leftovers!
—Jill Burwell, Renton, WA

Takes: 25 min. • **Makes:** 4 cups

- ½   cup butter, cubed
- 8   green onions, thinly sliced
- 1   small green pepper, finely chopped
- 1   lb. peeled and deveined cooked shrimp (61-70 per lb.)
- 1   jar (4 oz.) diced pimientos, drained
- 2   garlic cloves, minced
- 2   tsp. Creole seasoning
- 1   pkg. (8 oz.) cream cheese, cubed
  Chopped fresh parsley
  French bread baguette slices or assorted crackers

In a Dutch oven, melt butter over medium heat. Add green onions and green pepper; cook and stir until tender, 3-4 minutes. Add the shrimp, pimientos, garlic and Creole seasoning. Cook and stir until heated through. Stir in cream cheese until melted; sprinkle with parsley. Serve with baguette slices or crackers.
¼ cup: 136 cal., 11g fat (7g sat. fat), 73mg chol., 217mg sod., 2g carb. (1g sugars, 0 fiber), 7g pro.

MINI CHEESE BALLS

These mini cheese balls are the perfect quick appetizer for any party. For even more flavor, roll them in toasted sesame seeds, fresh rosemary and/or paprika.
—Judy Spivey, Ennice, NC

Prep: 30 min. + chilling
Makes: 36 cheese balls

- 1   pkg. (8 oz.) cream cheese, softened
- 2   cups shredded sharp cheddar cheese
  Optional toppings: Toasted sesame seeds, minced fresh rosemary and paprika
  Optional garnishes: Halved rye crisps and rolled tortilla chips

In a large bowl, combine cheeses. Shape into 36 balls; roll balls in toppings as desired. Cover and refrigerate balls for 8 hours or overnight. To serve, if desired, press a rye crisp or rolled corn chip into the top of each cheese ball.
1 cheese ball: 47 cal., 4g fat (2g sat. fat), 13mg chol., 61mg sod., 1g carb. (0 sugars, 0 fiber), 2g pro.

BEER DIP

Ranch dressing mix and beer flavor this fast dip packed with shredded cheese. Once you start eating it, you can't stop!
—Michelle Long, New Castle, CO

Takes: 5 min. • **Makes:** 3½ cups

- 2   pkg. (8 oz. each) cream cheese, softened
- ⅓   cup beer or nonalcoholic beer
- 1   envelope ranch salad dressing mix
- 2   cups shredded cheddar cheese
  Pretzels

In a large bowl, beat the cream cheese, beer and dressing mix until smooth. Stir in the cheddar cheese. Serve with pretzels.
2 Tbsp.: 89 cal., 8g fat (5g sat. fat), 26mg chol., 177mg sod., 1g carb. (0 sugars, 0 fiber), 3g pro.

TEST KITCHEN TIP

This dip has a little heat from the Creole seasoning—a blend of pepper, garlic powder, onion powder and dried herbs—but if you want to make it even spicier, add your favorite hot sauce and a little bit of acidity with a squeeze of fresh lemon juice.

HOT
SHRIMP DIP

CASHEW CHEESE

Spread this vegan cashew cheese on your favorite crackers, layer it on a toasted bagel or serve with fresh vegetables. It also makes a delicious, out-of-the-ordinary sandwich spread. What a tasty surprise!
—*Taste of Home* Test Kitchen

Prep: 1 hour + chilling • **Makes:** ¾ cup

- 1 **cup raw cashews**
- ⅓ **cup water**
- 2 **Tbsp. nutritional yeast**
- 2 **tsp. lemon juice**
- ½ **tsp. salt**
- ⅛ **tsp. garlic powder**

Place cashews in a small bowl. Add enough warm water to cover completely. Soak cashews for 1-2 hours; drain and discard water. Add cashews and the remaining ingredients to food processor. Cover and process until smooth, 1-2 minutes, scraping down sides occasionally. Transfer to serving dish. Cover and refrigerate for at least 1 hour before serving.

1 Tbsp.: 56 cal., 4g fat (1g sat. fat), 0 chol., 101mg sod., 3g carb. (1g sugars, 0 fiber), 2g pro. **Diabetic exchanges:** 1 fat.

ASK SARAH

WHAT IS CASHEW CHEESE?

Cashew cheese is a non-dairy, vegan substitute for cheese. It is typically made of blended cashews, nutritional yeast, water and a blend of seasonings.

CASHEW CHEESE

FRIED LEMON-PEPPER WINGS

These lemon-pepper wings are perfect for game day. Try them out if you've been stuck in a rut with your chicken wing recipe. Add grated lemon zest to the butter mixture for a more pronounced lemon flavor.
—*Taste of Home* Test Kitchen

Prep: 20 min. • **Cook:** 10 min./batch
Makes: 2 dozen

- 2½ lbs. chicken wings
- ½ cup all-purpose flour
- 2 tsp. salt
- ¼ tsp. pepper
  Oil for deep-fat frying
- 2 Tbsp. butter, melted
- 1½ tsp. lemon-pepper seasoning
- 2 Tbsp. minced fresh parsley

1. Cut wings into 3 sections; discard wing tip sections. In a large bowl, combine flour, salt and pepper. Add wings, a few at a time, and toss to coat.
2. In an electric skillet or deep fryer, heat oil to 375°. Fry wings, a few at a time, until no longer pink, 3-4 minutes on each side. Drain on paper towels. In a large bowl, combine butter and lemon-pepper seasoning. Add wings; toss to coat. Sprinkle with parsley. Serve immediately.
1 piece: 107 cal., 9g fat (2g sat. fat), 18mg chol., 92mg sod., 1g carb. (0 sugars, 0 fiber), 5g pro.

FROZEN BRANDY
OLD-FASHIONEDS

TASTE OF HOME
TEST
KITCHEN
RECIPE OF THE YEAR
★ ★ ★ ★ ★

FROZEN BRANDY OLD-FASHIONEDS

Both sides of my family are midwestern, so our brandy-loving tradition is evident in the slush we make for holidays and in the brandy old-fashioned cocktails we enjoy all year. I decided to combine those two recipes into something completely new. This goes very quickly at gatherings!
—Stephanie Vaughan, Madison, WI

Prep: 15 min. + freezing
Makes: 12 servings (about 2½ qt. slush mix)

- 6 cups water
- 1 cup sugar
- 2 cups brandy
- 1 can (12 oz.) frozen orange juice concentrate, thawed
- ¼ cup maraschino cherry juice
- ¼ cup bitters

EACH SERVING
- ¼ cup lemon-lime soda, chilled
  Optional: Maraschino cherries and orange wedges

1. In a large saucepan, bring water and sugar to a boil. Cook and stir until the sugar is dissolved; cool completely. Stir in brandy, orange juice concentrate, juice and bitters. Pour into a 3-qt. freezer container. Freeze overnight or until set.
2. For each serving, scoop ¾ cup slush into a rocks glass. Pour lemon-lime soda into the glass; serve with fruit as desired.
1 serving: 246 cal., 0 fat (0 sat. fat), 0 chol., 9mg sod., 38g carb. (32g sugars, 0 fiber), 1g pro.

CHILLED PEA SOUP SHOOTERS

Enjoy pea soup in a whole new way! The garnish is curried crab, which will catch everyone by surprise.
—*Taste of Home* Test Kitchen

Prep: 20 min. + chilling • **Makes:** 2 dozen

  1   pkg. (16 oz.) frozen peas, thawed
  1   cup chicken broth
  ¼   cup minced fresh mint
  1   Tbsp. lime juice
  1   tsp. ground cumin
  ¼   tsp. salt
  1½ cups plain yogurt
CURRIED CRAB
  2   Tbsp. minced fresh mint
  4   tsp. lime juice
  4   tsp. canola oil
  2   tsp. red curry paste
  ⅛   tsp. salt
  1   cup lump crabmeat, drained

1. Place the peas, broth, mint, lime juice, cumin and salt in a blender. Cover and process until smooth. Add yogurt; process until blended. Refrigerate for at least 1 hour.
2. For curried crab, in a small bowl, whisk the mint, lime juice, oil, curry paste and salt. Add the crabmeat; toss to coat. Chill until serving.
3. To serve, pour soup into shot glasses; garnish with crab mixture.
1 serving: 40 cal., 1g fat (0 sat. fat), 20mg chol., 216mg sod., 4g carb. (2g sugars, 1g fiber), 3g pro. **Diabetic exchanges:** ½ starch.

MUSHROOM & OLIVE BRUSCHETTA

MUSHROOM & OLIVE BRUSCHETTA

I tried this delicious bruschetta toast at a party and knew I had to make it myself. I couldn't find the person who brought the dish, so I duplicated the recipe on my own. The original was made on an English muffin, but party rye or baguette slices work, too.
—Lynne German, Buford, GA

Prep: 15 min. • **Bake:** 10 min.
Makes: 4 dozen

  1½ cups finely shredded cheddar
      cheese
  ½   cup canned mushroom stems and
      pieces, drained and chopped
  ½   cup chopped green onions
  ½   cup chopped pitted green olives
  ½   cup chopped ripe olives
  ½   cup mayonnaise
  ¼   tsp. curry powder
  2   French bread baguettes
      (10½ oz. each), cut into ½-in. slices
      Julienned green onions, optional

1. Preheat oven to 400°. In a large bowl, combine the first 7 ingredients. Cut each baguette into 24 slices; place on ungreased baking sheets. Bake 5 minutes, or until bread is lightly toasted.
2. Top with cheese mixture. Bake until the cheese is melted, 4-5 minutes. If desired, top with julienned green onions.
Freeze option: Cover and freeze unbaked, topped baguette slices on a parchment-lined baking sheet until firm. Transfer to a freezer container; return to freezer. To use, bake baguette slices on ungreased baking sheets in a preheated 400° oven until heated through, 8-10 minutes.
1 appetizer: 66 cal., 3g fat (1g sat. fat), 4mg chol., 161mg sod., 7g carb. (0 sugars, 0 fiber), 2g pro.

ORANGE-FENNEL SALSA

I love salsa! Enjoy this citrus variation with tortilla chips or serve as a garnish with your favorite meat. Its sweet and tangy flavor profile goes well with ham, pork and poultry.
—Nancy Heishman, Las Vegas, NV

Prep: 20 min. + chilling • **Makes:** 3 cups

- 3   large navel oranges
- 1   medium fennel bulb, finely chopped, plus 1 Tbsp. chopped fennel fronds
- ½   cup finely chopped red onion
- ⅓   cup minced fresh cilantro
- 1   jalapeno pepper, seeded and finely chopped
- 4   large fresh basil leaves, finely chopped
- 2   tsp. rice vinegar
- 2   tsp. olive oil
- ¼   tsp. garlic salt

1. Cut a thin slice from the top and bottom of each orange; stand orange upright on a cutting board. Cut off the peel and outer membrane from the orange. Working over a bowl to catch the juices, cut along the membrane of each segment to remove fruit. Finely chop the oranges; add to bowl with reserved juices.

2. Add remaining ingredients; toss to coat. Refrigerate, covered, until serving.

½ cup: 77 cal., 2g fat (0 sat. fat), 0 chol., 130mg sod., 16g carb. (11g sugars, 4g fiber), 2g pro.

CRUDITE DIP

To bring out this dip's tangy flavor, chill it before serving. This will allow the flavors time to blend.
—*Taste of Home* Test Kitchen

Prep: 5 min. + chilling • **Makes:** 1½ cups

- 1   cup sour cream
- ½   cup mayonnaise
- 2   green onions, finely chopped
- 1   Tbsp. lemon juice
- 1   Tbsp. minced fresh parsley
- 1   tsp. dill weed
- 1   garlic clove, minced
- ½   tsp. seasoned salt
- ⅛   tsp. pepper
    Assorted fresh vegetables

Combine the first 9 ingredients; mix well. Cover and refrigerate at least 2 hours. If desired, sprinkle with additional parsley. Serve with vegetables.

2 Tbsp.: 102 cal., 11g fat (3g sat. fat), 5mg chol., 117mg sod., 1g carb. (1g sugars, 0 fiber), 1g pro.

TEST KITCHEN TIP

Crudites are traditional French appetizers—raw, crisp veggies paired with a dipping sauce like this tangy, sour cream-based dip. Crudites are easy appetizers for small and large groups alike.

ORANGE-FENNEL SALSA

BANH MI SKEWERS

I love banh mi sandwiches but wanted to make them a little easier to serve for a party. These skewers are a fun twist. For simple prep on the day of the party, make the meatballs in advance and freeze them.
—Elisabeth Larsen, Pleasant Grove, UT

- -

Prep: 45 min. + chilling • **Cook:** 10 min./batch
Makes: 12 servings

- 1 **cup white vinegar or rice vinegar**
- ¼ **cup sugar**
- ½ **tsp. salt**
- 1 **English cucumber, thinly sliced**
- 2 **medium carrots, thinly sliced**
- 4 **radishes, thinly sliced**
- 1 **cup mayonnaise**
- 1 **Tbsp. Sriracha chili sauce**
- 2 **Tbsp. minced fresh cilantro**
- 2 **green onions, thinly sliced**
- 1 **Tbsp. soy sauce**
- 1 **garlic clove, minced**
- ¼ **tsp. cayenne pepper**
- 1½ **lbs. ground pork**
- 2 **Tbsp. canola oil**
- 1 **French bread baguette (10½ oz.), cut into 24 slices**

1. In a large bowl, combine vinegar, sugar and salt; whisk until sugar is dissolved. Add the cucumber, carrots and radishes; let stand until serving. Combine mayonnaise and chili sauce; refrigerate until serving.
2. In another large bowl, combine cilantro, green onions, soy sauce, garlic and cayenne. Add pork; mix lightly but thoroughly. Shape into 36 balls.
3. In a large skillet, heat oil over medium heat. Cook meatballs in batches until cooked through, turning occasionally.
4. Drain vegetable mixture. On 12 metal or wooden skewers, alternately thread the vegetables, meatballs and baguette slices. Serve with Sriracha mayonnaise.
1 skewer with about 1 Tbsp. sauce: 336 cal., 24g fat (5g sat. fat), 39mg chol., 416mg sod., 16g carb. (2g sugars, 1g fiber), 13g pro.

TOMATO FRITTERS

TOMATO FRITTERS

A friend gave me the basic recipe for these fritters, then I tweaked it for my family's tastes. It's one of our favorite snacks in the summer. We love them right after they've been fried, when they're still hot and crispy.
—Pam Halter, Bridgeton, NJ

- -

Prep: 15 min. • **Cook:** 5 min./batch
Makes: about 2½ dozen

- 1 **cup all-purpose flour**
- 1 **tsp. baking powder**
- ½ **tsp. salt**
  Dash dried basil
  Dash dried oregano
  Dash pepper
- 1 **large tomato, finely chopped**
- ½ **cup chopped onion**
- ½ **cup shredded Parmesan cheese**
- 1 **jalapeno pepper, seeded and finely chopped**
- 1 **garlic clove, minced**
- 1 **to 6 Tbsp. water, optional**
  Oil for deep-fat frying

1. In a large bowl, whisk flour, baking powder, salt, basil, oregano and pepper. Gently stir in tomato, onion, cheese, jalapeno and garlic just until moistened. If the batter seems thick, add water 1 Tbsp. at a time to thin it slightly until it loosens up and mixes easily.
2. In a cast-iron or other heavy skillet, heat oil to 375°. Drop the batter by rounded tablespoonfuls, a few at a time, into hot oil. Fry until golden brown, about 1½ minutes per side. Drain on paper towels.
1 fritter: 40 cal., 2g fat (0 sat. fat), 1mg chol., 79mg sod., 4g carb. (0 sugars, 0 fiber), 1g pro.

TEST KITCHEN TIP

The water in this recipe is optional. It will depend on how ripe and juicy your tomato is. Fry 1 fritter as a test. If the middle is still undercooked when the exterior is golden brown, add some water to the batter to loosen it and make a slightly thinner fritter.

EASY PUPPY CHOW

This simple version of everyone's favorite sweet-salty snack mix uses a whole box of cereal, so there's less measuring. And there's enough to feed a hungry crowd.
—*Taste of Home* Test Kitchen

Takes: 15 min. • **Makes:** 13 cups

- 1 box (12 oz.) Corn Chex
- 2 cups semisweet chocolate chips
- ¾ cup creamy peanut butter
- ⅓ cup butter, cubed
- 3 cups confectioners' sugar

1. Pour cereal into a very large bowl. In a large microwave-safe bowl, combine the chocolate chips, peanut butter and butter. Microwave on high 30 seconds. Stir gently. Continue microwaving on high, stirring every 30 seconds, until melted and blended. Pour over cereal; gently stir to coat.

2. In batches, place confectioners' sugar in a large airtight container, add cereal mixture and shake until well coated. Spread cereal out on a baking sheet. Let stand until set. Store in airtight containers.

½ cup: 229 cal., 10g fat (5g sat. fat), 6mg chol., 146mg sod., 35g carb. (23g sugars, 2g fiber), 3g pro.

MAPLE PULLED
PORK BUNS

MAPLE PULLED PORK BUNS

Maple syrup is my sweet secret to these irresistible buns. Slow-cooking the yummy pork couldn't be easier, and the buns are quick to roll up. We love them for parties. They serve a packed house.
—Rashanda Cobbins, Food Editor

Prep: 25 min. + rising • **Cook:** 5½ hours **Makes:** 16 servings

- 1 boneless pork shoulder butt roast (2½ lbs.)
- 1½ tsp. ground mustard
- 1 tsp. salt
- ½ tsp. cayenne pepper
- ½ tsp. ground ginger
- 1 cup thinly sliced onion
- 2 garlic cloves, peeled
- 1 cup maple syrup, divided
- ½ cup water
- 3 Tbsp. cider vinegar
- 2 loaves (1 lb. each) frozen bread dough, thawed
- 1 cup barbecue sauce
- 1 cup shredded pepper jack cheese
  Chopped green onions and crushed red pepper flakes

1. Season pork with mustard, salt, cayenne pepper and ginger; place in a 4-qt. slow cooker. Top with onion and garlic; pour in ½ cup maple syrup, water and cider vinegar. Cook, covered, on low 5-7 hours or until meat is tender. Shred meat with 2 forks; discard cooking liquid and vegetables.

2. On a lightly floured surface, roll 1 loaf of dough into a 16x10-in. rectangle. Combine barbecue sauce with remaining syrup; brush ¼ cup sauce mixture to within ½ in. of dough edges. Top with half of pork. Roll up jelly-roll style, starting with a long side; pinch seam to seal. Cut crosswise into 8 slices. Place in a 9-in. pie plate, cut side down. Repeat with remaining dough and additional pie plate. Cover with kitchen towels; let rise in a warm place until dough doubles, about 1 hour. Reserve remaining sauce mixture. Preheat oven to 400°.

3. Bake 20 minutes or until golden brown. Sprinkle with cheese and bake until melted, 5-10 minutes longer. Serve with reserved sauce mixture; sprinkle with green onions and red pepper flakes.

1 roll: 358 cal., 12g fat (4g sat. fat), 50mg chol., 727mg sod., 41g carb. (14g sugars, 2g fiber), 20g pro.

CHICKEN PICCATA MEATBALLS

The classic chicken piccata entree is my favorite dish, but I wanted another way to enjoy all the same flavors. These chicken piccata meatballs are the perfect solution, whether served alone or with a sauce like marinara or Buffalo. Serve over buttered noodles for a main dish or stick toothpicks in them for appetizers.
—Dawn Collins, Rowley, MA

Prep: 20 min. • **Cook:** 25 min.
Makes: 2 dozen

- ½ cup dry bread crumbs
- ⅓ cup grated Parmesan cheese
- 1 large egg, lightly beaten
- 1 tsp. garlic powder
- ¼ tsp. salt
- ⅛ tsp. pepper
- 1 lb. ground chicken
- 2 Tbsp. canola oil, divided
- 2 garlic cloves, minced
- ⅓ cup chicken broth
- ¼ cup white wine
- 1 jar (3½ oz.) capers, drained
- 1 Tbsp. lemon juice
- 2 Tbsp. butter
  Shredded Parmesan cheese
  and lemon wedges

1. In a large bowl, combine the first 6 ingredients. Add chicken; mix lightly but thoroughly. With wet hands, shape into 1-in. balls.
2. In a large skillet, heat 1 Tbsp. oil over medium heat. Brown meatballs in batches; drain. Remove and keep warm. In the same skillet, heat remaining 1 Tbsp. oil over medium heat. Add garlic; cook 1 minute.
3. Add broth and wine to pan; increase heat to medium-high. Cook 1 minute, stirring to loosen browned bits from the pan. Add the capers and lemon juice; bring to a boil. Add the meatballs. Reduce the heat; simmer, uncovered, until the meatballs are cooked through, 5-7 minutes, stirring occasionally. Remove from heat; stir in the butter until melted. Sprinkle with Parmesan cheese and serve with lemon wedges.
1 meatball: 63 cal., 4g fat (1g sat. fat), 24mg chol., 193mg sod., 2g carb. (0 sugars, 0 fiber), 4g pro.

CHICKEN PICCATA MEATBALLS

CHICKEN FRIES

Kid-friendly and quick, these crunchy oven-baked chicken fries are coated with a mixture of crushed potato chips, panko bread crumbs and Parmesan cheese. Dip them in ranch dressing, barbecue sauce or honey mustard.
—Nick Iverson, Denver, CO

Prep: 20 min. • **Bake:** 15 min.
Makes: 4 servings

- 2 large eggs, lightly beaten
- ½ tsp. salt
- ½ tsp. garlic powder
- ¼ to ½ tsp. cayenne pepper
- 2 cups finely crushed ridged potato chips
- 1 cup panko bread crumbs
- ½ cup grated Parmesan cheese
- 2 boneless skinless chicken breasts (6 oz. each), cut into ¼-in.-thick strips

Preheat oven to 400°. In a shallow bowl, whisk eggs, salt, garlic powder and cayenne. In a separate shallow bowl, combine chips, bread crumbs and cheese. Dip chicken in egg mixture, then in potato chip mixture, patting to help coating adhere. Transfer to a greased wire rack in a foil-lined rimmed baking sheet. Bake until golden brown, 12-15 minutes.
1 serving: 376 cal., 17g fat (6g sat. fat), 149mg chol., 761mg sod., 27g carb. (1g sugars, 2g fiber), 27g pro.

ROASTED BRUSSELS SPROUTS WITH SRIRACHA AIOLI

This dish constantly surprises you—it's crispy, easy to eat, totally shareable and yet it's a vegetable! This recipe is also gluten-free, dairy-free and paleo, and it can be vegan if you use vegan mayo.
—Molly Winsten, Brookline, MA

Prep: 20 min. • Cook: 20 min.
Makes: 8 servings

- 1 lb. fresh Brussels sprouts, trimmed and halved
- 2 Tbsp. olive oil
- 2 to 4 tsp. Sriracha chili sauce, divided
- ½ tsp. salt, divided
- ½ tsp. pepper, divided
- ½ cup mayonnaise
- 2 tsp. lime juice
- 1 Tbsp. lemon juice

1. Preheat oven to 425°. Place Brussels sprouts on a rimmed baking sheet. Drizzle with oil and 1 tsp. chili sauce; sprinkle with ¼ tsp. salt and ¼ tsp. pepper. Toss to coat. Roast until crispy, about 20-25 minutes.
2. Meanwhile, mix ¼ tsp. salt and ¼ tsp. pepper, the remaining 1-3 tsp. chili sauce, mayonnaise and lime juice. Drizzle lemon juice over Brussels sprouts before serving with the aioli.
4 halves with 1 Tbsp. sauce: 146 cal., 14g fat (2g sat. fat), 1mg chol., 310mg sod., 6g carb. (2g sugars, 2g fiber), 2g pro.

FLORENTINE CIABATTA

I came up with this appetizer because of my love for white pizza. I've served my ciabatta pizza at many parties, and it's always a big hit with kids and adults alike.
—Noreen McCormick Danek, Cromwell, CT

Prep: 20 min. + cooling • Bake: 15 min.
Makes: 16 servings

- ½ cup olive oil
- 2 garlic cloves, minced
- ¾ tsp. dried basil
- ¼ tsp. kosher salt
- ¼ tsp. dried oregano
  Dash crushed red pepper flakes
- 1 loaf (16 oz.) ciabatta bread, cut into 16 slices
- ⅓ cup chopped oil-packed sun-dried tomatoes
- ⅓ cup chopped roasted sweet red peppers
- ¼ cup frozen chopped spinach, thawed and squeezed dry
- 1½ cups shredded mozzarella cheese
- ⅓ cup pine nuts, toasted

1. In a small saucepan, heat oil over medium heat. Add garlic; cook 1 minute. Remove from heat: stir in basil, salt, oregano and red pepper flakes. Cool completely.
2. Preheat oven to 400°. Place bread on ungreased baking sheets. Bake until golden brown, 5-7 minutes on each side. Spread with garlic oil. Top with sun-dried tomatoes, roasted peppers and spinach; sprinkle with cheese. Bake 3-5 minutes longer, or until cheese is melted. Sprinkle with pine nuts. Serve immediately.
1 slice: 200 cal., 12g fat (3g sat. fat), 8mg chol., 258mg sod., 19g carb. (1g sugars, 1g fiber), 5g pro.

TOASTED RAVIOLI

While visiting a friend in St. Louis, I ordered toasted ravioli, a local specialty, at almost every restaurant we tried. When I got home, I had replicate the hot, crispy bites. This recipe comes pretty close.
—Cristina Carrera, Kenosha, WI

Prep: 15 min. • Cook: 20 min.
Makes: about 1½ dozen

- 1 cup seasoned bread crumbs
- ¼ cup shredded Parmesan cheese
- 2 tsp. dried basil
- 1 cup all-purpose flour
- 2 large eggs, lightly beaten
- 1 pkg. (9 oz.) frozen beef ravioli, thawed
  Oil for deep-fat frying
  Optional: Fresh minced basil and additional shredded Parmesan cheese
- 1 cup marinara sauce

1. In a shallow bowl, mix bread crumbs, Parmesan cheese and basil. Place flour and eggs in separate shallow bowls. Dip ravioli in flour to coat both sides; shake off excess. Dip in egg, then in crumb mixture, patting to help coating adhere.
2. In a deep cast-iron or electric skillet, heat ½ in. of oil to 375°. Fry ravioli, a few at a time, until golden brown, 1-2 minutes on each side. Drain on paper towels. Immediately sprinkle with basil and cheese, if desired. Serve warm with marinara sauce.
1 piece: 73 cal., 5g fat (1g sat. fat), 6mg chol., 117mg sod., 6g carb. (1g sugars, 1g fiber), 2g pro.

We host pasta dinners, and these easy bites make great appetizers. Prepare them in the air fryer if you want to eliminate the oil.
—AMY GLANDER, EDITOR

TOASTED
RAVIOLI

BANG BANG SHRIMP CAKE SLIDERS

Make this cabbage slaw dressing and shrimp patties a day early. When ready to serve, toss the slaw and sear the patties, then assemble and enjoy.
—Kim Banick, Turner, OR

- -

Prep: 30 min. + chilling • **Cook:** 10 min./batch
Makes: 12 sliders

- 1 lb. uncooked shrimp (41-50 per lb.), peeled and deveined
- 1 large egg, lightly beaten
- ½ cup finely chopped sweet red pepper
- 6 green onions, chopped and divided
- 1 Tbsp. minced fresh gingerroot
- ¼ tsp. salt
- 1 cup panko bread crumbs
- ¼ cup mayonnaise
- 1 Tbsp. Sriracha chili sauce
- 1 Tbsp. sweet chili sauce
- 5 cups shredded Chinese or napa cabbage
- 12 mini buns or dinner rolls
- 3 Tbsp. canola oil
  Additional Sriracha chili sauce, optional

1. Place shrimp in a food processor; pulse until chopped. In a large bowl, combine the egg, red pepper, 4 green onions, ginger and salt. Add the shrimp and bread crumbs; mix gently. Shape into twelve ½-in.-thick patties. Refrigerate 20 minutes.
2. In a large bowl, combine mayonnaise and the chili sauces; stir in the cabbage and remaining green onions. Place buns on a baking sheet, cut sides up. Broil buns 3-4 in. from heat until golden brown, 2-3 minutes.
3. In a large cast-iron or other heavy skillet, heat oil over medium heat. Add shrimp cakes in batches; cook until golden brown on each side, 4-5 minutes. Serve on toasted buns with slaw; secure with toothpicks. If desired, serve with additional chili sauce.
1 slider: 210 cal., 10g fat (1g sat. fat), 63mg chol., 321mg sod., 20g carb. (3g sugars, 1g fiber), 11g pro.

BANG BANG SHRIMP
CAKE SLIDERS

MEATBALLS WITH CHIMICHURRI SAUCE

Serve some of this South American herb sauce featuring fresh cilantro and parsley on the side. You'll want plenty for extra dipping.
—Amy Chase, Vanderhoof, BC

Takes: 30 min.
Makes: about 20 (⅔ cup sauce)

- 1 pkg. (22 oz.) frozen fully cooked Angus beef meatballs
- 3 garlic cloves, peeled
- 1 cup packed Italian flat leaf parsley
- ¼ cup packed fresh cilantro leaves
- 1 tsp. salt
- ¼ tsp. coarsely ground pepper
- 2 Tbsp. red wine vinegar
- ½ cup extra virgin olive oil

1. Prepare beef meatballs according to package directions.
2. Meanwhile, place garlic in a small food processor; pulse until chopped. Add parsley, cilantro, salt and pepper; pulse until finely chopped. Add vinegar. While processing, gradually add oil in a steady stream.
3. In a large bowl, toss meatballs with a little more than half of the chimichurri sauce. Transfer to a platter. Serve with remaining sauce for dipping.

1 meatball with about 2 tsp. sauce: 130 cal., 12g fat (4g sat. fat), 17mg chol., 318mg sod., 2g carb. (0 sugars, 0 fiber), 4g pro.

BAKED ASPARAGUS DIP

BLT BITES

These hors d'oeuvres may be mini, but their bacon and tomato flavor is full size. I serve them at parties, brunches and picnics, and they're always a hit.
—Kellie Remmen, Detroit Lakes, MN

Prep: 25 min. + chilling
Makes: 20 appetizers

- 20 cherry tomatoes
- 1 lb. sliced bacon, cooked and crumbled
- ½ cup mayonnaise
- ⅓ cup chopped green onions
- 3 Tbsp. grated Parmesan cheese
- 2 Tbsp. snipped fresh parsley

1. Cut a thin slice off each tomato top. Scoop out and discard pulp. Invert the tomatoes on a paper towel to drain.
2. In a small bowl, combine the remaining ingredients. Spoon into cherry tomatoes. Refrigerate for several hours.

1 stuffed tomato: 113 cal., 10g fat (3g sat. fat), 11mg chol., 206mg sod., 1g carb. (1g sugars, 0 fiber), 3g pro.

BAKED ASPARAGUS DIP

No one can believe how quick and easy this comforting dip is. The flavors of the fresh asparagus and Parmesan cheese work so well together.
—Sandra Baratka, Phillips, WI

Takes: 30 min. • **Makes:** about 2 cups

- 1 lb. diced cooked fresh asparagus, drained
- 1 cup grated Parmesan cheese
- 1 cup mayonnaise
  Baked pita chips

In a large bowl, combine the asparagus, cheese and mayonnaise. Place in a 6-in. cast-iron skillet or 2-cup ovenproof bowl. Bake at 375° until heated through, about 20 minutes. Serve warm with pita chips.

2 Tbsp.: 120 cal., 11g fat (2g sat. fat), 5mg chol., 162mg sod., 2g carb. (1g sugars, 0 fiber), 2g pro.

CHEESY CARAMELIZED
ONION SKILLET BREAD

CHEESY CARAMELIZED ONION SKILLET BREAD

While this app is perfect for a football game or informal party, it actually came about because I have two sons who are always hungry. I need time to get dinner on the table after coming home from work. They love the skillet bread for the flavor; I love it because it keeps them in the kitchen to chat while I prepare the rest of dinner! If you'd like, you can use homemade biscuits instead of prepared.
—Mary Leverette, Columbia, SC

Prep: 45 min. • **Bake:** 20 min.
Makes: 8 servings

- 2 tsp. caraway seeds
- 1 Tbsp. olive oil
- 1 large onion, chopped
- ¼ tsp. salt
- 1 cup shredded sharp cheddar cheese
- ½ cup butter, melted
- 1 tube (16.3 oz.) large refrigerated buttermilk biscuits
- 1 Tbsp. minced fresh thyme, optional

1. Preheat oven to 350°. In a 10-in. cast-iron or other ovenproof skillet, toast caraway seeds until fragrant, about 1 minute. Remove and set aside.
2. In the same skillet, heat oil over medium heat. Add onion; cook and stir until softened, 5-6 minutes. Reduce heat to medium-low; cook 30-40 minutes, stirring occasionally, until deep golden brown. Stir in salt; remove from the heat and cool slightly.
3. Sprinkle cheese over onions in skillet. Place melted butter and caraway seeds in a shallow bowl. Cut each biscuit into fourths. Dip biscuit pieces in butter mixture; place in a single layer over onion mixture in skillet.
4. Bake until puffed and golden brown, 20-25 minutes. Cool in skillet 5 minutes before inverting onto a serving plate. If desired, sprinkle with thyme. Serve warm.
1 serving: 352 cal., 25g fat (13g sat. fat), 45mg chol., 874mg sod., 27g carb. (4g sugars, 1g fiber), 7g pro

CHOCOLATE PEANUT BUTTER SHAKES

CHOCOLATE PEANUT BUTTER SHAKES

These rich chocolate peanut butter shakes will make you feel like you're sitting in a 1950s soda fountain. Make it modern with an over-the-top garnish like skewered doughnut holes.
—*Taste of Home* Test Kitchen

Takes: 10 min. • **Makes:** 2 cups

- ¾ cup 2% milk
- 1½ cups chocolate ice cream
- ¼ cup creamy peanut butter
- 2 Tbsp. chocolate syrup
  Optional toppings: Sweetened whipped cream and miniature peanut butter cups, quartered

In a blender, combine the milk, ice cream, peanut butter and syrup; cover and process until smooth. If desired, garnish with some whipped cream, peanut butter cups and additional chocolate syrup.
1 cup: 501 cal., 29g fat (11g sat. fat), 41mg chol., 262mg sod., 51g carb (43g sugars, 3g fiber), 14g pro.

WATERMELON CUPS

This lovely appetizer is almost too pretty to eat! Sweet watermelon cubes hold a refreshing topping that showcases cucumber, red onion and fresh herbs.
—*Taste of Home* Test Kitchen

Takes: 25 min. • **Makes:** 16 appetizers

- 16 seedless watermelon cubes (1 in.)
- ⅓ cup finely chopped cucumber
- 5 tsp. finely chopped red onion
- 2 tsp. minced fresh mint
- 2 tsp. minced fresh cilantro
- ½ to 1 tsp. lime juice

1. Using a small melon baller or measuring spoon, scoop out the center of each watermelon cube, leaving a ¼-in. shell (save pulp for another use).
2. In a small bowl, combine the remaining ingredients; spoon into watermelon cubes.
1 piece: 7 cal., 0 fat (0 sat. fat), 0 chol., 1mg sod., 2g carb. (2g sugars, 0 fiber), 0 pro.

LOADED HUEVOS RANCHEROS
WITH ROASTED POBLANO PEPPERS
PAGE 68

Breakfasts

Jump-start your day with our favorite breakfast recipes. Whether you're craving something savory or a little sweet, we've got you covered with this nourishing roundup of comforting egg bakes, fluffy waffles and more.

CHILES RELLENOS BREAKFAST BAKE

We love southwestern flavor, so I turned chiles rellenos into a breakfast casserole. My family members became fans in an instant.
—Joan Hallford, North Richland Hills, TX

Prep: 10 min. • **Bake:** 35 min. + standing
Makes: 15 servings

- 1 pkg. (20 oz.) refrigerated shredded hash brown potatoes
- 1 can (27 to 28 oz.) whole green chiles
- 1 cup chunky salsa
- 1 lb. bulk pork sausage or fresh chorizo, cooked, drained and crumbled
- 2 cups shredded Mexican cheese blend
- 6 large eggs
- ½ cup 2% milk
- ¼ tsp. ground cumin
  Salt and pepper to taste
  Optional ingredients: Warm flour tortillas (8 in.), sour cream and salsa

1. Preheat oven to 350°. In a greased 13x9-in. baking dish, layer half the potatoes; all the chiles, opened flat; all the salsa; half of the sausage; and half the cheese. Repeat the layers with remaining potatoes, sausage and cheese.
2. Beat eggs and milk; add cumin, salt and pepper. Pour over potato mixture.
3. Bake, uncovered, until eggs are set in center, 35-40 minutes. Let stand 15 minutes. If desired, serve with tortillas, sour cream and additional salsa.
1 piece: 210 cal., 13g fat (5g sat. fat), 105mg chol., 440mg sod., 11g carb. (3g sugars, 1g fiber), 10g pro.

TEST KITCHEN TIP

If you use chorizo instead of pork sausage in this breakfast dish, the final product will have a bit more heat. Paprika or chili powder gives chorizo its rich red color.

QUICK STOVETOP GRANOLA

QUICK STOVETOP GRANOLA

The fiber-rich oats in this granola will quell your cravings with just a small serving. Keep some handy in a small airtight container for moments when your stomach takes over. For even longer-lasting fullness, pair the treat with protein-packed yogurt.
—*Taste of Home* Test Kitchen

Takes: 15 min. • **Makes:** 3 cups

- 2 cups quick-cooking oats
- 2 Tbsp. brown sugar
- 2 Tbsp. honey
- 1 Tbsp. butter
- ¼ cup slivered almonds
- 2 Tbsp. golden raisins
- 2 Tbsp. sweetened shredded coconut

1. In a large nonstick skillet, toast oats over medium heat until golden brown. Remove and set aside. In the same skillet, cook and stir the brown sugar, honey and butter over medium-low heat until bubbly, 1-2 minutes.
2. Stir in the almonds, raisins, coconut and oats until coated. Cool granola, then store in an airtight container.
¼ cup: 102 cal., 3g fat (1g sat. fat), 3mg chol., 14mg sod., 16g carb. (6g sugars, 2g fiber), 3g pro. **Diabetic exchanges:** 1 starch, ½ fat.

STICKY CINNAMON-SUGAR MONKEY BREAD

You can do all the prep work for this monkey bread the night before. I prepare the dough pieces and put all the sauce ingredients in the pan so it's ready to go in the morning.
—Diana Kunselman, Rimersburg, PA

Prep: 20 min. + rising • **Bake:** 20 min.
Makes: 16 servings

    2   loaves (1 lb. each) frozen bread
        dough, thawed
    1   cup packed brown sugar
    ¾   cup butter, cubed
    1   pkg. (3 oz.) cook-and-serve vanilla
        pudding mix
    2   Tbsp. 2% milk
    2   tsp. ground cinnamon

1. Cut dough into 1-in. pieces; place in a greased 13x9-in. baking dish. In a large saucepan, combine remaining ingredients; bring to a boil. Cook and stir 1 minute; remove from heat. Pour over dough pieces.
2. Cover loosely with parchment or nonstick foil; let rise in a warm place until almost doubled, about 45 minutes. Preheat oven to 350°. Bake, uncovered, until golden brown, 20-25 minutes. Immediately invert onto a serving plate.
1 serving: 247 cal., 9g fat (4g sat. fat), 18mg chol., 339mg sod., 36g carb. (16g sugars, 2g fiber), 5g pro.

SALMON & ARTICHOKE QUICHE SQUARES

SALMON & ARTICHOKE QUICHE SQUARES

Salmon, goat cheese and artichoke hearts make this quiche feel a little fancy and taste extra delicious. Baked in a handy 11x7-inch dish, it makes enough to serve a hungry brunch crowd.
—Jeanne Holt, Mendota Heights, MN

Prep: 15 min. • **Bake:** 40 min. + cooling
Makes: 15 servings

    1   tube (8 oz.) refrigerated
        crescent rolls
    ⅔   cup shredded Parmesan
        cheese, divided
    ½   cup crumbled goat cheese
    1   cup thinly sliced smoked salmon
        fillets
    1   cup water-packed artichoke
        hearts, drained
    ¼   cup chopped green onions (green
        portion only)
    2   Tbsp. finely chopped fresh dill
    ¼   tsp. pepper
    5   large eggs
    1   cup heavy whipping cream

1. Preheat oven to 350°. Unroll crescent roll dough into a long rectangle; place in ungreased 11x7-in. baking dish. Press dough over bottom and up sides of dish, pressing perforations to seal.
2. Sprinkle with ⅓ cup Parmesan cheese. Top with goat cheese, salmon and artichoke hearts. Sprinkle with onions, chopped dill and pepper. Whisk eggs and cream; pour over salmon mixture. Sprinkle with remaining Parmesan cheese.
3. Bake until a knife inserted in center comes out clean, 40-45 minutes (loosely cover with foil if edges are getting too dark). Cool for 20 minutes. Cut into squares.
1 square: 179 cal., 13g fat (7g sat. fat), 89mg chol., 330mg sod., 8g carb. (2g sugars, 0 fiber), 8g pro.

EVERYTHING BREAKFAST SLIDERS

These little sliders combine your favorite morning foods into one tasty package.
—Rashanda Cobbins, Food Editor

- -

Prep: 30 min. • **Bake:** 15 min.
Makes: 8 servings

- 8 **large eggs**
- ¼ **cup 2% milk**
- 2 **green onions, thinly sliced**
- ¼ **tsp. pepper**
- 8 **Tbsp. spreadable chive and onion cream cheese**
- 8 **miniature bagels, split**
- 8 **slices cheddar cheese, halved**
- 8 **slices Canadian bacon**
- 8 **cooked bacon strips, halved**

GLAZE

- 2 **Tbsp. butter, melted**
- 1½ **tsp. maple syrup**
- ⅛ **tsp. garlic powder**
- 2 **Tbsp. everything seasoning blend**

1. Preheat oven to 375°. Heat a large nonstick skillet over medium heat. In a large bowl, whisk eggs, milk, green onions and pepper until blended; pour into skillet. Cook and stir until eggs are thickened and no liquid egg remains; remove from heat.
2. Spread cream cheese over bagel bottoms; place in a greased 13x9-in. baking dish. Layer each with a half-slice of cheese and Canadian bacon. Spoon scrambled eggs over top. Layer with remaining halved cheese slices, bacon and bagel tops. Stir together butter, maple syrup and garlic powder; brush over bagel tops. Sprinkle tops with everything seasoning blend.
3. Bake until tops are golden brown and cheese is melted, 12-15 minutes.
1 slider: 415 cal., 26g fat (13g sat. fat), 253mg chol., 1070mg sod., 18g carb. (4g sugars, 1g fiber), 24g pro.

CINNAMON BLUEBERRY FRENCH TOAST

I like to prep this breakfast in the afternoon, let it chill, and then put it in the slow cooker when I wake up the next morning. By the time we're ready for brunch, it's done just right. Yum!
—Angela Lively, Conroe, TX

- -

Prep: 15 min. + chilling • **Cook:** 3 hours
Makes: 6 servings

- 3 **large eggs**
- 2 **cups 2% milk**
- ¼ **cup sugar**
- 1 **tsp. ground cinnamon**
- 1 **tsp. vanilla extract**
- ¼ **tsp. salt**
- 9 **cups cubed French bread (about 9 oz.)**
- 1 **cup fresh or frozen blueberries, thawed**
  Maple syrup

1. Whisk together the first 6 ingredients. Place half of the cubed bread in a greased 5-qt. slow cooker; top with ½ cup blueberries and half of the milk mixture. Repeat the layers. Refrigerate, covered, 4 hours or overnight.
2. Remove from refrigerator while oven heats. Cook, covered, on low until a knife inserted in the center comes out clean, 3-4 hours. Serve warm with syrup.
1 cup: 265 cal., 6g fat (2g sat. fat), 100mg chol., 430mg sod., 42g carb. (18g sugars, 2g fiber), 11g pro.

EVERYTHING BREAKFAST SLIDERS

EASY MORNING
WAFFLES

EASY MORNING WAFFLES

The irresistible touch of cinnamon in these homemade waffles takes them way beyond any store-bought kind.
—*Taste of Home* Test Kitchen

- -

Prep: 20 min. • **Cook:** 5 min./batch
Makes: 14 waffles (1 cup syrup)

- 2   cups all-purpose flour
- 1   Tbsp. brown sugar
- 2   tsp. baking powder
- ½   tsp. salt
- ½   tsp. ground cinnamon
- 3   large eggs, separated, room temperature
- 2   cups 2% milk
- ¼   cup canola oil
- ¾   tsp. vanilla extract

SYRUP
- ½   cup butter, cubed
- ½   cup honey
- 1   tsp. ground cinnamon

1. In a large bowl, combine the flour, brown sugar, baking powder, salt and cinnamon. In a small bowl, whisk the egg yolks, milk, oil and vanilla; stir into the dry ingredients just until moistened. In a small bowl, beat egg whites until stiff peaks form; fold into batter.

2. Bake waffles in a preheated waffle maker according to manufacturer's directions until golden brown.

3. In a microwave, melt the butter, honey and cinnamon; stir until smooth. Serve waffles with syrup.

2 waffles with about 2 Tbsp. syrup: 464 cal., 25g fat (10g sat. fat), 130mg chol., 442mg sod., 53g carb. (26g sugars, 1g fiber), 9g pro.

ASK SARAH

CAN I FREEZE WAFFLES?
You bet! Arrange waffles in a single layer on sheet pans and freeze until firm. Transfer waffles to a freezer container. Freeze up to 2 months.

SLOW-COOKER BREAKFAST BURRITOS

Prep these tasty, hearty burritos the night before for a quick breakfast in the morning, or let them cook while you are away on a weekend afternoon for an easy supper.
—Anna Miller, Churdan, IA

- -

Prep: 25 min. • **Cook:** 3¾ hours + standing
Makes: 12 servings

- 1   lb. bulk pork sausage
- 1   pkg. (28 oz.) frozen O'Brien potatoes, thawed
- 2   cups shredded sharp cheddar cheese
- 12 large eggs
- ½   cup 2% milk
- ¼   tsp. seasoned salt
- ⅛   tsp. pepper
- 12 flour tortillas (8 in.)
     Optional toppings: Salsa, sliced jalapenos, chopped tomatoes, sliced green onions and cubed avocado

1. In a large skillet, cook the sausage over medium heat 8-10 minutes or until no longer pink, breaking into crumbles; drain.

2. In a greased 4- or 5-qt. slow cooker, layer the potatoes, sausage and cheese. In a large bowl, whisk the eggs, milk, seasoned salt and pepper until blended; pour over top.

3. Cook, covered, on low 3¾-4¼ hours or until eggs are set and a thermometer reads 160°. Uncover and let stand for 10 minutes. Serve in tortillas with the toppings of your choice.

1 burrito: 359 cal., 15g fat (6g sat. fat), 205mg chol., 480mg sod., 39g carb. (2g sugars, 3g fiber), 16g pro.

SLOW-COOKER
BREAKFAST BURRITOS

EASY CHEESY CAULIFLOWER BREAKFAST CASSEROLE

I love finding new ways to add veggies to my meals. This twist on a breakfast favorite swaps in riced cauliflower for the usual hash browns to make it keto-friendly.
—Robyn Warren, Lakeway, AR

- -

Prep: 30 min. • **Bake:** 40 min. + standing
Makes: 12 servings

- 1   lb. bacon strips, chopped
- 1   cup chopped sweet onion
- ½   large sweet red pepper, chopped
- ½   large green pepper, chopped
- 9   large eggs, lightly beaten
- 1½ cups whole-milk ricotta cheese
- 4   cups frozen riced cauliflower, thawed
- 2   cups shredded cheddar cheese
- 1   cup shredded Swiss cheese
- ½   tsp. pepper
- ¼   tsp. salt

1. Preheat oven to 350°. In a large skillet, cook bacon over medium heat until crisp, stirring occasionally. Remove with a slotted spoon; drain on paper towels. Discard the drippings, reserving 1 Tbsp. in pan.

2. Add onion and chopped peppers to the drippings; cook and stir over medium-high heat until tender, 6-8 minutes. In a large bowl, whisk eggs and ricotta. Stir in riced cauliflower, shredded cheeses, bacon, onion mixture, pepper and salt. Pour into a greased 13x9-in. baking dish. Bake, uncovered, until a knife inserted near the center comes out clean, 40-45 minutes. Let stand 10 minutes before serving.

Freeze option: Cool the baked casserole completely; cover and freeze. To use, partially thaw in refrigerator overnight. Remove from the refrigerator 30 minutes before baking. Preheat oven to 350°. Bake the casserole as directed, increasing time as necessary to heat through and for a thermometer inserted in center to read 165°.

1 piece: 307 cal., 22g fat (11g sat. fat), 194mg chol., 534mg sod., 7g carb. (4g sugars, 2g fiber), 21g pro.

EASY CHEESY CAULIFLOWER BREAKFAST CASSEROLE

MAKEOVER HASH & EGGS

A diner classic goes home-style in this better-than-ever version that delivers fresh flavors with a healthy dose of fiber.
—*Taste of Home* Test Kitchen

Takes: 30 min. • **Makes:** 4 servings

- 1 large onion, chopped
- 1 Tbsp. canola oil, divided
- 6 medium red potatoes (about 1½ lbs.), cut into ½-in. cubes
- ¼ cup water
- 3 pkg. (2 oz. each) thinly sliced deli corned beef, coarsely chopped
- ¼ tsp. pepper
- 4 large eggs
  Additional pepper, optional

1. In a large nonstick skillet, saute onion in 2 tsp. oil until tender. Stir in the potatoes and water. Bring to a boil. Reduce heat; cover and simmer for 15-20 minutes or until potatoes are tender. Stir in corned beef and pepper; heat through.

2. Meanwhile, in a large nonstick skillet, fry eggs in remaining oil as desired. Season with additional pepper if desired. Serve with corned beef hash.

1 egg with 1 cup hash: 301 cal., 12g fat (3g sat. fat), 239mg chol., 652mg sod., 31g carb. (4g sugars, 4g fiber), 18g pro. **Diabetic exchanges:** 2 starch, 2 medium-fat meat, ½ fat.

BERRY RICOTTA PUFF PANCAKE

This slightly sweet berry pancake has a custardy texture that puffs up beautifully when baked. It makes an easy yet impressive breakfast dish.
—Jessi Smith, Fort Myers, FL

Prep: 20 min. • **Bake:** 25 min.
Makes: 8 slices

- 3 Tbsp. butter
- 5 large eggs, room temperature
- 1½ cups reduced-fat ricotta cheese
- ½ cup fat-free milk
- 1½ tsp. vanilla extract
- ½ tsp. grated lemon zest
- ¾ cup all-purpose flour
- ¼ cup sugar
- ½ tsp. baking powder
- ½ tsp. salt
- ½ cup sliced fresh strawberries
- ½ cup fresh raspberries
- ½ cup fresh blueberries
  Confectioners' sugar

1. Preheat oven to 400°. Place butter in a 12-in. cast-iron or other ovenproof skillet. Place in oven 4-5 minutes or until butter is melted; carefully swirl to coat evenly.

2. Meanwhile, in a blender, process eggs, ricotta, milk, vanilla and lemon zest until blended. Add flour, sugar, baking powder and salt and process until blended. Pour into hot skillet. Top with berries.

3. Bake until puffed, and sides are golden brown and crisp, 25-30 minutes. Remove the pancake from the oven; serve immediately with confectioners' sugar.

1 slice: 287 cal., 13g fat (6g sat. fat), 186mg chol., 406mg sod., 29g carb. (15g sugars, 2g fiber), 13g pro.

BERRY RICOTTA PUFF PANCAKE

ROASTED
VEGETABLE STRATA

ROASTED VEGETABLE STRATA

With the abundance of zucchini my family has in the fall, this is the perfect dish to use some of what we have. Cheesy and rich, the warm, classic breakfast dish is always sure to please!
—Colleen Doucette, Truro, NS

Prep: 55 min. + chilling • **Bake:** 40 min.
Makes: 8 servings

- 3 large zucchini, halved lengthwise and cut into ¾-in. slices
- 1 each medium red, yellow and orange peppers, cut into 1-in. pieces
- 2 Tbsp. olive oil
- 1 tsp. dried oregano
- ½ tsp. salt
- ½ tsp. pepper
- ½ tsp. dried basil
- 1 medium tomato, chopped
- 1 loaf (1 lb.) unsliced crusty Italian bread
- ½ cup shredded sharp cheddar cheese
- ½ cup shredded Asiago cheese
- 6 large eggs
- 2 cups fat-free milk

1. Preheat oven to 400°. Toss zucchini and peppers with oil and seasonings; transfer to a 15x10x1-in. pan. Roast 25-30 minutes or until tender, stirring once. Stir in tomato; cool mixture slightly.
2. Trim ends from bread; cut bread into 1-in. slices. In a greased 13x9-in. baking dish, layer half of each of the following: bread, roasted vegetables and cheeses. Repeat layers. Whisk the eggs and milk; pour evenly over top. Refrigerate, covered, 6 hours or overnight.
3. Preheat oven to 375°. Remove casserole from the refrigerator while the oven heats. Bake, uncovered, 40-50 minutes or until golden brown. Let strata stand 5-10 minutes before cutting.
Freeze option: Cover and freeze unbaked strata. To use, partially thaw in refrigerator overnight. Remove from the refrigerator 30 minutes before baking. Preheat oven to 375°. Bake casserole as directed, increasing the time as necessary to heat through and for a thermometer inserted in the center of the casserole to read 165°.
1 piece: 349 cal., 14g fat (5g sat. fat), 154mg chol., 642mg sod., 40g carb. (9g sugars, 4g fiber), 17g pro. **Diabetic exchanges:** 2 starch, 1 medium-fat meat, 1 vegetable, 1 fat.

COCONUT-MACADAMIA SHEET-PAN PANCAKES

These tropical pancakes are great for when you want to serve a group without standing over the stove. To make them even more fun, swap the usual butter and maple syrup topping for pineapple-flavored ice cream.
—Trisha Kruse, Eagle, ID

Prep: 15 min. + standing • **Bake:** 15 min.
Makes: 10 servings

- 3½ cups complete buttermilk pancake mix
- ½ cup sweetened shredded coconut
- 2 cups 2% milk
- 1 Tbsp. coconut oil or butter, softened
- ½ cup macadamia nuts, coarsely chopped
- 2 medium bananas, sliced
    Butter and maple syrup

1. Preheat oven to 425°. In a large bowl, combine pancake mix and coconut. Stir in the milk just until the dry ingredients are moistened; let stand 10 minutes. Meanwhile, line a 15x10x1-in. baking pan with parchment; grease parchment with coconut oil.
2. Spread batter into prepared pan; sprinkle with macadamia nuts. Bake until puffy and golden brown, 15-20 minutes. Cool in pan on a wire rack 5 minutes. Remove from pan by lifting with parchment. Top with bananas; serve with butter and syrup.
1 piece: 288 cal., 11g fat (4g sat. fat), 4mg chol., 642mg sod., 44g carb. (13g sugars, 2g fiber), 7g pro.

What a fun take on a staple! I even cut the pancake into individual servings and stashed them in the freezer for quick, tasty breakfasts on busy days.

—MARK HAGEN, EXECUTIVE EDITOR

COCONUT-MACADAMIA
SHEET-PAN PANCAKES

BLUEBERRY CORNMEAL PANCAKES

These pancakes are one of my family's favorite breakfasts. No time to make it from scratch? No problem! My grandmother's standby of store-bought muffin mix makes quick work of the job.
—Carolyn Eskew, Dayton, OH

- -

Takes: 30 min. • **Makes:** 10 pancakes

1   pkg. (8½ oz.) cornbread/muffin mix
1   cup fresh or frozen blueberries
⅓   cup canned white or shoepeg corn
    Maple syrup

In a large bowl, prepare muffin mix according to the package directions. Gently stir in the blueberries and corn. Lightly grease a griddle; warm over medium heat. Pour the batter by ¼ cupfuls onto the griddle; flatten slightly. Cook until the bottoms are golden brown. Turn; cook until the second sides are golden brown. Serve with syrup.
2 pancakes: 251 cal., 7g fat (2g sat. fat), 39mg chol., 454mg sod., 41g carb. (14g sugars, 4g fiber), 6g pro.

COASTAL CAROLINA
MUFFIN-TIN FRITTATAS

COASTAL CAROLINA MUFFIN-TIN FRITTATAS

Incorporating the flavors of a low country South Carolina crab boil, these frittatas are easy to make and fun to eat. If you have leftover cooked potatoes (roasted or boiled), try dicing them and substituting them for the refrigerated shredded potatoes in this recipe!
—Shannon Kohn, Summerville, SC

- -

Prep: 30 min. • **Bake:** 30 min.
Makes: 1 dozen

½   cup mayonnaise
1   Tbsp. lemon juice
2   tsp. sugar
1   tsp. seafood seasoning
2   cups refrigerated shredded hash
    brown potatoes
1½ cups chopped smoked sausage
1   can (8 oz.) jumbo lump crabmeat,
    drained
¼   cup chopped roasted sweet
    red peppers
7   large eggs
¾   cup heavy whipping cream
1   Tbsp. Louisiana-style hot sauce
½   tsp. salt
12 bacon strips, cooked and crumbled
¼   cup thinly sliced green onions

1. Preheat oven to 350°. In a small bowl, combine mayonnaise, lemon juice, sugar and seafood seasoning. Refrigerate until serving.
2. Meanwhile, in a large bowl, combine the potatoes, sausage, crab and red peppers. Divide among 12 greased jumbo muffin cups. In another large bowl, whisk the eggs, cream, hot sauce and salt. Pour over potato mixture. Top with bacon.
3. Bake until a knife inserted in center comes out clean, 30-35 minutes. Serve with sauce and green onions.
1 frittata: 292 cal., 23g fat (8g sat. fat), 164mg chol., 768mg sod., 7g carb. (2g sugars, 1g fiber), 13g pro.

TEST KITCHEN TIP
Lump crabmeat is worth the splurge in these frittatas because the flavor really shines through.

BANANA BLUEBERRY OATMEAL BAKE

When my brother, sister and I were young, Mom would bake this cinnamon-scented oatmeal before driving us to school. Whenever I make it, I am filled with lots of happy memories.
—Vincent Taylor, Houston, TX

- -

Prep: 15 min. • **Bake:** 30 min. + standing
Makes: 4 servings

- 1½ cups unsweetened almond milk or 2% milk
- ⅓ cup honey
- 1 tsp. vanilla extract
- ½ tsp. ground cinnamon
- ⅛ tsp. salt
- 1¼ cups old-fashioned oats
- 2 medium bananas, sliced
- 1 cup fresh or frozen blueberries

TOPPING
- ¼ cup packed brown sugar
- 2 Tbsp. all-purpose flour
- 2 Tbsp. butter, softened
- ½ cup chopped pecans

1. Preheat oven to 350°. In a bowl, whisk the first 5 ingredients until blended. Stir in the oats.
2. Arrange banana slices in a single layer in a greased 9-in. square baking pan; sprinkle with blueberries. Pour oatmeal mixture over top, spreading evenly. Bake 25-30 minutes or until set. Remove from oven. Preheat broiler.
3. For topping, in a small bowl, mix brown sugar, flour and butter with a fork until crumbly; stir in the pecans. Sprinkle over oatmeal. Broil 7-8 in. from heat 2-3 minutes or until lightly browned. Let stand 10 minutes before serving.
1 cup: 483 cal., 19g fat (5g sat. fat), 15mg chol., 193mg sod., 78g carb. (49g sugars, 7g fiber), 6g pro.

BANANA BLUEBERRY OATMEAL BAKE

AIR-FRYER HAM & EGG POCKETS

Refrigerated crescent roll dough makes these breakfast pockets a snap to prepare.
—*Taste of Home* Test Kitchen

- -

Takes: 25 min. • **Makes:** 2 servings

- 1 large egg
- 2 tsp. 2% milk
- 2 tsp. butter
- 1 oz. thinly sliced deli ham, chopped
- 2 Tbsp. shredded cheddar cheese
- 1 tube (4 oz.) refrigerated crescent rolls

1. Preheat air fryer to 300°. In a small bowl, combine egg and milk. In a small skillet, heat butter until hot. Add the egg mixture; cook and stir over medium heat until the eggs are completely set. Remove from the heat. Fold in ham and cheese.
2. Separate the crescent dough into 2 rectangles. Seal perforations; spoon half the filling down the center of each. Fold the dough over the filling; pinch to seal. Place in a single layer on greased tray in air-fryer basket. Cook pastries until golden brown, 8-10 minutes.
1 serving: 326 cal., 20g fat (5g sat. fat), 118mg chol., 735mg sod., 25g carb. (6g sugars, 0 fiber), 12g pro.

GREEK SALAD-INSPIRED
QUICHE

GREEK SALAD-INSPIRED QUICHE

I love using my cast-iron skillet to create this family-sized Greek quiche for a flavorful breakfast. The quiche is meatless, but you can serve it with a side of sausage or bacon if you have meat lovers in the family. It also makes a great dinner entree with pita bread and a green salad.
—Donna Ryan, Topsfield, MA

Prep: 20 min. • **Bake:** 20 min. + standing
Makes: 6 servings

- 1 Tbsp. olive oil
- 1 cup cherry tomatoes, halved
- ⅔ cup finely chopped green pepper
- ½ cup thinly sliced red onion
- ⅔ cup chopped fresh spinach
- 2 garlic cloves, minced
- 1 cup crumbled feta cheese
- ½ cup pitted Greek olives, sliced
- 6 large eggs
- 1 cup 2% milk
- 1 Tbsp. minced fresh oregano or 1 tsp. dried oregano
- ½ tsp. salt
- ⅛ to ¾ tsp. crushed red pepper flakes

1. In a 9-in. cast-iron or other ovenproof skillet, heat oil over medium-high heat. Add the tomatoes, green peppers and onion; cook and stir until the vegetables are tender, 6-7 minutes; drain. Add spinach and garlic; cook and stir until the spinach is wilted, 1-2 minutes. Remove from heat and stir in feta and olives.
2. In a large bowl, whisk eggs, milk, oregano, salt and pepper flakes until blended. Pour over vegetables.
3. Bake until a knife inserted in the center comes out clean, 20-25 minutes. Let stand 10 minutes before serving.
1 piece: 354 cal., 22g fat (9g sat. fat), 175mg chol., 778mg sod., 25g carb. (5g sugars, 2g fiber), 12g pro.

COFFEE & CREAM DOUGHNUTS

Craving something sweet? You can make these decadent doughnuts in no time!
—*Taste of Home* Test Kitchen

Takes: 30 min. • **Makes:** 10 doughnuts

  Oil for deep-fat frying
- 2 tubes (10.2 oz. each) large refrigerated buttermilk biscuits
- 3 Tbsp. heavy whipping cream
- 1 Tbsp. plus 1 tsp. instant coffee granules
- 6 oz. cream cheese, softened
- ⅔ cup Nutella
  Confectioners' sugar and baking cocoa

1. In an electric skillet or deep fryer, heat oil to 375°. Drop biscuits, a few at a time, into hot oil. Fry until golden brown on both sides. Drain on paper towels.
2. Meanwhile, place the whipping cream in a small microwave-safe bowl. Microwave, uncovered, on high until hot; stir in coffee granules until dissolved. Add cream cheese and Nutella; beat until smooth.
3. Cut a small hole in the corner of a pastry or plastic bag; insert a very small tip. Fill bag with coffee mixture. Push the tip through the side of each doughnut to fill with cream. Dust tops with confectioners' sugar and cocoa. Serve immediately.
1 serving: 413 cal., 28g fat (9g sat. fat), 27mg chol., 659mg sod., 37g carb. (15g sugars, 1g fiber), 7g pro.

DID YOU KNOW?
Pietro Ferrero, an Italian pastry maker, created Nutella following World War II. Cocoa was very scarce, and Ferrero's sweet hazelnut and sugar paste used just a small amount of cocoa to deliver rich, chocolaty flavor.

BERRY SMOOTHIE BOWL

We turned one of our favorite smoothies into a smoothie bowl and topped it with even more fresh fruit and toasted nuts for a little crunch.
—*Taste of Home* Test Kitchen

Takes: 5 min. • **Makes:** 2 servings

- 1 cup fat-free milk
- 1 cup frozen unsweetened strawberries
- ½ cup frozen unsweetened raspberries
- 3 Tbsp. sugar
- 1 cup ice cubes
  Optional: Sliced fresh strawberries, fresh raspberries, chia seeds, fresh pumpkin seeds, unsweetened shredded coconut and sliced almonds

Place the milk, berries and sugar in a blender; cover and process until smooth. Add ice cubes; cover and process until smooth. Divide mixture between 2 serving bowls. Add optional toppings as desired.
1½ cups: 155 cal., 0 fat (0 sat. fat), 2mg chol., 54mg sod., 35g carb. (30g sugars, 2g fiber), 5g pro.

FLUFFY BUNNY PANCAKES

Kids will love that it's as tasty as it is cute. If you're in a rush, you can substitute pancake mix so you can hightail it out of the kitchen in no time.
—Shannon Norris, Senior Food Stylist

Takes: 15 min. • **Makes:** 2 servings

- 1 cup all-purpose flour
- 1 Tbsp. sugar
- 2 tsp. baking powder
- ½ tsp. salt
- 1 large egg, room temperature
- ¾ cup milk
- ¼ cup butter, melted

TOPPINGS

Banana slices, miniature semisweet chocolate chips, whipped cream and sweetened shredded coconut

1. Preheat griddle over medium-high heat. Whisk together flour, sugar, baking powder and salt. Combine the egg, milk and melted butter; stir into the dry ingredients just until moistened.

2. For each bunny, make a pancake 4 in. wide for the body, a pancake 2½ in. wide for the head, 2 small oval-shaped pancakes for the feet and two small triangular pancakes for the ears. Spoon batter onto griddle; cook until bubbles form on top of pancakes. Turn; cook until second side is golden brown.

3. To form bunny, place ears at the top of a plate. Place head slightly overlapping the bottom of the ears; top with the body slightly overlapping the head and the feet slightly overlapping the body. Place a banana slice on each foot; arrange mini chocolate chips at the end of each foot for toes. Dollop the whipped cream on the body just above the feet; sprinkle whipped cream with coconut for the tail. Serve immediately.

1 bunny: 547 calories, 29g fat (17g saturated fat), 163mg cholesterol, 1329mg sodium, 59g carbohydrate (11g sugars, 2g fiber), 13g protein.

APPLE BUTTER BISCUIT BREAKFAST BAKE

My grandma created this recipe to use up leftovers from Christmas Eve dinner. By combining leftover ham and biscuits with her homemade apple butter, milk and eggs, she could serve a warm, tasty breakfast and still have lots of time to spend with family.
—Mary Leverette, Columbia, SC

- -

Prep: 30 min. + chilling
Bake: 50 min. + standing • **Makes:** 12 servings

- 10   leftover biscuits (3-in. diameter)
- ¾   cup apple butter
- 2   cups shredded sharp cheddar cheese
- 1½   cups cubed fully cooked ham
- ¼   cup minced fresh parsley
- 6   large eggs
- 2½   cups 2% milk
- 1   tsp. salt
- ½   tsp. pepper
- ¼   tsp. ground mustard

1. Split biscuits. Spread apple butter over cut sides of biscuits; replace the tops. Cut each biscuit into quarters; place in a single layer in a greased 13x9-in. baking dish. Top with the cheese, ham and parsley.
2. In a large bowl, whisk eggs, milk, salt, pepper and mustard. Pour over biscuits. Cover and refrigerate overnight.
3. Preheat oven to 325°. Remove strata from refrigerator while oven heats. Bake strata, uncovered, until puffed and edges are golden brown, 50-60 minutes. Let stand 10 minutes before cutting.
1 piece: 331 cal., 15g fat (7g sat. fat), 126mg chol., 976mg sod., 31g carb. (12g sugars, 1g fiber), 16g pro.

APPLE CINNAMON OVERNIGHT OATS

Many folks love this oatmeal cold, but I like to heat it up a little since I'm not a big fan of it right out of the fridge. Add a handful of nuts for crunch, flavor and extra health benefits.
—Sarah Farmer, Executive Culinary Director

- -

Prep: 5 min. + chilling • **Makes:** 1 serving

- ½   cup old-fashioned oats
- ½   medium Gala or Honeycrisp apple, chopped
- 1   Tbsp. raisins
- 1   cup 2% milk
- ¼   tsp. ground cinnamon
  Dash salt
  Toasted chopped nuts, optional

In a small container or Mason jar, combine all ingredients. Seal; refrigerate overnight.
1½ cups: 349 cal., 8g fat (4g sat. fat), 20mg chol., 263mg sod., 59g carb. (28g sugars, 7g fiber), 14g pro.

This easy, no-cook method for making homemade oats is a lifesaver on busy days. I like to add sliced banana or blueberries on top for extra nutrients.
—JAZMIN DELGADO, GRAPHIC DESIGNER

APPLE CINNAMON OVERNIGHT OATS

FETA ASPARAGUS FRITTATA

Asparagus and feta cheese come together to make this frittata extra special. It's perfect for a lazy Sunday or to serve with a tossed salad for a light lunch.
—Mildred Sherrer, Fort Worth, TX

- -

Takes: 30 min. • **Makes:** 2 servings

- 12 fresh asparagus spears, trimmed
- 6 large eggs
- 2 Tbsp. heavy whipping cream
  Dash salt
  Dash pepper
- 1 Tbsp. olive oil
- 2 green onions, chopped
- 1 garlic clove, minced
- ½ cup crumbled feta cheese

1. Preheat oven to 350°. Place ½ in. of water and asparagus in a large skillet; bring to a boil. Cook, covered, until the asparagus is crisp-tender, 3-5 minutes; drain. Cool slightly.
2. In a bowl, whisk together eggs, cream, salt and pepper. Chop 2 asparagus spears. In an 8-in. cast-iron or other ovenproof skillet, heat oil over medium heat until hot. Saute green onions, garlic and chopped asparagus 1 minute. Stir in egg mixture; cook, covered, over medium heat until eggs are nearly set, 3-5 minutes. Top with whole asparagus spears and cheese.
3. Bake until the eggs are completely set, 7-9 minutes.
½ frittata: 425 cal., 31g fat (12g sat. fat), 590mg chol., 1231mg sod., 8g carb. (3g sugars, 3g fiber), 27g pro.

LOADED HUEVOS RANCHEROS WITH ROASTED POBLANO PEPPERS

This is a unique but tasty version of huevos rancheros. It's similar to a cowboy hash, because the potatoes take the place of the corn tortillas.
—Joan Hallford, North Richland Hills, TX

- -

Prep: 15 min. + standing • **Cook:** 20 min.
Makes: 4 servings

- 1 poblano pepper
- ½ lb. fresh chorizo or bulk spicy pork sausage
- 4 cups frozen O'Brien potatoes, thawed
- ½ cup shredded pepper jack cheese
- 1 tsp. smoked paprika
- ½ tsp. kosher salt
- ½ tsp. garlic powder
- ½ tsp. pepper
- 4 large eggs
  Salsa, sour cream and minced fresh cilantro

1. Place pepper in a 12-in. cast-iron or other ovenproof skillet. Broil 4 in. from heat until skin blisters, rotating pepper with tongs until all sides are blistered and blackened, about 5 minutes. Immediately place pepper in a small bowl; let stand, covered, 20 minutes.
2. Peel off and discard charred skin. Remove the stems and seeds. Finely chop the pepper; set aside.
3. In the same skillet, cook the chorizo over medium heat 6-8 minutes or until cooked through, breaking into crumbles; drain. Add the potatoes; cook and stir 8-10 minutes or until tender. Stir in cheese, smoked paprika, kosher salt, garlic powder and pepper.
4. With the back of a spoon, make 4 wells in potato mixture. Break an egg in each well. Cook, covered, on medium-low until egg whites are completely set and yolks begin to thicken but are not hard, 5-7 minutes. Serve with reserved roasted pepper, salsa, sour cream and cilantro.
1 serving: 426 cal., 26g fat (10g sat. fat), 251mg chol., 1114mg sod., 20g carb. (2g sugars, 3g fiber), 24g pro.

TASTE OF HOME
TEST KITCHEN
RECIPE OF THE YEAR
★ ★ ★ ★ ★

LOADED HUEVOS RANCHEROS WITH ROASTED POBLANO PEPPERS

CARAMEL-SCOTCH CREAM
CHEESE COFFEE CAKE

PEANUT BUTTER & JELLY OVERNIGHT OATS

These peanut butter and jelly overnight oats give everyone's favorite sandwich a healthy twist. Switch to crunchy peanut butter and sprinkle chopped peanuts over the top if you like the extra crunch.
—*Taste of Home* Test Kitchen

Prep: 10 min. + chilling • **Makes:** 4 servings

- ¼ **cup creamy peanut butter**
- 2 **Tbsp. honey**
- 1½ **cups 2% milk**
- 1⅓ **cups old-fashioned oats**
- ¼ **cup strawberry jelly**

1. In a small bowl, beat peanut butter and honey until smooth. Gradually add the milk until smooth. Add the oats and mix to combine. Refrigerate, covered, overnight.
2. Whisk the jelly slightly and swirl 1 Tbsp. into each serving.

1 serving: 323 cal., 12g fat (3g sat. fat), 7mg chol., 112mg sod., 48g carb. (27g sugars, 3g fiber), 10g pro.

CARAMEL-SCOTCH CREAM CHEESE COFFEE CAKE

I came up with this cream cheese coffee cake recipe so I could make a delicious brunch treat using convenience pastry for the base. Serving it when it's cold means that all the cozy filling stays in each slice.
—Sherry Little, Sherwood, AR

Prep: 25 min. • **Bake:** 20 min. + chilling
Makes: 8 servings

- 1 **tube (12 oz.) large refrigerated buttery crescent rolls**
- 1 **carton (7½ oz.) spreadable brown sugar and cinnamon cream cheese**
- ⅓ **cup butterscotch-caramel ice cream topping**
- ½ **cup chopped pecans**
- ⅓ **cup packed brown sugar**
- ¼ **cup all-purpose flour**
- 2 **Tbsp. cold butter**
- 1 **large egg, beaten**

1. Preheat oven to 375°. Unroll crescent dough into a long rectangle; place on a parchment-lined baking sheet. Press the perforations to seal. Spread cream cheese down center third of rectangle. Drizzle with ice cream topping; sprinkle with pecans. Combine brown sugar and flour; cut in the butter until crumbly. Sprinkle half of the mixture over pecans.
2. On each long side of dough, cut 8 strips at an angle, about 2 in. into the center. Fold 1 strip from each side over filling and pinch ends together; repeat. Brush with the beaten egg. Sprinkle the top with the remaining brown sugar mixture.
3. Bake coffee cake until deep golden brown, 18-22 minutes. Cool 5 minutes before removing from pan to a wire rack to cool completely. Refrigerate until cold.

1 piece: 381 cal., 19g fat (8g sat. fat), 16mg chol., 472mg sod., 47g carb. (25g sugars, 2g fiber), 5g pro.

THE BEST
QUICHE LORRAINE

MIXED BERRY FRENCH TOAST BAKE

I love this recipe! It's perfect for fuss-free holiday breakfasts or serving company. It's scrumptious and so easy to put together the night before.
—Amy Berry, Poland, ME

- -

Prep: 20 min. + chilling • **Bake:** 45 min.
Makes: 8 servings

- 6 large eggs
- 1¾ cups fat-free milk
- 1 tsp. sugar
- 1 tsp. ground cinnamon
- 1 tsp. vanilla extract
- ¼ tsp. salt
- 1 loaf (1 lb.) French bread, cubed
- 1 pkg. (12 oz.) frozen unsweetened mixed berries
- 2 Tbsp. cold butter
- ⅓ cup packed brown sugar
  Optional: Confectioners' sugar and maple syrup

1. Whisk together first 6 ingredients. Place bread cubes in a 13x9-in. or 3-qt. baking dish coated with cooking spray. Pour the egg mixture over top. Refrigerate, covered, 8 hours or overnight.
2. Preheat oven to 350°. Remove berries from freezer and French toast from the refrigerator and let stand while oven heats. Bake, covered, 30 minutes.
3. In a small bowl, cut butter into brown sugar until crumbly. Top French toast with berries; sprinkle with brown sugar mixture. Bake, uncovered, until a knife inserted in the center comes out clean, 15-20 minutes. If desired, dust with confectioners' sugar and serve with syrup.
1 serving: 310 cal., 8g fat (3g sat. fat), 148mg chol., 517mg sod., 46g carb. (17g sugars, 3g fiber), 13g pro.

THE BEST QUICHE LORRAINE

Nestled in a buttery, rustic crust, this quiche is filled with sweet onions, bacon bits and cheese. It's the perfect addition to brunch.
—Shannon Norris, Senior Food Stylist

- -

Prep: 1 hour. • **Bake:** 1¼ hours + cooling
Makes: 8 servings

- Pastry for single-crust pie
- 1 pkg. (12 oz.) thick-sliced bacon strips, coarsely chopped
- 3 large sweet onions, chopped
- 1 Tbsp. minced fresh thyme
- ½ tsp. coarsely ground pepper
- ⅛ tsp. ground nutmeg
- 1½ cups shredded Gruyere cheese
- ½ cup grated Parmesan cheese
- 8 large eggs
- 2 cups whole milk
- 1 cup heavy whipping cream

1. On a lightly floured surface, roll dough to a 14-in. circle. Transfer to a 9-in. springform pan; press firmly against bottom and sides. Refrigerate while preparing filling.
2. In a large skillet, cook bacon over medium heat until crisp, stirring occasionally. Remove with a slotted spoon; drain on paper towels. Discard drippings, reserving 1 Tbsp. in pan. Add onions to the drippings; cook and stir over medium heat 20-25 minutes or until caramelized. Stir in the thyme, pepper and nutmeg; remove from the heat. Cool slightly. Stir in cheeses and reserved bacon; spoon into crust. Preheat oven to 350°. In a large bowl, whisk the eggs, milk and cream until blended; pour over top. Place springform pan on a rimmed baking sheet.
3. Bake on a lower oven rack until a knife inserted near the center comes out clean, 75-85 minutes. Cool on a wire rack for 15 minutes. Loosen sides from pan with a knife. Remove rim from pan.
1 piece: 609 cal., 44g fat (24g sat. fat), 295mg chol., 789mg sod., 29g carb. (11g sugars, 2g fiber), 24g pro.
Pastry for a single-crust deep-dish pie (9 in.): Combine 1½ cups all-purpose flour and ¼ tsp. salt; cut in ⅔ cup cold butter until crumbly. Gradually add 3-6 Tbsp. ice water, tossing with a fork until dough holds together when pressed. Wrap and refrigerate 1 hour.

MIXED BERRY
FRENCH TOAST BAKE

GREEN ONION ROLLS
PAGE 77

Breads, Biscuits & More

We all love bread, rolls and other baked beauties straight from the oven. From easy quick breads to more complex loaves, the *Taste of Home* Test Kitchen has dozens of recipes perfect for beginner and seasoned bread-makers alike. Rely on these foolproof recipes and tips for classic bakes that will complement any meal!

HONEY-SQUASH
DINNER ROLLS

HONEY-SQUASH ROLLS

Squash gives a rich color to these fluffy rolls. Any variety of squash works well.
—Marcia Whitney, Gainesville, FL

Prep: 40 min. + rising • **Bake:** 20 min.
Makes: 2 dozen

- 2 pkg. (¼ oz. each) active dry yeast
- 2 tsp. salt
- ¼ tsp. ground nutmeg
- 6 to 6½ cups all-purpose flour
- 1¼ cups 2% milk
- ½ cup butter, cubed
- ½ cup honey
- 1 pkg. (12 oz.) frozen mashed winter squash, thawed (about 1⅓ cups)
- 1 large egg, lightly beaten
  Poppy seeds, salted pumpkin seeds or pepitas, or sesame seeds

1. In a large bowl, mix yeast, salt, nutmeg and 3 cups flour. In a small saucepan, heat milk, butter and honey to 120°-130°. Add to the dry ingredients; beat on medium speed for 2 minutes. Add the squash; beat on high 2 minutes. Stir in enough remaining flour to form a soft dough (dough will be sticky).
2. Turn dough onto a floured surface; knead until smooth and elastic, 6-8 minutes. Place in a greased bowl, turning once to grease the top. Cover and let rise in a warm place until doubled, about 1 hour.
3. Punch down dough. Turn onto a lightly floured surface; divide dough and shape into 24 balls. Divide between 2 greased 9-in. cast-iron skillets or round baking pans. Cover with kitchen towels; let rise in a warm place until doubled, about 45 minutes.
4. Preheat oven to 375°. Brush tops with beaten egg; sprinkle with seeds. Bake until dark golden brown, 20-25 minutes. Cover loosely with foil during the last 5-7 minutes if needed to prevent overbrowning. Remove from pans to wire racks; serve warm.
1 roll: 186 cal., 5g fat (3g sat. fat), 19mg chol., 238mg sod., 32g carb. (6g sugars, 1g fiber), 4g pro. **Diabetic exchanges:** 2 starch, 1 fat.

DOWN EAST BLUEBERRY BUCKLE

This buckle won a contest at my daughter's college. They shipped us four lobsters, but the real prize was seeing the smile on our daughter's face.
—Dianne van der Veen, Plymouth, MA

Prep: 15 min. • **Bake:** 30 min.
Makes: 9 servings

- 2 cups all-purpose flour
- ¾ cup sugar
- 2½ tsp. baking powder
- ¼ tsp. salt
- 1 large egg, room temperature
- ¾ cup 2% milk
- ¼ cup butter, melted
- 2 cups fresh or frozen blueberries

TOPPING
- ½ cup sugar
- ⅓ cup all-purpose flour
- ½ tsp. ground cinnamon
- ¼ cup butter, softened

1. Preheat oven to 375°. In a large bowl, whisk flour, sugar, baking powder and salt. In another bowl, whisk egg, milk and melted butter until blended. Add to flour mixture; stir just until moistened. Fold in blueberries. Transfer mixture to a greased 9-in. square baking pan.
2. For topping, in a small bowl, mix sugar, flour and cinnamon. Using a fork, stir in softened butter until mixture is crumbly. Sprinkle over batter.
3. Bake until a toothpick inserted in center comes out clean (do not overbake), 30-35 minutes. Cool in pan on a wire rack. Serve warm or at room temperature.
1 piece: 354 cal., 12g fat (7g sat. fat), 49mg chol., 277mg sod., 59g carb. (32g sugars, 2g fiber), 5g pro.

MOIST IRISH SODA BREAD

I'm allergic to yeast, so I appreciate recipes that don't call for that ingredient, such as quick breads, biscuits and this soda bread. This tender loaf dotted with raisins is my favorite way to enjoy toast for breakfast.
—Carol Fritz, Fulton, IL

Prep: 20 min. • **Bake:** 40 min.
Makes: 1 loaf (16 slices)

- 4 cups all-purpose flour
- 1 Tbsp. sugar
- 1½ tsp. baking soda
- 1 tsp. baking powder
- ½ tsp. salt
- ¼ cup cold butter
- 1 cup golden raisins
- 1¾ cups buttermilk

1. In a large bowl, combine the flour, sugar, baking soda, baking powder and salt. Cut in butter until the mixture resembles coarse crumbs. Add raisins. Stir in buttermilk just until moistened. Turn onto a lightly floured surface; gently knead 6-8 times.
2. Place on an ungreased baking sheet; pat into a 7-in. round loaf. Using a sharp knife, cut a 1-in. cross about ¼ in. deep on top of the loaf. Bake at 375° for 40-45 minutes or until golden brown. Cool on a wire rack.
1 slice: 181 cal., 3g fat (2g sat. fat), 9mg chol., 265mg sod., 33g carb. (0 sugars, 1g fiber), 4g pro. **Diabetic exchanges:** 1½ starch, ½ fruit, ½ fat.

> I've made this a couple times, and it's really good bread. Simple recipe, too. I pair it with butter and it's simply divine.
> —ARIELLE ANTTONEN, GRAPHIC DESIGNER

GRANOLA BLUEBERRY MUFFINS

I wanted to put a new spin on muffins, so I mixed in some granola. I brought a batch to work the next morning—success. The granola I used contained lots of nuts, pumpkin seeds and shredded coconut.
—Megan Weiss, Menomonie, WI

Prep: 20 min. • **Bake:** 15 min.
Makes: 1 dozen

- 1½ cups whole wheat flour
- ½ cup all-purpose flour
- ¼ cup packed brown sugar
- 2 tsp. baking powder
- ½ tsp. salt
- ½ tsp. baking soda
- 1 cup granola without raisins, divided
- 1 large egg, room temperature
- 1 cup buttermilk
- ¼ cup canola oil
- 2 Tbsp. orange juice
- 1 Tbsp. lemon juice
- 1 cup fresh or frozen unsweetened blueberries

1. Preheat oven to 400°. In a small bowl, whisk flours, brown sugar, baking powder, salt and baking soda. Stir in ½ cup granola. In another bowl, whisk egg, buttermilk, oil and juices until blended. Add to flour mixture; stir just until moistened. Fold in blueberries.
2. Fill 12 greased muffin cups three-fourths full; sprinkle remaining granola over batter. Bake 12-15 minutes or until a toothpick inserted in center comes out clean. Cool 5 minutes before removing from pan to a wire rack.
Freeze option: Freeze cooled muffins in freezer containers. To use, thaw at room temperature or, if desired, microwave each muffin on high for 20-30 seconds or until heated through.
1 muffin: 188 cal., 7g fat (1g sat. fat), 18mg chol., 251mg sod., 28g carb. (8g sugars, 4g fiber), 6g pro. **Diabetic exchanges:** 2 starch, 1 fat.

I LIKE TO EAT APPLES & BANANAS BREAD

I LIKE TO EAT APPLES & BANANAS BREAD

My children love to bake (and eat) all kinds of homemade banana bread. They make this all by themselves, with just a little help from me to put it in the oven.
—Kristin Metcalf, Charlton, MA

Prep: 20 min. • **Bake:** 50 min. + cooling
Makes: 1 loaf (16 slices)

- 1½ cups mashed ripe bananas (4-5 medium)
- 1½ cups chopped peeled apples (2 medium)
- ½ cup sugar
- ½ cup packed brown sugar
- 2 Tbsp. water
- 2 Tbsp. butter, melted
- 1½ cups all-purpose flour
- 1 tsp. baking soda
- 1 tsp. baking powder
- ¼ tsp. salt
- 1 cup sweetened shredded coconut
- ½ cup caramel sundae syrup
- ¼ tsp. sea salt

1. Preheat oven to 350°. Combine bananas, apples, sugars and water. Stir in melted butter. In another bowl, whisk flour, baking soda, baking powder and salt. Stir into banana mixture. Transfer to a greased and floured 9x5-in. loaf pan.
2. Bake until a toothpick inserted in center comes out clean, 50-60 minutes. Cool in pan 10 minutes before removing to a wire rack to cool completely.
3. Meanwhile, toast the coconut, stirring occasionally, in a shallow pan at 350° until golden brown, 4-6 minutes. Cool slightly. Mix toasted coconut with caramel syrup and sea salt; spread over loaf.
1 slice: 187 cal., 4g fat (3g sat. fat), 4mg chol., 232mg sod., 38g carb. (25g sugars, 1g fiber), 2g pro.

GREEN ONION ROLLS

Better double the batch—these savory, elegant rolls will disappear fast!
—Jane Kroeger, Key Largo, FL

- -

Prep: 30 min. + rising • **Bake:** 20 min.
Makes: 1 dozen

- 1 Tbsp. butter
- 1½ cups chopped green onions
- ½ tsp. pepper
- ¾ tsp. garlic salt, optional
- 1 loaf (1 lb.) frozen bread dough, thawed
- ½ cup shredded part-skim mozzarella cheese
- ⅓ cup grated Parmesan cheese

1. Preheat oven to 375°. In a large skillet, heat butter over medium-high heat; saute green onions until tender. Stir in pepper and, if desired, garlic salt. Remove from heat.
2. On a lightly floured surface, roll dough into a 12x8-in. rectangle. Spread with onion mixture. Sprinkle with cheeses.
3. Roll up jelly-roll style, starting with a long side; pinch seam to seal. Cut into 12 slices; place in greased muffin cups. Cover; let rolls rise in a warm place until doubled, about 30 minutes. Preheat oven to 375°.
4. Bake until golden brown, 18-20 minutes. Remove from pan to a wire rack. Serve the rolls warm.
1 roll: 142 cal., 4g fat (1g sat. fat), 7mg chol., 415mg sod., 20g carb. (2g sugars, 2g fiber), 6g pro.

SWEET ITALIAN HOLIDAY BREAD

This is authentic ciambellotto, a sweet loaf my great-grandmother used to bake in Italy. I still use her traditional recipe—the only update I made was for modern appliances.
—Denise Perrin, Vancouver, WA

- -

Prep: 15 min. • **Bake:** 45 min.
Makes: 1 loaf (20 slices)

- 4 cups all-purpose flour
- 1 cup sugar
- 2 Tbsp. grated orange zest
- 3 tsp. baking powder
- 3 large eggs, room temperature
- ½ cup 2% milk
- ½ cup olive oil
- 1 large egg yolk, lightly beaten
- 1 Tbsp. coarse sugar

1. Preheat oven to 350°. In a large bowl, whisk flour, sugar, orange zest and baking powder. In another bowl, whisk eggs, milk and oil until blended. Add to flour mixture; stir just until moistened.
2. Shape dough into a 6-in. round loaf on a greased baking sheet. Brush top with egg yolk; sprinkle with coarse sugar. Bake until a toothpick inserted in center comes out clean, 45-50 minutes. Cover top loosely with foil during the last 10 minutes if needed to prevent overbrowning. Remove from pan to a wire rack; serve warm.
1 slice: 197 cal., 7g fat (1g sat. fat), 38mg chol., 87mg sod., 30g carb. (11g sugars, 1g fiber), 4g pro.

GREEN ONION ROLLS

GRANDMA'S ONION SQUARES

EASY CAST-IRON PEACH BISCUIT ROLLS

I used to love going to the local coffee shop and enjoying their fresh peach cinnamon rolls. Being a busy mom of three, I no longer have the time, so I developed this no-yeast recipe that is quick and easy to make!
—Heather Karow, Burnett, WI

- -

Prep: 25 min. • **Bake:** 25 min. + cooling
Makes: 1 dozen

- 1 cup packed brown sugar
- ¼ cup butter, softened
- 3 tsp. ground cinnamon

DOUGH

- 2 cups all-purpose flour
- 2 Tbsp. sugar
- 1 Tbsp. baking powder
- 1 tsp. salt
- 3 Tbsp. butter
- ¾ cup 2% milk
- 1 can (15 oz.) sliced peaches in juice, undrained
- 1 cup confectioners' sugar

1. Preheat oven to 350°. In a small bowl, mix brown sugar, butter and cinnamon until crumbly. Reserve half for topping. Sprinkle remaining crumb mixture onto bottom of a 10-in. cast-iron or other ovenproof skillet.
2. For dough, in a large bowl, mix flour, sugar, baking powder and salt. Cut in butter until crumbly. Add milk; stir to form a soft dough (dough will be sticky). Roll into an 18x12-in. rectangle. Sprinkle reserved topping to within ½ in. of edges.
3. Drain peaches, reserving 2 Tbsp. juice for glaze. Chop peaches; place over topping. Roll up jelly-roll style, starting with a long side; pinch seam to seal. Cut into 12 slices. Place in prepared skillet, cut side down.
4. Bake until lightly browned, 25-30 minutes. Cool on a wire rack 10 minutes. For glaze, combine confectioners' sugar and 1-2 Tbsp. of the reserved peach juice to reach desired consistency. Drizzle over warm rolls.
1 roll: 279 cal., 7g fat (4g sat. fat), 19mg chol., 746mg sod., 52g carb. (35g sugars, 1g fiber), 3g pro.

GRANDMA'S ONION SQUARES

My grandma brought this recipe with her when she emigrated from Italy as a young wife and mother. It is still a family favorite.
—Janet Eddy, Stockton, CA

- -

Prep: 40 min. • **Bake:** 35 min.
Makes: 9 servings

- 2 Tbsp. olive oil
- 2 cups sliced onions
- 1 tsp. salt, divided
- ¼ tsp. pepper
- 2 cups all-purpose flour
- 3 tsp. baking powder
- 5 Tbsp. shortening
- ⅔ cup 2% milk
- 1 large egg, room temperature
- ¾ cup sour cream

1. Preheat oven to 400°. In a large skillet, heat oil over medium heat. Add onions; cook and stir until softened, 8-10 minutes. Reduce heat to medium-low; cook until deep golden brown, 30-40 minutes, stirring occasionally. Stir in ½ tsp. salt and the pepper.
2. Meanwhile, in a large bowl, combine flour, baking powder and remaining ½ tsp. salt. Cut in shortening until mixture resembles coarse crumbs. Stir in the milk just until moistened. Press into a greased 9-in. square baking pan; top with onions.
3. Combine egg and sour cream; spread over the onion layer. Bake until golden brown, 35-40 minutes. Cut into squares. Serve warm.
1 piece: 256 cal., 15g fat (5g sat. fat), 27mg chol., 447mg sod., 25g carb. (3g sugars, 1g fiber), 5g pro.

EASY CAST-IRON
PEACH BISCUIT ROLLS

LEMON RICOTTA FRITTERS

ASK SARAH

IS THERE A SUBSTITUTE FOR BAKING POWDER?

Absolutely! If you're out of baking powder, follow this simple formula using baking soda and lemon juice. Use ¼ tsp. baking soda for each 1 tsp. baking powder and add ½ tsp. lemon juice to the recipe's wet ingredients. The acid in the juice will create the reaction your goodies need to puff up.

LEMON RICOTTA FRITTERS

These lemony fritters are golden brown outside, soft and cakelike inside.
—Tina Mirilovich, Johnstown, PA

- -

Takes: 30 min. • **Makes:** about 2 dozen

1	cup all-purpose flour
2	tsp. baking powder
1½	tsp. grated lemon zest
	Pinch salt
3	large eggs, room temperature
1	cup whole-milk ricotta cheese
3	Tbsp. sugar
½	tsp. lemon extract
	Oil for deep-fat frying
	Confectioners' sugar
	Honey or strawberry jam

1. In a large bowl, whisk flour, baking powder, lemon zest and salt. In another bowl, whisk eggs, cheese, sugar and extract. Add to dry ingredients, stirring just until moistened.
2. In a deep cast-iron skillet or deep-fat fryer, heat the oil to 375°. Drop batter by tablespoonfuls, several at a time, into hot oil. Fry 2-3 minutes or until golden brown. Drain on paper towels. Dust with confectioners' sugar. Serve warm with honey or jam.
1 fritter: 60 cal., 3g fat (1g sat. fat), 24mg chol., 58mg sod., 5g carb. (2g sugars, 0 fiber), 2g pro.

APPLE-WALNUT MUFFIN MIX

Keep this mix on hand for small-batch baking. Each muffin comes out with a nice, rounded top, a crunchy sugar topping and hints of cinnamon, walnuts and apples.
—*Taste of Home* Test Kitchen

- -

Takes: 15 min.
Makes: 6 batches (2 muffins per batch)

- 1   **cup all-purpose flour**
- 1   **cup whole wheat flour**
- ¾   **cup sugar**
- ⅓   **cup chopped dried apples**
- ⅓   **cup chopped walnuts**
- 2   **tsp. baking powder**
- ½   **tsp. baking soda**
- ¼   **tsp. ground cinnamon**
- ⅛   **tsp. salt**

ADDITIONAL INGREDIENTS
- 2   **Tbsp. fat-free milk**
- 2   **Tbsp. reduced-fat plain yogurt**
- 2   **tsp. canola oil**
- 1   **tsp. coarse sugar**

In a large bowl, combine the first 9 ingredients. Store muffin mix in an airtight container for up to 2 months.
To prepare muffins: Place ½ cup muffin mix in a small bowl. Whisk the milk, yogurt and oil. Stir into dry ingredients just until moistened. Coat muffin cups with cooking spray or use foil liners; fill three-fourths full with batter. Sprinkle with coarse sugar. Bake at 400° for 10-12 minutes or until a toothpick inserted in the center comes out clean. Cool for 5 minutes before removing from pan to a wire rack. Serve warm.
1 muffin: 212 cal., 7g fat (1g sat. fat), 1mg chol., 164mg sod., 34g carb. (18g sugars, 2g fiber), 4g pro. **Diabetic exchanges:** 2 starch, 1½ fat.

CRUSTY HOMEMADE BREAD

CRUSTY HOMEMADE BREAD

Homemade bread makes an average day extraordinary. Enjoy this recipe as written, or stir in a few favorites like cheese, garlic, herbs or dried fruits.
—Megumi Garcia, Milwaukee, WI

- -

Prep: 20 min. + rising • **Bake:** 50 min.
Makes: 1 loaf (16 slices)

- 1½   **tsp. active dry yeast**
- 1¾   **cups warm water (110° to 115°)**
- 3½   **cups plus 1 Tbsp. all-purpose flour, divided**
- 2   **tsp. salt**
- 1   **Tbsp. cornmeal or additional flour**

1. In a large bowl, dissolve yeast in warm water. Using a rubber spatula, stir in 3½ cups flour and salt to form a soft, sticky dough. Do not knead. Cover and let rise at room temperature 1 hour.
2. Stir down dough (dough will be sticky). Turn onto a floured surface; with floured hands pat into a 9-in. square. Fold square into thirds, forming a 9x3-in. rectangle. Fold rectangle into thirds, forming a 3-in. square.

Place in a large greased bowl, turning once to grease the top. Cover and let rise at room temperature until almost doubled, 1 hour.
3. Punch down dough and repeat folding process. Return dough to bowl; refrigerate, covered, overnight.
4. Grease the bottom of a disposable foil roasting pan with sides at least 4 in. high; dust pan with cornmeal. Turn dough onto a floured surface. Knead gently 6-8 times; shape into a 6-in. round loaf. Place into prepared pan; dust the top with remaining 1 Tbsp. flour. Cover pan and let rise at room temperature until dough expands to a 7½-in. loaf, about 1¼ hours.
5. Preheat oven to 500°. Using a sharp knife, make a slash (¼ in. deep) across top of loaf. Cover pan tightly with foil. Bake on lowest oven rack 25 minutes.
6. Reduce oven setting to 450°. Remove foil; bake bread until deep golden brown, 25-30 minutes. Remove loaf to a wire rack to cool.
1 slice: 105 cal., 0 fat (0 sat. fat), 0 chol., 296mg sod., 22g carb. (0 sugars, 1g fiber), 3g pro.

SIMPLE BISCUITS

It's super easy to whip up a batch of these buttery biscuits to serve with breakfast or dinner. The dough is easy to work with, so there's no need to roll with a rolling pin; just pat it to the ideal thickness.
—*Taste of Home* Test Kitchen

Takes: 25 min. • **Makes:** 15 biscuits

- 2 cups all-purpose flour
- 3 tsp. baking powder
- 1 tsp. salt
- ⅓ cup cold butter, cubed
- ⅔ cup 2% milk

1. Preheat oven to 450°. In a large bowl, whisk flour, baking powder and salt. Cut in butter until mixture resembles coarse crumbs. Add milk; stir just until moistened.
2. Turn onto a lightly floured surface; knead gently 8-10 times. Pat the dough to ½-in. thickness. Cut with a 2½-in. biscuit cutter.
3. Place 1 in. apart on an ungreased baking sheet. Bake until biscuits are golden brown, 10-15 minutes. Serve warm.
1 biscuit: 153 cal., 7g fat (4g sat. fat), 18mg chol., 437mg sod., 20g carb. (1g sugars, 1g fiber), 3g pro.

BEST EVER CRESCENT ROLLS

My daughter and I have cranked out dozens of homemade crescent rolls over the years. I cut the dough into pie-shaped wedges; she rolls them up. It's a team effort, and we love the results! Best of all, you can freeze these rolls easily so you're always ready to serve oven-fresh crescents.
—Irene Yeh, Birmingham, AL

Prep: 40 min. + chilling • **Bake:** 10 min./batch
Makes: 32 rolls

- 3¾ to 4¼ cups all-purpose flour
- 2 pkg. (¼ oz. each) active dry yeast
- 1 tsp. salt
- 1 cup 2% milk
- ½ cup butter, cubed
- ¼ cup honey
- 3 large egg yolks, room temperature
- 2 Tbsp. butter, melted

1. Combine 1½ cups flour, yeast and salt. In a small saucepan, heat milk, cubed butter and honey to 120°-130°. Add to dry ingredients; beat on medium speed 2 minutes. Add egg yolks; beat on high 2 minutes. Stir in enough remaining flour to form a soft dough (dough will be sticky).
2. Turn dough onto a floured surface; knead until smooth and elastic, 6-8 minutes. Place in a greased bowl, turning once to grease the top. Cover and let rise in a warm place until doubled, about 45 minutes.
3. Punch down the dough. Cover and refrigerate overnight.
4. To bake, turn dough onto a lightly floured surface; divide in half. Roll each portion into a 14-in. circle; cut each circle into 16 wedges. Lightly brush wedges with melted butter. Roll up from wide ends, pinching pointed ends to seal. Place 2 in. apart on parchment-lined baking sheets, point side down. Cover with lightly greased plastic wrap; let rise in a warm place until doubled, about 45 minutes.
5. Preheat oven to 375°. Bake until golden brown, 9-11 minutes. Remove from pans to wire racks; serve warm.
Freeze option: Immediately after shaping, freeze rolls on parchment-lined baking sheets until firm. Transfer to a freezer container. Freeze up to 4 weeks. To use, let rise; bake as directed, increasing rise time to 2½-3 hours.
1 roll: 104 cal., 4g fat (3g sat. fat), 28mg chol., 107mg sod., 14g carb. (3g sugars, 1g fiber), 2g pro.

BEST EVER
CRESCENT ROLLS

CHEESE-FILLED GARLIC ROLLS

I added mozzarella cheese to change up plain old dinner rolls one night. Now my family requests them at every gathering. I don't mind, even in a time crunch.
—Rosalie Fittery, Philadelphia, PA

- -

Prep: 20 min. + rising • **Bake:** 15 min.
Makes: 2 dozen

- 1 loaf (1 lb.) frozen bread dough, thawed
- 24 cubes part-skim mozzarella cheese (¾ in. each, about 10 oz.)
- 3 Tbsp. butter, melted
- 2 tsp. minced fresh parsley
- 1 garlic clove, minced
- ½ tsp. Italian seasoning
- ½ tsp. crushed red pepper flakes
- 2 Tbsp. grated Parmigiano-Reggiano cheese

1. Divide the dough into 24 portions. Shape each portion around a cheese cube to cover completely; pinch to seal. Place each roll in a greased muffin cup, seam side down. Cover with kitchen towels; let rise in a warm place until doubled, about 30 minutes. Preheat oven to 350°.

2. In a small bowl, mix butter, parsley, garlic, Italian seasoning and pepper flakes. Brush over rolls; sprinkle with cheese. Bake until golden brown, 15-18 minutes.

3. Cool 5 minutes before removing from pans. Serve warm.

1 roll: 103 cal., 5g fat (2g sat. fat), 12mg chol., 205mg sod., 10g carb. (1g sugars, 1g fiber), 5g pro.

JALAPENO BUTTERMILK CORNBREAD

JALAPENO BUTTERMILK CORNBREAD

If you're from the South, you know a good cornbread recipe is a must. Here's a lighter version of my mom's traditional cornbread.
—Debi Mitchell, Flower Mound, TX

- -

Prep: 15 min. • **Bake:** 20 min.
Makes: 8 servings

- 1 cup self-rising flour
- 1 cup yellow cornmeal
- 1 cup buttermilk
- ¼ cup egg substitute
- 3 Tbsp. canola oil, divided
- 2 Tbsp. honey
- 1 Tbsp. reduced-fat mayonnaise
- ¼ cup fresh or frozen corn, thawed
- 3 Tbsp. shredded reduced-fat cheddar cheese
- 3 Tbsp. finely chopped sweet red pepper
- ½ to 1 jalapeno pepper, seeded and finely chopped

1. Preheat oven to 425°. In a large bowl, whisk flour and cornmeal. In another bowl, whisk buttermilk, egg substitute, 2 Tbsp. oil, honey and mayonnaise. Pour remaining oil into an 8-in. cast-iron or other ovenproof skillet; place skillet in oven 4 minutes.

2. Meanwhile, add buttermilk mixture to flour mixture; stir just until moistened. Fold in corn, cheese and peppers.

3. Carefully tilt and rotate skillet to coat bottom with oil; add batter. Bake until a toothpick inserted in center comes out clean, 20-25 minutes. Serve warm.

1 wedge: 180 cal., 4g fat (1g sat. fat), 4mg chol., 261mg sod., 32g carb. (6g sugars, 2g fiber), 6g pro. **Diabetic exchanges:** 2 starch, 1 fat.

CAST-IRON CHOCOLATE
CHIP BANANA BREAD

CAST-IRON CHOCOLATE CHIP BANANA BREAD

I love this cast-iron banana bread because it cooks evenly every time. The end result is so moist and delicious!
—Ashley Hudd, Holton, MI

- -

Prep: 20 min. • **Bake:** 25 min. + cooling
Makes: 10 servings

- ¼ cup butter, softened
- 1 cup sugar
- 1 large egg, room temperature
- 3 medium ripe bananas, mashed (about 1¼ cups)
- 1 tsp. vanilla extract
- 2 cups all-purpose flour
- 1 tsp. baking soda
- ½ tsp. salt
- 1 cup semisweet chocolate chips, divided
  Dried banana chips, optional

1. Preheat oven to 350°. In a large bowl, beat butter and sugar until crumbly. Beat in egg, bananas and vanilla. In another bowl, whisk flour, baking soda and salt; gradually beat into the banana mixture. Stir in ½ cup of the chocolate chips.
2. Transfer to a greased 10-in. cast-iron or other ovenproof skillet; sprinkle batter with remaining ½ cup chocolate chips. If desired, top with banana chips. Bake until a toothpick inserted in the center comes out clean, 25-30 minutes. Cool in pan on a wire rack.
1 slice: 330 cal., 10g fat (6g sat. fat), 31mg chol., 290mg sod., 58g carb. (34g sugars, 3g fiber), 4g pro.

> ### TEST KITCHEN TIP
> Homemade bread lasts 3-5 days at room temperature. To maximize time, place bread in a plastic bag and seal shut to keep moist. Make sure there's no condensation in the bag.

APPLE QUINOA SPOON BREAD

This spoon bread acts as a side but it's almost hearty enough for an entree!
—Christine Wendland, Browns Mills, NJ

- -

Prep: 25 min. • **Bake:** 25 min.
Makes: 9 servings

- ⅔ cup water
- ⅓ cup quinoa, rinsed
- 1 Tbsp. canola oil
- 1 small apple, peeled and diced
- 1 small onion, finely chopped
- 1 small parsnip, peeled and diced
- ½ tsp. celery seed
- 1¼ tsp. salt, divided
- 1 Tbsp. minced fresh sage
- ¾ cup yellow cornmeal
- ¼ cup all-purpose flour
- 1 Tbsp. sugar
- 1 tsp. baking powder
- 1 large egg, room temperature
- 1½ cups 2% milk, divided

1. Preheat oven to 375°. In a small saucepan, bring water to a boil. Add quinoa. Reduce heat; simmer, covered, until the liquid is absorbed, 12-15 minutes. Fluff with a fork; cool slightly.
2. Meanwhile, in a large skillet, heat oil over medium heat; saute apple, onion and parsnip with celery seed and ½ tsp. of the salt until softened, 4-5 minutes. Remove from heat; stir in sage.
3. In a large bowl, whisk together cornmeal, flour, sugar, baking powder and remaining ¾ tsp. salt. In another bowl, whisk together egg and 1 cup milk. Add to the cornmeal mixture, stirring just until moistened. Fold in quinoa and apple mixture.
4. Transfer to a greased 8-in. square baking dish. Pour remaining milk over top.
5. Bake, uncovered, until edges are golden brown, 25-30 minutes. Let stand 5 minutes before serving.
1 serving: 153 cal., 4g fat (1g sat. fat), 24mg chol., 412mg sod., 26g carb. (6g sugars, 2g fiber), 5g pro. **Diabetic exchanges:** 1½ starch, 1 fat.

HAM & GREEN ONION BISCUITS

I started with my grandmother's biscuits and added a bit of my personality. When I make these biscuits with my kids, it feels as if she's with us.
—Amy Chase, Vanderhoof, BC

- -

Prep: 20 min. • **Bake:** 10 min.
Makes: about 1 dozen

- 2 cups all-purpose flour
- 3 tsp. baking powder
- 1 tsp. sugar
- ¼ tsp. garlic salt
  Dash pepper
- 6 Tbsp. cold butter, cubed
- 1 cup finely chopped fully cooked ham
- 2 green onions, chopped
- ¾ cup 2% milk

1. Preheat oven to 450°. In a large bowl, whisk the first 5 ingredients. Cut in butter until mixture resembles coarse crumbs. Stir in ham and green onions. Add milk; stir just until moistened.
2. Turn dough onto a lightly floured surface; knead gently 8-10 times. Pat or roll dough to ½-in. thickness; cut with a floured 2½-in. biscuit cutter. Place biscuits 2 in. apart on an ungreased baking sheet. Bake 10-12 minutes or until golden brown. Serve warm.
1 biscuit: 151 cal., 7g fat (4g sat. fat), 23mg chol., 315mg sod., 17g carb. (1g sugars, 1g fiber), 5g pro.

PESTO PINWHEEL BUNS

An easy spinach-basil pesto gives delectable flavor to these rolls.
—*Taste of Home* Test Kitchen

Prep: 30 min. + rising • **Bake:** 25 min.
Makes: 1 dozen

- 1 pkg. (¼ oz.) active dry yeast
- 3 Tbsp. warm water (110° to 115°)
- ½ cup warm 2% milk (110° to 115°)
- 2 Tbsp. butter, softened
- 1 large egg, room temperature
- 1 Tbsp. sugar
- ¾ tsp. salt
- 2¼ to 2¾ cups all-purpose flour

PESTO
- 1 cup fresh baby spinach
- 1 cup fresh basil leaves
- 2 garlic cloves
- ¼ cup walnut halves, toasted
- ¼ cup grated Parmesan cheese
- ⅛ tsp. pepper
- ¼ cup olive oil

1. In a large bowl, dissolve yeast in warm water. Add the milk, butter, egg, sugar, salt and 1½ cups flour. Beat until smooth. Stir in enough of the remaining flour to form a firm dough.
2. Turn onto a lightly floured surface; knead until smooth and elastic, 6-8 minutes. Place in a greased bowl, turning once to grease the top. Cover and let rise in a warm place until doubled, about 1 hour.
3. Meanwhile, place the baby spinach, basil, garlic, walnuts, cheese and pepper in a food processor; cover and process until blended. While processing, gradually add olive oil in a steady stream. Set aside.
4. Punch dough down. Turn onto a lightly floured surface. Roll dough into a 12x10-in. rectangle. Spread pesto to within ½ in. of edges. Roll up jelly-roll style, starting with a long side; pinch seam to seal. Cut into 12 rolls.
5. Place the rolls cut side up in a greased 13x9-in. baking pan. Cover and let rise until doubled, about 40 minutes.

APRICOT & MACADAMIA EGGNOG BREAD

6. Bake rolls at 350° until golden brown, 25-30 minutes. Remove from pan to a wire rack. Serve warm. Refrigerate leftovers.
1 bun: 181 cal., 9g fat (3g sat. fat), 25mg chol., 200mg sod., 20g carb. (2g sugars, 1g fiber), 5g pro.

APRICOT & MACADAMIA EGGNOG BREAD

Holidays and nut breads are made for each other. My spiced quick bread has three of the ingredients I can't resist—eggnog, apricots and macadamia nuts.
—Nancy Heishman, Las Vegas, NV

Prep: 20 min. • **Bake:** 50 min. + cooling
Makes: 2 loaves (12 slices each)

- 4¾ cups all-purpose flour
- ¾ cup sugar
- 2 Tbsp. baking powder
- ½ tsp. salt
- 1 tsp. ground cinnamon
- 1 tsp. ground nutmeg
- 2 large eggs, room temperature
- 2½ cups eggnog
- ½ cup canola oil
- 1 Tbsp. grated orange zest
- ¼ cup orange juice
- ¾ cup chopped dried apricots
- ¾ cup chopped macadamia nuts

GLAZE
- ¾ cup confectioners' sugar
- 1 to 2 Tbsp. eggnog

1. Preheat oven to 350°. In a large bowl, whisk the first 6 ingredients. In another bowl, whisk eggs, 2½ cups eggnog, oil, orange zest and orange juice until blended. Add the liquid ingredients to the flour mixture; stir just until moistened. Fold in chopped apricots and macadamia nuts.
2. Transfer to 2 greased 9x5-in. loaf pans. Bake 50-60 minutes or until a toothpick inserted in center comes out clean. Cool in pans 10 minutes before removing to wire racks to cool completely.
3. For glaze, in a bowl, mix confectioners' sugar and enough eggnog to reach drizzling consistency. Spoon over loaves.
Freeze option: Securely wrap cooled loaves in foil, then freeze. To use, thaw at room temperature.
1 slice: 242 cal., 10g fat (2g sat. fat), 32mg chol., 186mg sod., 35g carb. (15g sugars, 1g fiber), 5g pro.

SOCCA

Socca is a traditional flatbread from Nice, France. It's common to see it cooked on grills as street food, served chopped in a paper cone and sprinkled with salt, pepper or other delicious toppings. Bonus: It's gluten-free.
—*Taste of Home* Test Kitchen

Prep: 5 min. + standing • **Cook:** 5 minutes
Makes: 6 servings

 1   **cup chickpea flour**
 1   **cup water**
 2   **Tbsp. extra virgin olive oil, divided**
 ¾   **tsp. salt**
     Optional toppings: Za'atar seasoning, sea salt flakes, coarsely ground pepper and additional extra virgin olive oil

1. In a small bowl, whisk chickpea flour, water, 1 Tbsp. oil and salt until smooth. Let stand 30 minutes.
2. Meanwhile, preheat broiler. Place a 10-in. cast-iron skillet in oven until hot, about 5 minutes. Add remaining 1 Tbsp. oil to the pan; swirl to coat. Pour batter into the hot pan and tilt to coat evenly.
3. Broil 6 in. from heat until edges are crisp and browned and center just begins to brown, 5-7 minutes. Cut into wedges. If desired, top with optional ingredients.
1 wedge: 113 cal., 6g fat (1g sat. fat), 0 chol., 298mg sod., 12g carb. (2g sugars, 3g fiber), 4g pro. **Diabetic exchanges:** 1 fat, ½ starch.

CHEDDAR CORN DOG MUFFINS

I wanted a change from typical hot dogs in a bun, so I made corn dog muffins. I added jalapenos to this kid-friendly recipe...and that won my husband over, too.
—Becky Tarala, Palm Coast, FL

Takes: 25 min. • **Makes:** 9 muffins

 1   **pkg. (8½ oz.) cornbread/muffin mix**
 ⅔   **cup 2% milk**
 1   **large egg, lightly beaten, room temperature**
 5   **turkey hot dogs, sliced**
 ½   **cup shredded sharp cheddar cheese**
 2   **Tbsp. finely chopped pickled jalapeno, optional**

1. Preheat oven to 400°. Line 9 muffin cups with foil liners or grease 9 nonstick muffin cups.
2. In a small bowl, combine the muffin mix, milk and egg; stir in hot dogs, cheese and, if desired, jalapeno. Fill prepared muffin cups three-fourths full.
3. Bake until a toothpick inserted in center comes out clean, 14-18 minutes. Cool for 5 minutes before removing from pan to a wire rack. Serve warm. Refrigerate leftovers.
Freeze option: Freeze cooled muffins in freezer containers. To use, microwave each muffin on high until heated through, 30-60 seconds.
1 muffin: 216 cal., 10g fat (4g sat. fat), 46mg chol., 619mg sod., 23g carb. (7g sugars, 2g fiber), 8g pro.

SOCCA

SPICY PUMPKIN
FRITTERS

LEMON POPOVERS WITH PECAN HONEY BUTTER

I received this recipe from my mom many years ago. We love the delicate lemon flavor with the pecan honey butter. The popovers are a nice addition to any dinner but they're especially delicious at breakfast with fruit.
—Joan Hallford, North Richland Hills, TX

- -

Prep: 10 min. • **Bake:** 25 min.
Makes: 6 servings

- 2 large eggs, room temperature
- 1 cup 2% milk
- 1 cup all-purpose flour
- ½ tsp. salt
- 5 Tbsp. finely chopped toasted pecans, divided
- ¾ tsp. grated lemon zest
- 2 tsp. lemon juice
- 6 Tbsp. butter, softened
- 6 Tbsp. honey

1. Preheat oven to 450°. In a large bowl, whisk eggs and milk until blended. Whisk in the flour and salt until smooth (do not overbeat). Stir in 3 Tbsp. pecans, lemon zest and lemon juice.
2. Generously grease a 6-cup popover pan with nonstick spray; fill cups half full with batter. Bake 15 minutes. Reduce oven setting to 350° (do not open oven door). Bake until deep golden brown, 10-15 minutes longer (do not underbake).
3. Meanwhile, combine butter, honey and remaining 2 Tbsp. pecans. Immediately remove popovers from pan to a wire rack. Pierce side of each popover with a sharp knife to let steam escape. Serve immediately with pecan honey butter.
1 popover with about 2 Tbsp. honey butter: 325 cal., 18g fat (9g sat. fat), 96mg chol., 332mg sod., 36g carb. (20g sugars, 1g fiber), 6g pro.

SPICY PUMPKIN FRITTERS

My husband is a lifelong veggie hater, but he tried these deep-fried pumpkin bites and fell in love. I serve them with chipotle mayo or ranch dressing.
—Trisha Kruse, Eagle, ID

- -

Prep: 10 min. • **Cook:** 5 min./batch
Makes: about 3 dozen

- 1½ cups all-purpose flour
- 2 tsp. baking powder
- 1¼ tsp. salt
- ¾ tsp. chili powder
- ½ tsp. onion powder
- ¼ tsp. crushed red pepper flakes
- 2 large eggs, room temperature
- 1 can (15 oz.) pumpkin
- ½ cup 2% milk
- 2 Tbsp. butter, melted
  Oil for deep-fat frying
  Chipotle mayonnaise, optional

1. In a large bowl, whisk the first 6 ingredients. In another bowl, whisk the eggs, pumpkin, milk and melted butter until blended. Add to dry ingredients, stirring just until moistened.
2. In an deep cast-iron skillet or deep-fat fryer, heat oil to 375°. Drop the batter by tablespoonfuls, a few at a time, into hot oil. Fry each side until golden brown, 1½-2 minutes. Drain on paper towels. Serve warm. If desired, serve with chipotle mayonnaise.
1 fritter: 50 cal., 3g fat (1g sat. fat), 11mg chol., 105mg sod., 5g carb. (1g sugars, 0 fiber), 1g pro.

LEMON POPOVERS
WITH PECAN HONEY BUTTER

SWIRL CINNAMON BREAD

If you like cinnamon, you'll love this quick bread! It's crusty on top, soft and moist inside—and one of our very most-searched recipes. Consider making extra loaves for the holidays and giving them to your family and friends.
—*Taste of Home* Test Kitchen

Prep: 25 min. • **Bake:** 45 min. + cooling
Makes: 1 loaf (12 slices)

- 2 cups all-purpose flour
- ¾ cup sugar
- ½ tsp. baking soda
- ½ tsp. plus 1½ tsp. ground cinnamon, divided
- ¼ tsp. salt
- 1 large egg, room temperature
- 1 cup reduced-fat plain yogurt
- ¼ cup canola oil
- 1 tsp. vanilla extract
- ¼ cup packed brown sugar

1. Preheat oven to 350°. In a large bowl, combine flour, sugar, baking soda, ½ tsp. cinnamon and salt. In a small bowl, whisk egg, yogurt, oil and vanilla. Stir into dry ingredients just until moistened. In a small bowl, combine the brown sugar and remaining cinnamon.

2. Spoon a third of the batter into an 8x4-in. loaf pan coated with cooking spray. Top with a third of the brown sugar mixture. Repeat layers twice. Cut through batter with a knife to swirl the brown sugar mixture.

3. Bake 45-55 minutes or until a toothpick inserted in the center comes out clean. Cool 10 minutes before removing from pan to a wire rack.

1 slice: 203 cal., 6g fat (1g sat. fat), 19mg chol., 124mg sod., 35g carb. (19g sugars, 1g fiber), 4g pro.

SWIRL CINNAMON
BREAD

STOLLEN
BUTTER ROLLS

STOLLEN BUTTER ROLLS

Our family enjoys my stollen so much they say it's just too good to be served only as a holiday sweet bread. I created this buttery, less sweet dinner roll so we can satisfy our stollen cravings anytime.
—Mindy White, Nashville, TN

- -

Prep: 45 min. + rising • **Bake:** 15 min.
Makes: 2 dozen

1	pkg. (¼ oz.) active dry yeast
¼	cup warm water (110° to 115°)
1	cup 2% milk
2	large eggs, room temperature
½	cup butter, softened
1	Tbsp. sugar
1	tsp. salt
4¼ to 4¾	cups all-purpose flour
¾	cup chopped mixed candied fruit
¾	cup dried currants
½	cup cold butter, cut into 24 pieces (1 tsp. each)

1. In a small bowl, dissolve yeast in warm water. In a large bowl, combine milk, eggs, butter, sugar, salt, yeast mixture and 3 cups flour; beat on medium speed until smooth. Stir in enough remaining flour to form a soft dough (dough will be sticky).
2. Turn dough onto a floured surface; knead until smooth and elastic, 6-8 minutes. Place in a greased bowl, turning once to grease the top. Cover and let rise in a warm place until doubled, about 1 hour.
3. Punch dough down; turn onto floured surface. Knead candied fruit and dried currants into dough (knead in more flour if necessary). Divide and shape into 24 balls; flatten slightly. Place 1 tsp. cold butter in center of each circle. Fold circles in half over butter; press edges to seal. Place in a greased 15x10x1-in. baking pan. Cover and let rise in a warm place until doubled, about 45 minutes.
4. Preheat oven to 375°. Bake until golden brown, 15-20 minutes. Cool in pan 5 minutes; serve warm.
Freeze option: Freeze cooled rolls in airtight containers. To use, microwave each roll on high until warmed, 30-45 seconds.
1 roll: 198 cal., 9g fat (5g sat. fat), 37mg chol., 178mg sod., 28g carb. (9g sugars, 1g fiber), 4g pro.

ORANGE CHOCOLATE CHIP SCONES

My family asks for these scones all the time, but I like to save them as a special treat for celebrations. They are a wonderful add-on to any brunch or potluck.
—Leslie Parker, Sioux Falls, SD

- -

Prep: 20 min. • **Bake:** 15 min.
Makes: 16 scones

3	cups all-purpose flour
⅓	cup sugar
2½	tsp. baking powder
½	tsp. baking soda
¼	tsp. salt
¾	cup cold butter, cubed
1	cup semisweet chocolate chips
1	cup buttermilk
4	tsp. grated orange zest
1	tsp. orange extract
2	Tbsp. sugar
¼	tsp. ground cinnamon
1	Tbsp. heavy whipping cream

1. Preheat oven to 400°. In a large bowl, whisk the first 5 ingredients. Cut in butter until mixture resembles coarse crumbs. Stir in chocolate chips. In another bowl, mix milk, orange zest and extract until blended; stir into flour mixture just until moistened.
2. Turn dough onto a lightly floured surface; knead gently 10 times. Divide dough in half. Pat each portion into an 8-in. circle. Cut each into 8 wedges. Place wedges on a greased baking sheet.
3. In a small bowl, mix sugar and cinnamon. Lightly brush scones with cream; sprinkle with cinnamon-sugar mixture. Bake 15-17 minutes or until golden brown. Serve warm.
1 scone: 245 cal., 13g fat (8g sat. fat), 25mg chol., 238mg sod., 31g carb. (12g sugars, 1g fiber), 3g pro.

HONEY CORNBREAD

It's a pleasure to serve this moist cornbread to family and guests. Honey gives it a slightly sweet taste. Most people find it's difficult to eat just one piece.

—Adeline Piscitelli, Sayreville, NJ

Takes: 30 min. • **Makes:** 9 servings

1	cup all-purpose flour
1	cup yellow cornmeal
¼	cup sugar
3	tsp. baking powder
½	tsp. salt
2	large eggs, room temperature
1	cup heavy whipping cream
¼	cup canola oil
¼	cup honey

1. In a bowl, combine flour, cornmeal, sugar, baking powder and salt. In a small bowl, beat the eggs. Add cream, oil and honey; beat well. Stir into the dry ingredients just until moistened. Pour into a greased 9-in. square baking pan.

2. Bake at 400° for 20-25 minutes or until a toothpick inserted in the center comes out clean. Serve warm.

1 piece: 318 cal., 17g fat (7g sat. fat), 83mg chol., 290mg sod., 37g carb. (14g sugars, 2g fiber), 5g pro.

HONEY CORNBREAD

MARCIE'S BANANA CHOCOLATE CHIP MUFFINS

These tender banana muffins are a big hit at our house. I use mini muffin tins because they are a better size for children, but you can make them full-size, too. I sprinkle a few mini chips on top before baking because the muffins look prettier that way.
—Marcie Trebe, Santa Rosa, CA

Prep: 25 min. • **Bake:** 20 min.
Makes: 1½ dozen

½ cup butter, softened
½ cup sugar
½ cup packed brown sugar
2 large eggs, room temperature
1¼ cups mashed ripe bananas (about 3 medium)
1 tsp. vanilla extract
1½ cups white whole wheat flour
½ cup all-purpose flour
1 tsp. baking soda
½ tsp. salt
¼ cup sour cream
½ cup 2% milk
¾ cup miniature semisweet chocolate chips, divided

1. Preheat oven to 350°. In a large bowl, cream butter and sugars until light and fluffy, 5-7 minutes. Add eggs, 1 at a time, beating well after each addition. Beat in mashed bananas and vanilla.
2. In another bowl, whisk flours, baking soda and salt. Add to creamed mixture, alternating with the sour cream and milk; stir just until moistened. Fold in ½ cup chocolate chips.
3. Fill greased or paper-lined muffin cups two-thirds full. Sprinkle with remaining chocolate chips.
4. Bake 18-20 minutes or until a toothpick inserted in center comes out clean. Cool 5 minutes before removing from pans to a wire rack. Serve warm.
Freeze option: Freeze cooled muffins in airtight freezer containers. To use, thaw at room temperature or, if desired, microwave each muffin on high for 20-30 seconds or until heated through.
1 muffin: 210 cal.,9g fat (5g sat. fat), 37mg chol.,191g sod., 31 carb. (18 sugars, 2g fiber), 3g pro.

MARCIE'S BANANA CHOCOLATE CHIP MUFFINS

MEATBALL ALPHABET
SOUP, PAGE 107

Soups, Salads & Sandwiches

Soup's on! And grab a big plate for a salad or sandwich, too. The fun, hearty and creative flavor combinations in these recipes shake up dull lunch and dinnertime routines. Whether you enjoy a fresh mix of greens as a light lunch on a warm day or hot, hearty soup and a sub to fortify your family on a chilly night, you'll agree this is comfort food at its finest.

THAT GOOD
SALAD

THAT GOOD SALAD

When a friend shared this recipe, it had a fancy French name. Our children can never remember it, so they say, "Mom, please make that good salad." Now our friends and neighbors request it for potluck dinners.
—Betty Lamb, Orem, UT

Takes: 20 min. • **Makes:** 14 servings

- ¾ cup canola oil
- ¼ cup lemon juice
- 2 garlic cloves, minced
- ½ tsp. salt
- ½ tsp. pepper
- 2 bunches (1 lb. each) romaine, torn
- 2 cups chopped tomatoes
- 1 cup shredded Swiss cheese
- ⅔ cup slivered almonds, toasted, optional
- ½ cup grated Parmesan cheese
- 8 bacon strips, cooked and crumbled
- 1 cup Caesar salad croutons

1. In a jar with a tight-fitting lid, combine the oil, lemon juice, garlic, salt and pepper; cover and shake well. Chill in the refrigerator.
2. In a large serving bowl, toss the romaine, tomatoes, Swiss cheese, almonds if desired, Parmesan cheese and bacon.
3. Shake dressing; pour over salad and toss. Add croutons and serve immediately.
1 cup: 193 cal., 17g fat (4g sat. fat), 13mg chol., 257mg sod., 5g carb. (1g sugars, 1g fiber), 6g pro.

YUMMY CORN CHIP SALAD

Corn chips give crunch and unexpected flavor to this potluck-favorite salad. Bacon adds a hint of smokiness while cranberries bring a touch of sweetness. It's the perfect picnic companion!
—Nora Friesen, Aberdeen, MS

Takes: 25 min. • **Makes:** 12 servings

- ¾ cup canola oil
- ¼ cup cider vinegar
- ¼ cup mayonnaise
- 2 Tbsp. yellow mustard
- ½ tsp. salt
- ¾ cup sugar
- ½ small onion
- ¾ tsp. poppy seeds

SALAD
- 2 bunches leaf lettuce, chopped (about 20 cups)
- 1 pkg. (9¼ oz.) corn chips
- 8 bacon strips, cooked and crumbled
- 1 cup shredded part-skim mozzarella cheese
- 1 cup dried cranberries

1. For dressing, place first 7 ingredients in a blender. Cover; process until smooth. Stir in poppy seeds.
2. Place salad ingredients in a large bowl; toss with dressing. Serve immediately.
1⅓ cups: 436 cal., 30g fat (4g sat. fat), 12mg chol., 456mg sod., 38g carb. (24g sugars, 2g fiber), 7g pro.

DUTCH-OVEN BARBECUED PORK SANDWICHES

These fabulous pulled pork sandwiches have a sweet, tangy flavor. If you want a smokier taste, you can add a little liquid smoke to the pulled pork before returning the meat to the Dutch oven.
—*Taste of Home* Test Kitchen

Prep: 15 min. • **Cook:** 4 hours
Makes: 8 servings

- 1 can (8 oz.) tomato sauce
- 1 large onion, chopped
- 1 cup barbecue sauce
- 3 tsp. chili powder
- 1 tsp. ground cumin
- ½ tsp. ground cinnamon
- 1 boneless pork sirloin roast (2 lbs.)
- 8 seeded hamburger bun, split

1. In a Dutch oven, combine the first 6 ingredients; add pork. Spoon some of the sauce over pork. Bring to a boil; reduce heat and simmer, covered, until meat is tender, 3-4 hours.
2. Remove meat; shred with 2 forks. Return to pan and heat through. Spoon ½ cup onto each bun.
1 sandwich: 357 cal., 9g fat (3g sat. fat), 68mg chol., 771mg sod., 40g carb. (16g sugars, 2g fiber), 28g pro.

TEST KITCHEN TIP

If you don't want to stand over the stovetop to fry bacon or want to cook a large amount at once, try the easy oven-bake method. Line a 15x10x1-in. sheet pan with aluminum foil. Arrange bacon in a single layer and bake at 400° to desired doneness, which will take 16-25 minutes. Remove bacon to paper towels. With this simple method, there's no need turn the bacon while cooking, and all the strips of bacon will bake up evenly. And because the grease collects on the foil, cleanup is a breeze.

MARINATED TENDERLOIN & AVOCADO ON BAGUETTE TOASTS

There's never any waste with tenderloin (and leftovers are rare). You can dress it up by substituting baguette toppings and having fun with it.
—Bonnie Hawkins, Elkhorn, WI

- -

Prep: 20 min. • **Cook:** 15 min. + marinating
Makes: 2 servings

- 2 beef tenderloin steaks (1 in. thick and 4 oz. each)
- 1 Tbsp. olive oil
- 1 Tbsp. canola oil
- 1 Tbsp. red wine vinegar
- ½ tsp. salt
- ½ tsp. Dijon mustard
- 4 slices red onion, separated into rings
- 8 slices French bread baguette (½ in. thick), toasted
- ½ medium ripe avocado, peeled and sliced
- 1 Tbsp. minced fresh parsley

1. Heat a large nonstick skillet over medium heat until hot. Place steaks in skillet; cook until meat reaches desired doneness (for medium-rare, a thermometer should read 135°; medium, 140°; medium-well, 145°), 5-7 minutes per side. Let stand 10 minutes; cut into thin slices.
2. In a small bowl, combine oils, vinegar, salt and mustard. Add onion and steak; turn to coat. Refrigerate overnight.
3. Drain beef, discarding the marinade. Layer toasts with beef, onion and avocado; sprinkle with parsley.
1 serving: 432 cal., 26g fat (5g sat. fat), 49mg chol., 817mg sod., 22g carb. (1g sugars, 3g fiber), 29g pro.

KALE CAESAR SALAD

I love Caesar salads, so I created this blend of kale and romaine lettuces with a creamy homemade Caesar dressing. It's perfect paired with grilled chicken or steak for a light weeknight meal.
—Rashanda Cobbins, Food Editor

- -

Takes: 15 min. • **Makes:** 8 servings

- 4 cups chopped fresh kale
- 4 cups torn romaine
- 1 cup Caesar salad croutons
- ½ cup shredded Parmesan cheese
- ½ cup mayonnaise
- 2 Tbsp. lemon juice
- 1 Tbsp. Worcestershire sauce
- 2 tsp. Dijon mustard
- 2 tsp. anchovy paste
- 1 garlic clove, minced
- ¼ tsp. salt
- ¼ tsp. pepper

In a large salad bowl, toss the chopped kale, romaine, croutons and cheese. For dressing, combine remaining ingredients in a small bowl; pour over the salad and toss to coat. Serve immediately.
1 cup: 148 cal., 13g fat (3g sat. fat), 10mg chol., 417mg sod., 6g carb. (1g sugars, 1g fiber), 3g pro. **Diabetic exchanges:** 2½ fat, 1 vegetable.

DID YOU KNOW?

Anchovies are fish related to herring and are usually purchased canned in oil or packed in salt. Anchovy paste is made from cured anchovies ground into a paste. It's usually sold in a tube in the canned seafood section.

KALE CAESAR SALAD

DILLY CHICKPEA SALAD SANDWICHES

PRESSURE-COOKER HOMEMADE CHICKEN & RICE SOUP

We love homemade chicken and rice soup and thought it would make a great pressure-cooker recipe. It doesn't disappoint.
—*Taste of Home* Test Kitchen

Takes: 15 min. • **Makes:** 10 servings (2½ qt.)

- 3 qt. chicken broth or water
- 4 bone-in chicken breast halves (about 3 lbs.)
- ¾ tsp. salt
- ¼ tsp. pepper
- ¼ tsp. poultry seasoning
- 1 tsp. chicken bouillon granules
- 3 medium carrots, chopped
- 2 celery ribs, chopped
- 1 small onion, chopped
- ½ cup uncooked long grain rice
  Minced fresh parsley, optional

1. Place all ingredients in a 6-qt. electric pressure cooker. Lock lid; close pressure-release valve. Adjust to pressure-cook on high for 5 minutes; quick-release pressure.
2. With a slotted spoon, remove chicken. When cool enough to handle, remove meat from bones; discard skin and bones. Cut the chicken into bite-sized pieces. Skim fat from broth; add chicken. Select saute setting and adjust for low heat; cook until the chicken is heated through. If desired, sprinkle with minced parsley.

1 cup: 223 cal., 7g fat (2g sat. fat), 72mg chol., 1690mg sod., 12g carb. (3g sugars, 1g fiber), 26g pro.

DILLY CHICKPEA SALAD SANDWICHES

This chickpea salad is super flavorful and contains less fat and cholesterol than chicken salad. These really make delightful picnic sandwiches.
—Deanna Wolfe, Muskegon, MI

Takes: 15 min. • **Makes:** 6 servings

- 1 can (15 oz.) chickpeas or garbanzo beans, rinsed and drained
- ½ cup finely chopped onion
- ½ cup finely chopped celery
- ½ cup reduced-fat mayonnaise or vegan mayonnaise
- 3 Tbsp. honey mustard or Dijon mustard
- 2 Tbsp. snipped fresh dill
- 1 Tbsp. red wine vinegar
- ¼ tsp. salt
- ¼ tsp. paprika
- ¼ tsp. pepper
- 12 slices multigrain bread
  Optional: Romaine leaves, tomato slices, dill pickle slices and sweet red pepper rings

Place chickpeas in a large bowl; mash to desired consistency. Stir in onion, celery, mayonnaise, mustard, dill, vinegar, salt, paprika and pepper. Spread over each of 6 bread slices; layer with toppings of your choice and remaining bread.

1 sandwich: 295 cal., 11g fat (2g sat. fat), 7mg chol., 586mg sod., 41g carb. (9g sugars, 7g fiber), 10g pro.

**ROASTED BEET SALAD
WITH ORANGE VINAIGRETTE**

BEST ITALIAN SAUSAGE SANDWICHES

Need a different type of sandwich? The rich tomato sauce simmers all afternoon in the slow cooker, ready to top some freshly grilled Italian sausages. It's a delicious combination with lots of crowd appeal!
—*Taste of Home* Test Kitchen

Prep: 10 min. • **Cook:** 4 hours
Makes: 10 servings

- 2 jars (24 oz. each) pasta sauce
- 2 medium green peppers, cut into strips
- 2 medium onions, thinly sliced
- ½ tsp. garlic powder
- ½ tsp. fennel seed, crushed
- 2 pkg. (20 oz. each) Italian turkey sausage links
- 10 hoagie buns, split

1. In a 3-qt. slow cooker, combine the first 5 ingredients. Cook, covered, on low for about 4 hours or until vegetables are tender.
2. Grill the sausages according to package directions. Serve on buns with sauce.

Freeze option: Freeze the cooled sauce in freezer containers. To use, partially thaw in refrigerator overnight. Heat through in a saucepan, stirring occasionally; add water if necessary.

1 sandwich: 454 cal., 15g fat (3g sat. fat), 68mg chol., 1716mg sod., 52g carb. (17g sugars, 4g fiber), 29g pro.

ROASTED BEET SALAD WITH ORANGE VINAIGRETTE

I fill my salad bowl with beets, oranges and baby spinach. Beets are good for you and colorful, too. This fresh medley makes an appealing side for any occasion.
—Nancy Heishman, Las Vegas, NV

Prep: 25 min. • **Bake:** 50 min. + cooling
Makes: 12 servings

- 3 medium fresh beets (about 1 lb.)
- 3 Tbsp. olive oil
- 1 tsp. grated orange zest
- 2 Tbsp. orange juice
- 1 Tbsp. white wine vinegar
- 2 tsp. honey
- 1 tsp. Dijon mustard
- ½ tsp. salt
- ¼ tsp. pepper
- 3 Tbsp. minced fresh tarragon, divided
- 1 pkg. (6 oz.) fresh baby spinach
- 4 cups torn mixed salad greens
- 2 medium navel oranges, peeled and sectioned
- 4 oz. crumbled goat cheese
- ½ cup chopped walnuts, toasted

1. Preheat oven to 425°. Scrub beets and trim tops to 1 in. Wrap in foil; place on a baking sheet. Bake 50-60 minutes or until tender. Remove foil; cool completely. Peel beets and cut into wedges.
2. In a small bowl, whisk oil, orange zest, orange juice, vinegar, honey, mustard, salt and pepper until blended; stir in 1 Tbsp. tarragon. In a large bowl, combine spinach, salad greens and remaining tarragon. Drizzle with vinaigrette and toss gently to coat.
3. Transfer to a platter or divide among 12 salad plates. Top with orange sections and beets; sprinkle with cheese and walnuts. Serve immediately.

1 cup: 125 cal., 9g fat (2g sat. fat), 12mg chol., 195mg sod., 10g carb. (6g sugars, 2g fiber), 4g pro. **Diabetic exchanges:** 2 vegetable, 2 fat.

BEST ITALIAN SANGE SANDWICHES
BEST ITALIAN SAUSAGE SANDWICHES

ASK SARAH

WHAT IS FENNEL SEED?

Fennel seed is the fruit of the vegetable of the same name. It has a slightly sweet and licorice-like flavor, similar to anise. It is frequently used in baked goods, sausage, pork and seafood dishes, and in cuisines from around the world.

QUICK HAM &
BEAN SOUP

QUICK HAM & BEAN SOUP

If you like ham and bean soup but don't want to spend hours in the kitchen, this version is the one for you. It's delicious and takes just 30 minutes from start to finish.
—*Taste of Home* Test Kitchen

- -

Takes: 30 min. • **Makes:** 7 servings

  2   medium carrots, sliced
  2   celery ribs, chopped
  ½   cup chopped onion
  2   Tbsp. butter
  4   cans (15½ oz. each) great
      northern beans, rinsed and drained
  4   cups chicken broth
  2   cups cubed fully cooked ham
  1   tsp. chili powder
  ½   tsp. minced garlic
  ¼   tsp. pepper
  1   bay leaf

In a large saucepan, saute carrots, celery and onion in butter until tender. Stir in the remaining ingredients. Bring mixture to a boil. Reduce heat; cook for 15 minutes or until heated through. Discard bay leaf.
1 cup: 168 cal., 7g fat (3g sat. fat), 30mg chol., 1242mg sod., 14g carb. (3g sugars, 4g fiber), 12g pro.

TEST KITCHEN TIP

Bay leaves are sold whole, and may be fresh or dried. Their savory, spicy and aromatic flavor makes them ideal for enhancing the flavor of soups, stews, meats, casseroles and other dishes. You can find fresh bay leaves with other herbs in the produce section of most supermarkets. Although they are nontoxic, bay leaves are not meant to be eaten. Don't forget to remove them before serving.

EASY SLOW-COOKER POTATO SOUP

This hearty slow-cooker potato soup tastes just like a loaded baked potato. Pop in the ingredients before heading to work in the morning for a quick and easy supper.
—*Taste of Home* Test Kitchen

- -

Prep: 10 min. • **Cook:** 6 hours
Makes: 8 servings

- 1   carton (32 oz.) chicken broth
- 1   pkg. (30 oz.) frozen shredded
     hash brown potatoes, thawed
- 1   small onion, finely chopped
- 2   garlic cloves, minced
- ¼   tsp. pepper
- 1   pkg. (8 oz.) cream cheese,
     softened and cubed
- 1   cup half-and-half cream
- 1   cup shredded cheddar cheese
     Optional: Crumbled cooked bacon
     and chopped green onions

1. In a 4- or 5-qt. slow cooker, combine broth, potatoes, onion, garlic and pepper. Cook, covered, on low 6-8 hours or until vegetables are tender.
2. Mash potatoes to desired consistency. Whisk in cream cheese until melted. Stir in half-and-half. Cook, covered, until heated through, 5-10 minutes longer. Serve with cheese and, if desired, crumbled bacon and green onions.
1 cup: 294 cal., 18g fat (10g sat. fat), 60mg chol., 711mg sod., 24g carb. (4g sugars, 1g fiber), 9g pro.

GRILLED CHEESE & AVOCADO SANDWICH

Who doesn't love a grilled cheese sandwich? This grown-up version kicks it up a notch with avocado, five kinds of cheese and extra-crispy bread.
—Josh Rink, Food Stylist

- -

Takes: 25 min. • **Makes:** 4 servings

- 6   Tbsp. butter, softened, divided
- 8   slices sourdough bread
- ½   cup shredded sharp white
     cheddar cheese
- ½   cup shredded Monterey Jack cheese
- ½   cup shredded Gruyere cheese
- 3   Tbsp. mayonnaise
- 3   Tbsp. finely shredded Manchego
     or Parmesan cheese
- ⅛   tsp. onion powder
- 4   oz. Brie cheese, rind removed,
     sliced
- 2   medium ripe avocado,
     peeled and sliced

1. Spread 3 Tbsp. butter on 1 side of bread slices. Place bread, butter side down, in a large cast-iron skillet or on an electric griddle over medium-low heat until golden brown, 2-3 minutes; remove. In a small bowl, combine the cheddar, Monterey Jack and Gruyere. In another bowl, mix together remaining 3 Tbsp. butter, mayonnaise, Manchego cheese and onion powder.
2. To assemble sandwiches, top toasted side of 4 bread slices with sliced Brie; add avocado slices. Sprinkle cheddar cheese mixture evenly over avocado slices. Top with remaining bread slices, toasted side facing inward. Spread butter-mayonnaise mixture on the outside of each sandwich. Place in same skillet and cook until golden brown and cheese is melted, 5-6 minutes on each side. Serve immediately.
1 sandwich: 773 cal., 60g fat (28g sat. fat), 122mg chol., 1023mg sod., 36g carb. (3g sugars, 6g fiber), 26g pro.

GRILLED CHEESE & AVOCADO SANDWICH

TURKEY WAFFLEWICHES

Who knew lunch could be so fun? You'll see smiles around the table when you serve this decadent waffle-inspired sandwich.
—*Taste of Home* Test Kitchen

- -

Takes: 15 min. • **Makes:** 4 servings

3	oz. cream cheese, softened
¼	cup whole-berry cranberry sauce
1	Tbsp. maple pancake syrup
¼	tsp. pepper
8	slices white bread
¾	lb. sliced deli turkey
2	Tbsp. butter, softened

1. In a small bowl, beat the cream cheese, cranberry sauce, syrup and pepper until combined. Spread over 4 slices of bread; top with the turkey and remaining bread. Spread butter over both sides of sandwiches.
2. Bake in a preheated waffle iron or indoor grill according to manufacturer's directions until golden brown, 2-3 minutes.
1 sandwich: 407 cal., 17g fat (8g sat. fat), 67mg chol., 1179mg sod., 41g carb. (10g sugars, 2g fiber), 23g pro.

TEST KITCHEN TIP

Deli meat is typically lean, like the turkey used in these sandwiches, but it can also be high in sodium. Switch over to low-sodium lunch meat or even leftover cooked turkey or chicken to keep your salt intake in check.

CRUNCHY LEMON-PESTO GARDEN SALAD

I use fresh vegetables straight from the garden to prepare this salad. If I pick the squash and cucumbers early enough, their skins are so tender they don't need to be removed. This salad is very adaptable—substitute any fresh veggie from your garden for these with delicious results!
—Carmell Childs, Orangeville, UT

- -

Takes: 25 min. • **Makes:** 6 servings

5	Tbsp. prepared pesto
1	Tbsp. lemon juice
2	tsp. grated lemon zest
1½	tsp. Dijon mustard
¼	tsp. garlic salt
¼	tsp. pepper
2½	cups thinly sliced yellow summer squash
1¾	cups thinly sliced mini cucumbers
¾	cup fresh peas
½	cup shredded Parmesan cheese
¼	cup thinly sliced green onions
5	thick-sliced bacon strips, cooked and crumbled

In a small bowl, whisk together the first 6 ingredients until blended. In a large salad bowl, combine squash, cucumbers, peas, Parmesan and green onions. Pour dressing over salad; toss to coat. Top with crumbled bacon to serve.
¾ cup: 159 cal., 11g fat (3g sat. fat), 13mg chol., 586mg sod., 8g carb. (4g sugars, 2g fiber), 8g pro. **Diabetic exchanges:** 2 fat, 1 vegetable.

CRUNCHY LEMON-PESTO GARDEN SALAD

SPICY PERUVIAN
POTATO SOUP

HEALTHY GAZPACHO FOR 2

Nutritious vegetables are the basis of this tasty chilled soup. We recommend using spicy V8 juice for a more kicked-up version.
—*Taste of Home* Test Kitchen

Prep: 20 min. + chilling • **Makes:** 2 servings

- 2 **medium tomatoes,
  seeded and chopped**
- ½ **small green pepper, chopped**
- ⅓ **cup chopped peeled cucumber**
- ⅓ **cup chopped red onion**
- 1⅓ **cups reduced-sodium tomato juice**
- ¼ **tsp. dried oregano**
- ¼ **tsp. dried basil**
- ⅛ **tsp. salt**
- 1 **small garlic clove, minced
  Dash pepper
  Dash hot pepper sauce**
- 1 **Tbsp. minced chives
  Chopped sweet yellow pepper,
  optional**

1. In a large bowl, combine the tomatoes, green pepper, cucumber and onion. In another bowl, combine the tomato juice, oregano, basil, salt, garlic, pepper and pepper sauce; pour over vegetables.
2. Cover and refrigerate for at least 4 hours or overnight. Just before serving, sprinkle with chives and, if desired, yellow pepper.
1½ cups: 81 cal., 0 fat (0 sat. fat), 0 chol., 252mg sod., 17g carb. (11g sugars, 4g fiber), 3g pro. **Diabetic exchanges:** 1 starch.

SPICY PERUVIAN
POTATO SOUP

This robust Peruvian soup (known there as locro de papa) has the comfort of potatoes and the warming spiciness of chiles. Light enough for a simple lunch, it's also satisfying served as a main dish for dinner.
—*Taste of Home* Test Kitchen

Prep: 35 min. • **Cook:** 4 hours
Makes: 8 servings (2 qt.)

- 1 **Tbsp. olive oil**
- 1 **medium onion, chopped**
- 1 **medium sweet red pepper,
  cut into 1-in. pieces**
- 3 **garlic cloves, minced**
- 1 **carton (32 oz.) chicken stock**
- 2 **large Yukon Gold potatoes,
  peeled and cut into 1-in. cubes**
- 1 **can (4 oz.) chopped green chiles**
- ½ **cup minced fresh cilantro, divided**
- ½ **to 1 serrano pepper, seeded
  and finely chopped**
- 2 **tsp. ground cumin**
- 1 **tsp. dried oregano**
- ¼ **tsp. salt**
- ¼ **tsp. pepper**
- 1 **fully cooked Spanish chorizo
  link (3 oz.), chopped
  Optional toppings: Sour cream
  and cubed avocado**

1. In a large skillet, heat oil over medium-high heat. Add onion and sweet pepper; cook and stir until crisp-tender, 6-8 minutes. Add the garlic; cook 1 minute longer. Transfer to a 4- or 5-qt. slow cooker. Add the chicken stock, potatoes, chiles, ¼ cup cilantro, serrano pepper and seasonings. Cook, covered, on low 4-6 hours, until potatoes are tender.
2. Remove soup from heat; cool slightly. Process in batches in a blender until smooth. Return to slow cooker. Stir in chorizo and remaining ¼ cup cilantro; heat through. If desired, serve with sour cream and avocado.
1 cup: 153 cal., 5g fat (1g sat. fat), 7mg chol., 472mg sod., 23g carb. (3g sugars, 2g fiber), 6g pro. **Diabetic exchanges:** 1½ starch, 1 fat.

MEATBALL
ALPHABET SOUP

MEATBALL ALPHABET SOUP

Bite-sized meatballs made from ground turkey perk up this fun alphabet soup. A variety of vegetables are mixed in a rich tomato broth seasoned with herbs.
—*Taste of Home* Test Kitchen

- -

Prep: 20 min. • **Cook:** 35 min.
Makes: 9 servings (about 3½ qt.)

- 1 large egg, lightly beaten
- 2 Tbsp. quick-cooking oats
- 2 Tbsp. grated Parmesan cheese
- ¼ tsp. garlic powder
- ¼ tsp. Italian seasoning
- ½ lb. lean ground turkey
- 1 cup chopped onion
- 1 cup chopped celery
- 1 cup chopped carrots
- 1 cup diced peeled potatoes
- 1 Tbsp. olive oil
- 2 garlic cloves, minced
- 4 cans (14½ oz. each) reduced-sodium chicken broth
- 1 can (28 oz.) diced tomatoes, undrained
- 1 can (6 oz.) tomato paste
- ¼ cup minced fresh parsley
- 1 tsp. dried basil
- 1 tsp. dried thyme
- ¾ cup uncooked alphabet pasta

1. In a bowl, combine the first 5 ingredients. Crumble turkey over mixture and mix lightly but thoroughly. Shape into ½-in. balls. In a nonstick skillet, brown the meatballs in small batches over medium heat until no longer pink. Remove from the heat; set aside.
2. In a large saucepan or Dutch oven, saute the onion, celery, carrots and potatoes in oil for 5 minutes or until crisp-tender. Add the garlic; saute 1 minute longer. Add the broth, tomatoes, tomato paste, parsley, basil and thyme; bring to a boil. Add pasta; cook for 5-6 minutes. Reduce heat; add meatballs. Simmer, uncovered, for 15-20 minutes or until vegetables are tender.
1½ cups: 192 cal., 5g fat (1g sat. fat), 39mg chol., 742mg sod., 26g carb. (8g sugars, 4g fiber), 13g pro.

MICHIGAN CHERRY SALAD

MICHIGAN CHERRY SALAD

This salad brings to mind what I love about my home state: apple picking with my kids, buying greens at the farmers market and tasting cherries while on vacation.
—Jennifer Gilbert, Brighton, MI

- -

Takes: 15 min. • **Makes:** 8 servings

- 7 oz. fresh baby spinach (about 9 cups)
- 3 oz. spring mix salad greens (about 5 cups)
- 1 large apple, chopped
- ½ cup coarsely chopped pecans, toasted
- ½ cup dried cherries
- ¼ cup crumbled Gorgonzola cheese

DRESSING
- ¼ cup fresh raspberries
- ¼ cup red wine vinegar
- 3 Tbsp. cider vinegar
- 3 Tbsp. cherry preserves
- 1 Tbsp. sugar
- 2 Tbsp. olive oil

1. In a large salad bowl, combine the first 6 ingredients.
2. Place raspberries, vinegars, cherry preserves and sugar in a blender. While processing, gradually add oil in a steady stream. Drizzle over salad; toss to coat.
1½ cups: 172 cal., 10g fat (2g sat. fat), 3mg chol., 78mg sod., 21g carb. (16g sugars, 3g fiber), 3g pro. **Diabetic exchanges:** 2 vegetable, 2 fat, 1 starch.

KOHLRABI, CUCUMBER & TOMATO SALAD

This chilled, refreshing salad is wonderful on hot days. It has a nice crunch and a delicious balance of sweet and spicy flavors.
—Kristina Segarra, Yonkers, NY

- -

Prep: 30 min. + chilling • **Makes:** 6 servings

- 2   **Tbsp. olive oil**
- 1   **medium red onion, finely chopped**
- 2   **pickled hot cherry peppers, seeded and finely chopped**
- 2   **garlic cloves, minced**
- 2   **Tbsp. cider vinegar**
- 1   **tsp. salt**
- 1   **kohlrabi, peeled and cut into ½-in. pieces**
- 2   **large yellow tomatoes, seeded and chopped**
- 2   **mini cucumbers, cut into ½-in. pieces**
- 2   **Tbsp. minced fresh cilantro**

1. In a small skillet, heat oil over medium-high heat. Add onion; cook and stir 2-3 minutes or until crisp-tender. Add peppers and garlic; cook 2 minutes longer. Stir in vinegar and salt; remove from heat.
2. In a large bowl, combine the kohlrabi, tomatoes and cucumbers. Pour in onion mixture; gently toss to coat. Chill for 1 hour. Sprinkle with cilantro before serving.
¾ cup: 59 cal., 4g fat (1g sat. fat), 0 chol., 372mg sod., 6g carb. (2g sugars, 2g fiber), 2g pro. **Diabetic exchanges:** 1 vegetable, ½ fat.

VIETNAMESE CRUNCHY CHICKEN SALAD

VIETNAMESE CRUNCHY CHICKEN SALAD

When I lived in Cleveland, I frequently dined at a stellar Vietnamese restaurant. This chicken salad quickly became my favorite. Because I had it so often, I figured out the components and flavors and created my own easy-to-make version.
—Erin Schillo, Northfield, OH

- -

Prep: 30 min. + marinating • **Cook:** 10 min.
Makes: 4 servings

- 3   **Tbsp. olive oil**
- 2   **Tbsp. lime juice**
- 1   **Tbsp. minced fresh cilantro**
- 1½ **tsp. grated lime zest**
- ½   **tsp. salt**
- ½   **tsp. pepper**
- ¼   **tsp. cayenne pepper**
- 1   **lb. boneless skinless chicken breasts, cut into thin strips**

DRESSING
- ½   **cup olive oil**
- ¼   **cup lime juice**
- 2   **Tbsp. rice vinegar**
- 2   **Tbsp. sugar**
- 1   **Tbsp. grated lime zest**
- ¾   **tsp. salt**
- ½   **tsp. crushed red pepper flakes**
- ¼   **tsp. pepper**

SALAD
- 5   **cups thinly sliced cabbage (about 1 lb.)**
- 1   **cup minced fresh cilantro**
- 1   **cup julienned carrots**
- 1   **cup salted peanuts, coarsely chopped**

1. In a large bowl, mix the first 7 ingredients; add chicken and toss to coat. Refrigerate, covered, 30 minutes. In a small bowl, whisk dressing ingredients.
2. In a large skillet over medium-high heat, stir-fry half the chicken mixture until no longer pink, 4-5 minutes. Remove from pan; repeat with remaining chicken. Cool slightly.
3. In a large bowl, combine the cabbage, minced cilantro, carrots and chicken; toss to combine. Add chopped peanuts and dressing; toss to coat. Serve immediately.
2 cups: 743 cal., 59g fat (9g sat. fat), 63mg chol., 1068mg sod., 25g carb. (12g sugars, 7g fiber), 35g pro.

EASY BUTTERNUT SQUASH SOUP

When the weather turns cold, get cozy with a bowl of this butternut squash soup. The cream adds richness, but if you're looking to cut calories, it can be omitted.
—*Taste of Home* Test Kitchen

Takes: 30 min. • **Makes:** 9 servings (2¼ qt.)

- 1 Tbsp. olive oil
- 1 large onion, chopped
- 3 garlic cloves, minced
- 1 medium butternut squash (3 lbs.), peeled and cubed
- 4 cups vegetable broth
- ¾ tsp. salt
- ¼ tsp. pepper
- ½ cup heavy whipping cream
- Optional: Additional heavy whipping cream and crispy sage leaves

1. In a large saucepan, heat oil over medium heat. Add onion; cook and stir until tender. Add garlic; cook 1 minute longer.
2. Stir in squash, broth, salt and pepper; bring to a boil. Reduce the heat; simmer, covered, 10-15 minutes or until squash is tender. Puree the soup using an immersion blender. Or cool slightly and puree soup in batches in a blender; return to pan. Add cream; cook and stir until heated through. If desired, garnish with additional heavy whipping cream and crispy sage.
1 cup: 157 cal., 7g fat (4g sat. fat), 17mg chol., 483mg sod., 23g carb. (6g sugars, 6g fiber), 3g pro.

MELON-BERRY SALAD

The best way to cool down on a warm day is to serve up a chilled fruit salad—the best of summer's bounty! The dressing gives this salad a creamy and rich texture, and the coconut milk makes it even more decadent. This can be served at breakfast or brunch, or as dessert. Wait until just before serving to garnish the salad. Otherwise the toasted coconut will get soggy.
—Carrie Hirsch, Hilton Head Island, SC

Takes: 20 min. • **Makes:** 12 servings

- 1 cup fat-free vanilla Greek yogurt
- ½ cup coconut milk
- ½ cup orange juice
- 4 cups cubed cantaloupe (½ in.)
- 4 cups cubed watermelon (½ in.)
- 2 medium navel oranges, sectioned
- 1 cup fresh raspberries
- 1 cup fresh blueberries
- ½ cup sweetened shredded coconut, toasted

1. For dressing, whisk together the yogurt, coconut milk and orange juice. Refrigerate until serving.
2. To serve, place fruit in a large bowl; toss gently with dressing. Sprinkle with coconut.
¾ cup: 105 cal., 3g fat (3g sat. fat), 0 chol., 30mg sod., 19g carb. (16g sugars, 2g fiber), 3g pro. **Diabetic exchanges:** 1 fruit, ½ fat.

EASY BUTTERNUT SQUASH SOUP

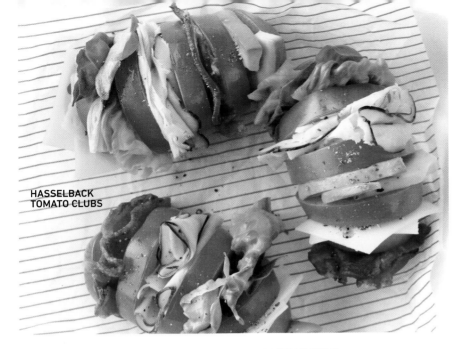

HASSELBACK TOMATO CLUBS

CHIPOTLE SWEET POTATO SALAD

I love the velvety taste and texture of sweet potatoes. A friend served sweet potatoes cooked with peppers and they tasted delicious together. I took those flavors and developed them into this creamy, smoky potato salad.

—Carolyn Eskew, Dayton, OH

Prep: 20 min. • **Bake:** 25 min. + cooling
Makes: 9 servings

- 3 lbs. sweet potatoes, peeled and cut into ¾-in. pieces (about 7 cups)
- ¼ cup finely chopped sweet onion
- ¼ cup finely chopped celery
- ¼ cup finely chopped seeded fresh poblano pepper
- 1 jalapeno pepper, seeded and finely chopped
- 1 cup mayonnaise
- 2 Tbsp. lime juice
- ½ to 1 tsp. ground chipotle pepper
- ½ tsp. salt
- ¼ tsp. pepper
  Minced fresh cilantro

1. Preheat oven to 425°. Place the sweet potatoes in a parchment-lined 15x10x1-in. baking pan; cover tightly with foil. Roast until tender, 25-30 minutes. Cool. Transfer to a large bowl.
2. Add onion, celery, poblano and jalapeno. Combine mayonnaise, lime juice, chipotle pepper, salt and pepper; pour over potato mixture and toss gently to coat. Refrigerate, covered, until serving. Sprinkle with cilantro.
¾ cup: 322 cal., 18g fat (3g sat. fat), 2mg chol., 278mg sod., 38g carb. (16g sugars, 5g fiber), 3g pro.

TEST KITCHEN TIP

If you're going to chill this salad for more than a couple of hours before serving, stir in just half of the dressing mixture. Add the rest right before serving.

HASSELBACK TOMATO CLUBS

This no-fuss, no-bread riff on a classic is perfect during tomato season. Make it for lunch or pair it with your favorite pasta salad for a light dinner.

—*Taste of Home* Test Kitchen

Takes: 15 min. • **Makes:** 2 servings

- 4 plum tomatoes
- 2 slices Swiss cheese, quartered
- 4 cooked bacon strips, halved
- 4 slices deli turkey
- 4 Bibb lettuce leaves
- ½ medium ripe avocado, peeled and cut into 8 slices
  Cracked pepper

Cut 4 crosswise slices in each tomato, leaving them intact at the bottom. Fill each slice with cheese, bacon, turkey, lettuce and avocado. Sprinkle with pepper.
2 stuffed tomatoes: 272 cal., 17g fat (5g sat. fat), 48mg chol., 803mg sod., 9g carb. (3g sugars, 4g fiber), 21g pro.

TURKEY PITAS WITH CREAMY SLAW

Pack these tasty pockets for school, work or a weekend picnic—or just eat them at home. Toss in a few slices of red pepper for extra color and crunch.

—*Taste of Home* Test Kitchen

Takes: 10 min. • **Makes:** 4 servings

- 3 cups coleslaw mix
- ¼ cup golden raisins
- 3 Tbsp. chopped red onion
- ⅓ cup reduced-fat mayonnaise
- 3 Tbsp. mango chutney
- 8 pita pocket halves
- ½ lb. sliced deli turkey
- 8 ready-to-serve fully cooked bacon strips, warmed
- 1 medium cucumber, thinly sliced

In a large bowl, combine coleslaw mix, raisins and onion. Add the mayonnaise and chutney; toss to coat. Line the pita pocket halves with turkey, bacon and cucumber slices; fill with coleslaw mixture.
2 filled pita halves: 427 cal., 12g fat (2g sat. fat), 27mg chol., 1257mg sod., 57g carb. (18g sugars, 3g fiber), 21g pro.

CHIPOTLE SWEET
POTATO SALAD

SWISS CHARD
BEAN SOUP

SWISS CHARD BEAN SOUP

This hearty soup combines nutritious Swiss chard with other garden favorites. Its light broth is surprisingly rich in flavor, and the grated Parmesan packs an additional punch.
—*Taste of Home* Test Kitchen

Prep: 25 min. • **Cook:** 30 min.
Makes: 10 servings (2½ qt.)

- 1 medium carrot, coarsely chopped
- 1 small zucchini, coarsely chopped
- 1 small yellow summer squash, coarsely chopped
- 1 small red onion, chopped
- 2 Tbsp. olive oil
- 2 garlic cloves, minced
- 3 cans (14½ oz. each) reduced-sodium chicken broth
- 4 cups chopped Swiss chard
- 1 can (15½ oz.) great northern beans, rinsed and drained
- 1 can (14½ oz.) diced tomatoes, undrained
- 1 tsp. dried thyme
- ½ tsp. salt
- ½ tsp. dried oregano
- ¼ tsp. pepper
- ¼ cup grated Parmesan cheese

1. In a Dutch oven, saute carrot, zucchini, yellow squash and onion in oil until tender. Add garlic; saute 1 minute longer. Add the chicken broth, Swiss chard, beans, tomatoes, thyme, salt, oregano and pepper.

2. Bring to a boil. Reduce the heat; simmer, uncovered, for 15 minutes or until the chard is tender. Just before serving, sprinkle with Parmesan cheese.

1 cup: 94 cal., 4g fat (1g sat. fat), 2mg chol., 452mg sod., 12g carb. (3g sugars, 4g fiber), 5g pro.

PRESSURE-COOKER CHILI CON CARNE

Although multicookers can't replace every tool in the kitchen, they sure are coming close. Chili con carne is one of our favorite dishes to re-create in them. This cooks up fast but tastes like it simmered all day!
—*Taste of Home* Test Kitchen

Takes: 15 min. + releasing • **Makes:** 7 servings

- 1 can (16 oz.) pinto beans, rinsed and drained
- 1 can (14½ oz.) Mexican diced tomatoes, undrained
- 1 can (8 oz.) tomato sauce
- 1 medium green pepper, chopped
- 1 medium onion, chopped
- 1 cup beef broth
- 1 jalapeno pepper, seeded and minced
- 2 Tbsp. chili powder
- ¼ tsp. salt
- ¼ tsp. pepper
- 1½ lbs. lean ground beef (90% lean)
  Optional: Sour cream and sliced jalapeno

1. Combine the first 10 ingredients in a 6-qt. electric pressure cooker. Crumble beef over top; stir to combine. Lock lid; close pressure-release valve. Adjust to pressure-cook on high for 5 minutes.
2. Allow the pressure to naturally release for 10 minutes, then quick-release any remaining pressure. Stir chili. If desired, serve with sour cream and additional jalapenos.
1 cup: 248 cal., 9g fat (3g sat. fat), 61mg chol., 687mg sod., 18g carb. (5g sugars, 5g fiber), 24g pro. **Diabetic exchanges:** 3 lean meat, 1 starch.

PEAR & POMEGRANATE SALAD

PEAR & POMEGRANATE SALAD

Pomegranate and Boursin cheese add zip to this cool salad of Bosc pears over lettuce. Look for the 5.2-ounce Boursin, which is more firm than the spreadable version.
—Erika Monroe-Williams, Scottsdale, AZ

Takes: 25 min. • **Makes:** 4 servings

- ¼ cup apple juice
- 2 Tbsp. canola oil
- 1 Tbsp. cider vinegar
- 1 Tbsp. white balsamic vinegar or white wine vinegar
- ⅛ tsp. onion powder
- ⅛ tsp. coarsely ground pepper
  Dash salt
- 3 medium Bosc pears
- 1 head Boston or Bibb lettuce (about 6 oz.), torn
- 1 cup pomegranate seeds
- 1 cup coarsely chopped pecans, toasted
- ¾ cup crumbled Boursin garlic and fine herbs cheese (half of a 5.2-oz. pkg.) or garlic and herb feta cheese

1. In a blender, combine first 7 ingredients. Cut 1 pear lengthwise in half; peel, core and coarsely chop 1 pear half. Add chopped pear to blender; cover and process until blended. Cut remaining pears and pear half lengthwise into ¼-in. slices.
2. Arrange lettuce on 4 plates. Top with pears, pomegranate seeds and pecans; sprinkle with cheese. Drizzle with dressing; serve immediately.
1 serving: 388 cal., 29g fat (4g sat. fat), 6mg chol., 74mg sod., 34g carb. (23g sugars, 7g fiber), 4g pro.

TEST KITCHEN TIPS

- Do not buy spreadable cheese for this recipe, which needs a cheese with firmer texture.

- To toast pecans for this salad, bake them in a shallow pan in a 350° oven for 5-10 minutes or cook in a skillet over low heat until lightly browned, stirring nuts occasionally.

SWEET CLUB SANDWICH

I first tasted this delicious layered loaf at a potluck at work. It seems fancy with its raspberry jam surprise, yet it's convenient because it can be assembled ahead of time and then warmed just before serving.
—Joanne Klopfenstein, North Liberty, IN

- -

Prep: 20 min. + cooling • **Bake:** 10 min.
Makes: 8 servings

- 2 tubes (8 oz. each) refrigerated crescent rolls
- 2 Tbsp. butter
- 4 Tbsp. honey, divided
- 6 oz. thinly sliced deli turkey
- 6 oz. sliced Muenster or Monterey Jack cheese
- 6 oz. thinly sliced deli ham
- 1/3 cup raspberry preserves
- 1 Tbsp. sesame seeds

1. Unroll each tube of crescent roll dough into 2 rectangles. Place 4 dough portions 2 in. apart on ungreased baking sheets; press perforations to seal.
2. In a small bowl, combine the butter and 2 Tbsp. honey. Brush over dough. Bake at 375° for 10-12 minutes or until lightly browned. Cool on pans for 15 minutes.
3. Carefully transfer 1 crust to a greased 15x10x1-in. baking pan. Layer with turkey, second crust, cheese and ham. Add third crust; spread with preserves.
4. Top with remaining crust; spread with the remaining honey. Sprinkle with sesame seeds. Bake, uncovered, at 375° until crust is golden brown and loaf is heated through, 10-15 minutes. Carefully cut into slices.
1 slice: 343 cal., 18g fat (8g sat. fat), 49mg chol., 938mg sod., 30g carb. (19g sugars, 0 fiber), 15g pro.

MIXED GREENS WITH ORANGE-GINGER VINAIGRETTE

Zingy vinaigrette starts with orange juice, ginger and a flick of cayenne. Just whisk, toss with greens and top the salad your way.
—Joy Zacharia, Clearwater, FL

- -

Takes: 20 min. • **Makes:** 8 servings

- 1/4 cup orange juice
- 1/4 cup canola oil
- 2 Tbsp. white vinegar
- 2 Tbsp. honey
- 2 tsp. grated fresh gingerroot
- 1/2 tsp. salt
- 1/4 tsp. cayenne pepper

SALAD
- 12 cups torn mixed salad greens
- 2 medium navel oranges, peeled and sliced crosswise
- 1 cup thinly sliced red onion

In a small bowl, whisk the first 7 ingredients until blended. In a large bowl, toss the salad greens with 1/4 cup vinaigrette; transfer to a serving dish. Top with orange slices and onion. Serve salad immediately with the remaining vinaigrette.
1 1/2 cups: 119 cal., 7g fat (1g sat. fat), 0 chol., 202mg sod., 15g carb. (9g sugars, 3g fiber), 2g pro. **Diabetic exchanges:** 1 1/2 fat, 1 vegetable, 1/2 starch.

MIXED GREENS WITH ORANGE-GINGER VINAIGRETTE

**PRESSURE-COOKER
CHICKEN & BACON WHITE CHILI**

TASTE OF HOME
**TEST
KITCHEN**
RECIPE OF THE YEAR
★★★★★

PRESSURE-COOKER CHICKEN & BACON WHITE CHILI

I made a creative twist on my favorite white chicken chili and used my pressure cooker, which made it quick and easy. I serve it with avocado, cilantro and onions.
—Teri Rasey, Cadillac, MI

- -

Prep: 10 min. • **Cook:** 15 min. + releasing
Makes: 16 servings (4 qt.)

- ½ lb. bacon strips, coarsely chopped
- 6 boneless skinless chicken thighs
- 1 pkg. (20 oz.) frozen corn
- 2 cans (15 oz. each) cannellini beans, rinsed and drained
- 2 cans (15 oz. each) black beans, rinsed and drained
- 2 cans (11 oz. each) diced tomatoes and green chiles
- 1 can (4 oz.) chopped green chiles
- 1 cup reduced-sodium chicken broth
- 1 Tbsp. chili powder
- 1 tsp. ground cumin
- 1 tsp. onion powder
- 1 tsp. minced garlic
- 1 envelope (1 oz.) ranch salad dressing mix
- 12 oz. cream cheese
- 2 cups shredded cheddar cheese
  Optional: Cubed avocado and sliced jalapeno

1. Select saute or browning setting on a 6-qt. electric pressure cooker; adjust for medium heat. Cook bacon until crisp, 5-6 minutes; remove bacon and reserve. Brown chicken in the bacon drippings until lightly browned, 5-6 minutes. Return the bacon to pan; top with the corn and next 11 ingredients in the order listed.

2. Lock lid; close the pressure-release valve. Adjust to pressure-cook on high for 15 minutes. Let pressure release naturally for 10 minutes; quick-release any remaining pressure. Stir in the cheese until melted. If desired, serve with avocado and jalapeno.

1 cup: 387 cal., 21g fat (10g sat. fat), 73mg chol., 1033mg sod., 29g carb. (2g sugars, 6g fiber), 20g pro.

SHAVED FENNEL SALAD

This salad tastes even more impressive than it looks. It's got an incredible crunch thanks to the cucumbers, radishes and apples, and the fennel fronds add just the faintest hint of licorice flavor.
—William Milton III, Clemson, SC

- -

Takes: 15 min. • **Makes:** 8 servings

- 1 large fennel bulb, fronds reserved
- 1 English cucumber
- 1 medium Honeycrisp apple
- 2 Tbsp. extra virgin olive oil
- ½ tsp. kosher salt
- ¼ tsp. coarsely ground pepper
- 2 radishes, thinly sliced

With a mandoline or vegetable peeler, cut fennel, cucumber and apple into very thin slices. Transfer to a large bowl; toss with the olive oil, salt and pepper. Top with radishes and reserved fennel fronds to serve.

¾ cup: 55 cal., 4g fat (1g sat. fat), 0 chol., 138mg sod., 6g carb. (4g sugars, 2g fiber), 1g pro.

TEST KITCHEN TIP

It's easy to modify this recipe based on your taste and what you have on hand. You can add more or less fennel and apple. Try adding a squeeze of lemon. The acid complements the dressing.

MOLASSES STEAK SANDWICHES

The classic combination of steak and Swiss gets some added down-home sweetness thanks to a molasses-based marinade. This familiar yet distinctive sandwich is special enough to serve at any get-together.
—*Taste of Home* Test Kitchen

Prep: 15 min. + marinating • **Grill:** 15 min.
Makes: 4 servings

- ¼ cup molasses
- 2 Tbsp. brown sugar
- 2 Tbsp. olive oil, divided
- 1 Tbsp. Dijon mustard
- 4 beef tenderloin steaks (1 in. thick and 4 oz. each)
- 2 large portobello mushrooms, stems removed
- 4 kaiser rolls, split
- 4 slices Swiss cheese

1. In a shallow dish, mix molasses, brown sugar, 1 Tbsp. oil and mustard. Add steaks and turn to coat. Cover; refrigerate up to 2 hours.

2. Drain beef, discarding marinade. Brush mushrooms with remaining oil. Grill steaks, covered, over medium heat 5-7 minutes on each side or until meat reaches desired doneness (for medium-rare, a thermometer should read 135°; medium, 140°; medium-well, 145°). Grill mushrooms, covered, until tender, 8-10 minutes, turning occasionally. Remove steaks and mushrooms from grill; let stand 5 minutes.

3. Grill rolls, cut side down, for 2-3 minutes or until lightly toasted. Cut mushrooms and steaks into slices. Serve in rolls with cheese.

1 sandwich: 452 cal., 17g fat (5g sat. fat), 59mg chol., 367mg sod., 40g carb. (9g sugars, 2g fiber), 34g pro.

THE BEST CHICKEN & DUMPLINGS

THE BEST CHICKEN & DUMPLINGS

Chicken and dumplings harken back to my childhood and chilly days when we devoured those cute little balls of dough swimming in hot, rich broth.
—Erika Monroe-Williams, Scottsdale, AZ

- -

Prep: 25 min. • **Cook:** 1 hour 10 min.
Makes: 8 servings (3 qt.)

¾	cup all-purpose flour, divided
½	tsp. salt
½	tsp. freshly ground pepper
1	broiler/fryer chicken (about 3 lbs.), cut up
2	Tbsp. canola oil
1	large onion, chopped
2	medium carrots, chopped
2	celery ribs, chopped
3	garlic cloves, minced
6	cups chicken stock
½	cup white wine or apple cider
2	tsp. sugar
2	bay leaves
5	whole peppercorns

DUMPLINGS

1⅓	cups all-purpose flour
2	tsp. baking powder
¾	tsp. salt
⅔	cup 2% milk
1	Tbsp. butter, melted

SOUP

½	cup heavy whipping cream
2	tsp. minced fresh parsley
2	tsp. minced fresh thyme
	Additional salt and pepper to taste

1. In a shallow bowl, mix ½ cup flour, salt and pepper. Add chicken, 1 piece at a time, and toss to coat; shake off excess. In a 6-qt. stockpot, heat oil over medium-high heat. Brown chicken in batches on all sides; remove from pan.

2. Add onion, carrots and celery to same pan; cook and stir 6-8 minutes or until onion is tender. Add garlic; cook and stir 1 minute longer. Stir in ¼ cup flour until blended. Gradually add stock, stirring constantly. Stir in wine, sugar, bay leaves and peppercorns. Return chicken to pan; bring to a boil. Reduce heat; simmer, covered, 20-25 minutes or until chicken juices run clear.

3. For dumplings, in a bowl, whisk flour, baking powder and salt. In another bowl, whisk milk and melted butter until blended. Add to flour mixture; stir just until moistened (do not overmix). Drop by rounded tablespoonfuls onto a parchment-lined baking sheet; set aside.

4. Remove chicken from stockpot; cool slightly. Discard bay leaves and skim fat from soup. Remove skin and bones from chicken and discard. Using 2 forks, coarsely shred meat into 1- to 1½-in. pieces; return to soup. Cook, covered, on high until mixture reaches a simmer.

5. Drop dumplings on top of simmering soup, a few at a time. Reduce heat to low; cook, covered, 15-18 minutes or until a toothpick inserted in center of dumplings comes out clean (do not lift cover while simmering). Gently stir in cream, parsley and thyme. Season with additional salt and pepper to taste.

1½ cups: 470 cal., 24g fat (8g sat. fat), 104mg chol., 892mg sod., 29g carb. (5g sugars, 2g fiber), 32g pro.

**PESTO CORN SALAD
WITH SHRIMP, PAGE 131**

Fish, Seafood & Meatless Dinners

Whether you enjoy an occasional meatless meal, follow a vegetarian diet or just want to take your dinner seaside for a night, these hearty fish, seafood and vegetarian dishes are so good, you'll forget all about meat.

SPANISH-STYLE PAELLA

If you enjoy ethnic foods, you'll love this hearty rice dish. Omit the chorizo and chicken and use vegetable broth if you want to make it meatless.
—*Taste of Home* Test Kitchen

Prep: 10 min. • **Cook:** 35 min.
Makes: 8 servings

- ½ lb. Spanish chorizo links, sliced
- ½ lb. boneless skinless chicken breasts, cubed
- 1 Tbsp. olive oil
- 1 garlic clove, minced
- 1 cup uncooked short grain rice
- 1 cup chopped onion
- 1½ cups chicken broth
- 1 can (14½ oz.) stewed tomatoes, undrained
- ½ tsp. paprika
- ¼ tsp. ground cayenne pepper
- ¼ tsp. salt
- 10 strands saffron, crushed or ⅛ tsp. ground saffron
- ½ lb. uncooked medium shrimp, peeled and deveined
- ½ cup sweet red pepper strips
- ½ cup green pepper strips
- ½ cup frozen peas
  Optional: Minced fresh parsley and lemon wedges

1. In a large saucepan or skillet over medium-high heat, cook the sausage and chicken in oil for 5 minutes or until sausage is lightly browned and chicken is no longer pink, stirring frequently. Add garlic; cook 1 minute longer. Drain if necessary.
2. Stir in rice and onion. Cook until onion is tender and rice is lightly browned, stirring frequently. Add the chicken broth, tomatoes, paprika, cayenne, salt and saffron. Bring to a boil. Reduce heat to low; cover and cook for 10 minutes.
3. Stir in the shrimp, peppers and peas. Cover and cook 10 minutes longer or until rice is tender, shrimp turn pink and liquid is absorbed. Top with fresh parsley and lemon wedges, if desired.

1 cup: 237 cal., 7g fat (2g sat. fat), 62mg chol., 543mg sod., 27g carb. (5g sugars, 2g fiber), 16g pro.

LEMON-BASIL GRILLED SHRIMP & COUSCOUS

The basil and lemon flavors in this grilled shrimp dish are a perfect complement to each other. Make sure to use fresh basil and fresh lemon juice and zest—you will notice the difference!
—Trisha Kruse, Eagle, ID

Takes: 30 min. • **Makes:** 6 servings

- 1½ cups uncooked pearl (Israeli) couscous
- ⅓ cup lemon juice
- ¼ cup olive oil
- 2 Tbsp. Dijon mustard
- 3 garlic cloves, minced
- ½ tsp. salt
- ¼ tsp. pepper
- ½ cup minced fresh basil, divided
- 2 lbs. uncooked large shrimp, peeled and deveined
- 2 tsp. grated lemon zest

1. Cook couscous according to package directions; remove from heat. Meanwhile, in a large bowl, whisk lemon juice, olive oil, Dijon mustard, garlic, salt and pepper until blended; stir in ¼ cup fresh basil. Stir ¼ cup dressing into cooked couscous; reserve remaining dressing.
2. Thread the shrimp onto metal or soaked wooden skewers. Grill shrimp, covered, on an oiled grill rack over medium-high heat until pink, 2-3 minutes on each side.
3. Remove shrimp from skewers; toss with reserved dressing. Serve with couscous. Sprinkle with the lemon zest and remaining minced basil.

8 shrimp with ½ cup couscous: 363 cal., 12g fat (2g sat. fat), 184mg chol., 497mg sod., 34g carb. (0 sugars, 0 fiber), 29g pro.

ARTICHOKE COD WITH SUN-DRIED TOMATOES

I serve cod over a bed of greens, pasta or quinoa. A squeeze of lemon gives it another layer of freshness.
—Hiroko Miles, El Dorado Hills, CA

Takes: 30 min. • **Makes:** 6 servings

- 1 can (14 oz.) quartered water-packed artichoke hearts, drained
- ½ cup julienned soft sun-dried tomatoes (not packed in oil)
- 2 green onions, chopped
- 3 Tbsp. olive oil
- 1 garlic clove, minced
- 6 cod fillets (6 oz. each)
- 1 tsp. salt
- ½ tsp. pepper
  Optional: Salad greens and lemon wedges

1. Preheat oven to 400°. In a small bowl, combine the first 5 ingredients; toss well to combine.
2. Sprinkle both sides of cod fillets with salt and pepper; place in a 13x9-in. baking dish coated with cooking spray. Top with the artichoke mixture.
3. Bake, uncovered, 15-20 minutes or until the fish just begins to flake easily with a fork. If desired, serve over salad greens with lemon wedges.

1 fillet with ⅓ cup artichoke mixture: 231 cal., 8g fat (1g sat. fat), 65mg chol., 665mg sod., 9g carb. (3g sugars, 2g fiber), 29g pro. **Diabetic exchanges:** 4 lean meat, 1½ fat, 1 vegetable.

BLACK BEAN BURGERS WITH CHIPOTLE SLAW

We like to eat meatless at least one day a week, so I always keep cans of various beans in the pantry for quick meals like this one.
—Deborah Biggs, Omaha, NE

- -

Prep: 25 min. + chilling • **Cook:** 10 min.
Makes: 4 servings

- 1   can (15 oz.) black beans, rinsed and drained
- 6   Tbsp. panko bread crumbs
- ¼   cup finely chopped onion
- ¼   cup finely chopped sweet red pepper
- ¼   cup minced fresh cilantro
- 2   large egg whites, lightly beaten
- 1   garlic clove, minced
- ¼   tsp. salt
- 2   Tbsp. red wine vinegar
- 1   Tbsp. plus 4 tsp. olive oil, divided
- 1   Tbsp. minced chipotle pepper in adobo sauce
- 1½   tsp. sugar
- 2¼   cups coleslaw mix
- 2   green onions, chopped
- 4   whole wheat hamburger buns, split

1. In a large bowl, mash beans. Add the panko, onion, red pepper, cilantro, egg whites, garlic and salt; mix well. Shape bean mixture into 4 patties; refrigerate patties for 30 minutes.

2. Meanwhile, in a small bowl, whisk the vinegar, 1 Tbsp. oil, chipotle pepper and sugar; stir in coleslaw mix and onions. Chill until serving.

3. In a large nonstick skillet, cook burgers in remaining oil over medium heat until a thermometer reads 160°, 3-5 minutes on each side. Serve on buns with slaw.

1 burger: 327 cal., 10g fat (1g sat. fat), 0 chol., 635mg sod., 48g carb. (9g sugars, 9g fiber), 12g pro. **Diabetic exchanges:** 3 starch, 1½ fat, 1 lean meat.

QUINOA & BLACK BEAN-STUFFED PEPPERS

If you're thinking about a meatless meal, give these no-fuss peppers a try. They come together with just a few ingredients and put a tasty spin on a low-fat dinner!
—Cindy Reams, Philipsburg, PA

- -

Takes: 30 min. • **Makes:** 4 servings

- 1½   cups water
- 1   cup quinoa, rinsed
- 4   large green peppers
- 1   jar (16 oz.) chunky salsa, divided
- 1   can (15 oz.) black beans, rinsed and drained
- ½   cup reduced-fat ricotta cheese
- ½   cup shredded Monterey Jack cheese, divided

1. Preheat oven to 400°. In a small saucepan, bring water to a boil. Add quinoa. Reduce heat; simmer, covered, until the water is absorbed, 10-12 minutes.

2. Meanwhile, cut and discard tops from peppers; remove seeds. Place in a greased 8-in. square baking dish, cut side down. Microwave, uncovered, on high until peppers are crisp-tender, 3-4 minutes. Turn peppers cut side up.

3. Reserve ⅓ cup salsa; add remaining salsa to quinoa. Stir in beans, ricotta cheese and ¼ cup Monterey Jack cheese. Spoon mixture into peppers; sprinkle with the remaining cheese. Bake, uncovered, until the filling is heated through, 10-15 minutes. Top with the reserved salsa.

1 stuffed pepper: 393 cal., 8g fat (4g sat. fat), 20mg chol., 774mg sod., 59g carb. (10g sugars, 10g fiber), 18g pro.

QUINOA & BLACK BEAN-STUFFED PEPPERS

ASIAN
SALMON TACOS

VEGETARIAN FARRO SKILLET

Farro is a type of wheat that was popular in ancient Rome. A good source of fiber, it includes more protein than most grains, making it a smart choice for meatless meals.
—*Taste of Home* Test Kitchen

- -

Prep: 20 min. • **Cook:** 30 min.
Makes: 4 servings

1	Tbsp. canola oil
1	medium onion, chopped
1	medium sweet red pepper, chopped
3	garlic cloves, minced
1	can (14½ oz.) vegetable broth
1	can (14½ oz.) diced tomatoes
1	can (15 oz.) garbanzo beans or chickpeas, rinsed and drained
1	small zucchini, halved and cut into ½-in. slices
1	cup farro, rinsed
1	cup frozen corn
¾	tsp. ground cumin
¼	tsp. salt
¼	tsp. pepper
	Chopped fresh cilantro

Heat oil in a large skillet over medium-high heat. Add onion and pepper; cook and stir until tender, 2-3 minutes. Add garlic; cook 1 minute longer. Stir in broth, tomatoes, beans, zucchini, farro, corn, cumin, salt and pepper. Bring to a boil. Reduce the heat; cover and simmer until the farro is tender, 25-30 minutes. Sprinkle with cilantro.

1½ cups: 416 cal., 8g fat (0 sat. fat), 0 chol., 757mg sod., 73g carb. (10g sugars, 15g fiber), 14g pro.

ASIAN SALMON TACOS

This Asian/Mexican fusion dish is ready in minutes—perfect for an on-the-run meal! If the salmon begins to stick in the skillet, just add 2-3 tablespoons of water and continue cooking.
—Marisa Raponi, Vaughan, ON

- -

Takes: 20 min. • **Makes:** 4 servings

1	lb. salmon fillet, skin removed, cut into 1-in. cubes
2	Tbsp. hoisin sauce
1	Tbsp. olive oil
	Shredded lettuce
8	corn tortillas (6 in.), warmed
1½	tsp. black sesame seeds
	Mango salsa, optional

1. Toss salmon with hoisin sauce. In a large nonstick skillet, heat oil over medium-high heat. Cook salmon until it begins to flake easily with a fork, 3-5 minutes, turning gently to brown all sides.
2. Serve salmon and lettuce in tortillas; sprinkle with sesame seeds. If desired, top with salsa.

2 tacos: 335 cal., 16g fat (3g sat. fat), 57mg chol., 208mg sod., 25g carb. (3g sugars, 3g fiber), 22g pro. **Diabetic exchanges:** 3 lean meat, 2 starch, 1 fat.

DID YOU KNOW?

Hoisin sauce is used as a sauce, glaze and condiment in both Chinese and Vietnamese cuisines. It is sweet and salty in taste, but the flavor can vary between brands, so feel free to adjust the amount used to suit your personal preference.

LINGUINE WITH BROCCOLI RABE & PEPPERS

SEARED SCALLOPS WITH CITRUS HERB SAUCE

Be sure to pat the scallops with a paper towel to remove any excess moisture. This will help create perfectly browned and flavorful scallops.
—April Lane, Greeneville, TN

- -

Takes: 20 min. • **Makes:** 2 servings

¾	lb. sea scallops
¼	tsp. salt
¼	tsp. pepper
⅛	tsp. paprika
3	Tbsp. butter, divided
1	garlic clove, minced
2	Tbsp. dry sherry or chicken broth
1	Tbsp. lemon juice
⅛	tsp. minced fresh oregano
⅛	tsp. minced fresh tarragon

1. Pat scallops dry with paper towels; sprinkle with salt, pepper and paprika. In a large skillet, heat 2 Tbsp. butter over medium-high heat. Add scallops; sear for 1-2 minutes on each side or until golden brown and firm. Remove from the skillet; keep warm.
2. Wipe skillet clean if necessary. Saute garlic in remaining butter until tender; stir in the sherry. Cook until the liquid is almost evaporated; stir in the remaining ingredients. Serve with scallops.
3 scallops with 1½ tsp. sauce: 314 cal., 18g fat (11g sat. fat), 101mg chol., 691mg sod., 6g carb. (0 sugars, 0 fiber), 29g pro.

LINGUINE WITH BROCCOLI RABE & PEPPERS

Broccoli rabe is one of my favorite veggies, and this recipe makes using it a snap, since it cooks right with the pasta. Before you know it, dinner is served!
—Gilda Lester, Millsboro, DE

- -

Takes: 25 min. • **Makes:** 6 servings

1	lb. broccoli rabe
1	pkg. (16 oz.) linguine
3	Tbsp. olive oil
2	anchovy fillets, finely chopped, optional
3	garlic cloves, minced
½	cup sliced roasted sweet red peppers
½	cup pitted Greek olives, halved
½	tsp. crushed red pepper flakes
¼	tsp. pepper
⅛	tsp. salt
½	cup grated Romano cheese

1. Cut ½ in. off ends of broccoli rabe; trim woody stems. Cut stems and leaves into 2-in. pieces. Cook linguine according to package directions, adding broccoli rabe during the last 5 minutes of cooking. Drain, reserving ½ cup pasta water.
2. Meanwhile, in a large skillet, heat oil over medium-high heat. Add anchovies and garlic; cook and stir 1 minute. Stir in red peppers, olives, pepper flakes, pepper and salt.
3. Add linguine and broccoli rabe to skillet; toss to combine, adding reserved pasta water as desired to moisten. Serve with Romano cheese.
1¼ cups: 429 cal., 15g fat (4g sat. fat), 2mg chol., 487mg sod., 60g carb. (4g sugars, 5g fiber), 17g pro.

SEARED SCALLOPS
WITH CITRUS HERB SAUCE

ASK SARAH

HOW DO I STORE FRESH HERBS?

Storing fresh herbs in water can extend their freshness by weeks. Simply place herbs in a jar of water. Cover the jar with a plastic bag and cinch the bottom with a rubber band. Replace water every few days.

KIMCHI FRIED RICE

Forget ordinary fried rice! Kimchi fried rice is just as easy, but it packs a flavorful punch. You can freeze this for up to three months. When reheating, add a little extra soy sauce so it doesn't dry out.
—*Taste of Home* Test Kitchen

Takes: 20 min. • **Makes:** 4 servings

- 2 Tbsp. canola oil, divided
- 1 small onion, chopped
- 1 cup kimchi, coarsely chopped
- ½ cup matchstick carrots
- ¼ cup kimchi juice
- 1 garlic cloves, minced
- 1 tsp. minced fresh gingerroot
- 3 cups leftover short grain rice
- 2 green onions, thinly sliced
- 3 tsp. soy sauce
- 1 tsp. sesame oil
- 4 large eggs
  Optional toppings: Sliced nori, green onions and black sesame seeds

1. In large skillet, heat 1 Tbsp. canola oil over medium-high heat. Add onion; cook and stir until tender, 2-4 minutes. Add the kimchi, carrots, kimchi juice, garlic and ginger; cook 2 minutes longer. Add rice, green onions, soy sauce and sesame oil; heat through, stirring frequently.

2. In another large skillet, heat remaining 1 Tbsp. canola oil over medium-high heat. Break eggs, 1 at a time, into pan; reduce the heat to low. Cook to desired doneness, turning after whites are set if desired. Serve over rice. If desired, sprinkle with nori, green onions and sesame seeds.

1 cup fried rice with 1 egg: 331 cal., 14g fat (2g sat. fat), 186mg chol., 546mg sod., 41g carb. (4g sugars, 2g fiber), 11g pro.

**KIMCHI
FRIED RICE**

CHICKPEA POTPIES

My family loves potpies, and with this recipe, no one even misses the meat. It's that tasty.
—Annette Woofenden, Middleboro, MA

Prep: 15 min. • **Bake:** 25 min.
Makes: 4 servings

- 1 small onion, chopped
- 6 Tbsp. butter
- 2 garlic cloves, minced
- 6 Tbsp. all-purpose flour
- ½ tsp. salt
- ¼ tsp. pepper
- 3 cups vegetable broth
- 2 cups frozen mixed vegetables, thawed
- 1 can (15 oz.) chickpeas or garbanzo beans, rinsed and drained
- 1¼ cups frozen cubed hash brown potatoes
- ¼ cup heavy whipping cream
- ¾ tsp. Italian seasoning
- 1 sheet refrigerated pie crust

1. Saute onion in butter in a large saucepan until tender. Add the garlic; cook 1 minute longer. Stir in the flour, salt and pepper until blended. Gradually add vegetable broth; bring to a boil. Cook and stir for 2 minutes or until thickened.
2. Stir in vegetables, chickpeas, potatoes, cream and Italian seasoning. Divide mixture among 4 ungreased 10-oz. ramekins.
3. Unroll pie crust; divide into 4 portions. Roll out each portion to fit ramekins; place crust over filling. Trim, seal and flute edges. Cut slits in crust. Place the ramekins on a baking sheet.
4. Bake at 400° for 25-30 minutes or until crust is golden brown.
1 potpie: 680 cal., 39g fat (20g sat. fat), 76mg chol., 1518mg sod., 72g carb. (10g sugars, 9g fiber), 11g pro.

DAD'S FAMOUS STUFFIES

DAD'S FAMOUS STUFFIES

The third of July is almost as important as the Fourth in my family. We make these stuffies on the third every year, and it's an event in and of itself!
—Karen Barros, Bristol, RI

Prep: 1¼ hours • **Bake:** 20 min.
Makes: 10 servings

- 20 fresh large quahog clams (about 10 lbs.)
- 1 lb. hot chourico or linguica (smoked Portuguese sausage) or fully cooked Spanish chorizo
- 1 large onion, chopped (about 2 cups)
- 3 tsp. seafood seasoning
- 1 pkg. (14 oz.) herb stuffing cubes
- 1 cup water
  Lemon wedges, optional
  Hot pepper sauce, optional

1. Add 2 in. water to a stockpot. Add clams and chourico; bring to a boil. Cover; steam until clams open, 15-20 minutes.
2. Remove the clams and sausage from pot, reserving 2 cups cooking liquid; cool slightly. Discard any unopened clams.
3. Preheat oven to 350°. Remove clam meat from shells. Separate shells; reserve 30 half-shells for stuffing. Place clam meat in a food processor; process until finely chopped. Transfer to a large bowl.
4. Remove the casings from sausage; cut sausage into 1½-in. pieces. Place in a food processor; process until finely chopped. Add the sausage, chopped onion and seafood seasoning to chopped clams. Stir in stuffing cubes. Add reserved cooking liquid and enough water to reach desired moistness, about 1 cup.
5. Spoon the clam mixture into reserved shells. Place in 15x10x1-in. baking pans. Bake until heated through, 15-20 minutes. Preheat broiler.
6. Broil clams 4-6 in. from heat 4-5 minutes or until golden brown. If desired, serve with lemon wedges and pepper sauce.
Freeze option: Cover and freeze unbaked stuffed clams in a 15x10x1-in. baking pan until firm. Transfer to freezer containers; return to freezer. To use, place 3 stuffed clams on a microwave-safe plate. Cover with paper towel; microwave on high 3-4 minutes.
Note: Find hot chourico at *michaelsprovision .com* and *gasparssausage.com*.
3 stuffed clams: 296 cal., 11g fat (3g sat. fat), 71mg chol., 1188mg sod., 34g carb. (3g sugars, 2g fiber), 18g pro.

VEGGIE-CASHEW STIR-FRY

Getting my meat-loving husband and two sons to eat more veggies was a struggle until I whipped up this stir-fry one night. I was shocked when they cleaned their plates and asked for seconds.
—Abbey Hoffman, Ashland, OH

Prep: 20 min. • **Cook:** 15 min.
Makes: 4 servings

¼ cup reduced-sodium soy sauce
¼ cup water
2 Tbsp. brown sugar
2 Tbsp. lemon juice
2 Tbsp. olive oil
1 garlic clove, minced
2 cups sliced fresh mushrooms
1 cup coarsely chopped fresh baby carrots
1 small zucchini, cut into ¼-in. slices
1 small sweet red pepper, coarsely chopped
1 small green pepper, coarsely chopped
4 green onions, sliced
2 cups cooked brown rice
1 can (8 oz.) sliced water chestnuts, drained
½ cup honey-roasted cashews

1. In a small bowl, mix soy sauce, water, brown sugar and lemon juice until smooth; set aside.

2. In a large skillet, heat oil over medium-high heat. Stir-fry garlic for 1 minute. Add the vegetables; cook until vegetables are crisp-tender, 6-8 minutes.

3. Stir the soy sauce mixture and add to pan. Bring to a boil. Add rice and water chestnuts; heat through. Top with cashews.

1½ cups: 385 cal., 16g fat (3g sat. fat), 0 chol., 671mg sod., 56g carb. (15g sugars, 6g fiber), 9g pro.

SURF & TURF

SURF & TURF

For an intimate dinner with close friends, serve this stunning dinner of tenderloin steaks and lobster tail. Your guests will think they are dining at a fine restaurant.
—*Taste of Home* Test Kitchen

Prep: 25 min. + chilling • **Bake:** 15 min.
Makes: 4 servings

2 garlic cloves, minced
2 tsp. plus 2 Tbsp. olive oil, divided
¼ cup minced fresh parsley
3 Tbsp. chopped green onions
2 Tbsp. minced fresh thyme
2 tsp. grated lemon zest
½ tsp. salt
¼ tsp. pepper
⅛ tsp. cayenne pepper
½ cup butter, softened
1 cup soft bread crumbs
¼ cup butter, melted
4 lobster tails (8 to 10 oz. each)
4 beef tenderloin steaks (4 oz. each)
4 tsp. coarsely ground pepper

1. In a small skillet, saute garlic in 2 tsp. oil until tender; remove from the heat. In a small bowl, combine the parsley, green onions, thyme, lemon zest, salt, pepper, cayenne pepper and reserved garlic. Set aside ½ cup for crumb topping.

2. Add softened butter to remaining herb mixture; mix well. Shape into a 1-in.-thick log; wrap and refrigerate for 30 minutes or until firm.

3. For crumb topping, combine the bread crumbs, melted butter and reserved herb mixture; set aside.

4. Split lobster tails in half lengthwise. With cut side up and using scissors, cut along the edge of shell to loosen the cartilage covering the tail meat from the shell; remove and discard cartilage.

5. Place lobster tails on a baking sheet; top with reserved crumb topping. Bake lobster, uncovered, at 375° until meat is firm and opaque and crumbs are golden brown, 15-20 minutes.

6. Meanwhile, sprinkle steaks with coarse pepper. In a large skillet over medium heat, cook the steaks in remaining oil until meat reaches desired doneness, 4-5 minutes on each side (for medium-rare, a thermometer should read 135°; medium, 140°; medium-well, 145°).

7. Unwrap herb butter; cut four ¼-in. slices from log. Place 1 slice on each steak. Serve with lobster. Rewrap remaining herb butter; refrigerate for 1 week or freeze for up to 3 months.

1 serving: 793 cal., 52g fat (26g sat. fat), 355mg chol., 1289mg sod., 10g carb. (1g sugars, 1g fiber), 69g pro.

CAULIFLOWER & TOFU CURRY

Cauliflower, garbanzo beans and tofu are subtle on their own, but together they make an awesome base for curry. We have this recipe weekly because one of us is always craving it.
—Patrick McGilvray, Cincinnati, OH

- -

Takes: 30 min. • **Makes:** 6 servings

- 1 Tbsp. olive oil
- 2 medium carrots, sliced
- 1 medium onion, chopped
- 3 tsp. curry powder
- ¼ tsp. salt
- ¼ tsp. pepper
- 1 small head cauliflower, broken into florets (about 3 cups)
- 1 can (14½ oz.) fire-roasted crushed tomatoes
- 1 pkg. (14 oz.) extra-firm tofu, drained and cut into ½-in. cubes
- 1 cup vegetable broth
- 1 can (15 oz.) garbanzo beans or chickpeas, rinsed and drained
- 1 can (13.66 oz.) coconut milk
- 1 cup frozen peas
  Hot cooked rice
  Chopped fresh cilantro

1. In a 6-qt. stockpot, heat oil over medium-high heat. Add carrots and onion; cook and stir until onion is tender, 4-5 minutes. Stir in seasonings.
2. Add cauliflower, tomatoes, tofu and broth; bring to a boil. Reduce heat; simmer, covered, 10 minutes. Stir in garbanzo beans, coconut milk and peas; return to a boil. Reduce heat to medium; cook, uncovered, stirring occasionally, until curry is slightly thickened and the cauliflower is tender, 5-7 minutes.
3. Serve with rice. Sprinkle with cilantro.
1⅓ cups: 338 cal., 21g fat (13g sat. fat), 0 chol., 528mg sod., 29g carb. (9g sugars, 7g fiber), 13g pro.

MUFFIN-TIN LASAGNAS

This is a super fun way to serve lasagna and a great way to surprise everyone at the table. Easy and quick, these little cups can be made with whatever ingredients your family likes best.
—Sally Kilkenny, Granger, IA

- -

Takes: 30 min. • **Makes:** 1 dozen

- 1 large egg, lightly beaten
- 1 carton (15 oz.) part-skim ricotta cheese
- 2 cups shredded Italian cheese blend, divided
- 1 Tbsp. olive oil
- 24 wonton wrappers
- 1 jar (24 oz.) garden-style pasta sauce
  Minced fresh parsley, optional

1. Preheat oven to 375°. In a bowl, mix beaten egg, ricotta cheese and 1¼ cups Italian cheese blend.
2. Generously grease 12 muffin cups with olive oil; line each with a wonton wrapper. Fill each with 1 Tbsp. ricotta mixture and 1½ Tbsp. pasta sauce. Top each with a second wrapper, rotating corners and pressing down centers. Repeat ricotta and sauce layers. Sprinkle with remaining cheese.
3. Bake until cheese melts, 20-25 minutes. If desired, sprinkle with parsley.
2 mini lasagnas: 414 cal., 19g fat (9g sat. fat), 83mg chol., 970mg sod., 36g carb. (8g sugars, 2g fiber), 22g pro.

CAULIFLOWER & TOFU CURRY

**PESTO CORN SALAD
WITH SHRIMP**

PESTO CORN SALAD WITH SHRIMP

This recipe showcases the beautiful bounty of summer with its fresh corn, tomatoes and delicious basil. Prevent browning by simply spritzing salad with lemon juice.
—Deena Bowen, Chico, CA

- -

Takes: 30 min. • **Makes:** 4 servings

- 4 medium ears sweet corn, husked
- ½ cup packed fresh basil leaves
- ¼ cup olive oil
- ½ tsp. salt, divided
- 1½ cups cherry tomatoes, halved
- ⅛ tsp. pepper
- 1 medium ripe avocado, peeled and chopped
- 1 lb. uncooked shrimp (31-40 per lb.), peeled and deveined

1. In a pot of boiling water, cook corn until tender, about 5 minutes. Drain; cool slightly. Meanwhile, in a food processor, pulse basil, oil and ¼ tsp. salt until blended.
2. Cut corn from cob and place in a bowl. Stir in tomatoes, pepper and remaining salt. Add avocado and 2 Tbsp. basil mixture; toss gently to combine.
3. Thread shrimp onto metal or soaked wooden skewers; brush with remaining basil mixture. Grill, covered, over medium heat until shrimp turn pink, 2-4 minutes per side. Remove shrimp from skewers; serve with corn mixture.
1 serving: 371 cal., 22g fat (3g sat. fat), 138mg chol., 450mg sod., 25g carb. (8g sugars, 5g fiber), 23g pro.

"Delicious flavors and great texture make this salad a summertime favorite at my house."
—CATHERINE WARD, PREP KITCHEN MANAGER

MAKEOVER MEATLESS LASAGNA

MAKEOVER MEATLESS LASAGNA

If you've never had tofu before, this is the best way to give it a try. It blends with all the other ingredients, adding protein without the fat and calories of ground beef.
—Mary Lou Moeller, Wooster, OH

- -

Prep: 30 min. • **Bake:** 45 min. + standing
Makes: 12 servings

- 10 uncooked whole wheat lasagna noodles
- 1½ cups sliced fresh mushrooms
- ¼ cup chopped onion
- 2 garlic cloves, minced
- 1 can (14½ oz.) Italian diced tomatoes, undrained
- 1 can (12 oz.) tomato paste
- 1 pkg. (14 oz.) firm tofu, drained and cubed
- 2 large eggs, lightly beaten
- 3 cups 2% cottage cheese
- ½ cup grated Parmesan cheese
- ½ cup packed fresh parsley leaves
- ½ tsp. pepper
- 2 cups shredded part-skim mozzarella cheese, divided

1. Preheat oven to 375°. Cook the noodles according to package directions for al dente. Meanwhile, in a large saucepan, cook the mushrooms and onion over medium heat until tender. Add garlic; cook 1 minute. Add tomatoes and tomato paste; cook and stir until heated through.
2. Pulse cubed tofu in a food processor until smooth. Add the next 5 ingredients; pulse until combined. Drain noodles.
3. Place 5 noodles into a 13x9-in. baking dish coated with cooking spray, overlapping as needed. Layer with half the tofu mixture, half the sauce and half the mozzarella. Top with remaining noodles, tofu mixture and sauce.
4. Bake, covered, 35 minutes. Sprinkle with remaining mozzarella. Bake, uncovered, until cheese is melted, 10-15 minutes. Let stand 10 minutes before serving.
1 piece: 258 cal., 9g fat (4g sat. fat), 48mg chol., 498mg sod., 26g carb. (9g sugars, 3g fiber), 19g pro. **Diabetic exchanges:** 2 medium-fat meat, 1½ starch.

GRILLED SALMON WITH CHORIZO-OLIVE SAUCE

Every one of the ingredients in this recipe brings a ton of flavor. Both the chorizo and salmon cook in a hurry, and garlic and citrus go beautifully with them.
—Charlene Chambers, Ormond Beach, FL

Takes: 25 min. • **Makes:** 4 servings

3   links (3 to 4 oz. each) fresh chorizo
4   green onions, chopped
2   garlic cloves, minced
1   can (14½ oz.) diced
    tomatoes, drained
¼   cup chopped pitted green olives
½   tsp. grated orange zest
¼   tsp. salt
¼   tsp. pepper
4   salmon fillets (6 oz. each)

1. Remove chorizo from casings. In a large ovenproof skillet on a stove or grill, cook and stir chorizo, green onions and garlic over medium-high heat until cooked through, 4-6 minutes, breaking chorizo into crumbles; drain.
2. Reduce heat to medium. Add tomatoes, olives and orange zest; stir to combine. Sprinkle salt and pepper over salmon.
3. On a greased grill rack, grill salmon, covered, over medium heat until fish just begins to flake easily with a fork, 3-4 minutes per side. Top with chorizo mixture.
1 salmon fillet with ½ cup sauce: 545 cal., 36g fat (10g sat. fat), 142mg chol., 1355mg sod., 7g carb. (4g sugars, 2g fiber), 43g pro.

FRESH CORN & TOMATO FETTUCCINE

This recipe combines delicious whole wheat pasta with the best of fresh garden produce. It's tossed with heart-healthy olive oil, and a little feta cheese gives it bite.
—Angela Spengler, Niceville, FL

Takes: 30 min. • **Makes:** 4 servings

8   oz. uncooked whole
    wheat fettuccine
2   medium ears sweet corn, husked
2   tsp. plus 2 Tbsp. olive oil, divided
½   cup chopped sweet red pepper
4   green onions, chopped
2   medium tomatoes, chopped
½   tsp. salt
½   tsp. pepper
1   cup crumbled feta cheese
2   Tbsp. minced fresh parsley

1. In a Dutch oven, cook the fettuccine according to package directions, adding corn during the last 8 minutes of cooking.
2. Meanwhile, in a small skillet, heat 2 tsp. oil over medium-high heat. Add red pepper and green onions; cook and stir until tender.
3. Drain pasta and corn; transfer pasta to a large bowl. Cool corn slightly; cut corn from cobs and add to pasta. Add tomatoes, salt, pepper, remaining oil and pepper mixture; toss to combine. Sprinkle with feta cheese and parsley.
2 cups: 422 cal., 15g fat (4g sat. fat), 15mg chol., 580mg sod., 56g carb. (6g sugars, 10g fiber), 17g pro.

FRESH CORN & TOMATO FETTUCCINE

TOMATO-GARLIC
LENTIL BOWLS

TUNA CAKES WITH MUSTARD MAYO

These patties take the cake! The recipe starts off simple with canned tuna. If you'd like, add more kick to the creamy mustard-mayo sauce with prepared horseradish.
—*Taste of Home* Test Kitchen

- -

Takes: 30 min. • **Makes:** 4 servings

- 2 **large eggs, beaten**
- 3 **Tbsp. minced fresh parsley, divided**
- ½ **tsp. seafood seasoning**
- 2 **cans (5 oz. each) light water-packed tuna, drained and flaked**
- ½ **cup seasoned bread crumbs**
- ½ **cup shredded carrot**
- 2 **Tbsp. butter, divided**
- 1 **pkg. (12 oz.) frozen peas**
- ¼ **tsp. pepper**
- ⅓ **cup mayonnaise**
- 1 **Tbsp. Dijon mustard**
- 1 **tsp. 2% milk**

1. In a large bowl, combine the eggs, 2 Tbsp. parsley and seafood seasoning. Stir in the tuna, bread crumbs and carrot. Shape into 8 patties.
2. In a large skillet, brown patties in 1 Tbsp. butter for 3-4 minutes on each side or until golden brown.
3. Meanwhile, microwave peas according to package directions. Stir in the pepper and remaining butter and parsley. Combine the mayonnaise, mustard and milk. Serve with tuna cakes and peas.
2 tuna cakes with ½ cup peas and 4 tsp. sauce: 433 cal., 25g fat (7g sat. fat), 149mg chol., 910mg sod., 24g carb. (6g sugars, 5g fiber), 28g pro.

TOMATO-GARLIC LENTIL BOWLS

An Ethiopian recipe inspired this feel-good dinner that's tangy, creamy and packed with hearty comfort.
—Rachael Cushing, Portland, OR

- -

Takes: 30 min. • **Makes:** 6 servings

- 1 **Tbsp. olive oil**
- 2 **medium onions, chopped**
- 4 **garlic cloves, minced**
- 2 **cups dried brown lentils, rinsed**
- 1 **tsp. salt**
- ½ **tsp. ground ginger**
- ½ **tsp. paprika**
- ¼ **tsp. pepper**
- 3 **cups water**
- ¼ **cup lemon juice**
- 3 **Tbsp. tomato paste**
- ¾ **cup fat-free plain Greek yogurt**
  Optional: Chopped tomatoes and minced fresh cilantro

1. In a large saucepan, heat the olive oil over medium-high heat; saute onions 2 minutes. Add the garlic; cook 1 minute. Stir in lentils, seasonings and water; bring to a boil. Reduce heat; simmer, covered, until the lentils are tender, 25-30 minutes.
2. Stir in lemon juice and tomato paste; heat through. Serve with yogurt and, if desired, tomatoes and cilantro.
¾ cup: 294 cal., 3g fat (0 sat. fat), 0 chol., 419mg sod., 49g carb. (5g sugars, 8g fiber), 21g pro. **Diabetic exchanges:** 3 starch, 2 lean meat, ½ fat.

"My whole family likes these. I make a double recipe on Sunday and eat it for lunches throughout the week. The yogurt, tomatoes and cilantro on top are a must!"

—ELLIE MARTIN CLIFFE, EXECUTIVE DIGITAL EDITOR

CRUNCHY CHILI CILANTRO LIME ROASTED SHRIMP

This shrimp recipe is dairy-free and comes together in about half an hour. The secret is in the bright, flavor-packed sauce. Serve over salad greens, store-bought coleslaw or cauliflower rice.
—Julie Peterson, Crofton, MD

Takes: 30 min. • **Makes:** 8 servings

- 2 lbs. uncooked shrimp (26-30 per lb.), peeled and deveined
- 4 garlic cloves, minced
- 1 tsp. paprika
- 1 tsp. ground ancho chili pepper
- 1 tsp. ground cumin
- ½ tsp. salt
- ¼ tsp. pepper
- 1 medium lime
- 1 cup crushed tortilla chips
- ¼ cup chopped fresh cilantro
- ¼ cup olive oil
- 1 cup cherry tomatoes, halved
- 1 medium ripe avocado, peeled and cubed

1. Preheat oven to 425°. Place the first 7 ingredients in a greased 15x10x1-in. pan. Finely grate zest from lime. Cut the lime crosswise in half; squeeze juice. Add zest and juice to shrimp mixture; toss to coat.
2. In a small bowl, combine crushed tortilla chips, cilantro and oil; sprinkle over shrimp mixture. Bake until the shrimp turn pink, 12-15 minutes. Top with tomatoes and avocado. If desired, serve with additional lime wedges and cilantro.

1 serving: 230 cal., 13g fat (2g sat. fat), 138mg chol., 315mg sod., 10g carb. (1g sugars, 2g fiber), 20g pro. **Diabetic exchanges:** 3 lean meat, 1½ fat, ½ starch.

VEGAN MAC & CHEESE

Buttery cashews and nutritional yeast create a rich, savory sauce in this vegan rendition of good ol' mac and cheese.
—*Taste of Home* Test Kitchen

Prep: 20 min. + standing • **Cook:** 10 min.
Makes: 6 servings

- 2 cups raw cashews
- 16 oz. uncooked elbow macaroni
- 1½ cups water
- ⅓ cup nutritional yeast
- 2 tsp. lemon juice
- 2 tsp. salt
- 2 tsp. onion powder
- 1½ tsp. paprika
- 1 tsp. pepper
- ⅛ tsp. cayenne pepper

1. Rinse cashews in cold water. Place in a large bowl; add water to cover by 3 in. Cover and let stand overnight.
2. Cook macaroni according to package directions. Drain and rinse the cashews, discarding liquid. Transfer nuts to a food processor. Add 1½ cups water, nutritional yeast, lemon juice and seasonings; cover and process until pureed, 3-4 minutes, scraping down sides as needed.
3. Drain macaroni; return to pan. Stir in the cashew mixture. Cook and stir over medium-low heat until heated through. Sprinkle with additional paprika if desired.
1⅔ cups: 497 cal., 18g fat (3g sat. fat), 0 chol., 803mg sod., 67g carb. (5g sugars, 5g fiber), 18g pro.

CRUNCHY CHILI CILANTRO
LIME ROASTED SHRIMP

BLACK BEAN & SWEET POTATO RICE BOWLS

With three hungry boys in my house, dinners need to be quick and filling, and it helps to get in some veggies, too. This is a favorite because it's hearty and fun to tweak with different ingredients.
—Kim Van Dunk, Caldwell, NJ

- -

Takes: 30 min. • **Makes:** 4 servings

- ¾ cup uncooked long grain rice
- ¼ tsp. garlic salt
- 1½ cups water
- 3 Tbsp. olive oil, divided
- 1 large sweet potato, peeled and diced
- 1 medium red onion, finely chopped
- 4 cups chopped fresh kale (tough stems removed)
- 1 can (15 oz.) black beans, rinsed and drained
- 2 Tbsp. sweet chili sauce
  Lime wedges, optional
  Additional sweet chili sauce, optional

1. Place rice, garlic salt and water in a large saucepan; bring to a boil. Reduce the heat; simmer, covered, until water is absorbed and rice is tender, 15-20 minutes. Remove from heat; let stand 5 minutes.

2. Meanwhile, in a large skillet, heat 2 Tbsp. olive oil over medium-high heat; saute sweet potato 8 minutes. Add onion; cook and stir until potato is tender, 4-6 minutes. Add kale; cook and stir until tender, 3-5 minutes. Stir in beans; heat through.

3. Gently stir 2 Tbsp. chili sauce and the remaining olive oil into rice; add to potato mixture. If desired, serve with lime wedges and additional chili sauce.

2 cups: 435 cal., 11g fat (2g sat. fat), 0 chol., 405mg sod., 74g carb. (15g sugars, 8g fiber), 10g pro.

BLACK BEAN & SWEET POTATO RICE BOWLS

CRAB-TOPPED TOMATO SLICES

When camping, my wife and I top large beefsteak tomatoes with spicy chunks of crabmeat. We warm this summer treat over the fire, but the stove works just as well.
—Thomas Faglon, Somerset, NJ

Takes: 30 min. • **Makes:** 4 servings

1   carton (8 oz.) mascarpone cheese
2   Tbsp. finely chopped
     sweet red pepper
1½ tsp. grated lemon zest
2   Tbsp. lemon juice
1   tsp. seafood seasoning
1   tsp. hot pepper sauce
½   tsp. salt
¼   tsp. freshly ground pepper
2   cans (6 oz. each) lump
     crabmeat, drained
8   slices tomato (½ in. thick)
     Minced chives

1. Preheat oven to 375°. In a large bowl, combine the first 8 ingredients; gently stir in crabmeat.
2. Place tomato slices on a foil-lined baking sheet; top with the crab mixture. Bake until heated through, 12-15 minutes. Sprinkle with minced chives.
1 serving: 325 cal., 27g fat (14g sat. fat), 153mg chol., 980mg sod., 3g carb. (1g sugars, 1g fiber), 20g pro.

AIR-FRYER CRUMB-TOPPED SOLE

Looking for a low-carb supper that's ready in a flash? These buttery sole fillets are covered with a rich sauce and topped with toasty bread crumbs. They're super speedy thanks to your air fryer.
—*Taste of Home* Test Kitchen

Prep: 10 min. • **Cook:** 10 min./batch
Makes: 4 servings

3   Tbsp. reduced-fat mayonnaise
3   Tbsp. grated Parmesan
     cheese, divided
2   tsp. mustard seed
¼   tsp. pepper
4   sole fillets (6 oz. each)
1   cup soft bread crumbs
1   green onion, finely chopped
½   tsp. ground mustard
2   tsp. butter, melted
     Cooking spray

1. Preheat air fryer to 375°. Combine the mayonnaise, 2 Tbsp. cheese, mustard seed and pepper; spread over tops of fillets.
2. Place fish in a single layer on greased tray in air-fryer basket. Cook until fish flakes easily with a fork, 3-5 minutes.
3. Meanwhile, in a small bowl, combine bread crumbs, onion, ground mustard and remaining 1 Tbsp. cheese; stir in butter. Spoon over fillets, patting gently to adhere; spritz topping with cooking spray. Cook until golden brown, 2-3 minutes longer. If desired, sprinkle with additional green onions.
1 fillet: 233 cal., 11g fat (3g sat. fat), 89mg chol., 714mg sod., 8g carb. (1g sugars, 1g fiber), 24g pro.

AIR-FRYER CRUMB-TOPPED SOLE

GULF COAST JAMBALAYA RICE

As the stew of the South, jambalaya is a definite staple. For ages, home cooks have been making their own renditions of the traditional recipe. This slow-cooked version is my personal favorite.
—Judy Batson, Tampa, FL

Prep: 20 min. • **Cook:** 3¼ hours
Makes: 8 servings

- 1 lb. boneless skinless chicken breasts, cut into 1-in. cubes
- 1 lb. smoked kielbasa, cut into ¼-in. slices
- 2 cups chicken stock
- 1 large green pepper, chopped
- 1 cup chopped sweet onion
- 2 celery ribs, chopped
- 2 garlic cloves, minced
- 2 tsp. Creole seasoning
- 1 tsp. seafood seasoning
- 1 tsp. pepper
- 1 lb. uncooked medium shrimp, peeled and deveined
- 2 cups uncooked instant rice

1. Place the first 10 ingredients in a 5-qt. slow cooker. Cook, covered, on low for 3-4 hours, until chicken is tender.
2. Stir in shrimp and rice. Cook, covered, 15-20 minutes longer, until the shrimp turn pink and rice is tender.
1⅓ cups: 395 cal., 18g fat (6g sat. fat), 138mg chol., 861mg sod., 25g carb. (3g sugars, 1g fiber), 31g pro.

BASIL-LEMON CRAB LINGUINE

This linguine looks and tastes like a meal from a five-star restaurant.
—Tonya Burkhard, Palm Coast, FL

Takes: 25 min. • **Makes:** 4 servings

- 1 pkg. (9 oz.) refrigerated linguine
- ⅓ cup butter, cubed
- 1 jalapeno pepper, seeded and finely chopped
- 1 garlic clove, minced
- 1 tsp. grated lemon zest
- 3 Tbsp. lemon juice
- 2 cans (6 oz. each) lump crabmeat, drained
- ¼ cup loosely packed basil leaves, thinly sliced
- ½ tsp. sea salt
- ¼ tsp. freshly ground pepper

1. Cook linguine according to the package directions. Meanwhile, in a large skillet, heat butter over medium heat. Add jalapeno and garlic; cook and stir for 1-2 minutes or until tender. Stir in lemon zest and juice. Add crab; heat through, stirring gently.
2. Drain linguine; add to skillet. Sprinkle with basil, salt and pepper; toss to combine.
1¼ cups: 392 cal., 18g fat (11g sat. fat), 161mg chol., 856mg sod., 35g carb. (1g sugars, 2g fiber), 23g pro.

BASIL-LEMON CRAB LINGUINE

FARMERS MARKET
ENCHILADAS

WHITE BEANS & BOW TIES

When we have fresh veggies, we toss them with pasta shapes like penne or bow ties. What a tasty way to enjoy a meatless meal!
—Angela Buchanan, Longmont, CO

- -

Takes: 25 min. • **Makes:** 4 servings

- 2½ cups uncooked whole wheat bow tie pasta (about 6 oz.)
- 1 Tbsp. olive oil
- 1 medium zucchini, sliced
- 2 garlic cloves, minced
- 2 large tomatoes, chopped (about 2½ cups)
- 1 can (15 oz.) cannellini beans, rinsed and drained
- 1 can (2¼ oz.) sliced ripe olives, drained
- ¾ tsp. freshly ground pepper
- ½ cup crumbled feta cheese

1. Cook pasta according to the package directions. Drain, reserving ½ cup of the pasta water.
2. Meanwhile, in a large skillet, heat oil over medium-high heat; saute the zucchini until crisp-tender, 2-4 minutes. Add garlic; cook and stir 30 seconds. Stir in tomatoes, beans, olives and pepper; bring to a boil. Reduce heat; simmer, uncovered, until tomatoes are softened, 3-5 minutes, stirring occasionally.
3. Stir in pasta and enough pasta water to moisten as desired. Stir in cheese.
1½ cups: 348 cal., 9g fat (2g sat. fat), 8mg chol., 394mg sod., 52g carb. (4g sugars, 11g fiber), 15g pro.

FARMERS MARKET ENCHILADAS

These vegetarian enchiladas incorporate garden favorites in a quick weeknight meal. Feel free to substitute whatever veggies you find at the farm stand or harvest from your own backyard patch—summer squash, eggplant and corn all taste great here, too.
—Elisabeth Larsen, Pleasant Grove, UT

- -

Prep: 20 min. • **Bake:** 45 min.
Makes: 7 servings

- 3 medium zucchini, quartered lengthwise and sliced
- 1 poblano pepper, seeded and chopped
- 8 oz. sliced fresh mushrooms
- 8 oz. cherry tomatoes
- 1 Tbsp. olive oil
- 1 tsp. ground cumin
- ½ tsp. salt
- ¼ tsp. cayenne pepper
- 2 cups shredded Monterey Jack cheese
- 1 cup crumbled queso fresco or feta cheese, divided
- ½ cup minced fresh cilantro, divided
- 2 Tbsp. lime juice
- 14 corn tortillas (6 in.), warmed
- 1 can (15 oz.) enchilada sauce

1. Preheat oven to 400°. In a large bowl, combine zucchini, poblano, mushrooms and tomatoes; drizzle with oil and sprinkle with cumin, salt and cayenne. Toss to coat. Divide vegetable mixture between 2 lightly greased 15x10x1-in. baking pans. Roast 15 minutes; rotate baking pans top to bottom. Roast an additional 10 minutes or until vegetables are tender. Return to bowl and cool slightly.
2. Stir in Monterey Jack cheese, ½ cup queso fresco, ¼ cup cilantro and lime juice. Place a scant ½ cup vegetable mixture off center on each tortilla. Roll up and place in a greased 13x9-in. baking dish, seam side down. Top with enchilada sauce; sprinkle with remaining queso fresco.
3. Bake, uncovered, until enchiladas are heated through and cheese is melted, about 20 minutes. Top with remaining cilantro.
2 enchiladas: 346 cal., 17g fat (9g sat. fat), 40mg chol., 780mg sod., 33g carb. (5g sugars, 5g fiber), 18g pro.

LENTIL
TACO CUPS

LENTIL TACO CUPS

My trusty muffin tin never fails to help me put fun and easy hand-held mains on the table for my family on busy weeknights. These festive vegetarian cups are always a hit with my kids; they're so flavorful, nobody misses the meat.
—Shauna Havey, Roy, UT

- -

Prep: 25 min. • **Bake:** 15 min.
Makes: 12 taco cups

- 12 mini flour tortillas, warmed
- 1 can (15 oz.) lentils, drained
- ¾ cup pico de gallo
- ½ cup enchilada sauce
- 2 Tbsp. taco seasoning
- 2 cups shredded Mexican cheese blend, divided

CREMA
- 1 cup sour cream
- ½ cup minced fresh cilantro
- 1 Tbsp. lime juice
- ¼ tsp. sea salt
  Shredded lettuce, sliced ripe olives and chopped tomatoes

1. Preheat oven to 425°. Press warm tortillas into 12 greased muffin cups, pleating sides as needed. In a large bowl, combine the lentils, pico de gallo, enchilada sauce and taco seasoning. Stir in 1½ cups cheese. Divide lentil mixture among cups. Sprinkle with remaining cheese.
2. Bake until heated through and cheese is melted, 12-15 minutes. Meanwhile, for the crema, combine sour cream, cilantro, lime juice and sea salt. Serve cups with crema, lettuce, olives and tomatoes.
2 taco cups: 303 cal., 20g fat (11g sat. fat), 43mg chol., 793mg sod., 17g carb. (3g sugars, 5g fiber), 14g pro.

PISTACHIO SALMON

PISTACHIO SALMON

This simple salmon gets its crunch from a coating of crushed pistachios, panko bread crumbs and Parmesan cheese. Add steamed veggies and rice and it's dinnertime!
—Anthony Oraczewski, Port St. Lucie, FL

- -

Takes: 25 min. • **Makes:** 4 servings

- ⅓ cup pistachios, finely chopped
- ¼ cup panko bread crumbs
- ¼ cup grated Parmesan cheese
- 1 salmon fillet (1 lb.)
- ½ tsp. salt
- ¼ tsp. pepper

1. Preheat oven to 400°. In a shallow bowl, toss the pistachios with the bread crumbs and cheese.
2. Place salmon on a greased foil-lined 15x10x1-in. pan, skin side down; sprinkle with salt and pepper. Top with pistachio mixture, pressing to adhere. Bake, uncovered, until fish just begins to flake easily with a fork, 15-20 minutes.
3 oz. cooked fish: 269 cal., 17g fat (3g sat. fat), 61mg chol., 497mg sod., 6g carb. (1g sugars, 1g fiber), 23g pro. **Diabetic exchanges:** 3 lean meat, 1 fat, ½ starch.

LEMON-PARSLEY TILAPIA

I like to include seafood in our weekly dinner rotation, but I just don't want to bother with anything complicated. My family adores this dish, and it's a breeze to prepare. Cod and snapper work well here, too—simply adjust the cooking time if needed.
—Trisha Kruse, Eagle, ID

Takes: 20 min. • **Makes:** 4 servings

 4 tilapia fillets (about 4 oz. each)
 2 Tbsp. lemon juice
 1 Tbsp. butter, melted
 2 Tbsp. minced fresh parsley
 2 garlic cloves, minced
 2 tsp. grated lemon zest
 ½ tsp. salt
 ¼ tsp. pepper

1. Preheat oven to 375°. Place tilapia in a parchment-lined 15x10x1-in. pan. Drizzle with lemon juice, then melted butter.
2. Bake until fish just begins to flake easily with a fork, 11-13 minutes. Meanwhile, mix remaining ingredients. Remove fish from oven; sprinkle with parsley mixture.
1 fillet: 124 cal., 4g fat (2g sat. fat), 63mg chol., 359mg sod., 1g carb. (0 sugars, 0 fiber), 21g pro. **Diabetic exchanges:** 3 lean meat, 1 fat.

PRESSURE-COOKER STEAMED MUSSELS WITH PEPPERS

Here's a worthy way to use your one-pot cooker. Serve French bread along with the mussels to soak up the deliciously seasoned broth. If you like your food spicy, add the jalapeno seeds.
—*Taste of Home* Test Kitchen

Prep: 30 min. • **Cook:** 5 min.
Makes: 4 servings

 2 lbs. fresh mussels, scrubbed and beards removed
 2 Tbsp. olive oil
 1 jalapeno pepper, seeded and chopped
 3 garlic cloves, minced
 1 bottle (8 oz.) clam juice
 ½ cup white wine or additional clam juice
 ⅓ cup chopped sweet red pepper
 3 green onions, sliced
 ½ tsp. dried oregano
 1 bay leaf
 2 Tbsp. minced fresh parsley
 ¼ tsp. salt
 ¼ tsp. pepper
    French bread baguette, sliced, optional

1. Tap mussels; discard any that do not close. Set aside. Select saute setting on a 6-qt. electric pressure cooker. Adjust for medium heat; add oil. When oil is hot, cook and stir jalapeno until crisp-tender, 2-3 minutes. Add garlic; cook 1 minute longer. Press cancel. Stir in mussels, clam juice, wine, red pepper, green onions, oregano and bay leaf. Lock lid; close pressure-release valve. Adjust to pressure-cook on high 2 minutes. Quick-release pressure.
2. Discard bay leaf and any unopened mussels. Sprinkle with parsley, salt and pepper. If desired, serve with baguette slices.
12 mussels: 293 cal., 12g fat (2g sat. fat), 65mg chol., 931mg sod., 12g carb. (1g sugars, 1g fiber), 28g pro.

PRESSURE-COOKER STEAMED MUSSELS WITH PEPPERS

MUSHROOM &
SWEET POTATO POTPIE

MUSHROOM & SWEET POTATO POTPIE

The last time I was in the U.S., I had a simply amazing mushroom and beer potpie at a brew pub. It was so rich and comforting, that I tried numerous versions when I got home and I think I've come pretty close!
—Iben Ravn, Copenhagen, Denmark

Prep: 45 min. • **Bake:** 30 min.
Makes: 8 servings

- ⅓ cup olive oil, divided
- 1 lb. sliced fresh shiitake mushrooms
- 1 lb. sliced baby portobello mushrooms
- 2 large onions, chopped
- 2 garlic cloves, minced
- 1 tsp. minced fresh rosemary, plus more for topping
- 1 bottle (12 oz.) porter or stout beer
- 1½ cups mushroom broth or vegetable broth, divided
- 2 bay leaves
- 1 Tbsp. balsamic vinegar
- 2 Tbsp. reduced-sodium soy sauce
- ¼ cup cornstarch
- 3 to 4 small sweet potatoes, peeled and thinly sliced
- ¾ tsp. coarsely ground pepper
- ½ tsp. salt

1. Preheat oven to 400°. In a Dutch oven, heat 1 Tbsp. oil over medium heat. Add shiitake mushrooms and cook in batches until dark golden brown, 8-10 minutes; remove with a slotted spoon. Repeat with 1 Tbsp. oil and the portobello mushrooms.

2. In same pan, heat 1 Tbsp. oil over medium heat. Add onions; cook and stir 8-10 minutes or until tender. Add the garlic and 1 tsp. rosemary; cook 30 seconds longer. Stir in beer, 1 cup broth, bay leaves, vinegar, soy sauce and sauteed mushrooms.

3. Bring to a boil. Reduce heat; simmer, uncovered, 10 minutes. In a small bowl, mix cornstarch and remaining broth until smooth; stir into mushroom mixture. Return to a boil, stirring constantly; cook and stir until thickened, 1-2 minutes. Remove and discard bay leaves; transfer mushroom mixture to 8 greased 8-oz. ramekins. Place on a rimmed baking sheet.

4. Layer the sweet potatoes in a circular pattern on top of each ramekin; brush with the remaining oil and sprinkle with pepper, salt and additional rosemary. Bake, covered, until potatoes are tender, 20-25 minutes. Remove cover and bake until potatoes are lightly browned, 8-10 minutes. Let stand 5 minutes before serving.

1 serving: 211 cal., 10g fat (1g sat. fat), 0 chol., 407mg sod., 26g carb. (10g sugars, 4g fiber), 5g pro.

CHEESY SUMMER SQUASH FLATBREADS

When you want a meatless meal with Mediterranean style, these flatbreads smothered with squash, hummus and mozzarella deliver the goods.
—Matthew Hass, Ellison Bay, WI

- -

Takes: 30 min. • **Makes:** 4 servings

- 3 small yellow summer squash, sliced ¼ in. thick
- 1 Tbsp. olive oil
- ½ tsp. salt
- 2 cups fresh baby spinach, coarsely chopped
- 2 naan flatbreads
- ⅓ cup roasted red pepper hummus
- 1 carton (8 oz.) fresh mozzarella cheese pearls
  Pepper

1. Preheat oven to 425°. Toss squash with oil and salt; spread evenly in a 15x10x1-in. baking pan. Roast until tender, roughly 8-10 minutes. Transfer to a bowl; stir in spinach.

2. Place naan on a baking sheet; spread with hummus. Top with the squash mixture and cheese. Bake on a lower oven rack just until the cheese is melted, 4-6 minutes. Sprinkle with pepper.

½ topped flatbread: 332 cal., 20g fat (9g sat. fat), 47mg chol., 737mg sod., 24g carb. (7g sugars, 3g fiber), 15g pro.

HOISIN-PINEAPPLE SALMON

HOISIN-PINEAPPLE SALMON

My mouth waters whenever I think of this sweet and tangy flavor. The pairing of sweet orange and slightly tart pineapple makes for a delicious contrast with the hoisin-glazed salmon. A sprinkle of fresh cilantro adds a lovely freshness.
—Naylet LaRochelle, Miami, FL

- -

Takes: 20 min. • **Makes:** 4 servings

- 4 salmon fillets (6 oz. each)
- 2 Tbsp. hoisin sauce
- ¼ tsp. pepper
- ½ cup unsweetened crushed pineapple
- ¼ cup orange marmalade
- 2 Tbsp. chopped fresh cilantro

1. Preheat oven to 400°. Spread salmon with hoisin sauce; sprinkle with pepper. Place on a greased foil-lined baking sheet, skin side down. Bake 12-15 minutes or until fish begins to flake easily with a fork.

2. Meanwhile, in a small saucepan, combine pineapple and marmalade. Bring to a boil, stirring occasionally; cook and stir roughly 4-6 minutes or until slightly thickened. Spoon over salmon; sprinkle with cilantro.

1 fillet with 2 Tbsp. sauce: 349 cal., 16g fat (3g sat. fat), 86mg chol., 226mg sod., 21g carb. (18g sugars, 1g fiber), 29g pro. **Diabetic exchanges:** 4 lean meat, 1½ starch.

ONE-PAN SWEET CHILI SHRIMP & VEGGIES

This recipe has everything I'm looking for in a weeknight family dinner: quick, flavorful, nutritious and all three of my kids will eat it! My oldest son loves shrimp, and I thought it could work really well as a sheet-pan supper.
—Elisabeth Larsen, Pleasant Grove, UT

Takes: 30 min. • **Makes:** 4 servings

- 1   lb. uncooked shrimp (16-20 per lb.), peeled and deveined
- 2   medium zucchini, halved and sliced
- ½   lb. sliced fresh mushrooms
- 1   medium sweet orange pepper, julienned
- 3   Tbsp. sweet chili sauce
- 1   Tbsp. canola oil
- 1   Tbsp. lime juice
- 1   Tbsp. reduced-sodium soy sauce
- 3   green onions, chopped
- ¼   cup minced fresh cilantro

1. Preheat oven to 400°. Place the shrimp, zucchini, mushrooms and orange pepper in a greased 15x10x1-in. baking pan. Combine chili sauce, oil, lime juice and soy sauce. Pour over shrimp mixture and toss to coat.
2. Bake until shrimp turn pink and vegetables are tender, 12-15 minutes. Sprinkle with the green onions and cilantro.
1 serving: 199 cal., 6g fat (1g sat. fat), 138mg chol., 483mg sod., 15g carb. (11g sugars, 3g fiber), 22g pro.

ONE-PAN SWEET CHILI SHRIMP & VEGGIES

TOFU
SALAD

GORGONZOLA SHRIMP PASTA

This creamy pasta dish is so quick and easy. It's perfect for weeknights but feels special enough for company.
—Robin Haas, Hyde Park, MA

- -

Takes: 30 min. • **Makes:** 6 servings

- 12 oz. uncooked penne pasta
- 2 Tbsp. olive oil
- 1 lb. uncooked shrimp (31-40 per lb.), peeled and deveined
- 3 garlic cloves, minced
- ½ cup dried cranberries
- ½ cup dry white wine or reduced-sodium chicken broth
- 6 oz. fresh baby spinach (about 3 cups)
- 4 oz. reduced-fat cream cheese, cubed
- ½ cup crumbled Gorgonzola cheese
- 3 Tbsp. minced fresh parsley
- ¼ tsp. salt
- ⅓ cup chopped walnuts

1. Cook the penne according to package directions for al dente. Meanwhile, in a large cast-iron skillet or Dutch oven, heat oil over medium heat. Add shrimp and garlic; cook until shrimp are pink, 5-10 minutes. Remove from pan and keep warm.
2. Stir cranberries and wine into same pan. Bring to a boil; cook until liquid is almost evaporated, 5 minutes.
3. Drain penne, reserving 1 cup of pasta water; add penne to pan. Stir in spinach, cream cheese, Gorgonzola cheese, parsley, salt and reserved shrimp. Cook and stir until mixture is heated through and cheeses are melted, about 5 minutes, adding enough reserved pasta water to reach desired consistency. Top with chopped walnuts.
2 cups: 486 cal., 18g fat (6g sat. fat), 114mg chol., 422mg sod., 57g carb. (13g sugars, 4g fiber), 26g pro.

TOFU SALAD

To make the tofu extra crispy, drain the liquid and cook it in a lot of oil at high heat.
—*Taste of Home* Test Kitchen

- -

Prep: 15 min. + marinating. • **Cook:** 10 min.
Makes: 4 servings

- 1 pkg. (16 oz.) extra-firm tofu, cut into 1-in. cubes
- ¼ cup rice vinegar
- ¼ cup reduced-sodium soy sauce
- 2 Tbsp. sesame oil
- 2 Tbsp. Sriracha chili sauce or 2 tsp. hot pepper sauce
- 2 Tbsp. creamy peanut butter
- ¼ tsp. ground ginger
- 2 Tbsp. canola oil
- 6 cups torn romaine
- 2 medium carrots, shredded
- 1 medium ripe avocado, peeled and sliced
- 1 cup cherry tomatoes, halved
- ½ small red onion, thinly sliced
- 2 Tbsp. sesame seeds, toasted

1. Blot tofu dry. Wrap in a clean kitchen towel; place on a plate and refrigerate for at least 1 hour.
2. In a large shallow dish, whisk vinegar, soy sauce, sesame oil, sriracha, peanut butter and ginger until smooth. Add tofu; turn to coat. Cover and refrigerate 3-5 hours, turning occasionally. Drain tofu reserving marinade; pat dry.
3. In a large skillet, heat canola oil over medium-high heat. Add tofu cubes; cook until crisp and golden brown, 5-7 minutes, stirring occasionally. Remove from pan; drain on paper towels. In a large bowl, combine romaine, carrots, avocado, tomatoes, onion and tofu. Pour reserved marinade over salad; toss to coat. Sprinkle with sesame seeds. Serve immediately.
2 cups: 414 cal., 31g fat (4g sat. fat), 0 chol., 1129mg sod., 24g carb. (12g sugars, 7g fiber), 15g pro.

GORGONZOLA
SHRIMP PASTA

CHEESE MANICOTTI

CHEESE MANICOTTI

This is the first meal I ever cooked for my husband, and all these years later he still enjoys my manicotti!
—Joan Hallford, North Richland Hills, TX

- -

Prep: 25 min. • **Bake:** 1 hour
Makes: 7 servings

- 1 carton (15 oz.) reduced-fat ricotta cheese
- 1 small onion, finely chopped
- 1 large egg, lightly beaten
- 2 Tbsp. minced fresh parsley
- ½ tsp. pepper
- ¼ tsp. salt
- 1 cup shredded part-skim mozzarella cheese, divided
- 1 cup grated Parmesan cheese, divided
- 4 cups marinara sauce
- ½ cup water
- 1 pkg. (8 oz.) manicotti shells

1. Preheat oven to 350°. In a small bowl, mix the first 6 ingredients; stir in ½ cup mozzarella cheese and ½ cup Parmesan cheese. In another bowl, mix marinara sauce and water; spread ¾ cup sauce onto bottom of a 13x9-in. baking dish coated with cooking spray. Fill uncooked manicotti shells with the ricotta mixture; arrange over sauce. Top with remaining sauce.
2. Bake, covered, 50 minutes or until pasta is tender. Sprinkle with remaining ½ cup mozzarella cheese and ½ cup Parmesan cheese. Bake, uncovered, 10-15 minutes longer or until cheese is melted. If desired, top with additional parsley.
2 stuffed manicotti: 361 cal., 13g fat (6g sat. fat), 64mg chol., 1124mg sod., 41g carb. (12g sugars, 4g fiber), 19g pro.
Diabetic exchanges: 3 starch, 2 lean meat, ½ fat.

SALMON FETTUCCINE ALFREDO

Alfredo sauce and salmon are a culinary dream team in this creamy pasta with crisp veggies. We love the flavor combo, but you could also make it with chicken or shrimp.
—*Taste of Home* Test Kitchen

Takes: 20 min. • **Makes:** 4 servings

- 8 oz. uncooked fettuccine
- 1 medium sweet red pepper, chopped
- 1 Tbsp. olive oil
- 2 garlic cloves, minced
- 2 jars (15 oz. each) Alfredo sauce
- 2 cups frozen broccoli florets
- 2 pouches (6 oz. each) boneless skinless pink salmon
- ½ tsp. dried basil

1. Cook fettuccine according to package directions. Meanwhile, in a large skillet, saute pepper in oil until tender. Add garlic; cook 1 minute longer.

2. Stir in the Alfredo sauce, broccoli, salmon and basil. Cook, uncovered, over medium heat for 5-7 minutes or until heated through. Drain fettuccine. Add to skillet; toss to coat.

1¼ cups: 678 cal., 33g fat (17g sat. fat), 96mg chol., 1329mg sod., 60g carb. (3g sugars, 5g fiber), 36g pro.

PINEAPPLE SHRIMP TACOS

PINEAPPLE SHRIMP TACOS

Taste the tropics with our cool and crispy take on shrimp tacos. Wrapping the shells in lettuce adds even more crunch, while keeping the tacos tidy after you take a bite.
—*Taste of Home* Test Kitchen

Takes: 25 min. • **Makes:** 4 servings

- 1 lb. uncooked large shrimp, peeled and deveined
- 3 tsp. olive oil, divided
- 1 large sweet orange pepper, sliced
- 1 large sweet red pepper, sliced
- 1 small onion, halved and sliced
- 1 cup pineapple tidbits
- 1 envelope fajita seasoning mix
- ⅓ cup water
- 8 corn tortillas (6 in.), warmed
- ½ cup shredded Cotija or mozzarella cheese
- 8 large romaine lettuce leaves

1. Cook shrimp in 2 tsp. oil in a large cast-iron or other heavy skillet over medium heat until shrimp turn pink, 4-6 minutes. Remove and keep warm.

2. In the same skillet, saute the peppers, onion and pineapple in remaining oil until tender. Add seasoning mix and water. Bring to a boil; cook and stir for 2 minutes. Return shrimp to the skillet; heat through. Spoon onto tortillas; top with cheese. Wrap lettuce around tortillas to serve.

2 tacos: 382 cal., 11g fat (4g sat. fat), 153mg chol., 1123mg sod., 44g carb. (13g sugars, 6g fiber), 27g pro.

BUFFALO CHICKEN
ENCHILADAS, PAGE 156

Beef, Chicken & Pork Entrees

Bored with your usual repertoire of beef, chicken and pork recipes? These meaty entrees make it easier than ever to transform weekday regulars into must-have dinner favorites. From the comforting classics you love to bold new specialties, these dishes are guaranteed to rise to the top of your list of greatest hits!

**MISO BUTTER
ROASTED CHICKEN**

MISO BUTTER ROASTED CHICKEN

I love this recipe for its simple front-end prep. You can spatchcock the chicken yourself or purchase a bird that is already spatchcocked at the grocery store or butcher's shop. The only work left to do is to chop the veggies!
—Stefanie Schaldenbrand, Los Angeles, CA

- -

Prep: 25 min. • **Bake:** 1½ hours + standing
Makes: 6 servings

- 1 **lb. medium fresh mushrooms**
- 1 **lb. baby red potatoes**
- 1 **lb. fresh Brussels sprouts, halved**
- 6 **garlic cloves, minced**
- 1 **Tbsp. olive oil**
- 1½ **tsp. minced fresh thyme**
  or ½ tsp. dried thyme
- ½ **tsp. salt**
- ½ **tsp. pepper**
- 1 **roasting chicken (5 to 6 lbs.)**
- ¼ **cup butter, softened**
- ¼ **cup white miso paste**

1. Preheat oven to 425°. Mix mushrooms, potatoes, Brussels sprouts and garlic; drizzle with olive oil. Sprinkle with the thyme, salt and pepper; toss to coat. Place in a shallow roasting pan.
2. Place chicken on a work surface, breast side down and tail end facing you. Using kitchen shears, cut along each side of the backbone; discard backbone. Turn chicken over so breast side is up; flatten by pressing down firmly on the breastbone until it cracks. Place the chicken on a rack over vegetables. Twist and tuck wings under to secure in place. Combine butter and miso paste; spread over skin (mixture will be thick).
3. Roast until a thermometer inserted in the thickest part of the thigh reads 170°-175°, 1½-1¾ hours, covering chicken loosely with aluminum foil after 45 minutes of cooking. (Miso mixture on chicken will appear very dark while roasting.)
4. Remove chicken from oven; tent with foil. Let stand for 15 minutes before carving. If desired, skim fat and thicken pan drippings for gravy. Serve with chicken. If desired, top with additional fresh thyme.
1 serving: 653 cal., 37g fat (13g sat. fat), 170mg chol., 912mg sod., 25g carb. (3g sugars, 4g fiber), 54g pro.

CAST-IRON SKILLET STEAK

If you have never cooked steak at home before, it can be a little intimidating. That's why I came up with this simple steak recipe that's so easy, you could make it any day of the week.
—James Schend, Deputy Editor

- -

Prep: 5 min. + standing • **Cook:** 5 min.
Makes: 2 servings

- 3 **tsp. kosher salt, divided**
- 1 **beef New York strip or ribeye steak (1 lb.), 1 in. thick**

1. Remove steak from refrigerator and sprinkle with 2 tsp. salt; let stand for 45-60 minutes.
2. Preheat a cast-iron skillet over high heat until extremely hot, 4-5 minutes. Sprinkle remaining 1 tsp. salt in bottom of skillet; pat beef dry with paper towels. Place steak in skillet and cook until it is easily moved, 1-2 minutes; flip, placing steak in a different section of the skillet. Cook for 30 seconds and then begin moving steak, occasionally pressing slightly to ensure the steak has even contact with skillet.
3. Continue turning and flipping until steak is cooked to desired degree of doneness (for medium-rare, a thermometer should read 135°; medium, 140°; medium-well, 145°), 1-2 minutes.
6 oz. cooked beef: 494 cal., 36g fat (15g sat. fat), 134mg chol., 2983mg sod., 0 carb. (0 sugars, 0 fiber), 40g pro.

ASK SARAH

HOW DO I CHOOSE THE BEST STEAK AT THE STORE?

Steak should be evenly marbled with creamy white fat. Look for pieces with a bright, cherry red color. Avoid meat with gray or brown patches or cuts that look dried out. Packages shouldn't have any holes, tears or excessive liquid. If they do, it might indicate improper handling and storage.

SLOW-COOKER MONGOLIAN BEEF

This dish uses inexpensive ingredients to offer big flavor in a small amount of time. The slow cooker makes easy work of it as well—easier than getting takeout!
—*Taste of Home* Test Kitchen

Prep: 10 min. • **Cook:** 4¼ hours
Makes: 4 servings

- ¾ cup reduced-sodium chicken broth
- 2 Tbsp. reduced-sodium soy sauce
- 1 Tbsp. hoisin sauce
- 2 tsp. minced fresh gingerroot
- 2 tsp. sesame oil
- 1 tsp. minced garlic
- ½ tsp. salt
- ¼ tsp. crushed red pepper flakes
- 1 lb. beef flank steak, cut into thin strips
- 2 Tbsp. cornstarch
- 2 Tbsp. water
- 2 cups hot cooked rice
- 5 green onions, cut into 1-in. pieces
  Sesame seeds, optional

1. In a 4- or 5-qt. slow cooker, combine first 8 ingredients. Add beef and toss to coat. Cook, covered, on low 4-5 hours, until meat is tender.

2. In a small bowl, mix cornstarch and water until smooth; gradually stir into beef. Cook, covered, on high until sauce is thickened, 15-30 minutes. Serve over hot cooked rice. Sprinkle with green onions and, if desired, sesame seeds.

1 serving: 329 cal., 11g fat (4g sat. fat), 54mg chol., 530mg sod., 30g carb. (2g sugars, 1g fiber), 26g pro.

DRY-RUB GRILLED PORK CHOPS OVER CANNELLINI GREENS

DRY-RUB GRILLED PORK CHOPS OVER CANNELLINI GREENS

My family was not a huge fan of pork until I made this recipe. Feel free to incorporate your favorite herbs into the dry rub. You can use the rub on boneless skinless chicken breast or other meats, too.
—Michael Cirlincione, Stockton, NJ

Prep: 20 min. • **Cook:** 25 min
Makes: 4 servings

- 1 Tbsp. olive oil
- 1 medium onion, chopped
- 2 garlic cloves, minced
- 1 can (15 oz.) cannellini beans, rinsed and drained
- 1 cup water-packed artichoke hearts, drained and chopped
- ¾ cup pitted Greek olives, chopped
- ¼ cup dry white wine or chicken broth
- ¼ cup chicken broth
- ¼ tsp. salt
- ¼ tsp. smoked paprika
- ¼ tsp. pepper
- 4 bone-in pork loin chops (8 oz. each)
- 2 tsp. Greek seasoning or seasoning of your choice
- 5 oz. fresh baby spinach (about 6 cups)

1. In a large skillet, heat oil over medium-high heat. Add onion; cook and stir until tender, 4-5 minutes. Add the garlic; cook 1 minute longer. Stir in beans, artichokes, olives, wine, broth, salt. paprika and pepper. Bring to a boil; reduce heat. Simmer until the liquid is almost evaporated, 12-15 minutes.

2. Meanwhile, sprinkle chops with Greek seasoning. Grill over medium heat until a thermometer reads 145°, 6-8 minutes on each side. Let pork chops stand 5 minutes before serving.

3. Stir spinach into bean mixture; cook and stir until wilted, 2-3 minutes. Serve with pork.

1 serving: 530 cal., 29g fat (8g sat. fat), 111mg chol., 1345mg sod., 22g carb. (1g sugars, 6g fiber), 42g pro.

EASY CHICKEN PESTO STUFFED PEPPERS

On busy weeknights, I don't want to spend more than 30 minutes preparing dinner, nor do I want to wash a towering pile of dishes. This recipe delivers without having to sacrifice flavor.
—Olivia Cruz, Greenville, SC

- -

Takes: 25 min. • **Makes:** 4 servings

- 4 medium sweet yellow or orange peppers
- 1½ cups shredded rotisserie chicken
- 1½ cups cooked brown rice
- 1 cup prepared pesto
- ½ cup shredded Havarti cheese
  Fresh basil leaves, optional

1. Cut peppers lengthwise in half; remove stems and seeds. Place peppers on a baking sheet, skin side up. Broil 4 in. from heat until skins blister, about 5 minutes. Reduce oven temperature to 350°.

2. Meanwhile, in a large bowl, combine chicken, rice and pesto. When cool enough to handle, fill peppers with chicken mixture; return to baking sheet. Bake until heated through, about 5 minutes. Sprinkle with shredded cheese; bake until cheese is melted, 3-5 minutes. If desired, sprinkle with basil.

2 stuffed pepper halves: 521 cal., 31g fat (7g sat. fat), 62mg chol., 865mg sod., 33g carb. (7g sugars, 5g fiber), 25g pro.

WEEKNIGHT GOULASH

With this recipe, you can put in a full day's work, run some errands and still get dinner on the table in no time. Make it extra special by serving the meat sauce over spaetzle.
—Cyndy Gerken, Naples, FL

- -

Prep: 25 min. • **Cook:** 8½ hours
Makes: 2 servings

- 1 lb. beef stew meat
- 1 Tbsp. olive oil
- 1 cup beef broth
- 1 small onion, chopped
- ¼ cup ketchup
- 1 Tbsp. Worcestershire sauce
- 1½ tsp. brown sugar
- 1½ tsp. paprika
- ¼ tsp. ground mustard
- 1 Tbsp. all-purpose flour
- 2 Tbsp. water
  Hot cooked egg noodles or spaetzle

1. In a large skillet, brown beef in oil; drain. Transfer to a 1½-qt. slow cooker. Combine the broth, onion, ketchup, Worcestershire sauce, brown sugar, paprika and mustard. Pour over beef. Cover and cook on low for 8-10 hours, until meat is tender.

2. In a small bowl, combine flour and water until smooth. Gradually stir into the beef mixture. Cover and cook on high until thickened, about 30 minutes longer. Serve with noodles.

1 cup: 478 cal., 23g fat (7g sat. fat), 141mg chol., 1005mg sod., 20g carb. (14g sugars, 1g fiber), 45g pro.

EASY CHICKEN PESTO STUFFED PEPPERS

MANGO CHICKEN THIGHS
WITH BASIL-COCONUT SAUCE

MANGO CHICKEN THIGHS WITH BASIL-COCONUT SAUCE

This recipe brings restaurant flavor to my home kitchen effortlessly! The meal comes together quickly and fills the kitchen with wonderful aromas. If there are any leftovers, they are just as good reheated the next day.
—Kathi Jones-DelMonte, Rochester, NY

- -

Prep: 20 min. • **Cook:** 30 min.
Makes: 4 servings

- 4   boneless skinless chicken thighs (about 1 lb.)
- ½   tsp. salt
- ¼   tsp. pepper
- 1   Tbsp. olive oil
- 3   garlic cloves, minced
- 1   Tbsp. minced fresh gingerroot
- 1   can (13.66 oz.) coconut milk
- 1   medium mango, peeled and chopped
- 4   green onions, sliced
- ½   cup thinly sliced fresh basil, divided
- ¼   cup miso paste
- 2   tsp. Sriracha chili sauce
- 2   cups cooked jasmine rice
- 2   medium limes, quartered

1. Sprinkle chicken with salt and pepper. In a large skillet, heat oil over medium heat. Brown chicken on both sides. Add garlic and ginger; cook 1 minute longer.
2. Stir in coconut milk, mango, green onions, ¼ cup basil, miso paste and chili sauce. Cook and stir until sauce is slightly reduced and a thermometer inserted in chicken reads 170°, about 20 minutes. Sprinkle with remaining ¼ cup basil. Serve with rice and limes.
1 serving: 552 cal., 28g fat (18g sat. fat), 76mg chol., 1209mg sod., 46g carb. (17g sugars, 4g fiber), 28g pro.

TEST KITCHEN TIP

Choose plump mangoes with a sweet, fruity fragrance. Avoid those that are bruised or very soft. Ripe mangoes have green-yellow skin with a pronounced red blush. To ripen a mango, let stand at room temperature and out of sunlight. Then refrigerate the ripened mango until you are ready to use it.

BUFFALO CHICKEN ENCHILADAS

Filled with rotisserie chicken, lots of cheese and Buffalo sauce, these enchiladas will be the most craveable, easy and delicious dish you've ever tasted. The entire family will ask for them again and again.
—Becky Hardin, St. Peters, MO

- -

Prep: 15 min. • **Bake:** 25 min.
Makes: 10 servings

- 3   cups shredded rotisserie chicken
- 2   cups shredded cheddar cheese, divided
- 1   can (10 oz.) diced tomatoes and green chiles, drained
- 1   can (10 oz.) enchilada sauce
- ½   cup Buffalo wing sauce
- 1   can (10½ oz.) condensed cream of celery soup, undiluted
- 4   oz. reduced-fat cream cheese, cubed
- ½   cup blue cheese salad dressing
- 10   flour tortillas (8 in.)
- ⅓   cup crumbled blue cheese
    Optional: Chopped tomatoes, sliced celery, shredded lettuce, sliced green onions, minced fresh cilantro and additional cheddar cheese

1. Preheat oven to 350°. In a large bowl, combine chicken, 1¾ cups shredded cheese, diced tomatoes and green chiles, enchilada sauce and wing sauce. In a small saucepan, heat the soup, cream cheese, dressing and remaining ¼ cup shredded cheese over low heat until cheeses are melted, 5-10 minutes. Remove from heat.
2. Place ½ cup chicken mixture off center on each tortilla. Roll up and place in a greased 13x9-in. baking dish, seam side down. Top with sauce.
3. Bake, uncovered, until the enchiladas are heated through and cheese is melted, 25-30 minutes. Sprinkle with blue cheese and additional toppings of your choice.
1 enchilada: 472 cal., 26g fat (10g sat. fat), 76mg chol., 1387mg sod., 34g carb. (2g sugars, 3g fiber), 25g pro.

BUFFALO CHICKEN
ENCHILADAS

TASTE OF HOME
TEST
KITCHEN
RECIPE OF THE YEAR
★ ★ ★ ★

LARB GAI

LARB GAI

Larb gai is a wonderfully savory Thai dish.
—*Taste of Home* Test Kitchen

Takes: 30 minutes • **Makes:** 4 servings

- 1 lb. ground chicken
- 2 Tbsp. canola oil
- 2 green or red fresh chiles, seeded and chopped
- 2 shallots, thinly sliced
- 2 garlic cloves, minced
- 2 Tbsp. lime juice
- 3 Tbsp. fish sauce
- 1 Tbsp. sweet chili sauce
- 2 tsp. brown sugar
- 1 to 2 tsp. Sriracha chili sauce
- ¼ cup fresh cilantro leaves
- 2 Tbsp. minced fresh mint
  Hot cooked sticky rice
  Boston lettuce leaves, optional

In a skillet, cook chicken over medium heat until no longer pink, 8-10 minutes, breaking into crumbles; drain. In the same skillet, heat oil over medium heat. Add the shallots and chiles; cook and stir until tender, 3-4 minutes. Add garlic; cook 1 minute longer. Stir in the cooked chicken, lime juice, fish sauce, chili sauce, brown sugar and Sriracha. Cook and stir until heated through. Stir in cilantro and mint. Serve with sticky rice and, if desired, lettuce leaves.

½ cup: 262 cal., 16g fat (3g sat. fat), 75mg chol., 1211mg sod., 10g carb. (6g sugars, 0 fiber), 20g pro.

TEST KITCHEN TIP

For sticky rice, place 2 cups uncooked sweet rice in a 3-qt. microwave-safe dish. Cover with water; let stand for 1 hour. Drain rice and return to dish; add 2 cups water. Microwave, covered, on high until rice is tender, 8-12 minutes, stirring every 3 minutes. Let rice stand 10 minutes.

EPIPHANY HAM

I wanted to cook a ham but didn't have the ingredients for my usual glaze recipe, so I made substitutions. You can experiment, too. Instead of using black cherry soda, try another flavor, or use sweet and sour sauce in place of the duck sauce.
—Edith Griffith, Havre de Grace, MD

Prep: 10 min. • **Bake:** 3 hours
Makes: 12 servings

- 1   **fully cooked bone-in ham (8 to 10 lbs., not spiral cut)**
- 1   **can (12 oz.) black cherry soda**
- 2   **tsp. Chinese five-spice powder**
- ⅔   **cup duck sauce**

1. Preheat oven to 350°. Place ham on a rack in a baking pan or dish; pour soda over ham. Sprinkle with five-spice powder. Cover with aluminum foil; bake 30 minutes.
2. Remove foil and discard. Baste with duck sauce; return to oven and bake, uncovered, until a thermometer reads 140°, about 2½ hours, basting again halfway through.
6 oz. cooked ham: 303 cal., 8g fat (3g sat. fat), 133mg chol., 1659mg sod., 13g carb. (9g sugars, 0 fiber), 45g pro.

SHEET-PAN HONEY
MUSTARD CHICKEN

TASTE OF HOME
TEST KITCHEN
RECIPE OF THE YEAR
★★★★★

SHEET-PAN HONEY MUSTARD CHICKEN

This chicken dish is an easy gluten-free, low-carb meal ideal for busy weekdays. The chicken is tender, juicy and so delicious! It's now on the list of our favorite meals. You can substitute any low-carb vegetable for the green beans.
—Denise Browning, San Antonio, TX

Prep: 20 min. • **Bake:** 45 min.
Makes: 6 servings

- 6   **bone-in chicken thighs (about 2¼ lbs.)**
- ¾   **tsp. salt, divided**
- ½   **tsp. pepper, divided**
- 2   **medium lemons**
- ⅓   **cup olive oil**
- ⅓   **cup honey**
- 3   **Tbsp. Dijon mustard**
- 4   **garlic cloves, minced**
- 1   **tsp. paprika**
- ½   **cup water**
- ½   **lb. fresh green beans, trimmed**
- 6   **miniature sweet peppers, sliced into rings**
- ¼   **cup pomegranate seeds, optional**

1. Preheat oven to 425°. Place chicken in a greased 15x10x1-in. baking pan. Sprinkle with ½ tsp. salt and ¼ tsp. pepper. Thinly slice 1 lemon; place over chicken. Cut remaining lemon crosswise in half; squeeze juice into a small bowl. Whisk in oil, honey, mustard, garlic and paprika. Pour half the mixture over chicken; reserve remaining sauce for beans. Pour water into pan. Bake 25 minutes.
2. Meanwhile, combine the beans, sweet peppers, remaining sauce, ¼ tsp. salt and ¼ tsp. pepper; toss to coat. Arrange the vegetables around chicken in pan. Bake until a thermometer inserted in chicken reads 170°-175° and the beans are tender, 15-20 minutes. If desired, sprinkle with pomegranate seeds.
1 serving: 419 cal., 26g fat (6g sat. fat), 81mg chol., 548mg sod., 22g carb. (17g sugars, 2g fiber), 24g pro.

HAM & SWISS BAKED PENNE

As a kid I loved to eat the hot ham and Swiss sandwiches from a local restaurant. With its melty, gooey goodness, this bake makes me think of them.
—Ally Billhorn, Wilton, IA

- -

Takes: 30 min. • **Makes:** 6 servings

2⅓ cups uncooked penne pasta
3 Tbsp. butter
3 Tbsp. all-purpose flour
2 cups 2% milk
1 cup half-and-half cream
1½ cups shredded Swiss cheese
½ cup shredded Colby cheese
2 cups cubed fully cooked ham
TOPPING
¼ cup seasoned bread crumbs
¼ cup grated Parmesan cheese
2 Tbsp. butter, melted

1. Preheat oven to 375°. Cook the pasta according to the package directions for al dente; drain.
2. Meanwhile, in a large saucepan, melt butter over medium heat. Stir in flour until smooth; gradually whisk in milk and cream. Bring mixture to a boil, stirring constantly; cook and stir until thickened, 1-2 minutes. Gradually stir in the Swiss and Colby cheeses until melted. Add ham and drained pasta; toss to coat.
3. Transfer to a greased 11x7-in. baking dish. In a small bowl, mix the topping ingredients; sprinkle over pasta. Bake, uncovered, until bubbly, 15-20 minutes.
1 cup: 559 cal., 30g fat (18g sat. fat), 116mg chol., 905mg sod., 41g carb. (7g sugars, 2g fiber), 31g pro.

ASIAN CHICKEN THIGHS

Here, a thick, tangy sauce coats golden brown chicken. Serve the thighs over long grain rice or with ramen noodle slaw.
—Dave Farrington, Midwest City, OK

- -

Prep: 15 min. • **Cook:** 50 min.
Makes: 5 servings

ASIAN CHICKEN THIGHS

5 tsp. olive oil
5 bone-in chicken thighs (about 1¾ lbs.), skin removed
⅓ cup water
¼ cup packed brown sugar
2 Tbsp. orange juice
2 Tbsp. reduced-sodium soy sauce
2 Tbsp. ketchup
1 Tbsp. white vinegar
4 garlic cloves, minced
½ tsp. crushed red pepper flakes
¼ tsp. Chinese five-spice powder
2 tsp. cornstarch
2 Tbsp. cold water
Sliced green onions
Hot cooked rice, optional

1. In a large skillet, heat oil over medium heat. Add chicken; cook until golden brown, 8-10 minutes on each side. In a small bowl, whisk water, brown sugar, orange juice, soy sauce, ketchup, white vinegar, minced garlic, red pepper flakes and five-spice powder. Pour over chicken. Bring to a boil. Reduce heat; simmer, uncovered, until the chicken thighs are tender, 30-35 minutes, turning chicken occasionally.
2. In a small bowl, mix cornstarch and cold water until smooth; stir into pan. Bring to a boil; cook and stir until sauce is thickened,

about 1 minute. Sprinkle with green onions. If desired, serve with rice.
Freeze option: Cool chicken. Freeze in freezer containers. To use, partially thaw in refrigerator overnight. Heat slowly in a covered skillet until a thermometer inserted in chicken reads 165°, stirring occasionally and adding a little water if necessary.
1 chicken thigh: 292 cal., 14g fat (3g sat. fat), 87mg chol., 396mg sod., 15g carb. (13g sugars, 0 fiber), 25g pro. **Diabetic exchanges:** 3 lean meat, 1 starch, 1 fat.

"What I love about this recipe is that it's super easy and customizable, and the chicken thighs are so tender. Even if you don't have all of the seasoning ingredients, it will still taste good. It's so flavorful."

—RACHEL WILKE,
SENIOR SOCIAL MEDIA EDITOR/DESIGNER

EASY SLOW-COOKER POT ROAST

I love pot roast. First of all, it's delicious. Second, it's easy! I can't describe the feeling of walking into my house after a long day at work and smelling this dish that has been simmering in the slow cooker all day. There's nothing better.
—James Schend, Deputy Editor

Prep: 10 min. • **Cook:** 10 hours
Makes: 10 servings

- 1 boneless beef rump or chuck roast (3 to 3½ lbs.)
- 1 Tbsp. canola oil
- 6 medium carrots, cut into thirds
- 6 medium potatoes, peeled and quartered
- 1 large onion, quartered
- 3 tsp. Montreal steak seasoning
- 1 carton (32 oz.) beef broth
- 3 Tbsp. cornstarch
- 3 Tbsp. water

1. In a large skillet over medium heat, brown roast in oil on all sides. Place the carrots, potatoes and onion in a 6-qt. slow cooker. Place roast on top of vegetables; sprinkle with steak seasoning. Add beef broth. Cook, covered, on low 10-12 hours, until beef and vegetables are tender.
2. Remove roast and vegetables from slow cooker; keep warm.
3. Transfer cooking juices to a saucepan; skim fat. Bring juices to a boil. In a small bowl, mix the cornstarch and water until smooth; stir into juices. Return to a boil, stirring constantly; cook and stir until thickened, 1-2 minutes. Serve with roast and vegetables.

1 serving: 354 cal., 15g fat (5g sat. fat), 88mg chol., 696mg sod., 24g carb. (4g sugars, 3g fiber), 30g pro. **Diabetic exchanges:** 4 lean meat, 1½ starch, ½ fat.

GREEK CHICKEN & RICE

Here's a fresh take on comfort food! This dish is my go-to on busy weeknights and when unexpected company stops by. Toss in chopped spinach to boost the nutrition.
—Savannah Lay, Baker City, OR

Takes: 30 min. • **Makes:** 4 servings

- 1 lb. boneless skinless chicken breasts, cut into 1-in. cubes
- ¼ tsp. garlic powder
- ¼ tsp. pepper
- 2 tsp. olive oil
- 1 jar (12 oz.) marinated quartered artichoke hearts, drained and chopped
- 1 jar (12 oz.) roasted sweet red peppers, drained and chopped
- ⅓ cup oil-packed sun-dried tomatoes, chopped
- ⅓ cup Greek olives, sliced
- 1 pkg. (8.8 oz.) ready-to-serve brown rice
- 1 Tbsp. minced fresh parsley

1. Sprinkle chicken with garlic powder and pepper. In a large skillet, heat oil over medium heat. Add chicken; cook and stir until no longer pink, 8-10 minutes. Stir in the artichokes, roasted peppers, tomatoes and Greek olives. Cook and stir until heated through, 3-5 minutes.
2. Meanwhile, prepare rice according to package directions. Serve with chicken. Sprinkle with parsley.

1¼ cups: 436 cal., 21g fat (4g sat. fat), 63mg chol., 1008mg sod., 29g carb. (3g sugars, 7g fiber), 26g pro.

EASY SLOW-COOKER POT ROAST

POMEGRANATE
SHORT RIBS

POMEGRANATE SHORT RIBS

I like drizzling the pomegranate molasses sauce on top of simple roasted vegetables. It's a bit tangy and a bit sweet, and adds a nice depth of flavor.
—Shannon Sarna, South Orange, NJ

Prep: 25 min. + chilling • **Cook:** 6 hours
Makes: 8 servings

- 1 tsp. salt
- ½ tsp. ground cinnamon
- ½ tsp. pepper
- ¼ tsp. ground coriander
  Dash crushed red pepper flakes
- 8 bone-in beef short ribs (about 4 lbs.)
- 2 Tbsp. safflower oil
- 1 medium onion, chopped
- 3 garlic cloves, minced
- 1 Tbsp. tomato paste
- 1½ cups chicken or beef stock
- 1½ cups dry red wine or pomegranate juice
- 3 Tbsp. soy sauce, optional
- ⅓ cup pomegranate molasses
  Minced fresh parsley and pomegranate seeds

1. Combine the first 5 ingredients; rub over ribs. Refrigerate, covered, at least 2 hours. In a large skillet, heat oil over medium heat. Brown ribs on all sides in batches. Transfer to a 5-qt. slow cooker. Discard drippings, reserving 2 Tbsp. Add onion to drippings; cook and stir over medium-high heat until tender, 8-10 minutes. Add garlic and tomato paste; cook 1 minute longer.

2. Add red wine to the pan; increase heat to medium-high. Cook 10 minutes until slightly thickened, stirring to loosen browned bits from pan. Transfer to slow cooker. Add the stock, molasses and, if desired, soy sauce, making sure the ribs are fully submerged in liquid. Cook, covered, on low for 6-8 hours, until ribs are tender. Serve ribs with parsley and pomegranate seeds.

1 short rib: 267 cal., 14g fat (5g sat. fat), 55mg chol., 428mg sod., 11g carb. (7g sugars, 0 fiber), 19g pro.

ONE-POT
SALSA CHICKEN

ONE-POT SALSA CHICKEN

This skillet recipe is a colorful and healthy main dish that can be on the table in just over an hour. The subtle, sweet-spicy flavor is a nice surprise.
—Ann Sheehy, Lawrence, MA

Prep: 20 min. • **Cook:** 45 min.
Makes: 6 servings

- 2 Tbsp. canola oil
- 2 lbs. boneless skinless chicken thighs, cut into 1-in. pieces
- 1 tsp. pepper
- ½ tsp. salt
- 2 medium sweet potatoes, peeled and cubed
- 1 jar (16 oz.) medium salsa
- 2 medium nectarines, peeled and chopped
- 2 Tbsp. Tajin seasoning
- 1 cup uncooked instant brown rice
- 1 cup water
- ¼ cup minced fresh parsley
  Minced fresh chives

1. In a Dutch oven, heat the canola oil over medium-high heat. Sprinkle chicken with pepper and salt. Brown in batches; return all to pan. Add potatoes, salsa, nectarines and seasoning. Bring to a boil; reduce heat. Cover and simmer until potatoes are almost tender, about 15 minutes.

2. Stir in brown rice and water; bring to a boil. Reduce heat. Cover and simmer until the potatoes are tender, about 10 minutes. Stir in the minced parsley. Serve in bowls; sprinkle with chives.

1⅔ cups: 432 cal., 16g fat (3g sat. fat), 101mg chol., 1254mg sod., 39g carb. (13g sugars, 4g fiber), 31g pro.

TEST KITCHEN TIP

Tajin seasoning is a unique blend of lime, chile peppers and sea salt. Look for it in the spice aisle.

CURRY COCONUT CHICKEN

My husband and I love this yummy dish. It's a breeze to prepare in the slow cooker, and it tastes just like a meal you'd have at your favorite Indian or Thai restaurant.
—Andi Kauffman, Beavercreek, OR

- -

Prep: 20 min. • **Cook:** 4 hours
Makes: 2 servings

- 1 **medium potato, peeled and cubed**
- ¼ **cup chopped onion**
- 2 **boneless skinless chicken breast halves (4 oz. each)**
- ½ **cup light coconut milk**
- 2 **tsp. curry powder**
- 1 **garlic clove, minced**
- ½ **tsp. reduced-sodium chicken bouillon granules**
- ⅛ **tsp. salt**
- ⅛ **tsp. pepper**
- 1 **cup hot cooked rice**
- 1 **green onion, thinly sliced**
  Optional: Raisins, shredded coconut and chopped unsalted peanuts

1. Place potatoes and onion in a 1½- or 2-qt. slow cooker. In a large skillet coated with cooking spray, brown chicken on both sides. Transfer to slow cooker.
2. In a small bowl, combine the coconut milk, curry, garlic, bouillon, salt and pepper; pour over the chicken. Cover and cook on low for 4-5 hours, until meat is tender.
3. Serve the chicken and sauce with rice; sprinkle with green onions. If desired, garnish with raisins, coconut and peanuts.
1 serving: 353 cal., 7g fat (4g sat. fat), 63mg chol., 266mg sod., 42g carb. (3g sugars, 3g fiber), 27g pro.

ONE-POT BACON CHEESEBURGER PASTA

ONE-POT BACON CHEESEBURGER PASTA

When it's too chilly to grill burgers, I whip up a big pot of this cheesy pasta. Believe it or not, it tastes just like a bacon cheeseburger, and it's much easier for my young children to enjoy. It's great paired with Tater Tots or french fries.
—Carly Terrell, Granbury, TX

- -

Prep: 15 min. • **Cook:** 35 min.
Makes: 12 servings

- 8 **bacon strips, chopped**
- 2 **lbs. ground beef**
- ½ **large red onion, chopped**
- 12 **oz. uncooked spiral pasta**
- 4 **cups chicken broth**
- 2 **cans (15 oz. each) crushed tomatoes**
- 1 **can (8 oz.) tomato sauce**
- 1 **cup water**
- ¼ **cup ketchup**
- 3 **Tbsp. prepared mustard**
- 2 **Tbsp. Worcestershire sauce**
- ¼ **tsp. salt**
- ¼ **tsp. pepper**
- 2 **cups shredded cheddar cheese, divided**
- ⅓ **cup chopped dill pickle**
  Optional: Chopped tomatoes, shredded lettuce, sliced pickles and sliced red onion

1. In a 6-qt. stockpot, cook bacon over medium heat, stirring occasionally, until crisp, 6-8 minutes. Remove with a slotted spoon; drain bacon on paper towels. Discard drippings.
2. In the same pot, cook ground beef and onion over medium heat until meat is no longer pink, 6-8 minutes, breaking into crumbles; drain. Add next 10 ingredients; bring to a boil. Reduce heat; simmer, covered, until pasta is al dente, stirring occasionally, about 10 minutes.
3. Stir in 1 cup cheese, pickle and bacon; cook and stir until cheese is melted. Serve with the remaining cheese and, if desired, tomatoes, lettuce, pickles and red onions.
1⅓ cups: 390 cal., 18g fat (8g sat. fat), 73mg chol., 1023mg sod., 31g carb. (7g sugars, 3g fiber), 25g pro.

CHIPOTLE-ORANGE CHICKEN

Big on flavor and easy on the cook's time, this slow-cooker chicken recipe is a winner. The sweet-hot sauce gets its heat from the chipotle pepper. I serve this dish with a side of rice to use up every delectable drop of the sauce.
—Susan Hein, Burlington, WI

- -

Prep: 15 min. • **Cook:** 3 hours
Makes: 2 servings

- 2   boneless skinless chicken breast halves (6 oz. each)
- ⅛   tsp. salt
- Dash pepper
- ¼   cup chicken broth
- 3   Tbsp. orange marmalade
- 1½ tsp. canola oil
- 1½ tsp. balsamic vinegar
- 1½ tsp. minced chipotle pepper in adobo sauce
- 1½ tsp. honey
- ½   tsp. chili powder
- ⅛   tsp. garlic powder
- 2   tsp. cornstarch
- 1   Tbsp. cold water

1. Sprinkle chicken with salt and pepper. Transfer to a 1½-qt. slow cooker. In a small bowl, combine the broth, marmalade, oil, balsamic vinegar, chipotle pepper, honey, chili powder and garlic powder; pour over chicken. Cover and cook on low 3-4 hours, until a thermometer reads 165°.

2. Remove chicken to a serving platter and keep warm. Place the cooking juices in a small saucepan; bring to a boil. Combine the cornstarch and water until smooth. Gradually stir into pan. Bring to a boil; cook and stir until thickened, about 2 minutes. Serve with chicken.

Freeze option: Cool chicken mixture. Freeze in freezer containers. To use, partially thaw in refrigerator overnight. Heat through slowly in a covered skillet until a thermometer inserted in chicken reads 165°, stirring occasionally; add broth or water if necessary.

1 chicken breast half: 324 cal., 8g fat (1g sat. fat), 95mg chol., 414mg sod., 29g carb. (24g sugars, 1g fiber), 35g pro.

CHIPOTLE-ORANGE CHICKEN

TRIPLE-CITRUS STEAKS WITH JICAMA & MANGO

I came up with this recipe several years ago. It's one of our all-time favorites. It's colorful and easy to make.
—Sherry Little, Sherwood, AR

- -

Prep: 30 min. + marinating • **Cook:** 15 min.
Makes: 4 servings

- 1   medium orange
- 1   medium lemon
- 1   medium lime
- 4   Tbsp. honey
- 1¼ tsp. salt, divided
- 4   beef flat iron steaks or top sirloin steaks (6 oz. each and ¾ in. thick)
- ½   cup water
- 1   cup julienned peeled jicama
- 1   medium mango, peeled and cubed

1. Cut orange, lemon and lime crosswise in half; squeeze juice from fruits. Stir in honey and salt. Pour ⅓ cup marinade into a bowl or shallow dish. Add steaks and turn to coat. Refrigerate at least 3 hours, turning once. Cover and refrigerate remaining marinade.

2. Drain steaks, discarding marinade. Heat a large skillet over medium heat. Cook steaks until meat reaches desired doneness (for medium-rare, a thermometer should read 135°; medium, 140°; medium-well, 145°), 6-8 minutes on each side. Remove steaks and keep warm.

3. Add water and the reserved marinade. Bring to a boil; cook until liquid is reduced to 3 Tbsp., 10-12 minutes. Add jicama and mango; heat through. Serve with steaks. If desired, garnish servings with orange, lemon or lime slices.

1 serving: 412 cal., 18g fat (7g sat. fat), 109mg chol., 609mg sod., 29g carb. (24g sugars, 3g fiber), 34g pro.

**CHICKEN POTPIE GALETTE
WITH CHEDDAR-THYME CRUST**

CHICKEN POTPIE GALETTE WITH CHEDDAR-THYME CRUST

This gorgeous galette puts a fun open-faced spin on traditional chicken potpie. The rich filling and flaky cheddar-flecked crust make it taste so homey.
—Elisabeth Larsen, Pleasant Grove, UT

- -

Prep: 45 min. + chilling
Bake: 30 min. + cooling • **Makes:** 8 servings

1¼ cups all-purpose flour
½ cup shredded sharp cheddar cheese
2 Tbsp. minced fresh thyme
¼ tsp. salt
½ cup cold butter, cubed
¼ cup ice water
FILLING
3 Tbsp. butter
2 large carrots, sliced
1 celery rib, diced
1 small onion, diced
8 oz. sliced fresh mushrooms
3 cups julienned Swiss chard
3 garlic cloves, minced
1 cup chicken broth
3 Tbsp. all-purpose flour
½ tsp. salt
¼ tsp. pepper
2 cups shredded cooked chicken
½ tsp. minced fresh oregano
2 Tbsp. minced fresh parsley

1. Combine flour, cheese, thyme and salt; cut in butter until crumbly. Gradually add ice water, tossing with a fork until dough holds together when pressed. Shape into a disk; refrigerate 1 hour.
2. For filling, melt butter in a large saucepan over medium-high heat. Add carrots, celery and diced onion; cook and stir until slightly softened, 5-7 minutes. Add mushrooms; cook 3 minutes longer. Add Swiss chard and garlic; cook until chard is wilted, 2-3 minutes.
3. Whisk together chicken broth, flour, salt and pepper; slowly pour over vegetables, stirring constantly. Cook until thickened, 2-3 minutes. Stir in chicken and oregano.
4. Preheat oven to 400°. On a floured sheet of parchment, roll dough into a 12-in. circle. Transfer to a baking sheet. Spoon filling over crust to within 2 in. of edge. Fold crust edge over filling, pleating as you go, leaving center uncovered. Bake on a lower oven rack until crust is golden brown and filling is bubbly, 30-35 minutes. Cool for 15 minutes before slicing. Sprinkle with parsley.
1 piece: 342 cal., 21g fat (12g sat. fat), 81mg chol., 594mg sod., 22g carb. (2g sugars, 2g fiber), 16g pro.

GARLICKY CHICKEN DINNER

Bone-in chicken brings comforting flavor, which is enhanced by herbs, lemon and hearty vegetables.
—Shannon Norris, Senior Food Stylist

- -

Prep: 25 min. • **Bake:** 45 min.
Makes: 8 servings

1¼ lbs. small red potatoes, quartered
4 medium carrots, cut into ½-in. slices
1 medium red onion, cut into thin wedges
1 Tbsp. olive oil
6 garlic cloves, minced
2 tsp. minced fresh thyme, divided
1½ tsp. salt, divided
1 tsp. pepper, divided
1 tsp. paprika
4 chicken drumsticks
4 bone-in chicken thighs
1 small lemon, sliced
1 pkg. (5 oz.) fresh spinach

1. Preheat oven to 425°. In a large bowl, combine potatoes, carrots, onion, oil, garlic, 1 tsp. thyme, ¾ tsp. salt and ½ tsp. pepper; toss to coat. Transfer to a 15x10x1-in. baking pan coated with cooking spray.
2. In a small bowl, mix paprika and remaining thyme, salt and pepper. Sprinkle chicken with paprika mixture; arrange over vegetables. Top chicken with lemon slices. Roast until a thermometer inserted in chicken reads 170°-175° and vegetables are just tender, 35-40 minutes.
3. Remove chicken to a serving platter; keep warm. Top vegetables with spinach. Roast until vegetables are tender and spinach is wilted, 8-10 minutes longer. Stir vegetables to combine; serve with chicken.
1 piece chicken with 1 cup vegetables: 264 cal., 12g fat (3g sat. fat), 64mg chol., 548mg sod., 18g carb. (3g sugars, 3g fiber), 21g pro. **Diabetic exchanges:** 3 medium-fat meat, 1 starch, 1 vegetable, ½ fat.

GARLICKY
CHICKEN DINNER

BUFFALO CHICKEN STUFFED POBLANO PEPPERS

I'm not a fan of green bell peppers, so I decided to create a filling that would go well with my favorite pepper—the poblano. After a few taste tests with my family, this stuffed poblano peppers recipe is now one of our favorites. I've also added black beans to the filling, used Cubanelle peppers, and served cilantro lime rice on the side.
—Lorri Stout, Gaithersburg, MD

- -

Prep: 15 min. • **Bake:** 30 min.
Makes: 8 servings

- 4   poblano peppers
- 2   Tbsp. butter
- 4   green onions, thinly sliced, divided
- 3   cups shredded cooked
      chicken breast
- 1   cup frozen corn (about
      5 oz.), thawed
- 4   oz. cream cheese, cubed
- ¾   cup shredded Mexican
      cheese blend, divided
- ½   cup Buffalo wing sauce
- ¼   cup crumbled blue cheese
- 1   tsp. granulated garlic

1. Preheat oven to 350°. Cut the peppers lengthwise in half; remove seeds. Place in a greased 15x10-in. baking pan. In a large skillet, heat butter over medium-high heat. Add 3 green onions; cook and stir until tender, about 5 minutes. Add chicken, corn, cream cheese, ½ cup shredded cheese, wing sauce, blue cheese and garlic; cook and stir until cheeses are melted.
2. Fill pepper halves with chicken mixture. Bake, covered, 25-30 minutes. Sprinkle with remaining ¼ cup shredded cheese and green onion; bake, uncovered, until the cheese is melted, about 5 minutes.
1 stuffed pepper half: 246 cal., 14g fat (8g sat. fat), 75mg chol., 668mg sod., 9g carb. (3g sugars, 2g fiber), 21g pro.

BUFFALO CHICKEN STUFFED POBLANO PEPPERS

CONTEST-WINNING CHICKEN WILD RICE CASSEROLE

While this special dish is perfect for serving company, it's so good that I often make it for everyday meals. We enjoy it with rolls or French bread.
—Elizabeth Tokariuk, Lethbridge, AB

- -

Prep: 20 min. • **Bake:** 30 min.
Makes: 8 servings

- 1   small onion, chopped
- ⅓   cup butter
- ⅓   cup all-purpose flour
- 1½ tsp. salt
- ½   tsp. pepper
- 1   can (14½ oz.) chicken broth
- 1   cup half-and-half cream
- 4   cups cubed cooked chicken
- 4   cups cooked wild rice
- 2   jars (4½ oz. each) sliced mushrooms, drained
- 1   jar (4 oz.) diced pimientos, drained
- 1   Tbsp. minced fresh parsley
- ⅓   cup slivered almonds

1. In a large saucepan, saute onion in butter until tender. Stir in the flour, salt and pepper until blended. Gradually stir in broth; bring to a boil. Boil and stir for 2 minutes or until thickened and bubbly. Stir in the cream, chicken, rice, mushrooms, pimientos and parsley; heat through.
2. Transfer to a greased 2½-qt. baking dish. Sprinkle with almonds. Bake, uncovered, at 350° for 30-35 minutes or until bubbly.
1 cup: 382 cal., 19g fat (8g sat. fat), 98mg chol., 878mg sod., 26g carb. (3g sugars, 3g fiber), 27g pro.

THAI SLOPPY JOE CHICKEN & WAFFLES

Sloppy joes, chicken and waffles, and Thai food are family favorites at our house, so I decided to combine all three to create one tasty dish. The slaw with peanut dressing adds crunch and flavor.
—Arlene Erlbach, Morton Grove, IL

- -

Takes: 30 min. • **Makes:** 6 servings

- ¼   cup creamy peanut butter
- ½   cup minced fresh cilantro, divided
- 6   Tbsp. teriyaki sauce, divided
- 3   Tbsp. chili sauce, divided
- 2   Tbsp. lime juice
- 2   cups coleslaw mix
- 1   lb. ground chicken
- ⅓   cup canned coconut milk
- 1   tsp. ground ginger
- ¾   tsp. garlic powder
- 6   frozen waffles
     Sliced green onions, optional

1. Place the peanut butter, ¼ cup cilantro, 4 Tbsp. cup teriyaki sauce, 1 Tbsp. chili sauce and lime juice in a food processor; process until combined. Place coleslaw mix in a large bowl; add peanut butter mixture. Toss to coat; set aside.
2. In a large skillet, cook the chicken over medium heat until the meat is no longer pink, 6-8 minutes, breaking into crumbles; drain. Stir in coconut milk, ginger, garlic powder, remaining ¼ cup cilantro and 2 Tbsp. teriyaki sauce. Cook and stir until heated through.
3. Meanwhile, prepare waffles according to package directions. Top waffles with chicken mixture and coleslaw. If desired, sprinkle with green onions.
1 serving: 314 cal., 17g fat (5g sat. fat), 55mg chol., 1046mg sod., 24g carb. (7g sugars, 2g fiber), 18g pro.

THAI SLOPPY JOE CHICKEN & WAFFLES

OKTOBERFEST CASSEROLE

Folks love German-inspired dishes here in northeastern Ohio. This casserole is a mashup of three of my favorites: cheesy hash brown casserole; bratwursts and sauerkraut; and pretzels and beer cheese. It takes just minutes to prep and bakes all in one dish. It's sure to please everyone.
—Sarah Markley, Ashland, OH

- -

Prep: 15 min. • **Bake:** 1½ hours + standing
Makes: 12 servings

- 2 cans (10½ oz. each) condensed cheddar cheese soup, undiluted
- 1 cup beer or chicken broth
- 1 cup sour cream
- 1 pkg. (32 oz.) frozen cubed hash brown potatoes, thawed
- 1 pkg. (14 oz.) fully cooked bratwurst links, chopped
- 1 can (14 oz.) sauerkraut, rinsed and well drained
- 2 cups shredded cheddar cheese
- 2 cups pretzel pieces

Preheat oven to 350°. In a large bowl, whisk soup, beer and sour cream until combined. Stir in the potatoes, sauerkraut, chopped bratwurst and cheese. Transfer to a greased 13x9-in. baking dish. Cover and bake for 45 minutes. Uncover; bake for 30 minutes. Top with pretzel pieces. Bake until bubbly and heated through, 12-15 minutes longer. Let stand 10 minutes before serving.
1 serving: 356 cal., 21g fat (10g sat. fat), 49mg chol., 884mg sod., 29g carb. (4g sugars, 3g fiber), 13g pro.

GRILLED BASIL CHICKEN & TOMATOES

Relax after work with a cold drink while this savory chicken marinates in an herby tomato blend. Let it soak for an hour, then toss it on the grill. It tastes just like summer.
—Laura Lunardi, West Chester, PA

- -

Prep: 15 min. + marinating • **Grill:** 10 min.
Makes: 4 servings

- ¾ cup balsamic vinegar
- ¼ cup tightly packed fresh basil leaves
- 2 Tbsp. olive oil
- 1 garlic clove, minced
- ½ tsp. salt
- 8 plum tomatoes
- 4 boneless skinless chicken breast halves (4 oz. each)

1. For marinade, place the first 5 ingredients in a blender. Cut 4 tomatoes into quarters and add to blender; cover and process until blended. Halve the remaining 4 tomatoes for grilling.
2. In a bowl, combine chicken and ⅔ cup marinade; refrigerate, covered, 1 hour, turning occasionally. Reserve remaining marinade for serving.
3. Place chicken on an oiled grill rack over medium heat; discard marinade remaining in the bowl. Grill chicken, covered, until a thermometer reads 165°, 4-6 minutes per side. Grill tomatoes, covered, over medium heat until lightly browned, 2-4 minutes per side. Serve chicken and tomatoes with reserved marinade.
1 serving: 177 cal., 5g fat (1g sat. fat), 63mg chol., 171mg sod., 8g carb. (7g sugars, 1g fiber), 24g pro. **Diabetic exchanges:** 3 lean meat, 1 vegetable, ½ fat.

GRILLED BASIL CHICKEN & TOMATOES

CURRY-RUBBED
ROAST CHICKEN

CURRY-RUBBED ROAST CHICKEN

There is just something so right about serving a savory roasted chicken to loved ones. This recipe is simple—yet it's packed with spicy showoff flavors suitable for any special occasion.
—Merry Graham, Newhall, CA

- -

Prep: 20 min. • **Cook:** 1½ hours + standing
Makes: 6 servings

4   Tbsp. coconut oil, divided
2½ tsp. salt, divided
2   tsp. Madras curry powder
½   tsp. granulated garlic
1   roasting chicken (5 to 6 lbs.)
¼   tsp. pepper
1   cup chopped leeks
    (white portion only)
1   celery rib, coarsely chopped
3   green onions, chopped
1   medium lemon, quartered
1   cup reduced-sodium chicken broth
GRAVY
1   Tbsp. unsalted butter
1   Tbsp. all-purpose flour
1   cup reduced-sodium chicken broth
½   cup white wine
    Optional: Lemon slices, minced
    fresh parsley and minced chives

1. Preheat oven to 350°. Mix 2 Tbsp. coconut oil and 2 tsp. salt with curry powder and garlic. Carefully loosen skin from chicken breast and upper legs; rub coconut oil mixture under skin. Remove giblets from cavity; save for another use. Sprinkle cavity with pepper and remaining salt; rub inside and outside of chicken with remaining oil.
2. Combine leek, celery, green onions and lemon and toss lightly; loosely stuff cavity. Tuck wings under chicken; tie drumsticks together. Place breast side up on a rack in a shallow roasting pan.
3. Roast 45 minutes; add chicken broth to pan. Continue roasting until a thermometer reads 165° when inserted in the center of stuffing and at least 170° in the thigh, 45-60 minutes. (Cover loosely with foil if chicken browns too quickly.)
4. Pour juices from cavity into pan. Remove chicken to a platter; tent with foil. Let stand 15-20 minutes before removing stuffing.
5. For gravy, pour pan juices into a large saucepan; skim off fat. Bring juices to a boil over medium heat. Add butter and flour; cook and stir until slightly thickened. Add broth and wine; cook and stir until thickened, 2-3 minutes. Serve with chicken and, if desired, lemon slices, parsley and chives.
1 serving: 580 cal., 38g fat (17g sat. fat), 154mg chol., 1328mg sod., 6g carb. (2g sugars, 1g fiber), 49g pro.

PORK & ASPARAGUS SHEET-PAN DINNER

When time is of the essence, it's nice to have the right recipe at your fingertips. Not only is this delicious, but you can clean it up in a flash.
—Joan Hallford, North Richland Hills, TX

- -

Prep: 20 min. • **Bake:** 20 min.
Makes: 4 servings

¼   cup olive oil, divided
3   cups diced new potatoes
3   cups cut fresh asparagus
    (1-in. pieces)
¼   tsp. salt
¼   tsp. pepper
1   large gala or Honeycrisp apple,
    peeled and cut into 1-in. wedges
2   tsp. brown sugar
1   tsp. ground cinnamon
¼   tsp. ground ginger
4   boneless pork loin chops
    (1 in. thick and about 6 oz. each)
2   tsp. Southwest seasoning

1. Preheat oven to 425°. Line a 15x10x1-in. baking pan with aluminum foil; brush with 2 tsp. olive oil.
2. In a large bowl, toss the potatoes with 1 Tbsp. olive oil. Place in 1 section of prepared baking pan. In same bowl, toss asparagus with 1 Tbsp. olive oil; place in another section of pan. Sprinkle salt and pepper over potatoes and asparagus.
3. In same bowl, toss apple with 1 tsp. olive oil. In a small bowl, mix the brown sugar, cinnamon and ginger; sprinkle over apples and toss to coat. Transfer to a different section of pan.
4. Brush pork chops with remaining 1 Tbsp. olive oil; sprinkle both sides with Southwest seasoning. Place chops in remaining section of pan. Bake until a thermometer inserted in pork reads 145° and potatoes and apples are tender, 20-25 minutes. Let stand 5 minutes before serving.
1 serving: 486 cal., 23g fat (5g sat. fat), 82mg chol., 447mg sod., 32g carb. (10g sugars, 5g fiber), 37g pro.

SPICY PLUM PORK
MEATBALLS WITH BOK CHOY

SPICY PLUM PORK MEATBALLS WITH BOK CHOY

I'm a fan of sweet, salty and spicy flavors and trying to make healthier food choices. This is so satisfying, you won't miss any pasta or rice. If you don't care for spiralized zucchini, thin pasta noodles work, too.
—Susan Mason, Puyallup, WA

Prep: 30 min. • **Cook:** 30 min.
Makes: 4 servings

- 1 jar (7 oz.) plum sauce
- ½ cup hoisin sauce
- 3 Tbsp. reduced-sodium soy sauce
- 2 Tbsp. rice vinegar
- 1 Tbsp. Sriracha chili sauce
- 1 large egg, lightly beaten
- 1½ cups panko bread crumbs, divided
- 1 lb. ground pork
- 4 Tbsp. olive oil, divided
- 2 medium zucchini, spiralized
- 1 lb. bok choy, trimmed and cut into 1-in. pieces
  Sesame seeds, optional

1. Whisk together the first 5 ingredients. Reserve 1¼ cups for sauce. Pour remaining mixture into a large bowl; add egg and ½ cup bread crumbs. Add the pork; mix lightly but thoroughly. Shape into 16 balls. Place the remaining 1 cup bread crumbs in a shallow bowl. Roll meatballs in bread crumbs to coat.
2. In a large skillet, heat 3 Tbsp. oil over medium heat. In batches, cook meatballs until cooked through, turning occasionally. Remove and keep warm. Heat remaining 1 Tbsp. oil in the same skillet. Add zucchini and bok choy; cook and stir over medium-high heat until crisp-tender, 6-8 minutes. Add the meatballs and reserved sauce; heat through. If desired, sprinkle with sesame seeds.
1 serving: 647 cal., 34g fat (9g sat. fat), 123mg chol., 1656mg sod., 55g carb. (16g sugars, 4g fiber), 29g pro.

SPICE-CRUSTED STEAKS WITH CHERRY SAUCE

SPICE-CRUSTED STEAKS WITH CHERRY SAUCE

If you are hosting meat lovers for dinner, these impressive cast-iron skillet steaks are guaranteed to please. They're perfect for a special occasion without too much fuss.
—*Taste of Home* Test Kitchen

Prep: 20 min. + chilling • **Cook:** 45 min.
Makes: 4 servings

- ½ cup dried cherries
- ¼ cup port wine, warmed
- 3½ tsp. coarsely ground pepper
- 1 tsp. brown sugar
- ¾ tsp. garlic powder
- ¾ tsp. paprika
- ¾ tsp. ground coffee
- ½ tsp. kosher salt
- ¼ tsp. ground cinnamon
- ¼ tsp. ground cumin
- ⅛ tsp. ground mustard
- 4 beef tenderloin steaks (1¼ in. thick and 6 oz. each)
- 1 Tbsp. canola oil
- 1 large shallot, finely chopped
- 1 Tbsp. butter
- 1 cup reduced-sodium beef broth
- 1 tsp. minced fresh thyme
- ½ cup heavy whipping cream
  Crumbled blue cheese, optional

1. Preheat oven to 350°. In a small bowl, combine cherries and wine; set aside. In a shallow dish, combine the pepper, brown sugar, garlic powder, paprika, coffee, salt, cinnamon, cumin and mustard. Add 1 steak at a time and turn to coat. Cover and refrigerate for 30 minutes.
2. Place oil in a 10-in. cast-iron or other ovenproof skillet; tilt to coat bottom. Heat oil over medium-high heat; sear steaks, 2 minutes on each side. Bake, uncovered, until meat reaches desired doneness (for medium-rare, a thermometer should read 135°; medium, 140°; medium-well, 145°), about 15 minutes. Remove steaks from oven and keep warm.
3. Wipe skillet clean; saute shallot in butter until crisp-tender. Add broth and thyme. Bring to a boil; cook until liquid is reduced by half, about 8 minutes. Stir in the cream; bring to a boil. Cook until thickened, stirring occasionally, 8 minutes.
4. Stir in the reserved cherry mixture. Serve sauce over steaks. If desired, sprinkle with blue cheese.
1 steak with 3 Tbsp. sauce: 506 cal., 28g fat (13g sat. fat), 124mg chol., 381mg sod., 20g carb. (13g sugars, 1g fiber), 39g pro.

MEAT LOVER'S PIZZA RICE SKILLET

One night I needed a quick dinner, so I threw this together from what I had in the fridge and pantry. Add any other pizza toppings you desire. I often add black olive slices or mushrooms. My son calls it pizza rice.
—Teri Rasey, Cadillac, MI

Takes: 25 min. • **Makes:** 6 servings

- 1 lb. bulk Italian sausage
- 1 can (14½ oz.) diced tomatoes with basil, oregano and garlic
- 1 can (15½ oz.) cannellini beans, rinsed and drained
- 1½ cups water
- 1½ cups uncooked instant rice
- ¼ cup grated Parmesan cheese
- ½ cup (2 oz.) sliced mini pepperoni
  Optional: Additional grated Parmesan cheese and chopped fresh basil

1. In a large skillet, cook the sausage over medium heat 5-7 minutes or until no longer pink, breaking into crumbles; drain. Return to skillet with next 4 ingredients. Bring to a boil; cover and remove from heat. Let stand for 5 minutes.
2. Fluff with a fork; stir in Parmesan cheese. Top with mini pepperoni and, if desired, additional Parmesan cheese and basil.
1¼ cups: 390 cal., 20g fat (6g sat. fat), 48mg chol., 906mg sod., 35g carb. (2g sugars, 4g fiber), 15g pro.

BEEF SUYA

My Nigerian brother-in-law introduced me to beef suya, a spicy street food that is popular in western Africa. The spice rub is made with ground peanuts and a blend of seasonings. After lots of experimenting, this is my version.
—Elena Iorga, Helena, MT

Prep: 30 min. + marinating • **Grill:** 15 min.
Makes: 8 servings

- 1 cup salted peanuts
- 1 Tbsp. paprika
- 2 tsp. onion powder
- 2 tsp. ground ginger
- 1 tsp. crushed red pepper flakes
- 1 tsp. garlic powder
- 1 beef tri-tip roast or beef top sirloin steak (2 lbs.), thinly sliced against the grain
- 2 Tbsp. canola oil
- 1 tsp. salt
- 1 medium onion, cut into wedges
- 1 large tomato, cut into wedges
  Fresh cilantro leaves

1. Place the peanuts in a food processor; process until finely chopped. Add paprika, onion powder, ginger, pepper flakes and garlic powder; pulse until combined.
2. Place beef in a large bowl or shallow dish. Drizzle with oil; sprinkle with salt. Toss to coat. Add the peanut mixture; turn to coat. Refrigerate, covered, for 2 hours. Drain beef, discarding marinade.
3. Thread beef slices onto metal or soaked wooden skewers. Grill beef, covered, over medium-high heat until the meat reaches desired doneness, 10-15 minutes, turning occasionally. Serve with onion, tomato and fresh cilantro.
3 oz. cooked beef with 1 wedge tomato and onion: 329 cal., 21g fat (5g sat. fat), 68mg chol., 405mg sod., 7g carb. (2g sugars, 3g fiber), 29g pro.

BEEF SUYA

TASTE OF HOME
TEST KITCHEN
RECIPE OF THE YEAR
★★★★★

EGG ROLL NOODLE BOWL

SALSA STEAK GARLIC TOASTS

These open-faced steak sandwiches play up the popular combo of steak and garlic bread. The salsa, sour cream and garnish elevate it into quick, satisfying meal. Feel free to substitute chopped green onions or chives for the cilantro if desired.
—Arlene Erlbach, Morton Grove, IL

- -

Takes: 25 min. • **Makes:** 4 servings

  4   **slices frozen garlic Texas toast**
  1   **Tbsp. olive oil**
  1   **beef top sirloin steak**
       (1 lb.), thinly sliced
1½ **cups salsa**
       Sour cream and chopped
       fresh cilantro

1. Prepare the garlic toast according to package directions.
2. Meanwhile, in a large skillet, heat oil over medium heat. Saute steak until no longer pink, 3-5 minutes; drain. Stir in salsa; cook and stir until heated through. Serve over toast. Top with sour cream and cilantro.
1 garlic toast with ¾ cup steak mixture: 375 cal., 16g fat (4g sat. fat), 52mg chol., 721mg sod., 27g carb. (5g sugars, 1g fiber), 29g pro.

EGG ROLL NOODLE BOWL

We love Asian egg rolls, but they can be challenging to make. Simplify everything with this deconstructed egg roll made on the stovetop and served in a bowl.
—Courtney Stultz, Weir, KS

- -

Takes: 30 min. • **Makes:** 4 servings

  1   **Tbsp. sesame oil**
 ½ **lb. ground pork**
  1   **Tbsp. soy sauce**
  1   **garlic clove, minced**
  1   **tsp. ground ginger**
 ½ **tsp. salt**
 ¼ **tsp. ground turmeric**
 ¼ **tsp. pepper**
  6   **cups shredded cabbage**
       (about 1 small head)
  2   **large carrots, shredded**
       (about 2 cups)
  4   **oz. rice noodles**
  3   **green onions, thinly sliced**
       Additional soy sauce, optional

1. In a large cast-iron or other heavy skillet, heat oil over medium-high heat; cook and crumble pork until browned, 4-6 minutes. Stir in soy sauce, garlic and seasonings. Add cabbage and carrots; cook until tender, stirring occasionally, 4-6 minutes longer.
2. Cook rice noodles according to package directions; drain and immediately add to pork mixture, tossing to combine. Sprinkle with green onions. If desired, serve with additional soy sauce.
1½ cups: 302 cal., 12g fat (4g sat. fat), 38mg chol., 652mg sod., 33g carb. (2g sugars, 4g fiber), 14g pro. **Diabetic exchanges:** 2 medium-fat meat, 2 vegetable, 1½ starch, ½ fat.

"I started making this during the COVID-19 quarantine. Now it's in my regular meal rotation. It's such an easy weeknight dinner—and it's healthy! I usually swap ground turkey for the pork, since I have that on hand more often."

—EMILY PARULSKI, SENIOR DIGITAL EDITOR

COUNTRY FRENCH PORK WITH PRUNES & APPLES

The classic flavors of herbes de Provence, apples and dried plums make this amazing slow-cooked pork taste like a hearty meal at a French country cafe. For a traditional pairing, serve the pork with braised lentils.
—Suzanne Banfield, Basking Ridge, NJ

Prep: 20 min. • **Cook:** 4 hours + standing
Makes: 10 servings

- 2 Tbsp. all-purpose flour
- 1 Tbsp. herbes de Provence
- 1½ tsp. salt
- ¾ tsp. pepper
- 1 boneless pork loin roast (3 to 4 lbs.)
- 2 Tbsp. olive oil
- 2 medium onions, halved and thinly sliced
- 1 cup apple cider or unsweetened apple juice
- 1 cup beef stock
- 2 bay leaves
- 2 large tart apples, peeled, cored and chopped
- 1 cup pitted dried plums (prunes)

1. Mix flour, herbes de Provence, salt and pepper; rub over pork. In a large skillet, heat oil over medium-high heat. Brown roast on all sides. Place roast in a 5- or 6-qt. slow cooker. Add onions, apple cider, beef stock and bay leaves.
2. Cook, covered, on low 3 hours. Add the apples and dried plums. Cook, covered, on low 1-1½ hours longer or until apples and pork are tender. Remove roast, onions, apples and plums to a serving platter, discarding bay leaves; tent with foil. Let stand 15 minutes before slicing.
4 oz. cooked pork with ¾ cup fruit mixture: 286 cal., 9g fat (3g sat. fat), 68mg chol., 449mg sod., 22g carb. (13g sugars, 2g fiber), 28g pro.

MEXICAN TURKEY MEAT LOAF

MEXICAN TURKEY MEAT LOAF

Here's a zesty, flavorful meat loaf you can really sink your teeth into! Pair this easy entree with black beans, rice, green salad with lime vinaigrette or any of your favorite Tex-Mex sides.
—Kristen Miller, Glendale, WI

Prep: 25 min. • **Cook:** 3 hours + standing
Makes: 1 loaf (6 servings)

- 2 slices white bread, torn into small pieces
- ⅓ cup 2% milk
- 1 lb. lean ground turkey
- ½ lb. fresh chorizo
- 1 medium sweet red pepper, finely chopped
- 1 small onion, finely chopped
- 1 jalapeno pepper, seeded and finely chopped
- 2 large eggs, lightly beaten
- 2 Tbsp. minced fresh cilantro
- 2 garlic cloves, minced
- 2 tsp. chili powder
- 1 tsp. salt
- 1 tsp. ground cumin
- ½ tsp. dried oregano
- ½ tsp. pepper
- ¼ tsp. cayenne pepper
- ⅔ cup salsa, divided
  Additional minced fresh cilantro
  Hot cooked Spanish rice

1. Combine bread and milk in a large bowl; let stand until liquid is absorbed. Add the next 14 ingredients and ⅓ cup salsa; mix lightly but thoroughly.
2. On an 18x7-in. piece of heavy-duty foil, shape the meat mixture into a 10x6-in. oval loaf. Lifting with foil, transfer to a 6-qt. oval slow cooker. Press ends of foil up sides of slow cooker.
3. Cook meat loaf, covered, on low until a thermometer reads 165°, 3-4 hours. Lifting with foil, drain fat into slow cooker before removing meat loaf to a platter; top with remaining salsa and sprinkle with cilantro. Let stand 10 minutes before slicing. Serve with rice.
1 slice: 335 cal., 20g fat (6g sat. fat), 149mg chol., 1109mg sod., 11g carb. (4g sugars, 1g fiber), 27g pro.

**DUTCH-OVEN
ENCHILADAS**

DUTCH-OVEN ENCHILADAS

Scoop up a bite of this delicious Dutch-oven enchiladas recipe. It's simple to put together and is easily customizable based on your family's tastes!
—*Taste of Home* Test Kitchen

Prep: 30 min. • **Cook:** 1 hour
Makes: 6 servings

3	**cups shredded cooked chicken**
1	**can (15 oz.) black beans, rinsed and drained**
1	**can (10½ oz.) condensed cream of chicken soup, undiluted**
1	**can (10 oz.) green enchilada sauce**
1	**can (4 oz.) chopped green chiles**
¼	**cup minced fresh cilantro**
1	**Tbsp. lime juice**
9	**corn tortillas (6 in.)**
3	**cups shredded Colby-Monterey Jack cheese**
	Optional: Minced fresh cilantro, salsa, sour cream and lime wedges

1. Preheat oven to 350°. In a large bowl, combine first 7 ingredients. Spread ¼ cup chicken mixture over bottom of Dutch oven. Top with 3 tortillas, overlapping and tearing them to fit, a third of the chicken mixture and a third of the cheese. Repeat layers twice.
2. Bake, covered, until a thermometer reads 165°, 50-60 minutes. If desired, serve with additional cilantro, salsa, sour cream and lime wedges.
1 serving: 541 cal., 27g fat (15g sat. fat), 116mg chol., 1202mg sod., 36g carb. (2g sugars, 6g fiber), 39g pro.

CORNISH PASTIES

CORNISH PASTIES

My great-aunt Gladys was from a mining town in England where pasties were very popular. I loved to watch her craft each pasty, as she made them in different sizes depending on who was eating. I serve them with a green salad to make a lovely meal.
—Verna Hainer, Pueblo, CO

Prep: 30 min. + chilling • **Bake:** 50 min.
Makes: 8 servings

- 3 cups all-purpose flour
- 1½ tsp. salt
- ¾ tsp. baking powder
- 1 cup shortening
- 8 to 10 Tbsp. ice water

FILLING

- 1 lb. beef top round steak, cut into ½-in. pieces
- 1½ cups finely chopped onion
- 1½ cups cubed peeled potatoes (½-in. cubes)
- 1½ cups chopped peeled turnips (½-in. cubes)
- 1 tsp. salt
- ¼ tsp. pepper
- 4 Tbsp. butter
- ½ cup evaporated milk, optional
  Ketchup

1. In a large bowl, mix flour, salt and baking powder; cut in shortening until crumbly. Gradually add water, tossing with a fork until dough forms a ball. Cover and refrigerate for 30 minutes.

2. Preheat oven to 375°. In another large bowl, combine the beef, onion, potatoes, turnips, salt and pepper. Divide the dough into 4 equal portions. On a lightly floured surface, roll 1 portion into a 9-in. circle. Mound 1½ cups filling on half of circle and dot with 1 Tbsp. butter. Moisten edges with water; fold the dough over filling and press edges with a fork to seal.

3. Place on a parchment-lined rimmed 15x10x1-in. baking pan. Repeat with remaining dough, filling and butter. Cut slits in tops of pasties. Bake 30 minutes. If desired, pour milk into slits. Bake until golden brown, 20-30 minutes longer. Serve with ketchup.

Freeze option: Freeze cooled pasties in a freezer container. To use, reheat pasties on a parchment-lined baking sheet in a preheated 375° oven until heated through.

½ pasty: 556 cal., 32g fat (10g sat. fat), 47mg chol., 864mg sod., 46g carb. (3g sugars, 3g fiber), 19g pro.

CASHEW CHICKEN SHEET-PAN SUPPER

Enjoy a chicken sheet-pan meal that is tender, flavorful and tangy. The veggies brown up nicely and the cashews add something extra.
—Jennifer Gilbert, Brighton, MI

Prep: 20 min. • **Bake:** 15 min.
Makes: 4 servings

- ½ cup reduced-sodium soy sauce
- 2 shallots, minced
- 2 Tbsp. brown sugar
- 2 Tbsp. chili sauce
- 1 Tbsp. cider vinegar
- 1 Tbsp. sesame oil
- 2 tsp. rice vinegar
- ½ tsp. ground ginger
- ¼ tsp. garlic powder
- ¼ tsp. pepper
- 1 lb. chicken tenderloins, cubed
- 1 large sweet yellow pepper, cut into strips
- 1 large sweet red pepper, cut into strips
- 4 cups fresh broccoli florets
- 1 cup fresh sugar snap peas
- 1 cup salted cashews

Preheat oven to 400°. Whisk the first 10 ingredients until combined. Place chicken, peppers, broccoli and peas in a foil-lined 15x10x1-in. baking pan. Drizzle with soy sauce mixture; toss to coat. Sprinkle with cashews. Bake until chicken is no longer pink and vegetables are crisp-tender, 15-20 minutes.

1 serving: 492 cal., 22g fat (4g sat. fat), 56mg chol., 1553mg sod., 38g carb. (17g sugars, 6g fiber), 39g pro.

EASY PAD THAI

Skip the take-out restaurant and give this pad thai recipe a try if you need an easy and quick meal.
—James Schend, Deputy Editor

Takes: 30 min. • **Makes:** 4 servings

- 4   oz. uncooked thick rice noodles
- ½   lb. pork tenderloin, cut into thin strips
- 2   tsp. canola oil
- 2   shallots, thinly sliced
- 2   garlic cloves, minced
- 1   large egg, lightly beaten
- 3   cups coleslaw mix
- 4   green onions, thinly sliced
- ⅓   cup rice vinegar
- ¼   cup sugar
- 3   Tbsp. reduced-sodium soy sauce
- 2   Tbsp. fish sauce or additional reduced-sodium soy sauce
- 1   Tbsp. chili garlic sauce
- 1   Tbsp. lime juice
- 2   Tbsp. chopped salted peanuts
     Chopped fresh cilantro leaves, lime wedges and fresh bean sprouts

1. Cook the noodles according to the package directions.
2. In a large nonstick skillet or wok, stir-fry the pork in oil over high heat until lightly browned; remove and set aside. Add shallot to pan and cook until tender, about 1 minute; add garlic and cook 30 seconds. Make a well in the center of the onion mixture; add egg. Stir-fry for 1-2 minutes or until the egg is completely set.
3. Add the coleslaw mix, green onions, vinegar, sugar, soy sauce, fish sauce, chili garlic sauce, lime juice and peanuts; heat through. Return pork to pan and heat through. Drain noodles; toss with pork mixture. Garnish with cilantro, additional peanuts, lime wedges and bean sprouts.
1¼ cups: 361 cal., 8g fat (2g sat. fat), 78mg chol., 1669mg sod., 53g carb. (23g sugars, 2g fiber), 19g pro.

GARLIC HERBED BEEF TENDERLOIN

You don't need much seasoning to add flavor to this tender beef roast.
—Ruth Andrewson, Leavenworth, WA

Prep: 5 min. • **Bake:** 40 min. + standing
Makes: 12 servings

- 1   beef tenderloin roast (3 lbs.)
- 2   tsp. olive oil
- 2   garlic cloves, minced
- 1½   tsp. dried basil
- 1½   tsp. dried rosemary, crushed
- 1   tsp. salt
- 1   tsp. pepper

1. Tie the tenderloin at 2-in. intervals with kitchen string. Combine oil and garlic; brush over meat. Combine the basil, rosemary, salt and pepper; sprinkle evenly over meat. Place on a rack in a shallow roasting pan.
2. Bake, uncovered, at 425° until tenderloin reaches desired doneness (for medium-rare, a thermometer should read 135°; medium, 140°; medium-well, 145°), 40-50 minutes. Let stand for 10 minutes before slicing.
3 oz. cooked beef: 198 cal., 10g fat (4g sat. fat), 78mg chol., 249mg sod., 1g carb. (0 sugars, 0 fiber), 25g pro. **Diabetic exchanges:** 3 lean meat.

EASY PAD THAI

TACO
BOWLS

CHICKEN PARMESAN SLIDER BAKE

Sliders are the perfect finger food for any get-together, and this flavorful chicken Parmesan version won't disappoint.
—Nick Iverson, Denver, CO

Prep: 20 min. • **Bake:** 25 min.
Makes: 1 dozen

24	oz. frozen breaded chicken tenders
1	pkg. (12 oz.) Hawaiian sweet rolls
1	pkg. (7½ oz.) sliced provolone and mozzarella cheese blend
1	jar (24 oz.) marinara sauce

TOPPING

½	cup butter, cubed
1	tsp. garlic powder
1	tsp. crushed red pepper flakes
¼	cup grated Parmesan cheese
2	Tbsp. minced fresh basil

1. Preheat oven to 375°. Prepare chicken tenders according to package directions. Meanwhile, without separating rolls, cut horizontally in half; arrange roll bottoms in a greased 13x9-in. baking dish. Place half of cheese slices over roll bottoms. Bake until cheese is melted, 3-5 minutes.

2. Layer rolls with half of sauce, chicken tenders, remaining sauce and remaining cheese slices. Replace top halves of rolls.

3. For topping, microwave butter, garlic powder and red pepper flakes, covered, on high, stirring occasionally, until butter is melted. Pour over rolls; sprinkle with Parmesan cheese. Bake, uncovered, until golden brown and heated through, 20-25 minutes. Sprinkle with basil before serving.

1 slider: 402 cal., 23g fat (11g sat. fat), 62mg chol., 780mg sod., 34g carb. (10g sugars, 4g fiber), 17g pro.

TACO BOWLS

We love this dish for the super simple prep. And it's so easy to customize with toppings.
—Hope Wasylenki, Gahanna, OH

Prep: 15 min. • **Cook:** 7 hours
Makes: 10 servings

1	boneless beef chuck roast (2½ lbs.), cut in half
¼	cup beef broth
1	Tbsp. canola oil
1	small onion, finely chopped
1	jalapeno pepper, seeded and finely chopped
1	garlic clove, minced
3	tsp. chili powder
1½	tsp. ground cumin
	Dash salt
2	cups canned crushed tomatoes in puree
1	cup salsa verde
5	cups hot cooked brown rice
1	can (15 oz.) black beans, rinsed, drained and warmed
1	cup pico de gallo

Optional: Reduced-fat sour cream, shredded cheddar cheese, sliced avocado, lime wedges and warmed corn tortillas

1. Place beef and broth in a 5-qt. slow cooker. Cook, covered, on low 6-8 hours or until meat is tender.

2. Remove beef; discard juices. Return beef to slow cooker; shred with 2 forks.

3. In a large skillet, heat oil over medium heat; saute chopped onion and jalapeno until softened, 3-4 minutes. Add garlic and seasonings; cook and stir 1 minute. Stir in tomatoes and salsa; bring to a boil. Add to beef, stirring to combine. Cook, covered, on high for 1 hour or until flavors are blended.

4. For each serving, place ½ cup rice in a soup bowl. Top with beef mixture, beans and pico de gallo. Serve with optional ingredients as desired.

Freeze option: Freeze cooled meat mixture in freezer containers. To use, partially thaw in refrigerator overnight. Heat through in a saucepan, stirring occasionally.

1 serving: 389 cal., 13g fat (5g sat. fat), 74mg chol., 550mg sod., 38g carb. (4g sugars, 5g fiber), 28g pro. **Diabetic exchanges:** 3 lean meat, 2½ starch, ½ fat.

SMOKY MACARONI & CHEESE
PAGE 188

Side Dishes

Discover the perfect addition to your next menu. From speedy weeknight favorites to picnic and holiday crowd-pleasers, these side dishes rank among our most loved and most requested when we cook for our own families.

BACON MAC & CHEESE
CORNBREAD SKILLET

BACON MAC & CHEESE CORNBREAD SKILLET

My cast-iron skillet is a workhorse in my kitchen. I just love it for cooking and baking. And this cast-iron mac and cheese recipe can be served either as a main dish or as a smaller-portion side.
—Lisa Keys, Kennet Square, PA

- -

Prep: 35 min. • **Bake:** 30 min. + standing
Makes: 8 servings

- 1¾ cups uncooked elbow macaroni
- 8 bacon strips, chopped
- 1 cup shredded smoked Gouda or cheddar cheese
- 1 cup shredded pepper jack cheese
- 4 oz. cream cheese, cubed
- 6 large eggs, divided use
- 3 cups 2% milk, divided
- 4 green onions, chopped
- 1 tsp. kosher salt, divided
- ½ tsp. pepper, divided
- 1 pkg. (8½ oz.) cornbread/muffin mix
- ½ tsp. smoked paprika
  Additional green onions

1. Preheat oven to 400°. Cook macaroni according to package directions. Meanwhile, in a 12-in. cast-iron or other ovenproof skillet, cook chopped bacon over medium heat until crisp, stirring occasionally. Remove with a slotted spoon; drain on paper towels. Discard drippings, reserving 1 Tbsp. in pan.
2. Drain the macaroni; add macaroni to drippings. Stir in shredded cheeses and cream cheese; cook and stir over medium heat until cheese is melted, 2-3 minutes. Whisk 2 eggs, 1 cup milk, green onions, ½ tsp. kosher salt and ¼ tsp. pepper; pour the mixture into skillet. Cook and stir until slightly thickened, 3-4 minutes. Remove skillet from the heat.
3. Reserve ¼ cup bacon for topping; sprinkle the remaining bacon over macaroni. Place cornbread mix, paprika, remaining 4 eggs, 2 cups milk, ½ tsp. kosher salt and ¼ tsp. pepper in a blender; cover and process until smooth. Pour over bacon.

4. Bake until cornbread is puffed and golden brown, 30-35 minutes. Let stand 10 minutes before serving. Sprinkle with reserved ¼ cup bacon and additional green onions.
1 cup: 497 cal., 27g fat (13g sat. fat), 203mg chol., 978mg sod., 40g carb. (12g sugars, 3g fiber), 23g pro.

PERFECT SUSHI RICE

Sushi rice can be used for more than just sushi. Use it to create a healthy rice bowl, tuck it into a lettuce wrap topped with grilled meat or try it as a base for your favorite stir-fry.
—*Taste of Home* Test Kitchen

- -

Prep: 40 min. + standing • **Cook:** 15 min.
Makes: 8 servings

- 2 cups sushi rice
- ¼ cup rice vinegar
- 2 Tbsp. sugar
- ½ tsp. salt

PERFECT SUSHI RICE

1. In large bowl, wash rice in several changes of cold water until water is clear. Transfer to a large saucepan; add 2 cups water. Let stand for 30 minutes.
2. Cover saucepan and bring to boil over high heat. Reduce heat to low; cook until water is absorbed and rice is tender, 15-20 minutes. Remove from the heat. Let stand, covered, for 10 minutes.
3. Meanwhile, in small bowl, combine the vinegar, sugar and salt, stirring until sugar is dissolved.
4. Transfer rice to a shallow bowl; sprinkle with vinegar mixture. Set aside remaining vinegar mixture for assembly. With a wooden paddle or spoon, stir rice with a slicing motion until cooled. Cover with a damp cloth to keep moist. (The rice mixture may be made up to 6 hours ahead and stored at room temperature, covered, with a damp towel. Do not refrigerate.)
½ cup: 201 cal., 0 fat (0 sat. fat), 0 chol., 268mg sod., 45g carb. (6g sugars, 1g fiber), 3g pro.

LOADED MASHED POTATO BITES

Put leftover mashed potatoes to good use! Turn them into yummy hot bites loaded with bacon, cheese and onions.
—Becky Hardin, St. Peters, MO

- -

Prep: 15 min. + chilling • **Cook:** 10 min.
Makes: 1½ dozen

- 3 cups mashed potatoes
- 1½ cups shredded sharp cheddar cheese
- ¾ cup crumbled cooked bacon
- ½ cup chopped green onions
- 2 oz. Colby-Monterey Jack cheese, cut into eighteen ½-in. cubes
- ½ cup panko bread crumbs
- ½ cup grated Parmesan cheese
- ½ tsp. salt
- ½ tsp. pepper
- 1 large egg, beaten
  Oil for deep-fat frying

1. In a large bowl, combine the potatoes, shredded cheese, bacon and green onions. Divide into eighteen ¼-cup portions. Shape each portion around a cheese cube to cover completely, forming a ball. Refrigerate, covered, at least 30 minutes.
2. In a shallow bowl, mix bread crumbs, Parmesan cheese, salt and pepper. Place egg in a separate shallow bowl. Dip potato balls in egg, then in crumb mixture, patting to help coating adhere.
3. In an electric skillet or a deep-fat fryer, heat oil to 375°. Fry potato balls, a few at a time, until golden brown, for 2 minutes. Drain on paper towels.
1 piece: 227 cal., 19g fat (5g sat. fat), 30mg chol., 420mg sod., 8g carb. (1g sugars, 1g fiber), 7g pro.

MOIST CORN SPOON BREAD

Enjoy this easy take on a southern specialty by taking advantage of the convenience of your slow cooker. It's an excellent dish for Thanksgiving, Easter or any special feast.
—*Taste of Home* Test Kitchen

- -

Prep: 20 min. • **Cook:** 4 hours
Makes: 8 servings

- 1 pkg. (8 oz.) cream cheese, softened
- 2 Tbsp. sugar
- 2 large eggs, beaten
- 1 cup 2% milk
- 2 Tbsp. butter, melted
- ½ tsp. salt
- ¼ tsp. cayenne pepper
- ⅛ tsp. pepper
- 2 cups frozen corn
- 1 can (14¾ oz.) cream-style corn
- 1 cup yellow cornmeal
- 1 cup shredded Monterey Jack cheese
- 3 green onions, thinly sliced
  Optional: Coarsely ground pepper and thinly sliced green onions

1. In a large bowl, beat softened cream cheese and sugar until smooth. Gradually beat in eggs. Beat in the milk, butter, salt, cayenne and pepper until blended. Stir in remaining ingredients.
2. Pour into a greased 3-qt. slow cooker. Cover and cook on low for 4-5 hours, until a toothpick inserted in the center comes out clean. If desired, top with additional pepper and green onions.
1 serving: 350 cal., 18g fat (11g sat. fat), 54mg chol., 525mg sod., 38g carb. (8g sugars, 3g fiber), 12g pro.

MOIST CORN SPOON BREAD

**HEIRLOOM TOMATO
GALETTE WITH PECORINO**

HEIRLOOM TOMATO GALETTE WITH PECORINO

I found beautiful heirloom tomatoes and had to show them off. In this easy galette, the tomatoes are tangy and the crust is beyond buttery.
—Jessica Chang, Playa Vista, CA

- -

Prep: 10 min. + chilling
Bake: 25 min. + cooling • **Makes:** 6 servings

- 1 cup all-purpose flour
- 1 tsp. baking powder
- ¾ tsp. kosher salt, divided
- ½ cup cold unsalted butter, cubed
- ½ cup sour cream
- 2 cups cherry tomatoes, halved
- 3 oz. pecorino Romano cheese, thinly sliced

1. Whisk flour, baking powder and ½ tsp. salt; cut in butter until mixture resembles coarse crumbs. Stir in the sour cream until dough forms a ball. Shape into a disk; cover and refrigerate until firm enough to roll, about 2 hours.
2. Meanwhile, place tomatoes in a colander; toss with remaining salt. Let tomatoes stand 15 minutes.

3. Preheat oven to 425°. On a floured sheet of parchment, roll dough into a 12-in. circle. Transfer to a baking sheet.
4. Place cheese slices over crust to within 2 in. of edge; arrange tomatoes over cheese. Fold crust edges over filling, pleating as you go and leaving center uncovered. Bake until crust is golden brown and cheese is bubbly, about 25 minutes. Cool for 10 minutes before slicing.
1 piece: 317 cal., 23g fat (15g sat. fat), 68mg chol., 559mg sod., 19g carb. (2g sugars, 1g fiber), 9g pro.

"I love serving this to guests. The last time I made it, I didn't have pecorino Romano, so I used shredded Parmesan mixed with a little feta, and put a smear of sour cream over the crust before adding the toppings."
—HAZEL WHEATON, EDITOR

SPICED SWEET POTATO FRIES

This spicy homemade seasoning blend shakes up everyone's favorite finger food.
—*Taste of Home* Test Kitchen

- -

Takes: 25 min. • **Makes:** 6 servings

- 1 pkg. (19 oz.) frozen french-fried sweet potatoes
- ½ tsp. garlic powder
- ½ tsp. curry powder
- ½ tsp. pepper
- ¼ tsp. chili powder
- ⅛ tsp. ground cinnamon
- ⅛ tsp. salt

Bake fries according to package directions. Meanwhile, in a small bowl, combine the remaining ingredients. Sprinkle over fries; toss to coat.
1 serving: 129 cal., 3g fat (1g sat. fat), 0 chol., 241mg sod., 24g carb. (10g sugars, 2g fiber), 0 pro.

TEST KITCHEN TIP
You can also make these fries using 2-3 large fresh sweet potatoes, peeled and cut into ¼-inch julienned strips (about 2¼ pounds).

CRISPY FRIED ONION RINGS

SMOKY MACARONI & CHEESE

I found this recipe years ago in a magazine, and I kept adjusting the ingredients until I found the perfect combination.
—Stacey Dull, Gettysburg, OH

- -

Prep: 40 min. • **Grill:** 20 min. + standing
Makes: 2 casseroles (8 servings each)

- 6 cups small pasta shells
- 12 oz. Velveeta, cut into small cubes
- 2 cups shredded smoked cheddar cheese, divided
- 1 cup shredded cheddar cheese
- 1 cup 2% milk
- 4 large eggs, lightly beaten
- ¾ cup heavy whipping cream
- ⅔ cup half-and-half cream
- ½ cup shredded provolone cheese
- ½ cup shredded Colby-Monterey Jack cheese
- ½ cup shredded pepper jack cheese
- 1 tsp. salt
- ½ tsp. pepper
- ½ tsp. smoked paprika
- ½ tsp. liquid smoke, optional
  Dash cayenne pepper, optional
- 8 bacon strips, cooked and crumbled, optional

1. Preheat grill or smoker to 350°. Cook the pasta according to package directions for al dente. Drain and transfer to a large bowl. Stir in Velveeta, 1 cup smoked cheddar, cheddar cheese, milk, eggs, heavy cream, half-and-half, provolone, Colby-Monterey Jack, pepper jack, salt, pepper, paprika, and, if desired, liquid smoke and cayenne pepper.
2. Transfer to 2 greased 13x9-in. baking pans; sprinkle with remaining 1 cup smoked cheddar cheese. Place on grill or smoker rack. Grill or smoke, covered, until a thermometer reads at least 160°, 20-25 minutes, rotating pans partway through cooking. Do not overcook. Let stand for 10 minutes before serving; if desired, sprinkle with bacon.
1 cup: 403 cal., 23g fat (13g sat. fat), 117mg chol., 670mg sod., 30g carb. (4g sugars, 1g fiber), 18g pro.

CRISPY FRIED ONION RINGS

Enjoy these crispy rings on their own with dip or add them as a fun topper to burgers. They also give salads a little extra crunch.
—*Taste of Home* Test Kitchen

- -

Takes: 25 min. • **Makes:** 12 servings

- ½ cup all-purpose flour
- ½ cup water
- 1 large egg, lightly beaten
- 1 tsp. seasoned salt
- ½ tsp. baking powder
- 1 large onion, very thinly sliced
  Oil for deep-fat frying

In a shallow bowl, whisk first 5 ingredients. Separate onion slices into rings. Dip rings into batter. In a deep-fat fryer, heat 1 in. oil to 375°. In batches, fry onion rings until golden brown, 1-1½ minutes on each side. Drain on paper towels. Serve immediately.
½ cup: 71 cal., 5g fat (0 sat. fat), 16mg chol., 153mg sod., 5g carb. (1g sugars, 0 fiber), 1g pro.

Baked Onion Rings: Preheat oven to 425°. Beat egg in a shallow bowl. In another shallow bowl, mix ⅔ cup dry bread crumbs, ½ tsp. seasoned salt and ¼ tsp. pepper. Dip onion rings into egg, then roll in crumb mixture. Place on a baking sheet coated with cooking spray. Bake 15-18 minutes or until golden brown, turning once.

Red Onion Rings: Substitute a red onion for the onion. With the flour mixture, whisk in ¼ tsp. cayenne.

SMOKY MACARONI
& CHEESE

**BANANA-ORANGE
SWEET POTATO BAKE**

BANANA-ORANGE
SWEET POTATO BAKE

Welcome fall with this simple side dish. It's a pleasant change of pace from the traditional casserole with marshmallows, and it's quite popular at potlucks.
—Joan Hallford, North Richland Hills, TX

- -

Prep: 50 min. • **Bake:** 35 min.
Makes: 10 servings

5	medium sweet potatoes (about 3 lbs.), peeled and cubed
⅔	cup packed brown sugar
3	Tbsp. butter
¼	tsp. salt
¼	tsp. ground cloves
⅛	tsp. pepper
2	tsp. grated orange zest
⅓	cup orange juice
¼	cup orange liqueur, optional
3	medium ripe bananas, mashed
2	large eggs, lightly beaten

TOPPING

½	cup granola cereal
½	cup chopped pecans, toasted
¼	cup sweetened shredded coconut, toasted
2	Tbsp. brown sugar
¼	cup butter, melted

1. Preheat oven to 350°. Place the sweet potatoes in a large Dutch oven; add water to cover. Bring to a boil. Reduce heat; cook, covered, just until tender, 12-15 minutes. Drain; cool slightly. Return to pan; mash with brown sugar, butter, salt, cloves and pepper until smooth. Stir in orange zest, orange juice and, if desired, liqueur. Add bananas and eggs; mix well. Transfer to a greased 2-qt. baking dish.

2. For topping, mix the granola cereal, pecans, coconut and brown sugar; sprinkle over sweet potatoes. Drizzle with melted butter. Bake, uncovered, until heated through, 35-45 minutes.

¾ cup: 355 cal., 15g fat (7g sat. fat), 59mg chol., 160mg sod., 54g carb. (33g sugars, 5g fiber), 5g pro.

VEGETABLE BARLEY SAUTE

Here's a wonderful side dish you can easily adjust to suit your tastes. Try it with broccoli instead of green beans or sweet potato ribbons instead of carrots.
—*Taste of Home* Test Kitchen

Takes: 30 min. • **Makes:** 4 servings

- ½ **cup quick-cooking barley**
- ⅓ **cup water**
- 3 **Tbsp. reduced-sodium soy sauce**
- 2 **tsp. cornstarch**
- 1 **garlic clove, minced**
- 1 **Tbsp. canola oil**
- 2 **carrots, thinly sliced**
- 1 **cup cut fresh green beans (2-in. pieces)**
- 2 **green onions, sliced**
- ½ **cup unsalted cashews, optional**

1. Prepare barley according to package directions. In a small bowl, combine the water, soy sauce and cornstarch until smooth; set aside.
2. In a large skillet or wok, saute garlic in oil for 15 seconds. Add carrots and beans; stir-fry for 2 minutes. Add onions; stir-fry 1 minute longer. Stir soy sauce mixture; stir into skillet. Bring to a boil; cook and stir until thickened, about 1 minute. Add barley; heat through. If desired, stir in cashews.
⅔ cup: 148 cal., 4g fat (1g sat. fat), 0 chol., 458mg sod., 24g carb. (3g sugars, 6g fiber), 5g pro. **Diabetic exchanges:** 1½ starch, 1 fat.

AIR-FRYER CANDIED ACORN SQUASH SLICES

This acorn squash recipe was passed down to me from my grandma, who always served it at Thanksgiving. Now I make it in my air fryer whenever I'm feeling nostalgic.
—Rita Addicks, Weimar, TX

Prep: 15 min. • **Cook:** 15 min./batch
Makes: 6 servings

- 2 **medium acorn squash**
- ⅔ **cup packed brown sugar**
- ½ **cup butter, softened**

1. Preheat air fryer to 350°. Cut squash in half lengthwise; remove and discard seeds. Cut each half crosswise into ½-in. slices; discard ends. In batches, arrange squash in a single layer on greased tray in air-fryer basket. Cook until squash is just tender, about 5 minutes per side.
2. Combine sugar and butter; spread over squash. Cook 3 minutes longer.
1 serving: 320 cal., 16g fat (10g sat. fat), 41mg chol., 135mg sod., 48g carb. (29g sugars, 3g fiber), 2g pro.

TEST KITCHEN TIP
If you don't have an air fryer, you can make this recipe in an oven.

VEGETABLE BARLEY SAUTE

MASHED CAULIFLOWER

This side dish is lower in carbs than mashed potatoes but just as flavorful and satisfying. It makes an enticing addition to a special menu. Add chopped green onions for a festive garnish.
—Tina Martini, Sparks, NV

Takes: 25 min. • **Makes:** 2½ cups

- 1 medium head cauliflower, broken into florets
- ½ cup shredded Swiss cheese
- 1 Tbsp. butter
- ¾ tsp. salt
- ¼ tsp. pepper
- ⅛ tsp. garlic powder
- 2 to 3 Tbsp. 2% milk

1. In a large saucepan, bring 1 in. water to a boil. Add cauliflower; cook, covered, until very tender, 8-12 minutes. Drain.

2. Mash cauliflower, adding Swiss cheese, butter, seasonings and enough milk to reach desired consistency.

¾ cup: 160 cal., 10g fat (6g sat. fat), 28mg chol., 718mg sod., 11g carb. (4g sugars, 4g fiber), 9g pro.

"I'm digging the mashed cauliflower trend. This is the simplest method I've come across. Being able to swap carb-heavy mashed potatoes for something lighter is a huge win."

—EMILY PARULSKI, SENIOR DIGITAL EDITOR

GOLDEN BEET CURRY RISOTTO WITH CRISPY BEET GREENS

GOLDEN BEET CURRY RISOTTO WITH CRISPY BEET GREENS

I was delighted to find golden beets at the farmers market and knew they'd be perfect in this risotto.
—Merry Graham, Newhall, CA

Prep: 30 min. • **Cook:** 50 min.
Makes: 6 servings

- 3 medium fresh golden beets and beet greens
- 3 Tbsp. melted coconut oil, divided
- ¾ tsp. sea salt, divided
- 5 cups reduced-sodium chicken broth
- 1 cup chopped leeks (white portion only)
- 1 tsp. curry powder
- 1 tsp. garlic salt
- 1 cup medium pearl barley
- ½ cup white wine or unsweetened apple juice
- 1 cup grated Manchego cheese
- 3 Tbsp. lemon juice (Meyer lemons preferred)
- 4 tsp. grated lemon zest, divided
- ¼ tsp. coarsely ground pepper
- ¼ cup chopped fresh parsley Lemon slices

1. Preheat oven to 350°. Wash and trim the beet greens, removing stems; dry with paper towels. Place the greens in a single layer on parchment-lined baking sheets. Brush with 1 Tbsp. coconut oil; sprinkle with ¼ tsp. sea salt. Bake until dry and crisp, 15-18 minutes. Set aside.

2. Meanwhile, peel and dice beets. In a large saucepan, bring chicken broth to a boil. Add beets. Reduce heat; simmer, covered, until beets are tender, 15-18 minutes. Remove beets with a slotted spoon. Keep broth hot.

3. In another large saucepan, heat remaining coconut oil over medium heat. Add the leeks; cook and stir 2-3 minutes. Add curry powder, garlic salt and remaining sea salt; cook, stirring, until the leeks are tender, about 2-3 minutes. Increase heat to medium-high. Add pearl barley; stir constantly until lightly toasted, 2-3 minutes. Add wine; stir until liquid has evaporated.

4. Add enough broth, about 1 cup, to cover barley. Reduce heat to medium; cook and stir until the broth is absorbed. Add remaining broth, ½ cup at a time, cooking and stirring until broth is absorbed after each addition. Stir in beets with last addition of broth. Cook until barley is tender but firm to the bite and risotto is creamy, 25-30 minutes.

5. Remove from heat. Stir in cheese, lemon juice, 2½ tsp. grated lemon zest and pepper. Transfer to a serving dish. Sprinkle with fresh parsley and remaining lemon zest. Serve with crispy beet greens and lemon slices.

⅔ cup: 314 cal., 14g fat (11g sat. fat), 19mg chol., 1238mg sod., 37g carb. (7g sugars, 8g fiber), 12g pro.

MUSHROOM MARSALA WITH BARLEY

This tasty recipe is a vegetarian mashup of chicken Marsala and mushroom barley soup. It's great as a main entree, but can also be served, with or without the barley, as a side dish.

—Arlene Erlbach, Morton Grove, IL

- -

Prep: 20 min. • **Cook:** 4¼ hours
Makes: 6 servings

- 1½ lbs. baby portobello mushrooms, cut into ¾-in. chunks
- 1 cup thinly sliced shallots
- 3 Tbsp. olive oil
- ½ tsp. minced fresh thyme
- ¾ cup Marsala wine, divided
- 3 Tbsp. reduced-fat sour cream
- 2 Tbsp. all-purpose flour
- 1½ tsp. grated lemon zest
- ¼ tsp. salt
- ¼ cup crumbled goat cheese
- ¼ cup minced fresh parsley
- 2½ cups cooked barley

1. In a 4- or 5-qt. slow cooker, combine mushrooms, shallots, olive oil and thyme. Add ¼ cup Marsala wine. Cook, covered, on low for about 4 hours, until vegetables are tender.

2. Stir in sour cream, flour, lemon zest, salt and remaining Marsala. Cook, covered, on low 15 minutes longer. Sprinkle with goat cheese and minced parsley. Serve with hot cooked barley.

¾ cup: 235 cal., 9g fat (2g sat. fat), 7mg chol., 139mg sod., 31g carb. (6g sugars, 5g fiber), 7g pro. **Diabetic exchanges:** 2 starch, 2 fat, 1 vegetable.

MUSHROOM MARSALA WITH BARLEY

BROWN RICE & VEGETABLES

This nutritious rice dish, full of big chunks of butternut squash and sweet potatoes, is a standout combination of sweet and savory flavors. It's a winner every fall.

—*Taste of Home* Test Kitchen

- -

Prep: 20 min. • **Cook:** 5 hours
Makes: 12 servings

- 1 cup uncooked brown rice
- 1 medium butternut squash (about 3 lbs.), cubed
- 2 medium apples, coarsely chopped
- 1 medium sweet potato, peeled and cubed
- 1 medium onion, chopped
- 1 tsp. salt
- ½ tsp. pepper
- 1 can (14½ oz.) reduced-sodium chicken broth
- ½ cup raisins
- 1 Tbsp. minced fresh tarragon or 1 tsp. dried tarragon

1. Place rice in a greased 4- or 5-qt. slow cooker. In a large bowl, combine the squash, apples, sweet potato, onion, salt and pepper; add to slow cooker. Pour chicken broth over the vegetables.

2. Cover and cook on low 5-6 hours, until vegetables are tender. Stir in the raisins and tarragon.

¾ cup: 148 cal., 1g fat (0 sat. fat), 0 chol., 303mg sod., 35g carb. (11g sugars, 5g fiber), 3g pro. **Diabetic exchanges:** 2 starch.

BROWN RICE WITH ALMONDS & CRANBERRIES

I'm always looking to switch things up during the holiday season. This rice salad is just the ticket, as it's on the lighter side and uses ingredients I always have on hand.
—Joan Hallford, North Richland Hills, TX

- -

Prep: 35 min. • **Bake:** 1¼ hours
Makes: 10 servings

- 3 cans (14½ oz. each) beef broth
- ¼ cup butter, cubed
- 1 large onion, chopped
- 1 cup uncooked long grain brown rice
- ½ cup bulgur
- ½ cup slivered almonds
- ½ cup dried cranberries
- ¾ cup minced fresh parsley, divided
- ¼ cup chopped green onions
- ¼ tsp. salt
- ¼ tsp. pepper

1. Preheat oven to 375°. In a large saucepan, bring broth to a simmer; reduce heat to low and keep hot. In a large skillet, heat butter over medium heat. Add onion; cook and stir until tender, 3-4 minutes. Add rice, bulgur and slivered almonds; cook and stir until the rice is lightly browned and has a nutty aroma, 2-3 minutes.
2. Transfer to a greased 13x9-in. baking dish. Stir in the dried cranberries, ½ cup parsley, green onions, salt and pepper. Stir in hot beef broth. Bake, covered, for 45 minutes. Uncover and continue to cook until liquid is absorbed and rice is tender, 30-35 minutes longer. Remove from oven and fluff with a fork. Cover; let stand 5-10 minutes. Sprinkle with remaining parsley before serving.
¾ cup: 207 cal., 8g fat (3g sat. fat), 12mg chol., 658mg sod., 29g carb. (7g sugars, 4g fiber), 5g pro. **Diabetic exchanges:** 2 starch, 1½ fat.

CARROT RAISIN COUSCOUS

CARROT RAISIN COUSCOUS

Golden raisins add a slightly sweet flavor to this unique side dish featuring couscous and julienned carrots. The recipe will brighten any table.
—Jordan Sucher, Brooklyn, NY

- -

Prep: 15 min. • **Cook:** 20 min.
Makes: 10 servings

- ⅓ cup port wine or chicken broth
- ⅓ cup golden raisins
- 1 medium onion, chopped
- 3 Tbsp. olive oil, divided
- 1 pkg. (10 oz.) couscous
- 2 cups chicken broth
- ¼ tsp. salt, divided
- ¼ tsp. pepper, divided
- 4 medium carrots, julienned
- 1 Tbsp. sugar
- 1 tsp. molasses

1. In a small saucepan, heat wine until hot. In a small bowl, soak raisins in wine for 5 minutes. Drain raisins, reserving wine.
2. In a large saucepan, saute onion in 1 Tbsp. oil until tender. Stir in couscous. Cook and stir until lightly browned. Stir in the broth, raisins and half the salt and pepper. Bring to a boil. Cover and remove from the heat. Let stand for 5 minutes; fluff with a fork.
3. In a small skillet, saute the carrots in remaining oil until crisp-tender. Combine sugar, molasses, reserved wine and the remaining salt and pepper. Stir into carrots; heat through.
4. In a large bowl, combine the couscous mixture and carrots; toss to combine.
¾ cup: 188 cal., 5g fat (1g sat. fat), 1mg chol., 277mg sod., 32g carb. (8g sugars, 2g fiber), 5g pro. **Diabetic exchanges:** 1½ starch, 1 vegetable, 1 fat.

POTATO & CHORIZO CASSEROLE

I love the smoky flavor that chorizo gives this dish, but I've also made it with Italian sausage and substituted an Italian cheese blend for the Mexican cheese. Or you can use cream of mushroom soup and fresh mushrooms for a vegetarian option.
—Ana Beteta, Aberdeen, MD

- -

Prep: 25 min. • **Bake:** 40 min.
Makes: 12 servings

- 8 oz. fresh chorizo or bulk spicy pork sausage
- 1 pkg. (32 oz.) frozen cubed hash brown potatoes, thawed
- 1 can (10½ oz.) condensed cream of chicken soup, undiluted
- 2 cups shredded Mexican cheese blend
- 1 pkg. (8 oz.) cream cheese, cubed
- 1 medium onion, chopped
- 1 small sweet red pepper, chopped
- 1 small green pepper, chopped
- ½ tsp. crushed red pepper flakes
- ¾ cup panko bread crumbs
  Chopped fresh parsley and cilantro

1. Preheat oven to 375°. In a small skillet, cook the chorizo over medium heat until cooked through, breaking into crumbles, 5-7 minutes; drain. Transfer to a large bowl. Stir in the hash browns, soup, cheeses, onion, peppers and pepper flakes. Transfer to a greased 13x9-in. baking dish. Sprinkle with panko.
2. Bake, uncovered, until golden brown and bubbly, 40-45 minutes. Sprinkle with parsley and cilantro before serving.
¾ cup: 316 cal., 20g fat (9g sat. fat), 54mg chol., 611mg sod., 22g carb. (3g sugars, 2g fiber), 12g pro.

BALSAMIC BRUSSELS SPROUTS

These Brussels sprouts couldn't be easier to make—and you need only a few ingredients!
—Kallee Krong-McCreery, Escondido, CA

- -

Takes: 15 min. • **Makes:** 4 servings

- 3 to 4 Tbsp. extra virgin olive oil
- 1 pkg. (16 oz.) frozen Brussels sprouts, thawed
- 2 Tbsp. balsamic vinegar
- 2 Tbsp. torn fresh basil leaves
- ½ to 1 tsp. flaky sea salt
- ½ tsp. coarsely ground pepper

In a large skillet, heat oil over medium-high heat. Add Brussels sprouts to skillet and cook until heated through, 5-7 minutes. Transfer to a serving bowl. Drizzle with the vinegar; sprinkle with basil, salt and pepper.
⅔ cup: 145 cal., 11g fat (2g sat. fat), 0 chol., 252mg sod., 11g carb. (2g sugars, 4g fiber), 4g pro. **Diabetic exchanges:** 2 fat, 1 vegetable.

BALSAMIC BRUSSELS SPROUTS

SHIITAKE & BUTTERNUT RISOTTO

SPRING ONION PIMIENTO CHEESE GRITS

Grits were a breakfast staple when I was growing up. Even today, we still have them about three times a week. The trick with grits is the more you whisk, the creamier they'll be.
—Melissa Pelkey Hass, Waleska, GA

- -

Prep: 15 min. • **Cook:** 20 min.
Makes: 16 servings

- 2 cups uncooked stone-ground yellow grits
- 1 pkg. (8 oz.) cream cheese, softened
- ½ cup mayonnaise
- 3 cups shredded Monterey Jack cheese
- 1 jar (4 oz.) diced pimientos, drained
- 3 green onions, diced
- 1 tsp. sugar
  Dash cayenne pepper
- ¼ cup butter, softened
  Salt and pepper to taste

1. Prepare grits according to the package directions. Keep warm.
2. Meanwhile, using a mixer, beat cream cheese. Add mayonnaise; continue beating until creamy. Add next 5 ingredients, mixing until well blended.
3. Stir butter and pimiento cheese mixture into the warm grits; season to taste. Mix well.
¾ cup: 281 cal., 20g fat (10g sat. fat), 41mg chol., 231mg sod., 19g carb. (1g sugars, 1g fiber), 8g pro.

SHIITAKE & BUTTERNUT RISOTTO

I like to think of this recipe as a labor of love. The risotto takes a bit of extra attention, but once you take your first bite you'll know it was worth the effort.
—Stephanie Campbell, Elk Grove, CA

- -

Prep: 25 min. • **Cook:** 25 min.
Makes: 2 servings

- 1 cup cubed peeled butternut squash
- 2 tsp. olive oil, divided
  Dash salt
- 1¼ cups reduced-sodium chicken broth
- ⅔ cup sliced fresh shiitake mushrooms
- 2 Tbsp. chopped onion
- 1 small garlic clove, minced
- ⅓ cup uncooked arborio rice
  Dash pepper
- ¼ cup white wine or ¼ cup additional reduced-sodium chicken broth
- ¼ cup grated Parmesan cheese
- 1 tsp. minced fresh sage

1. Place squash in a greased 9-in. square baking pan. Add 1 tsp. olive oil and salt; toss to coat.
2. Bake, uncovered, at 350° until tender, 25-30 minutes, stirring occasionally.
3. Meanwhile, in a small saucepan, heat chicken broth and keep warm. In a small skillet, saute the mushrooms, onion and garlic in remaining 1 tsp. oil until tender, 3-4 minutes. Add rice and pepper; cook and stir for 2-3 minutes. Reduce the heat; stir in wine. Cook and stir until all the liquid is absorbed.
4. Add the heated broth, ¼ cup at a time, stirring constantly. Allow the liquid to absorb between additions. Cook just until risotto is creamy and the rice is almost tender, about 20 minutes. Stir in cheese until melted. Add squash and sage. Serve immediately.
¾ cup: 282 cal., 9g fat (3g sat. fat), 12mg chol., 567mg sod., 40g carb. (3g sugars, 3g fiber), 10g pro.

SLOW-COOKER POLENTA

GRILLED MEDITERRANEAN ZUCCHINI SALAD

Looking for the perfect side dish? Try my grilled zucchini salad with Mediterranean dressing. I also add summer squash, when it's in season, for a variation, or crumbled goat cheese when I want creaminess.
—Rashanda Cobbins, Food Editor

- -

Takes: 20 min. • **Makes:** 4 servings

    3   medium zucchini, thinly sliced
    ¼   cup olive oil, divided
    ¼   tsp. salt
    ¼   tsp. pepper
    ¼   cup chopped red onion
    3   Tbsp. minced fresh mint
    2   Tbsp. minced fresh parsley
    1   medium lemon, juiced and zested
    ⅓   cup crumbled feta cheese
    3   Tbsp. pine nuts, toasted

1. In a large bowl, combine zucchini and 2 Tbsp. olive oil. Add salt and pepper; toss to coat. Transfer to a grill wok or open grill basket; place on grill rack. Grill, covered, over medium-high heat until zucchini is crisp-tender, 5-10 minutes, turning occasionally.
2. Transfer zucchini to a serving bowl; sprinkle with remaining 2 Tbsp. olive oil and chopped red onion. When cooled slightly, sprinkle with mint, parsley, lemon juice and zest, and feta cheese. Stir gently. Sprinkle with pine nuts before serving.
1 cup: 220 cal., 20g fat (3g sat. fat), 5mg chol., 252mg sod., 8g carb. (4g sugars, 3g fiber), 5g pro.

TEST KITCHEN TIP

If you do not have a grill wok or basket, use a disposable foil pan. Poke holes in the bottom of the pan with a meat fork to allow liquid to drain.

SLOW-COOKER POLENTA

This Italian classic is so simple to make, you can now make it any night of the week.
—Elisabeth Matelski, Boston, MA

- -

Prep: 10 min. • **Cook:** 6 hours
Makes: 12 servings

    13 cups reduced-sodium
        chicken broth, divided
    3   cups cornmeal
    1   medium onion, finely chopped
    3   garlic cloves, minced
    2   bay leaves
    2   tsp. salt
    1   cup half-and-half cream
    1   cup shredded Parmesan cheese
    ¼   cup butter, cubed
    1   tsp. pepper
        Additional shredded Parmesan
        cheese

In a 6-qt. slow cooker, combine 12 cups broth, cornmeal, onion, garlic, bay leaves and salt. Cook, covered, on low 6-8 hours, until the liquid is absorbed and polenta is creamy. Remove bay leaves. Stir in cream, cheese, butter, pepper and remaining broth. If desired, serve with additional cheese.
1 cup: 255 cal., 8g fat (5g sat. fat), 25mg chol., 1168mg sod., 34g carb. (3g sugars, 2g fiber), 9g pro.

EASY GRILLED CORN
WITH CHIPOTLE-LIME BUTTER

ASK SARAH

HOW DO I PICK FRESH SWEET CORN?

Start by inspecting the husk. The freshest corn will have a husk that is bright green, wrapped tightly and slightly damp. Note the tassel, which is the fluff of silks at the top. It should be light brown or gold, and a little sticky. It should smell sweet with no signs of decay. Finally, give the corn a gentle squeeze. It should feel firm, and the kernels should feel plump.

EASY GRILLED CORN WITH CHIPOTLE-LIME BUTTER

Grilling corn in the husks is so easy. There's no need to remove the silk and tie the husk closed before grilling. Just soak, grill and add your favorite flavored butter.
—*Taste of Home* Test Kitchen

Prep: 5 min. + soaking • **Grill:** 25 min.
Makes: 8 servings

   8   large ears sweet corn in husks
   ½   cup butter, softened
 1½   tsp. grated lime zest
   1   tsp. minced fresh cilantro
   ½   tsp. salt
   ½   tsp. ground chipotle pepper
        Coarse sea salt, optional

1. In a large stockpot, cover corn with cold water. Soak 30 minutes; drain. Grill corn, covered, over medium heat until tender, turning occasionally, 25-30 minutes.
2. Meanwhile, combine the remaining ingredients. Carefully peel back husks; discard silk. Spread the butter mixture over corn.

1 ear of corn with 2 Tbsp. butter: 225 cal., 13g fat (8g sat. fat), 31mg chol., 265mg sod., 27g carb. (9g sugars, 3g fiber), 5g pro.

BACON & GARLIC SUGAR SNAP PEAS

This flavorful side dish calls for only four ingredients! Do use fresh sugar snap peas if you'd can!
—Tami Kuehl, Loup City, NE

Takes: 10 min. • **Makes:** 4 servings

- 2 bacon strips, coarsely chopped
- 1 pkg. (14 oz.) frozen sugar snap peas, thawed
- 1 shallot or small onion, thinly sliced
- 2 garlic cloves, thinly sliced

In a large skillet, cook chopped bacon over medium heat until crisp, stirring occasionally. Remove with a slotted spoon; drain on paper towels. Cook and stir peas in bacon drippings until heated through. Add shallot and garlic; cook 1 minute longer. Sprinkle with the reserved bacon.

½ cup: 126 cal., 6g fat (2g sat. fat), 9mg chol., 100mg sod., 13g carb. (5g sugars, 3g fiber), 5g pro. **Diabetic exchanges:** 1 starch, 1 fat.

BADGER STATE STUFFING

BADGER STATE STUFFING

Your family will love the contrasting sweet, savory and slightly tart flavors in this twist on a Thanksgiving classic. Feel free to use your favorite beer or dried fruit to make the dish your own.
—Andrea Fetting, Franklin, WI

Prep: 35 min. • **Bake:** 50 min. + standing
Makes: 8 servings

- ½ lb. bacon strips, diced
- ½ lb. sliced fresh mushrooms
- 1 medium onion, diced
- 1 cup chopped celery (about 3 stalks)
- 1 cup chopped carrot (about 4 medium carrots)
- 2 garlic cloves, minced
- 1 can (8 oz.) sauerkraut, rinsed and well drained
- ½ cup amber beer or chicken broth
- 5 cups cubed sourdough bread (½-in. cubes)
- 1 cup dried cherries or dried cranberries
- 1 large egg
- 1¼ cups chicken broth
- 3 Tbsp. minced fresh parsley
- 1 tsp. poultry seasoning
- ½ tsp. pepper

1. Preheat oven to 350°. In a large skillet, cook bacon over medium heat until crisp, stirring occasionally. Remove with a slotted spoon; drain on paper towels. Discard the drippings, reserving 3 Tbsp. in pan.

2. Add mushrooms, onion, celery and carrot to drippings; cook and stir over medium-high heat until tender, 8-10 minutes. Add garlic; cook 1 minute longer. Stir in sauerkraut and beer. Bring to a boil; cook, uncovered, until liquid is reduced by half.

3. In a large bowl, combine the bread cubes, cherries, bacon and sauerkraut mixture. In a small bowl, whisk egg, broth, parsley, poultry seasoning and pepper. Gradually stir into the bread mixture.

4. Transfer to a greased 2-qt. baking dish. Bake, covered, 20 minutes. Uncover; bake until lightly browned, 30-35 minutes longer. Let stand 10 minutes before serving.

1 cup: 271 cal., 11g fat (4g sat. fat), 39mg chol., 700mg sod., 35g carb. (18g sugars, 3g fiber), 9g pro.

PEPPER JACK HASH BROWN CASSEROLE

I found myself in need of an impromptu potato dish, but I had no fresh potatoes. Frozen hash browns and a plethora of cheeses offered me the solution to my side-dish dilemma.
—Cyndy Gerken, Naples, FL

Prep: 25 min. • **Bake:** 25 min.
Makes: 12 servings

- 1   pkg. (30 oz.) frozen shredded hash brown potatoes, thawed
- 1   can (10½ oz.) condensed cream of chicken soup, undiluted
- 2   cups shredded pepper jack cheese
- 1½ cups heavy whipping cream
- ½   cup butter, melted
- ½   cup sour cream
- ¼   cup shredded Parmesan cheese
- ½   tsp. salt
- ½   tsp. onion powder
- ¼   tsp. garlic powder
- ¼   tsp. pepper

TOPPING
- 1   cup crushed potato chips
- 5   bacon strips, cooked and crumbled
- ¾   cup shredded Parmesan cheese
- 1   tsp. paprika

1. Preheat oven to 350°. In a large bowl, combine the first 11 ingredients. Transfer to a greased 13x9-in. baking dish. For topping, combine potato chips, bacon and Parmesan; sprinkle over casserole. Top with paprika.
2. Bake, uncovered, until edges are bubbly and topping is golden brown, 25-30 minutes.
⅔ cup: 416 cal., 33g fat (19g sat. fat), 87mg chol., 682mg sod., 20g carb. (2g sugars, 2g fiber), 12g pro.

RUSTIC TOMATO PIE

Perk up your plate with this humble tomato pie. We like to use fresh-from-the-garden tomatoes and herbs, but store-bought produce will work in a pinch.
—*Taste of Home* Test Kitchen

Prep: 15 min. **Bake:** 30 min. + cooling
Makes: 8 servings

- Pastry for single-crust pie
- 1¾ lbs. mixed tomatoes, seeded and cut into ½-in. slices
- ¼   cup thinly sliced green onions
- ½   cup mayonnaise
- ½   cup shredded cheddar cheese
- 2   Tbsp. minced fresh basil
- ¼   tsp. salt
- ¼   tsp. pepper
- 2   bacon strips, cooked and crumbled
- 2   Tbsp. grated Parmesan cheese

1. Preheat oven to 400°. On a lightly floured surface, roll dough to a ⅛-in.-thick circle; transfer to a 9-in. pie plate. Trim crust to ½ in. beyond rim of plate.
2. Place half of the tomatoes and half of the onions in crust. Combine mayonnaise, cheddar cheese, fresh basil, salt and pepper; spread over tomatoes. Top with remaining onions and tomatoes. Fold crust edge over filling, pleating as you go and leaving an 8-in. opening in the center. Sprinkle with bacon and Parmesan cheese. Bake on a lower oven rack until until crust is golden and filling is bubbly, 30-35 minutes. Let stand 10 minutes before cutting. If desired, sprinkle pie with additional basil.
1 piece: 325 cal., 25g fat (11g sat. fat), 41mg chol., 409mg sod., 19g carb. (3g sugars, 2g fiber), 6g pro.
Pastry for single-crust pie (9 in.) Combine 1¼ cups all-purpose flour and ¼ tsp. salt; cut in ½ cup cold butter until crumbly. Gradually add 3-5 Tbsp. ice water, tossing with a fork until dough holds together when pressed. Wrap and refrigerate 1 hour.

RUSTIC TOMATO PIE

SPICY CHUCK
WAGON BEANS

SWEET & TANGY BEETS

Fresh beets are delicious when combined with aromatic spice and a hint of orange. These have the perfect balance of sweet and sour flavors.
—*Taste of Home* Test Kitchen

- -

Prep: 15 min. • **Cook:** 7 hours
Makes: 6 servings

2   lbs. small fresh beets, peeled and halved
½   cup sugar
¼   cup packed brown sugar
2   Tbsp. cornstarch
½   tsp. salt
¼   cup orange juice
¼   cup cider vinegar
2   Tbsp. butter
1½ tsp. whole cloves

1. Place beets in a 3-qt. slow cooker. Mix sugars, cornstarch and salt. Stir in orange juice and cider vinegar. Pour over beets; dot with butter.
2. Place cloves on a double thickness of cheesecloth. Gather corners of cloth to enclose cloves; tie securely with string. Place bag in slow cooker. Cook, covered, on low 7-8 hours, until beets are tender. Discard spice bag.
¾ cup: 214 cal., 4g fat (2g sat. fat), 10mg chol., 344mg sod., 44g carb. (38g sugars, 3g fiber), 3g pro. **Diabetic exchanges:** 2 vegetable, 1½ starch, 1 fat.

SPICY CHUCK WAGON BEANS

Baked beans don't get any easier than this! Just open some cans, chop an onion, and add a dash (or two) of hot sauce. They'll simmer to perfection in minutes.
—James Schend, Deputy Editor

- -

Takes: 30 min.
Makes: 24 servings

1   Tbsp. canola oil
1   medium onion, chopped
2   cans (28 oz. each) baked beans
3   cans (15 oz. each) chili beans, undrained
2   cans (15 oz. each) black beans, rinsed and drained
2   pkg. (7 oz. each) frozen fully cooked breakfast sausage links, thawed and cut into ½-in. pieces
1   cup beer or reduced-sodium chicken broth
2   chipotle peppers in adobo sauce, minced
1   to 2 Tbsp. hot pepper sauce

In a Dutch oven, heat oil over medium-high heat; saute onion until tender, 3-5 minutes. Stir in remaining ingredients; bring to a boil. Reduce heat; simmer, uncovered, until beans are thickened and flavors are blended, about 15 minutes, stirring occasionally.
⅔ cup: 221 cal., 8g fat (3g sat. fat), 15mg chol., 663mg sod., 30g carb. (2g sugars, 8g fiber), 10g pro.

TEST KITCHEN TIP

You can also make these baked beans in a greased 6-qt. slow cooker. Combine all ingredients, omitting oil. Cook, covered, on low 6-8 hours, until heated.

SIMPLE AU GRATIN POTATOES

These cheesy potatoes are always welcome at our dinner table, and they're so simple to make. A perfect complement to ham, this versatile, homey side dish also goes well with pork, chicken and other entrees.
—Cris O'Brien, Virginia Beach, VA

- -

Prep: 20 min. • **Bake:** 1½ hours
Makes: 8 servings

- 3   **Tbsp. butter**
- 3   **Tbsp. all-purpose flour**
- 1½ **tsp. salt**
- ⅛   **tsp. pepper**
- 2   **cups 2% milk**
- 1   **cup shredded cheddar cheese**
- 5   **cups thinly sliced peeled potatoes (about 6 medium)**
- ½   **cup chopped onion**
    Additional pepper, optional

1. Preheat oven to 350°. In a large saucepan, melt butter over low heat. Stir in flour, salt and pepper until smooth. Gradually add milk. Bring to a boil; cook and stir 2 minutes or until thickened. Remove from heat; stir in the cheese until melted. Add the potatoes and onion.
2. Transfer to a greased 2-qt. baking dish. Cover and bake for 1 hour. Uncover; bake until potatoes are tender, 30-40 minutes. If desired, top with additional pepper.
¾ cup: 224 cal., 10g fat (7g sat. fat), 35mg chol., 605mg sod., 26g carb. (4g sugars, 2g fiber), 7g pro.

RICE-STUFFED ACORN SQUASH

We often make this side dish in the fall, after harvesting fresh squash from our garden. A fun hint of Asian flavor offers a different, unexpected accent. I especially enjoy the pleasant flavor combination of mozzarella and ginger.
—Lydia Garcia, Gettysburg, PA

- -

Prep: 45 min. • **Bake:** 20 min.
Makes: 4 servings

- 2   **small acorn squash**
- ¾   **cup uncooked long grain rice**
- 1½ **cups water**
- 2   **Tbsp. soy sauce**
- 1   **medium onion, chopped**
- ¼   **cup butter, cubed**
- 2   **medium tart apples, peeled and chopped**
- 1   **cup shredded part-skim mozzarella cheese**
- ½   **cup chopped walnuts**
- ½   **cup half-and-half cream**
- ¼   **cup balsamic vinegar**
- 3   **Tbsp. honey**
- 3   **tsp. minced fresh gingerroot**
- 1   **tsp. curry powder**

1. Cut the squash in half; remove seeds. Place cut side down in a greased 13x9-in. baking dish. Cover and bake at 350° for 40-45 minutes or until tender.
2. Meanwhile, in a large saucepan, bring the rice, water and soy sauce to a boil. Reduce heat; cover and simmer for 15-18 minutes or until liquid is absorbed and rice is tender.
3. In a large skillet, saute onion in butter until almost tender. Add the apples; saute for 3 minutes. Remove from the heat; stir in the rice, cheese, walnuts, cream, vinegar, honey, ginger and curry.
4. Turn squash over; stuff with rice mixture. Bake, uncovered, for 20-25 minutes or until heated through.
1 stuffed squash half: 687 cal., 31g fat (14g sat. fat), 64mg chol., 767mg sod., 93g carb. (33g sugars, 8g fiber), 17g pro.

ROASTED RADISHES

Radishes aren't just for salads anymore. The springtime veggie makes a colorful side to nearly any meal.
—*Taste of Home* Test Kitchen

- -

Prep: 10 min. • **Bake:** 30 min.
Makes: 6 servings

- 2¼ **lbs. radishes, trimmed and quartered (about 6 cups)**
- 3   **Tbsp. olive oil**
- 1   **Tbsp. minced fresh oregano or 1 tsp. dried oregano**
- ¼   **tsp. salt**
- ⅛   **tsp. pepper**

1. Preheat oven to 425°. Toss radishes with remaining ingredients. Transfer to a greased 15x10x1-in. pan.
2. Roast until crisp-tender, 30 minutes, stirring once.
⅔ cup: 88 cal., 7g fat (1g sat. fat), 0mg chol., 165mg sod., 6g carb. (3g sugars, 3g fiber), 1g pro. **Diabetic exchanges:** 1 vegetable, 1½ fat.

JALAPENO & COTIJA CHEESE POTATO STACK PIE

LENTIL WHITE BEAN PILAF

Vegetarians will be happy to see this hearty meatless grain pilaf on the menu. I like to make this when I have extra cooked lentils, barley, quinoa and rice on hand.
—Juli Meyers, Hinesville, GA

- -

Prep: 35 min. • **Cook:** 15 min.
Makes: 10 servings

- 1 cup dried lentils, rinsed
- ½ cup quick-cooking barley
- ½ cup quinoa, rinsed
- ⅓ cup uncooked long grain rice
- ½ lb. sliced baby portobello mushrooms
- 3 medium carrots, finely chopped
- 3 celery ribs, finely chopped
- 1 large onion, finely chopped
- ¼ cup butter, cubed
- 3 garlic cloves, minced
- 2 tsp. minced fresh rosemary or ½ tsp. dried rosemary, crushed
- ½ cup vegetable broth
- ½ tsp. salt
- ½ tsp. pepper
- 2 cups canned cannellini beans, rinsed and drained

1. Cook the lentils, barley, quinoa and rice according to package directions; set aside.
2. In a Dutch oven, saute the mushrooms, carrots, celery and onion in butter until tender. Add garlic and rosemary; cook 1 minute longer. Add the broth, salt and pepper, stirring to loosen browned bits from pan. Stir in cannellini beans and cooked lentils, barley, quinoa and rice; heat through.
¾ cup: 259 cal., 6g fat (3g sat. fat), 12mg chol., 290mg sod., 41g carb. (3g sugars, 11g fiber), 11g pro.
Herbed Lentil White Bean Pilaf: Omit rosemary. With the broth, add ¾ tsp. dried basil, ½ tsp. dried oregano, ½ tsp. dried thyme and ¼ tsp. garlic powder.

JALAPENO & COTIJA CHEESE POTATO STACK PIE

Pie isn't just for dessert anymore. Stacking thinly sliced potatoes with layers of minced jalapenos and crumbled Cotija cheese helps turn ordinary spuds into something truly spectacular and memorable.
—Colleen Delawder, Herndon, VA

- -

Prep: 20 min. • **Bake:** 50 min.
Makes: 8 servings

- 2½ lbs. red potatoes, peeled and thinly sliced
- ¼ cup butter, melted
- ½ tsp. salt
- ¼ tsp. pepper
- 2 jalapeno peppers, seeded and minced
- 1¼ cups crumbled Cotija or feta cheese
  Salsa and sour cream, optional

1. Preheat oven to 375°. Line a 15x10x1-in. pan with parchment. Remove the bottom of a 9-in. springform pan and place the round outer edge in the middle of the parchment.

2. Place the potatoes, butter, salt and pepper in a large bowl; toss to coat. Layer a third of the potatoes evenly within the springform ring. Sprinkle with a third of the jalapenos and a third of the cheese. Repeat the layers. Top with remaining potatoes and jalapenos.
3. Bake for 35 minutes. Top with remaining cheese. Bake 15-20 minutes longer or until potatoes are tender. Let stand 5 minutes before removing ring. If desired, serve with salsa and sour cream.
1 serving: 223 cal., 12g fat (7g sat. fat), 34mg chol., 477mg sod., 23g carb. (2g sugars, 3g fiber), 7g pro.

TEST KITCHEN TIP

If jalapenos are spicier than you'd like, toss them with a little vodka and let them sit for 15 minutes. Then drain, rinse and proceed with the recipe.

VEGETABLE & BARLEY PILAF

Hearty, colorful, easy and fast were the reviews we gave this good-for-you dish. Barley boasts a healthy amount of soluble fiber, which aids digestion. And it can help to lower cholesterol, too! You can easily substitute any other fresh veggies you have on hand.
—Jesse Klausmeier, Burbank, CA

- -

Takes: 30 min. • **Makes:** 4 servings

- 1 large zucchini, quartered and sliced
- 1 large carrot, chopped
- 1 Tbsp. butter
- 2 cups reduced-sodium chicken broth
- 1 cup quick-cooking barley
- 2 green onions, chopped
- ½ tsp. dried marjoram
- ¼ tsp. salt
- ⅛ tsp. pepper

1. In a large saucepan, saute zucchini and carrot in butter until crisp-tender. Add the broth; bring to a boil. Stir in barley. Reduce heat; cover and simmer until barley is tender, 10-12 minutes.

2. Stir in the onions, marjoram, salt and pepper. Remove from the heat; cover and let stand for 5 minutes.

¾ cup: 219 cal., 4g fat (2g sat. fat), 8mg chol., 480mg sod., 39g carb. (3g sugars, 10g fiber), 9g pro.

Spinach Barley Pilaf: With the onions, stir in 1 cup chopped fresh spinach.

VEGETABLE & BARLEY PILAF

SUGAR SNAP PEA STIR-FRY

Fresh ginger, balsamic vinegar, soy sauce and sesame oil provide a nice blend of flavors in this Asian-inspired recipe for fresh sugar snap peas. This quick-to-cook recipe will complement most any spring entree, whether it's ham, lamb, chicken or fish. Best of all, it's easy to double for large crowds.
—*Taste of Home* Test Kitchen

- -

Takes: 20 min. • **Makes:** 6 servings

- 1 lb. fresh sugar snap peas
- 2 tsp. canola oil
- 1 garlic clove, minced
- 2 tsp. minced fresh gingerroot
- 1½ tsp. balsamic vinegar
- 1½ tsp. reduced-sodium soy sauce
- 1 tsp. sesame oil
  Dash cayenne pepper
- 1 Tbsp. minced fresh basil
  or 1 tsp. dried basil
- 2 tsp. sesame seeds, toasted

In a large nonstick skillet or wok, saute the peas in canola oil until crisp-tender. Add the garlic, ginger, vinegar, soy sauce, sesame oil and cayenne; saute 1 minute longer. Add basil; toss to combine. Sprinkle with the sesame seeds.

½ cup: 60 cal., 3g fat (0 sat. fat), 0 chol., 59mg sod., 6g carb. (3g sugars, 2g fiber), 3g pro. **Diabetic exchanges:** 1 vegetable, ½ fat.

ROASTED ASPARAGUS & LEEKS

No vegetable says spring like asparagus. Here, we combined pretty green spears with leeks. Crushed red pepper adds a bit of unexpected zest.

—*Taste of Home* Test Kitchen

Prep: 15 min. • **Bake:** 20 min.
Makes: 12 servings

- 3 lbs. fresh asparagus, trimmed
- 12 medium leeks (white portion only), halved lengthwise
- 4½ tsp. olive oil
- 1½ tsp. dill weed
- ½ tsp. salt
- ½ tsp. crushed red pepper flakes
- ¼ tsp. pepper

1. Place fresh asparagus and leeks on an ungreased 15x10x1-in. baking pan. Combine the remaining ingredients; pour over the vegetables.
2. Bake at 400° for 20-25 minutes or until tender, stirring occasionally.

1 serving: 83 cal., 2g fat (0 sat. fat), 0 chol., 98mg sod., 15g carb. (4g sugars, 3g fiber), 3g pro. **Diabetic exchanges:** 2 vegetable, ½ fat.

ROOT VEGETABLE PAVE

ROOT VEGETABLE PAVE

This truly is a stunning side dish to serve company. The robust blend features earthy root vegetables in a lightly herbed cream sauce. It's a perfect make-ahead dish for special occasions.

—Carla Mendres, Winnipeg, MB

Prep: 40 min. • **Bake:** 1¾ hours + standing
Makes: 8 servings

- 3 medium russet potatoes, peeled
- 2 large carrots
- 2 medium turnips, peeled
- 1 large onion, halved
- 1 medium fennel bulb, fronds reserved
- ½ cup all-purpose flour
- 1 cup heavy whipping cream
- 1 Tbsp. minced fresh thyme, plus more for topping
- 1 Tbsp. minced fresh rosemary
- ½ tsp. salt
- ½ tsp. pepper, plus more for topping
- 1 cup shredded Asiago cheese, divided

1. Preheat oven to 350°. With a mandoline or vegetable peeler, cut first 5 ingredients into very thin slices. Transfer to a large bowl; toss with flour. Stir in cream, thyme, 1 Tbsp. rosemary, salt and pepper.
2. Place half the vegetable mixture into a greased 9-in. springform pan. Sprinkle with ½ cup cheese. Top with remaining vegetable mixture. Place pan on a baking sheet and cover with a double thickness of foil.
3. Bake until the vegetables are tender and easily pierced with a knife, 1¾-2 hours. Remove from oven and top foil with large canned goods as weights. Let stand 1 hour. Remove cans, foil and rim from pan before cutting. Top with remaining cheese. Add the reserved fennel fronds and, as desired, additional fresh thyme and the pepper. Refrigerate leftovers.

1 slice: 248 cal., 15g fat (9g sat. fat), 46mg chol., 216mg sod., 23g carb. (4g sugars, 2g fiber), 7g pro.

**SMOKY QUINOA
WITH MUSHROOMS**

SMOKY QUINOA WITH MUSHROOMS

Add quinoa cooked with smoked paprika to your list of top sides. To warm the spinach leaves, quickly saute if desired.
—Ellen Kanner, Miami, FL

- -

Prep: 15 min. • **Cook:** 35 min.
Makes: 4 servings

- 4 tsp. olive oil
- 1 lb. sliced fresh mushrooms
- 3 garlic cloves, minced
- 3 Tbsp. tomato paste
- 2 Tbsp. smoked paprika
- 2 Tbsp. lemon juice
- 1 tsp. ground cumin
- ½ tsp. salt
- 1 cup water or vegetable broth
- ¾ cup quinoa, rinsed
- 4 cups fresh baby spinach
  Minced fresh cilantro and
  lemon wedges

1. In a large saucepan, heat olive oil over medium-high heat. Add mushrooms; cook and stir 6-8 minutes or until mushrooms are tender. Add garlic and cook 1 minute longer. Reduce heat to medium-low; cook, covered, 10 minutes.
2. Stir in tomato paste, paprika, lemon juice, cumin and salt until blended. Add water; bring to a boil. Add quinoa. Reduce heat; simmer, covered, 15-18 minutes or until liquid is absorbed. Remove from heat; fluff with a fork.
3. Arrange spinach on a serving plate; spoon quinoa over spinach. Sprinkle with cilantro; serve with lemon wedges.
⅔ cup quinoa mixture with 1 cup spinach:
217 cal., 8g fat (1g sat. fat), 0 chol., 337mg sod., 31g carb. (4g sugars, 6g fiber), 10g pro.
Diabetic exchanges: 2 vegetable, 1½ starch, 1 fat..

SOFT GIANT PRETZELS
PAGE 223

Odds & Ends

Is there anything better than homemade jam on biscuits or green beans you grew and canned yourself? Our recipes for condiments, sauces, canned fruits and veggies, and some surprising snacks spruce up any meal.

SWEET HOOSIER
DOG SAUCE

SWEET HOOSIER DOG SAUCE

In our area of Indiana, we love sweet coney sauce on hot dogs. A drive-in restaurant in our town is famous for its version.
—Jill Thomas, Washington, IN

- -

Takes: 30 min. • **Makes:** 5 cups

- 2   **lbs. ground beef**
- 1   **can (6 oz.) tomato paste**
- 1   **cup water**
- 1   **can (8 oz.) tomato sauce**
- ½   **cup sweet pickle relish**
- ¼   **cup dried minced onion**
- 2   **Tbsp. sugar**
- 1   **Tbsp. chili powder**
- 2   **tsp. Worcestershire sauce**
- 1   **tsp. salt**
- 1   **tsp. cider vinegar**
- 1   **tsp. yellow mustard**
- ½   **tsp. celery salt**
- ¼   **tsp. garlic powder**
- ¼   **tsp. onion powder**
- **Hot dogs and buns**
- **Optional: Diced onion, sliced pickles and shredded cheddar cheese**

In a Dutch oven, cook beef over medium heat until no longer pink, 8-10 minutes, breaking into crumbles; drain. Stir in tomato paste; cook and stir 3 minutes. Stir in next 13 ingredients. Bring to a boil; reduce heat. Simmer sauce, uncovered, until thickened, 15-20 minutes, stirring occasionally. Serve sauce over hot dogs in buns. Add optional toppings as desired.

Freeze option: Freeze the cooled sauce in freezer containers. To use, partially thaw in refrigerator overnight. Heat through in a covered saucepan, stirring gently; add water if necessary.

¼ cup: 111 cal., 5g fat (2g sat. fat), 28mg chol., 298mg sod., 7g carb. (4g sugars, 1g fiber), 9g pro.

HOMEMADE SAUERKRAUT

HOMEMADE SAUERKRAUT

Put down that jar! You only need two simple ingredients to make fresh, zippy sauerkraut at home. Get those brats ready!
—Josh Rink, Food Stylist

- -

Prep: 45 min. + standing
Makes: 40 servings (about 10 cups)

- 6   **lbs. cabbage (about 2 heads)**
- 3   **Tbsp. canning salt**
- **Optional: 2 peeled and thinly sliced Granny Smith apples, 2 thinly sliced sweet onions, 2 tsp. caraway seeds and 1 tsp. ground coriander**

1. Quarter cabbages and remove cores; slice ⅛ in. thick. In an extra-large bowl, combine salt and cabbage. With clean hands, squeeze cabbage until it wilts and releases its liquid, about 10 minutes. If desired, add any of the optional ingredients.

2. Firmly pack cabbage mixture into 4-qt. fermenting crock or large glass container, removing as many air bubbles as possible. If cabbage mixture is not covered by 1-2 in. of liquid, make enough brine to cover by 1-2 in. To make brine, combine 4½ tsp. canning salt per 1 qt. of water in a saucepan; bring to a boil until salt is dissolved. Cool brine before adding to crock.

3. Place crock weight over cabbage; the weight should be submerged in the brine. Or, place an inverted dinner plate or glass pie plate over cabbage. The plate should be slightly smaller than the container opening, but it should be large enough to cover most of the shredded cabbage mixture. Weigh down the plate with 2 or 3 sealed quart jars that are filled with water. If using a glass container with a lid, cover the opening loosely so that any gas produced by the fermenting cabbage can escape. Alternately, you can cover the opening with a clean, heavy towel. If using a crock, seal according to manufacturer's instructions.

4. Store crock, undisturbed, at 70°-75° for 3-4 weeks (bubbles will form and aroma will change). Cabbage must be kept submerged below the surface of the fermenting liquid throughout fermentation. Check the crock 2-3 times each week; skim and remove any scum that may form on top of the liquid. Fermentation is complete when the bubbling stops. Transfer the sauerkraut to individual containers. Cover and store in refrigerator for up to 3 months.

¼ cup: 11 cal., 0 fat (0 sat. fat), 0 chol., 344mg sod., 3g carb. (1g sugars, 1g fiber), 1g pro.

HOMEMADE EGGNOG

After just one taste, folks will know this homemade holiday treat came from the kitchen, not from the store.
—Pat Waymire, Yellow Springs, OH

Prep: 15 min. • **Cook:** 30 min. + chilling
Makes: 12 servings (3 qt.)

- 12 large eggs
- 1½ cups sugar
- ½ tsp. salt
- 8 cups whole milk, divided
- 2 Tbsp. vanilla extract
- 1 tsp. ground nutmeg
- 2 cups heavy whipping cream
  Additional nutmeg, optional

1. In a heavy saucepan, whisk together the eggs, sugar and salt. Gradually add 4 cups of the whole milk; cook and stir over low heat until a thermometer reads 160°-170°, 30-35 minutes. Do not allow mixture to boil. Immediately transfer to a large bowl.
2. Stir in vanilla, nutmeg and the remaining milk. Place bowl in an ice-water bath, stirring until the milk mixture is cool. (If the mixture separates, process it in a blender until smooth.) Refrigerate, covered, until cold, at least 3 hours.
3. To serve, beat cream until soft peaks form. Whisk gently into cooled milk mixture. If desired, sprinkle with additional nutmeg before serving.
1 cup: 411 cal., 25g fat (14g sat. fat), 247mg chol., 251mg sod., 35g carb. (35g sugars, 0 fiber), 13g pro.

QUICK JALAPENO HUSH PUPPIES

The crunchy exterior of these southern-style snacks is a nice contrast to the moist cornbread. Jalapeno peppers and hot sauce add a hint of heat.
—*Taste of Home* Test Kitchen

Prep: 15 min. • **Cook:** 5 min./batch
Makes: 2½ dozen

- 1½ cups yellow cornmeal
- ½ cup all-purpose flour
- 1 tsp. baking powder
- 1 tsp. salt
- 2 large eggs, lightly beaten
- ¾ cup 2% milk
- 2 jalapeno peppers, seeded and minced
- ¼ cup finely chopped onion
- 1 tsp. Louisiana-style hot sauce
  Oil for deep-fat frying

1. In a large bowl, combine the cornmeal, flour, baking powder and salt. In another bowl, beat the eggs, milk, jalapenos, onion and hot sauce. Stir into dry ingredients just until combined.
2. In a cast-iron or other heavy skillet, heat oil to 375°. Drop tablespoonfuls of batter, a few at a time, into hot oil. Fry until golden brown on both sides. Drain on paper towels. Serve warm.
1 hush puppy: 56 cal., 3g fat (0 sat. fat), 14mg chol., 94mg sod., 7g carb. (0 sugars, 1g fiber), 1g pro.

QUICK JALAPENO HUSH PUPPIES

PICKLED
GREEN BEANS

PICKLED GREEN BEANS

This recipe preserves my green beans for months...that's if we don't eat them all first! I crank up the heat with cayenne pepper.
—Marisa McClellan, Philadelphia, PA

- -

Prep: 20 min. • **Process:** 10 min.
Makes: 4 pints

   1¾ **lbs. fresh green beans, trimmed**
   1   **tsp. cayenne pepper**
   4   **garlic cloves, peeled**
   4   **tsp. dill seed or 4 fresh dill heads**
   2½ **cups water**
   2½ **cups white vinegar**
   ¼   **cup canning salt**

1. Pack beans into 4 hot 1-pint jars to within ½ in. of the top. Add cayenne, garlic and dill seed to jars.
2. In a large saucepan, bring water, vinegar and salt to a boil.
3. Carefully ladle hot liquid over the beans, leaving ½-in. headspace. Remove air bubbles and adjust headspace, if necessary, by adding hot mixture. Wipe rims. Center lids on jars; screw on bands until fingertip tight.
4. Place jars into canner with simmering water, ensuring that they are completely covered with water. Bring to a boil; process for 10 minutes. Remove jars and cool.
8 green beans: 9 cal., 0 fat (0 sat. fat), 0 chol., 83mg sod., 2g carb. (1g sugars, 1g fiber), 1g pro.

"Last summer we grew a bumper crop of green beans, so I canned a lot of them using this recipe. I love them so much I could almost eat an entire jar in one sitting!"

—ELLIE MARTIN CLIFFE, EXECUTIVE DIGITAL EDITOR

HOMEMADE BUTTERFINGER BITES

Bent on using up a stash of leftover candy corn, I decided to experiment. Turns out, if you melt it, mix it with peanut butter and coat the balls with chocolate, you get a softer, denser version of a Butterfinger bite. Who knew? They're delicious!
—Melissa Hansen, Ellison Bay, WI

- -

Prep: 30 min. + standing
Makes: about 4 dozen

   1   **cup candy corn**
   ⅔   **cup peanut butter**
   1   **cup semisweet chocolate chips**
   1   **tsp. coconut oil**

1. Microwave candy corn on high for 30 seconds; stir. Cook in 15-second intervals until melted; stir until smooth. Add peanut butter; microwave mixture until smooth, 45-60 seconds, stirring 3 times.
2. Gently shape teaspoonfuls of mixture into balls (if mixture becomes crumbly, reheat for 15-20 seconds). Place on waxed paper; let stand until set. In a microwave, melt the chocolate chips and oil; stir until smooth. Dip the balls in chocolate mixture, allowing excess to drip off. Place on waxed paper; let stand until set.
1 piece: 50 cal., 3g fat (1g sat. fat), 0 chol., 16mg sod., 6g carb. (6g sugars, 0 fiber), 1g pro.

THE BEST
MARINARA SAUCE

GIARDINIERA

Sweet and tangy, this Italian condiment is packed with peppers, cauliflower, carrots and other crisp-tender veggies. It's perfect to offer alongside pickles or olives on a relish tray.

—Alicia Rooker, Recipe Editor/Tester

- -

Prep: 1 hour • **Process:** 10 min./batch
Makes: 10 pints

6	cups white vinegar
3½	cups sugar
3	cups water
4½	tsp. canning salt
1	Tbsp. dried oregano
1	Tbsp. fennel seed
2	small heads cauliflower, broken into small florets (about 12 cups)
4	large carrots, sliced
4	celery ribs, cut into ½-in. slices
48	pearl onions, peeled and trimmed (about 1¼ lbs.)
4	large sweet red peppers, cut into ½-in. strips
4	serrano peppers, seeds removed and thinly sliced
10	bay leaves
20	whole peppercorns
10	garlic cloves, thinly sliced

1. In a large stockpot, combine vinegar, sugar, water, canning salt, oregano and fennel seed. Bring to a boil. Add cauliflower, carrots, celery and onions; return to a boil. Remove from heat; add peppers.
2. Carefully ladle hot mixture into 10 hot 1-pint jars, leaving ½- in. headspace. Add a bay leaf and 2 peppercorns to each jar; divide garlic slices among jars. Remove air bubbles and adjust headspace, if necessary, by adding more hot mixture. Wipe rims. Center lids on jars; screw on bands until fingertip tight.
3. Place jars into canner with simmering water, ensuring that they are completely covered with water. Bring to a boil; process for 10 minutes. Remove jars and cool.
¼ cup: 74 cal., 1g fat (0 sat. fat), 0 chol., 323mg sod., 16g carb. (15g sugars, 1g fiber), 1g pro.

THE BEST MARINARA SAUCE

I developed this recipe with a friend to make the most of a bumper crop of tomatoes. Now we like to make huge batches of the sauce and then give jars along with a pound of pasta as gifts around the holidays.

—Shannon Norris, Senior Food Stylist

- -

Prep: 1 hour + simmering • **Process:** 40 min.
Makes: 9 cups

3	Tbsp. olive oil
1	cup chopped onion
⅓	cup minced garlic, divided
12	lbs. plum tomatoes, quartered
2	cups water
1¼	cups minced fresh basil, divided
¼	cup minced fresh oregano
¼	cup tomato paste
2	tsp. kosher salt
1	tsp. coarsely ground pepper
¼	cup plus 1½ tsp. lemon juice

1. In a stockpot, heat oil over medium heat. Add the onion; cook and stir until softened, 3-4 minutes. Add 2 Tbsp. minced garlic; cook 1 minute longer. Add tomatoes, water and ½ cup basil; bring to a boil. Reduce the heat; simmer, covered, until the tomatoes are completely broken down and soft, about 1 hour, stirring occasionally.
2. Press tomato mixture through a food mill into a large bowl; discard skins and seeds. Return tomato mixture to stockpot; add ½ cup of remaining basil, oregano and the remaining garlic. Bring to a boil. Reduce the heat; simmer, uncovered, until thickened, 3½-4 hours, stirring occasionally. Add the tomato paste and remaining ¼ cup of basil; season with salt and pepper.
3. Add 1 Tbsp. plus 1½ tsp. lemon juice to each of 3 hot 1½-pint jars. Ladle hot mixture into jars, leaving ½-in. headspace. Remove any air bubbles and adjust the headspace, if necessary, by adding hot mixture. Wipe jar rims. Center lids on jars; screw on bands until fingertip tight.
4. Place jars into canner with simmering water, ensuring that they are completely covered with water. Bring to a boil; process for 40 minutes. Remove jars and cool.
¾ cup: 131 cal., 4g fat (1g sat. fat), 0 chol., 348mg sod., 22g carb. (13g sugars, 6g fiber), 5g pro. **Diabetic exchanges:** 1½ starch, 1 fat.

GIARDINIERA

CANNED BLUEBERRY JAM

Summer doesn't feel complete without at least one berry-picking trip and a batch of homemade blueberry jam. Eat atop fresh scones or biscuits for maximum enjoyment!
—Marisa McClellan, Philadelphia, PA

Prep: 35 min. • **Process:** 10 min./batch
Makes: 9 half-pints

- 8 cups fresh blueberries
- 6 cups sugar
- 3 Tbsp. lemon juice
- 2 tsp. ground cinnamon
- 2 tsp. grated lemon zest
- ½ tsp. ground nutmeg
- 2 pouches (3 oz. each) liquid fruit pectin

1. Place blueberries in a food processor; cover and process until blended. Transfer to a stockpot. Stir in the sugar, lemon juice, cinnamon, lemon zest and nutmeg. Bring to a full rolling boil over high heat, stirring constantly. Stir in pectin. Boil for 1 minute, stirring constantly.

2. Remove from the heat; skim off foam. Ladle hot mixture into hot sterilized half-pint jars, leaving ¼-in. headspace. Remove air bubbles; wipe rims and adjust lids. Process for 10 minutes in a boiling-water canner.

2 Tbsp.: 74 cal., 0 fat (0 sat. fat), 0 chol., 0 sod., 19g carb. (18g sugars, 0 fiber), 0 pro.

ASK SARAH

SHOULD I ADJUST PROCESSING TIME IF I LIVE AT A HIGHER ALTITUDE?

Yes, the air is thinner at higher altitudes, which causes water to boil at a lower temperature. Lower boiling temperatures are not as effective at killing bacteria. To compensate, increase the processing time or canner pressure.

CANNED BLUEBERRY JAM

OLD-FASHIONED ERMINE FROSTING

This old-timey frosting brings back fond memories of being in the kitchen with my grandmother. It was her go-to for cakes when she didn't have cornstarch or cream cheese on hand.
—Rashanda Cobbins, Food Editor

- -

Prep: 10 min. • **Cook:** 10 min. + chilling
Makes: 5 cups

- ½ cup all-purpose flour
- 2½ cups whole milk
- 1¾ cups sugar
- ½ tsp. salt
- 1¾ cups butter, softened
- 1½ tsp. vanilla extract

1. In a small heavy saucepan, whisk flour and milk until smooth. Cook and stir over medium heat until thickened and bubbly, 5-7 minutes.
2. Remove from heat; stir in sugar and salt until dissolved; transfer to a small bowl. Press plastic wrap onto surface. Refrigerate until cold.
3. In a large mixing bowl, beat butter until light and fluffy, about 5 minutes. Gradually beat in cooled mixture. Beat in the vanilla. Switch to whisk attachment; continue beating on medium speed until frosting is stiff and fluffy. Frost cake immediately.
2 Tbsp.: 60 cal., 4g fat (3g sat. fat), 11mg chol., 50mg sod., 5g carb. (5g sugars, 0 fiber), 0 pro.

NASHVILLE BBQ SAUCE

Nashville barbecue sauce is vinegar-forward with smoky undertones. Use it liberally on your favorite grilled or smoked meats.
—*Taste of Home* Test Kitchen

- -

Prep: 5 min. • **Cook:** 25 min.
Makes: 15 cups

- 1½ cups ketchup
- ½ cup packed brown sugar
- ⅓ cup cider vinegar
- 2 Tbsp. Worcestershire sauce
- 2 Tbsp. liquid smoke, optional
- 2 Tbsp. molasses
- 1 tsp. salt
- 1 tsp. ground mustard
- 1 tsp. chili powder
- ½ tsp. paprika
- ½ tsp. pepper

In a large saucepan, combine all ingredients. Bring to a boil. Reduce the heat; simmer, uncovered, until slightly thickened and darkened in color, 20-25 minutes.
2 Tbsp.: 30 cal., 0 fat (0 sat. fat), 0 chol., 231mg sod., 8g carb. (7g sugars, 0 fiber), 0 pro.

OLD-FASHIONED ERMINE FROSTING

MINI ZUCCHINI PIZZAS

This simple snack recipe is the perfect, low-carb way to satisfy your pizza cravings.
—*Taste of Home* Test Kitchen

Takes: 20 min. • **Makes:** about 2 dozen

- 1 large zucchini (about 11 oz.), cut diagonally into ¼-in. slices
- ⅛ tsp. salt
- ⅛ tsp. pepper
- ⅓ cup pizza sauce
- ¾ cup shredded part-skim mozzarella cheese
- ½ cup miniature pepperoni slices Minced fresh basil

1. Preheat broiler. Arrange the zucchini in a single layer on a greased baking sheet. Broil 3-4 in. from heat just until crisp-tender, 1-2 minutes per side.

2. Sprinkle zucchini with salt and pepper; top with sauce, cheese and pepperoni. Broil until the cheese is melted, about 1 minute. Sprinkle with basil.

1 appetizer: 29 cal., 2g fat (1g sat. fat), 5mg chol., 108mg sod., 1g carb. (1g sugars, 0 fiber), 2g pro.

BIRTHDAY CAKE SHOOTERS

These festive shots are a fun way to get a birthday party started. Use chocolate cake-flavored vodka and chocolate liqueur for a super chocolaty treat.
—*Taste of Home* Test Kitchen

Prep: 5 min. • **Makes:** 2 servings

Ice cubes
- 2 oz. cake-flavored vodka
- 1 oz. white chocolate liqueur Sweetened whipped cream Sprinkles

Fill cocktail shaker three-fourths full with ice. Add vodka and white chocolate liqueur; cover and shake until condensation forms on outside of shaker, 10-15 seconds. Strain into 2 shot glasses. Top shooters with whipped cream and sprinkles.

1½ oz.: 181 cal., 0 fat (0 sat. fat), 0 chol., 3mg sod., 17g carb. (0 sugars, 0 fiber), 0 pro.

MINI ZUCCHINI PIZZAS

AIR-FRYER MINI
CHIMICHANGAS

AIR-FRYER MINI CHIMICHANGAS

My family raves over my Mexican-inspired bites. Infused with green chile, these beefy snacks are guaranteed to liven up the party!
—Kathy Rogers, Hudson, OH

Prep: 1 hour • **Cook:** 10 min./batch
Makes: 14 servings

- 1 lb. ground beef
- 1 medium onion, chopped
- 1 envelope taco seasoning
- ¾ cup water
- 3 cups shredded Monterey Jack cheese
- 1 cup sour cream
- 1 can (4 oz.) chopped green chiles, drained
- 14 egg roll wrappers
- 1 large egg white, lightly beaten
   Cooking spray
   Salsa

1. In a large skillet, cook beef and onion over medium heat until meat is no longer pink; drain. Stir in taco seasoning and water. Bring to a boil. Reduce heat; simmer, uncovered, for 5 minutes, stirring occasionally. Remove from the heat; cool slightly.
2. Preheat air fryer to 375°. In a large bowl, combine cheese, sour cream and chiles. Stir in beef mixture. Place an egg roll wrapper on work surface with 1 point facing you. Place ⅓ cup filling in center. Fold bottom one-third of wrapper over filling; fold in sides.
3. Brush top point with egg white; roll up to seal. Repeat with remaining wrappers and filling. (Keep the remaining egg roll wrappers covered with waxed paper to avoid drying out.)
4. In batches, place chimichangas in a single layer on greased tray in air-fryer basket; spritz with cooking spray. Cook until golden brown, 3-4 minutes on each side. Serve warm with salsa and additional sour cream.
1 chimichanga: 294 cal., 15g fat (8g sat. fat), 48mg chol., 618mg sod., 23g carb. (1g sugars, 1g fiber), 16g pro.

MOM'S PICKLED CARROTS

My mom is the only other person I've known to make this recipe. In fact, whenever I take these carrots to a potluck or picnic, people are pleasantly surprised to try them for the first time. After that, they're hooked.
—Robin Koble, Fairview, PA

Prep: 15 min. + chilling • **Cook:** 20 min.
Makes: 6 cups

- 2 lbs. carrots, cut lengthwise into ¼-in.-thick strips
- 1½ cups sugar
- 1½ cups water
- 1½ cups cider vinegar
- ¼ cup mustard seed
- 3 cinnamon sticks (3 in.)
- 3 whole cloves

1. Place the carrots in a large saucepan; add enough water to cover. Bring to a boil. Cook, covered, until crisp-tender, 3-5 minutes. Drain. Transfer to a large bowl. In another large saucepan, combine the remaining ingredients. Bring to a boil. Reduce heat; simmer, uncovered, for 20 minutes. Pour mixture over carrots. Refrigerate, covered, overnight to allow flavors to blend.
2. Transfer mixture to jars. Cover and refrigerate up to 1 month.
¼ cup: 30 cal., 0 fat (0 sat. fat), 0 chol., 170mg sod., 7g carb. (6g sugars, 1g fiber), 1g pro.

SOFT GIANT
PRETZELS

SOFT GIANT PRETZELS

My husband, friends and family love these soft, chewy pretzels. Let your machine mix the dough; then all you have to do is shape and bake these fun snacks.
—Sherry Peterson, Fort Collins, CO

Prep: 20 min. + rising • **Bake:** 10 min.
Makes: 8 pretzels

- 1   cup plus 2 Tbsp. water (70° to 80°)
- 3   cups all-purpose flour
- 3   Tbsp. brown sugar
- 1½ tsp. active dry yeast
- 2   qt. water
- ½   cup baking soda
-     Coarse salt

1. In a bread machine pan, place 1 cup water and next 3 ingredients in order suggested by manufacturer. Select dough setting. Check dough after 5 minutes of mixing; if needed, add 1-2 Tbsp. water or flour.
2. When cycle is completed, turn dough onto a lightly floured surface. Divide dough into 8 balls. Roll each into a 20-in. rope; form into pretzel shape.
3. Preheat oven to 425°. In a large saucepan, bring 2 qt. water and the baking soda to a boil. Drop pretzels into boiling water, 2 at a time; boil for 10-15 seconds. Remove with a slotted spoon; drain on paper towels.
4. Place pretzels on greased baking sheets. Bake until golden brown, 8-10 minutes. Spritz or lightly brush with water. Sprinkle with salt.
1 pretzel: 193 cal., 1g fat (0 sat. fat), 0 chol., 380mg sod., 41g carb. (5g sugars, 1g fiber), 5g pro.

CHOCOLATE GANACHE PEANUT BUTTER CUPCAKES

I've been baking cakes and cupcakes for years and enjoy trying new flavors and textures. Here I blended the classic combo of chocolate and peanut butter. They are very much worth the prep time.
—Ronda Schabes, Vicksburg, MI

Prep: 55 min. • **Bake:** 20 min. + cooling
Makes: 2 dozen

- 2   cups sugar
- 1¾ cups all-purpose flour
- ¾   cup baking cocoa
- ½   tsp. salt
- ½   tsp. baking soda
- ½   tsp. baking powder
- 1   cup buttermilk
- 1   cup strong brewed coffee, room temperature
- ½   cup canola oil
- 2   large eggs, room temperature
- 1   tsp. vanilla extract

FILLING
- ½   cup creamy peanut butter
- 3   Tbsp. unsalted butter, softened
- 1   cup confectioners' sugar
- 2   to 4 Tbsp. 2% milk

GANACHE
- 2   cups semisweet chocolate chips
- ½   cup heavy whipping cream

PEANUT BUTTER FROSTING
- 1   cup packed brown sugar
- 4   large egg whites
- ¼   tsp. salt
- ¼   tsp. cream of tartar
- 1   tsp. vanilla extract
- 2   cups unsalted butter, softened
- ⅓   cup creamy peanut butter
-     Chocolate curls, optional

1. Preheat oven to 350°. In a large bowl, combine the first 6 ingredients. Whisk buttermilk, coffee, oil, eggs and vanilla until blended; add to the dry ingredients until combined. (Batter will be very thin.) Fill paper-lined muffin cups two-thirds full.
2. Bake 18-20 minutes or until a toothpick inserted in the center comes out clean. Cool

10 minutes before removing from pans to wire racks to cool completely.
3. In a small bowl, cream peanut butter, butter, confectioners' sugar and enough milk to achieve piping consistency. Cut a small hole in the corner of a pastry bag; insert a small round tip. Fill bag with peanut butter filling. Insert tip into the top center of each cupcake; pipe about 1 Tbsp. filling into each.
4. Place chocolate chips in a small bowl. In a small saucepan, bring cream just to a boil. Pour over chocolate; whisk until smooth. Dip the top of each cupcake into ganache; place on wire racks to set.
5. In a large heavy saucepan, combine the brown sugar, egg whites, salt and cream of tartar over low heat. With a hand mixer, beat on low speed 1 minute. Continue beating on low over low heat until frosting reaches 160°, 8-10 minutes. Pour into a large bowl; add vanilla. Beat on high until stiff peaks form, about 5 minutes.
6. Add butter, 1 Tbsp. at a time, beating well after each addition. If mixture begins to look curdled, place frosting bowl in another bowl filled with hot water for a few seconds. Continue adding butter and beating until smooth. Beat in peanut butter 1-2 minutes or until smooth.
7. Place frosting in a pastry bag with large star tip; pipe onto each cupcake. If desired, top with chocolate curls. Store in an airtight container in the refrigerator. Let stand at room temperature before serving.
1 cupcake: 498 cal., 33g fat (16g sat. fat), 69mg chol., 196mg sod., 50g carb. (39g sugars, 2g fiber), 6g pro.

STRAWBERRY BASIL JAM

I make this sweet and savory jam with fresh-picked strawberries and basil from my herb garden. The deep red jam, laced with flecks of green basil, is so pretty and makes a perfect gift. Just add a bright ribbon around the top with a gift tag.
—Julie O'Neil, Two Harbors, MN

- -

Prep: 25 min. • **Process:** 10 min./batch
Makes: 9 half-pints

- 5 cups crushed strawberries (about 3 lbs.)
- 1 tsp. butter
- 1 pkg. (1¾ oz.) powdered fruit pectin
- 7 cups sugar
- ½ cup minced fresh basil

1. In a Dutch oven, combine strawberries and butter. Stir in pectin. Bring to a full rolling boil over high heat, stirring constantly. Stir in sugar; return to a full rolling boil. Boil and stir 1 minute. Immediately stir in basil.
2. Remove from heat; skim off foam. Ladle hot mixture into 9 hot half-pint jars, leaving ¼-in. headspace. Remove air bubbles and adjust headspace, if necessary, by adding hot mixture. Wipe rims. Center lids on jars; screw on bands until fingertip tight.
3. Place jars into canner with simmering water, ensuring that they are completely covered with water. Bring to a boil; process for 10 minutes. Remove jars and cool.
2 Tbsp.: 81 cal., 0 fat (0 sat. fat), 0 chol., 1mg sod., 21g carb. (20g sugars, 0 fiber), 0 pro.

SPINACH-BASIL PESTO

SPINACH-BASIL PESTO

Toss this rich, garlicky pesto with pasta or use as a spread. It also freezes well.
—Jaye Beeler, Grand Rapids, MI

- -

Takes: 10 min. • **Makes:** 1¾ cups

- 6 garlic cloves, halved
- 3 cups fresh baby spinach
- 1½ cups loosely packed basil leaves
- ¾ cup chopped walnuts or pine nuts, toasted
- 1 cup grated Parmesan cheese
- ½ tsp. salt
  Dash pepper
- ¾ cup olive oil

Place garlic in a food processor; pulse until finely chopped. Add the spinach, basil and walnuts. Pulse until chopped. Add cheese, salt and pepper. Continue processing while gradually adding oil in a steady stream.
Freeze option: Freeze pesto in freezer containers. To use, thaw in refrigerator.
2 Tbsp.: 167 cal., 17g fat (3g sat. fat), 5mg chol., 177mg sod., 2g carb. (0 sugars, 1g fiber), 3g pro.

HOMEMADE STEAK SEASONING

Here's the perfect seasoning for your favorite cut.
—Sarah Farmer, Executive Culinary Director

- -

Takes: 5 min. • **Makes:** about ⅓ cup

- 2 Tbsp. coarsely ground pepper
- 2 Tbsp. kosher salt
- 2 tsp. onion powder
- 2 tsp. dried minced garlic
- 2 tsp. paprika
- 2 tsp. crushed coriander seeds
- 2 tsp. crushed red pepper flakes

In a small bowl, combine all ingredients. Store in an airtight container in a cool, dry place for up to 1 year.
½ tsp.: 3 cal., 0 fat (0 sat. fat), 0 chol., 360mg sod., 1g carb. (0 sugars, 0 fiber), 0 pro.

HOMEMADE PEANUT BUTTER CUPS

These irresistible homemade candies with gooey peanut butter centers are so easy to make. I choose pretty mini muffin liners and colored sprinkles to coordinate with whatever holiday we're celebrating.
—LaVonne Hegland, St. Michael, MN

Prep: 20 min. + chilling • **Makes:** 3 dozen

- 1 cup creamy peanut butter, divided
- ½ cup confectioners' sugar
- 4½ tsp. butter, softened
- ½ tsp. salt
- 2 cups semisweet chocolate chips
- 4 milk chocolate candy bars (1.55 oz. each), coarsely chopped
  Colored sprinkles, optional

1. In a bowl, combine ½ cup creamy peanut butter, confectioners' sugar, butter and salt until smooth.
2. In a microwave, melt chocolate chips, candy bars and remaining peanut butter; stir until smooth.
3. Drop 1 tsp. of chocolate mixture into paper-lined mini muffin cups. Drop a scant tsp. of peanut butter mixture into each cup; top with another tsp. of chocolate mixture. If desired, decorate with sprinkles. Refrigerate until set. Store in an airtight container.
1 piece: 123 cal., 8g fat (4g sat. fat), 2mg chol., 76mg sod., 12g carb. (10g sugars, 1g fiber), 3g pro.

HOMEMADE PEANUT BUTTER CUPS

ROASTED CURRY CHICKPEAS

We coated chickpeas with a few simple seasonings to make this low-fat snacking sensation. It rivals calorie-laden varieties sold in stores.
—*Taste of Home* Test Kitchen

Takes: 30 min. • **Makes:** 1 cup

- 1 can (15 oz.) chickpeas or garbanzo beans
- 2 Tbsp. olive oil
- 1 tsp. salt
- ¼ tsp. pepper
- 2 tsp. curry powder
- ½ tsp. crushed red pepper flakes

Rinse and drain chickpeas; place on paper towels and pat dry. Place in a greased 15x10x1-in. baking pan; drizzle with oil and sprinkle with seasonings. Toss to coat. Bake at 450° until crispy and golden brown, 25-30 minutes.
¼ cup: 162 cal., 9g fat (1g sat. fat), 0 chol., 728mg sod., 17g carb. (3g sugars, 5g fiber), 4g pro.

"In our family, we love snacks that have a little bit of heat. These seasoned chickpeas hit the spot."

—SARAH FARMER, EXECUTIVE CULINARY DIRECTOR

LEMONADE ICED TEA

I have always loved iced tea with lemon, and this great thirst-quencher just takes it one step further. Lemonade gives the drink a nice color, too. I dress up each glass with a slice of lemon on the rim.
—Gail Buss, New Bern, NC

Prep: 15 min. + chilling
Makes: 12 servings (3 qt.)

- 3 qt. water
- 9 tea bags
- ¾ to 1¼ cups sugar
- 1 can (12 oz.) frozen lemonade concentrate, thawed
  Lemon slices, optional

In a Dutch oven, bring the water to a boil. Remove from the heat; add tea bags. Cover and steep for 5 minutes. Discard tea bags. Stir in sugar and lemonade concentrate. Cover and refrigerate until chilled. Serve over ice. If desired, garnish with lemon slices.
1 cup: 100 cal., 0 fat (0 sat. fat), 0 chol., 1mg sod., 26g carb. (25g sugars, 0 fiber), 0 pro.

MARINA'S GOLDEN CORN FRITTERS

Just one bite of these fritters takes me back to when my kids were young. Nowadays for our get-togethers, I sometimes triple the recipe. Serve the fritters with maple syrup or agave nectar.
—Marina Castle Kelley, Canyon Country, CA

Takes: 30 min. • **Makes:** 32 fritters

- 2½ cups all-purpose flour
- 3 tsp. baking powder
- 2 tsp. dried parsley flakes
- 1 tsp. salt
- 2 large eggs, room temperature
- ¾ cup 2% milk
- 2 Tbsp. butter, melted
- 2 tsp. grated onion
- 1 can (15¼ oz.) whole kernel corn, drained
  Oil for deep-fat frying

1. In a large bowl, whisk flour, baking powder, parsley and salt. In another bowl, whisk eggs, milk, melted butter and onion until blended. Add to dry ingredients, stirring just until moistened. Fold in corn.
2. In an electric skillet or deep fryer, heat oil to 375°. Drop batter by tablespoonfuls, several at a time, into hot oil. Fry 2-3 minutes on each side or until golden brown. Drain on paper towels.
2 fritters: 162 cal., 8g fat (2g sat. fat), 28mg chol., 327mg sod., 18g carb. (2g sugars, 1g fiber), 4g pro.

MARINA'S GOLDEN CORN FRITTERS

SWIRLED PEPPERMINT MARSHMALLOWS

BASIL CITRUS COCKTAIL
This irresistible cocktail is fruity, fantastic and low in calories!
—*Taste of Home* Test Kitchen

- -

Takes: 10 min. • **Makes:** 1 serving

- 6 fresh basil leaves
- 1½ to 2 cups ice cubes
- 2 oz. white grapefruit juice
- 2 oz. mandarin orange juice
- ¾ oz. gin
- ½ oz. Domaine de Canton ginger liqueur

In a cocktail shaker, muddle basil leaves. Fill shaker three-fourths full with ice. Add the juices, gin and ginger liqueur; cover and shake until condensation forms on outside of shaker, 10-15 seconds. Strain into a chilled cocktail glass.

1 serving: 136 cal., 0 fat (0 sat. fat), 0 chol., 0 sod., 14g carb. (7g sugars, 0 fiber), 1g pro.

SWIRLED PEPPERMINT MARSHMALLOWS
The fluffy, airy texture of these handmade marshmallows will remind you of glistening snowflakes. What a treat!
—*Taste of Home* Test Kitchen

- -

Prep: 55 min. + standing • **Makes:** 1½ lb.

- 2 tsp. butter
- 3 envelopes unflavored gelatin
- 1 cup cold water, divided
- 2 cups sugar
- 1 cup light corn syrup
- ¼ tsp. salt
- ¾ tsp. peppermint extract
- 10 to 12 drops food coloring
- ¼ cup confectioners' sugar
- ¼ cup finely ground peppermint candies

1. Line a 13x9-in. pan with foil and grease the foil with butter; set aside.

2. In a large metal bowl, sprinkle gelatin over ½ cup water; set aside. In a large heavy saucepan, combine the sugar, corn syrup, salt and remaining water. Bring to a boil, stirring occasionally. Cook, without stirring, until a candy thermometer reads 240° (soft-ball stage).

3. Remove from the heat and gradually add to gelatin. Beat on high speed until mixture is thick and the volume is doubled, about 15 minutes. Beat in extract. Spread into prepared pan. Quickly drop food coloring over candy; cut through candy with a knife to swirl. Cover and let stand at room temperature for 6 hours or overnight.

4. Combine the confectioners' sugar and ground peppermint candies. Using foil, lift marshmallows out of pan. With a knife or pizza cutter coated with cooking spray, cut into 1-in. squares; toss in confectioners' sugar mixture. Store in an airtight container in a cool, dry place.

1 marshmallow: 24 cal., 0 fat (0 sat. fat), 0 chol., 8mg sod., 6g carb. (6g sugars, 0 fiber), 0 pro.

FLAVORFUL STRAWBERRY-RHUBARB JAM

I consider this sweet, flavorful jam a taste of summer in a jar! The fruity concoction is simply scrumptious.
—Peggy Woodward, Senior Food Editor

- -

Prep: 10 min. • **Process:** 5 min.
Makes: about 6 pints

    4   cups fresh strawberries, crushed
    2   cups chopped fresh rhubarb
    ¼   cup bottled lemon juice
    1   pkg. (1¾ oz.) powdered fruit pectin
    5½ cups sugar

1. In a Dutch oven, combine strawberries, rhubarb and lemon juice; stir in pectin. Bring to a full rolling boil, stirring constantly. Stir in sugar; return to a full rolling boil. Boil and stir 1 minute.
2. Remove from heat; skim off foam. Ladle hot mixture into 6 hot sterilized pint jars, leaving ¼-in. headspace. Remove air bubbles and adjust headspace, if necessary, by adding hot mixture. Wipe rims. Center lids on jars; screw on bands until fingertip tight.
3. Place jars into canner with simmering water, ensuring that they are completely covered with water. Bring to a boil; process for 5 minutes. Remove jars and cool.
2 Tbsp.: 99 cal., 0 fat (0 sat. fat), 0 chol., 1mg sod., 25g carb. (24g sugars, 0 fiber), 0 pro.

CARAMEL-PECAN MONKEY BREAD

The kids will get a kick out of pulling off gooey pieces of this delectable monkey bread. It's hard to resist the popular caramel-coated treat.
—*Taste of Home* Test Kitchen

- -

Prep: 20 min. + chilling
Bake: 30 min. + cooling • **Makes:** 20 servings

    1   pkg. (¼ oz.) active dry yeast
    ¼   cup warm water (110° to 115°)
    5   Tbsp. plus ½ cup butter, divided
    1¼   cups warm 2% milk (110° to 115°)

CARAMEL-PECAN MONKEY BREAD

    2   large eggs, room temperature
    1¼   cups sugar, divided
    1   tsp. salt
    5   cups all-purpose flour
    1   tsp. ground cinnamon
    CARAMEL
    ⅔   cup packed brown sugar
    ¼   cup butter, cubed
    ¼   cup heavy whipping cream
    ¾   cup chopped pecans, divided
    OPTIONAL GLAZE
    4   oz. cream cheese, softened
    ¼   cup butter, softened
    1½   cups confectioners' sugar
    3   to 5 Tbsp. 2% milk

1. Dissolve yeast in warm water. Melt 5 Tbsp. butter. Add milk, eggs and melted butter; stir in ¼ cup sugar, salt and 3 cups flour. Beat on medium speed for 3 minutes. Stir in enough remaining flour to form a firm dough.
2. Turn onto a floured surface; knead until smooth and elastic, 6-8 minutes. Place in a greased bowl, turning once to grease the top. Refrigerate, covered, overnight.

3. Punch dough down; shape into 40 balls (about 1¼ in. diameter). Melt remaining butter. In a shallow bowl, combine cinnamon and remaining sugar. Dip balls in butter, then roll in the sugar mixture.
4. For caramel, bring brown sugar, butter and cream to a boil in a small saucepan over medium heat. Cook and stir 3 minutes. Pour half of the caramel into a greased 10-in. fluted tube pan; layer with half the pecans and half the dough balls; repeat. Cover and let rise until doubled, about 45 minutes.
5. Preheat oven to 350°. Bake until golden brown, 30-40 minutes. (Cover loosely with foil for last 10 minutes if top browns too quickly.) Cool 10 minutes before inverting onto a serving plate.
6. For optional glaze, beat the cream cheese and butter until blended; gradually beat in confectioners' sugar. Add enough milk to reach desired consistency. Drizzle glaze over warm bread.
2 pieces: 334 cal., 15g fat (8g sat. fat), 52mg chol., 207mg sod., 45g carb. (21g sugars, 1g fiber), 5g pro.

SPICY ALMONDS

We like to venture out into the Selkirk mountain range surrounding our family cabin. These nuts never tasted better than when we enjoyed them together at the peak at the end of an amazing hike. Almonds are extremely nutritious. When dressed up with a wonderful blend of spices, they go from ordinary to awesome!
—Gina Myers, Spokane, WA

- -

Prep: 10 min. • **Bake:** 30 min. + cooling
Makes: 2½ cups

- 1   **Tbsp. sugar**
- 1½ **tsp. kosher salt**
- 1   **tsp. paprika**
- ½ **tsp. ground cinnamon**
- ½ **tsp. ground cumin**
- ½ **tsp. ground coriander**
- ¼ **tsp. cayenne pepper**
- 1   **large egg white, room temperature**
- 2½ **cups unblanched almonds**

Preheat oven to 325°. In a small bowl, combine the first 7 ingredients. In another small bowl, whisk egg white until foamy. Add almonds; toss to coat. Sprinkle with spice mixture; toss to coat. Spread in a single layer in a greased 15x10x1-in. baking pan. Bake for 30 minutes, stirring every 10 minutes. Spread on waxed paper to cool completely. Store in an airtight container.

¼ cup: 230 cal., 20g fat (2g sat. fat), 0 chol., 293mg sod., 9g carb. (3g sugars, 4g fiber), 8g pro.

DROP DOUGHNUTS

Remember this recipe after your next holiday dinner. I use any leftover mashed potatoes to make these light and fluffy doughnuts. My neighbor's mother-in-law created the recipe. The doughnuts are great for breakfast or as a snack.
—Marilyn Kleinfall, Elk Grove Village, IL

- -

Takes: 25 min. • **Makes:** 3½ dozen

- ½ **cup mashed potatoes (made with milk and butter)**
- ¼ **cup sugar**
- 1   **large egg, lightly beaten**
- ½ **cup sour cream**
- ½ **tsp. vanilla extract**
- 1½ **cups all-purpose flour**
- ½ **tsp. baking soda**
- ¼ **tsp. baking powder**
    Oil for deep-fat frying
    Additional sugar or confectioners' sugar, optional

1. In a large bowl, combine the potatoes, sugar, egg, sour cream and vanilla. Combine dry ingredients; stir in potato mixture.
2. Heat oil in an electric skillet or deep-fat fryer to 375°. Drop teaspoonfuls of batter, a few at a time, into hot oil. Fry until golden brown on both sides. Drain on paper towels. If desired, roll in sugar while warm.

1 doughnut: 42 cal., 2g fat (1g sat. fat), 5mg chol., 29mg sod., 5g carb. (1g sugars, 0 fiber), 1g pro.

SPICY ALMONDS

KEY LIME BLONDIE BARS
PAGE 248

Cookies, Brownies & Bars

Who doesn't love the first blissful bite into a warm, tender cookie or rich brownie or bar? With these deliciously fun recipes and a few simple pantry staples, you can whip up batches of bite-sized yumminess that your whole family is guaranteed to love!

CHOCOLATE CHIP
COOKIE BROWNIES

CHOCOLATE CHIP COOKIE BROWNIES

It was fun to experiment with this chippy brownie recipe. When my daughter tasted the final version, she told me she thought they were the best brownies ever. That sure does make a mom feel good.
—Dion Frischer, Ann Arbor, MI

- -

Prep: 15 min. • **Bake:** 50 min. + cooling
Makes: 1 dozen

- ¾ cup butter
- 1½ cups sugar
- ½ cup baking cocoa
- 3 large eggs, room temperature
- ¾ cup all-purpose flour
- ½ cup chopped walnuts

COOKIE LAYER

- ½ cup butter
- 1 cup packed brown sugar
- 1 large egg, room temperature
- 1 cup all-purpose flour
- ½ tsp. baking soda
- 1 cup semisweet chocolate chips

1. Preheat oven to 350°. Line a 9-in. square baking pan with foil, letting ends extend up sides; grease foil.
2. In a microwave, melt butter in a large microwave-safe bowl. Stir in sugar and cocoa. Add the eggs, 1 at a time, whisking to blend after each addition. Add the flour; stir just until combined. Stir in nuts. Spread into prepared pan. Bake 15 minutes.
3. Meanwhile, for cookie layer, melt butter in another microwave-safe bowl. Stir in the brown sugar. Whisk in egg. In a small bowl, whisk flour and baking soda; stir into butter mixture just until combined. Stir in chocolate chips. Spoon mixture over hot brownie layer.
4. Bake 35-40 minutes longer or until a toothpick inserted in the center comes out with moist crumbs. Cool completely in pan on a wire rack. Lifting foil, remove brownies from pan. Cut into bars.
1 brownie: 536 cal., 29g fat (15g sat. fat), 113mg chol., 236mg sod., 69g carb. (51g sugars, 2g fiber), 6g pro.

PEANUT BUTTER KISS COOKIES

Everyone who tries these classic peanut butter gems is amazed that they use only five simple ingredients. Baking doesn't get much easier than this!
—Dee Davis, Sun City, AZ

- -

Prep: 20 min. • **Bake:** 10 min./batch + cooling
Makes: about 2½ dozen

- 1 cup peanut butter
- 1 cup sugar
- 1 large egg, room temperature
- 1 tsp. vanilla extract
- 30 milk chocolate kisses

1. Preheat oven to 350°. Cream the peanut butter and sugar until light and fluffy. Beat in egg and vanilla.
2. Roll into 1¼-in. balls. Place 2 in. apart on ungreased baking sheets. Bake until tops are slightly cracked, 10-12 minutes. Immediately press 1 chocolate kiss into the center of each cookie. Cool for 5 minutes before removing from pans to wire racks.
1 cookie: 102 cal., 6g fat (2g sat. fat), 7mg chol., 43mg sod., 11g carb. (10g sugars, 1g fiber), 2g pro.

"I love the simplicity of these Peanut Butter Kiss Cookies at Christmastime. It's a welcome recipe in the mix of more complex and time-consuming ones."

—STEPHANIE MARCHESE,
VISUAL PRODUCTION EXECUTIVE DIRECTOR

PEANUT BUTTER
KISS COOKIES

GOOEY CARAMEL-TOPPED GINGERSNAPS

Making these cookies is therapeutic for me. These gingersnaps are quite popular at fundraisers. If you'd like, you can make variations by changing the cookie base or using different types of nuts.
—Deirdre Cox, Kansas City, MO

Prep: 30 min. + chilling • **Makes:** 3½ dozen

- 42 gingersnap cookies
- 1 pkg. (14 oz.) caramels
- ¼ cup 2% milk or heavy whipping cream
- 1 cup chopped honey-roasted peanuts
- 12 oz. white or dark chocolate candy coating, melted
  Chocolate jimmies or finely chopped honey-roasted peanuts

1. Arrange cookies in a single layer on waxed paper-lined baking sheets. In a microwave, melt caramels with milk; stir until smooth. Stir in 1 cup chopped peanuts. Spoon about 1 tsp. caramel mixture over each cookie; refrigerate until set.
2. Dip each cookie halfway into the candy coating; allow excess to drip off. Return to baking sheet; sprinkle with jimmies or finely chopped peanuts. Refrigerate until set.
1 cookie: 128 cal., 5g fat (3g sat. fat), 1mg chol., 70mg sod., 19g carb. (14g sugars, 0 fiber), 2g pro.

TIRAMISU COOKIES

TIRAMISU COOKIES

These tiramisu cookies bring out all the delicious flavors of tiramisu in sandwich style. Pack these treats in a decorative container for an easy, edible hostess gift.
—*Taste of Home* Test Kitchen

Prep: 30 min. • **Bake:** 15 min./batch + cooling
Makes: 1½ dozen

- 1 cup butter, softened
- ¾ cup sugar
- 2 large eggs, room temperature
- 1 tsp. vanilla extract
- ½ tsp. rum extract
- 2¼ cups all-purpose flour
- 1 tsp. baking powder
- ¼ tsp. salt

FILLING
- 1 carton (8 oz.) mascarpone cheese
- ¼ cup butter, softened
- 2 tsp. instant coffee granules
- 1 tsp. vanilla extract
- 3 cups confectioners' sugar
  Baking cocoa

1. Preheat oven to 350°. Cream butter and sugar until light and fluffy, 5-7 minutes. Beat in eggs and extracts. In another bowl, whisk flour, baking powder and salt; gradually beat into creamed mixture.

2. Drop dough by tablespoonfuls 2 in. apart onto parchment-lined baking sheets; flatten slightly with the bottom of a glass dipped in sugar. Bake until the edges begin to brown slightly, 12-14 minutes. Remove from pans to wire racks; cool completely.
3. For the filling, in a large bowl, beat the mascarpone cheese and butter until smooth. In a small bowl, dissolve the instant coffee in vanilla; beat into mascarpone mixture. Gradually beat in confectioners' sugar until smooth. Pipe or spread filling on bottoms of half the cookies; cover with remaining cookies. Dust cookies with cocoa. Store in the refrigerator.
1 sandwich cookie: 344 cal., 19g fat (11g sat. fat), 70mg chol., 176mg sod., 40g carb. (28g sugars, 0 fiber), 3g pro.

DID YOU KNOW?

Mascarpone is a soft fresh cheese with a milky white color. It has a rich, buttery, slightly sweet flavor and a smooth, thick, creamy texture.

SWEETHEART SLICES

Get the flavor of a snickerdoodle plus the texture of a shortbread in these cookies. Bake them for your sweeties, or make the cookies together to create fun memories!
—*Taste of Home* Test Kitchen

Prep: 20 min. + freezing • **Bake:** 15 min./batch
Makes: about 2 dozen

- 1 cup butter, softened
- ¾ cup sugar
- 4 large egg yolks
- 3 tsp. vanilla extract
- 2½ cups all-purpose flour
- 1½ tsp. ground cinnamon
- ⅓ cup miniature semisweet chocolate chips
  Red or pink paste food coloring

1. Cream butter and sugar until light and fluffy, 5-7 minutes. Add egg yolks, 1 at a time, beating well after each addition. Beat in vanilla . Whisk the flour and cinnamon; gradually add to the creamed mixture and mix well. Remove ⅔ of dough to another bowl; stir in chocolate chips. Tint remaining dough pink.

2. On a lightly floured surface, roll smaller portion to ½-in. thickness. Cut with a 1-in. heart-shaped cookie cutter. Brush 1 side of hearts with water and gently stack together to form two 5-in.-long logs, running a finger along sides to smooth edges. Refrigerate until firm, about 30 minutes.

3. Divide the chocolate chip dough into 10 portions. Roll each into a 5-in. coil. Brush outsides of heart logs with water; mold coils around heart logs, gently pressing to adhere. Roll to mold dough into smooth rolls. Place wrapped cookie logs in airtight containers. Freeze until firm, about 2 hours.

4. Preheat oven to 350°. Cut into ¼-in. slices. Place 2 in. apart on parchment-lined baking sheets. Bake until edges are lightly browned, 12-14 minutes. Cool on pans for 2 minutes. Remove to wire racks to cool.

1 cookie: 162 cal., 9g fat (6g sat. fat), 51mg chol., 63mg sod., 18g carb. (8g sugars, 1g fiber), 2g pro.

CHOCOLATE PEANUT BUTTER NO-BAKE COOKIES

These peanut butter and chocolate cookies bring back fond memories of my mom. The no-bake recipe was her favorite, and she always made a batch whenever she knew company was coming.
—Jacquie McTaggart, Independence, IA

Prep: 20 min. + chilling • **Makes:** 2½ dozen

- 2 cups sugar
- ½ cup butter or margarine, cubed
- ½ cup 2% milk
- 3 Tbsp. baking cocoa
  Dash salt
- ½ cup creamy peanut butter
- 1 tsp. vanilla extract
- 3 cups old-fashioned oats

1. In large saucepan, combine the first 5 ingredients. Bring to a boil, stirring constantly. Cook and stir 3 minutes.

2. Remove from heat; stir in peanut butter and vanilla until blended. Stir in oats. Drop mixture by tablespoonfuls onto waxed paper-lined baking sheets. Refrigerate until set. Store in airtight containers.

1 cookie: 139 cal., 6g fat (3g sat. fat), 8mg chol., 50mg sod., 20g carb. (14g sugars, 1g fiber), 2g pro.

SWEETHEART
SLICES

GLAZED ITALIAN FRUITCAKE COOKIES

I grew up in Italy and enjoyed these cookies every Christmas. Now I make them every year and give some to friends.
—Trisha Kruse, Eagle, ID

Prep: 25 min. + chilling • **Bake:** 10 min./batch
Makes: 4 dozen

- 1 cup butter, softened
- ⅓ cup half-and-half cream
- 1 tsp. vanilla extract
- 3 cups all-purpose flour
- ¾ cup sugar
- 4 tsp. baking powder
- ½ tsp. salt
- ½ cup chopped walnuts, toasted
- ½ cup chopped mixed dried fruit

GLAZE
- 1 oz. unsweetened chocolate
- 1½ tsp. butter
- 1 cup confectioners' sugar
- ½ tsp. vanilla extract
- 2 to 3 Tbsp. 2% milk

1. In a large bowl, beat butter, cream and vanilla until blended. In another bowl, whisk the flour, sugar, baking powder and salt; gradually beat into creamed mixture. Stir in the walnuts and dried fruit (mixture will be crumbly). Press the mixture together to form a ball.

2. Divide dough in half; shape each into an 8-in.-long roll. Place wrapped rolls in airtight containers. Refrigerate 1 hour or until firm.

3. Preheat oven to 350°. Uncover and cut dough crosswise into ¼-in. slices. Place 1 in. apart on ungreased baking sheets. Bake 10-12 minutes or until the edges are light brown. Remove cookies from pans to wire racks to cool completely.

4. Meanwhile, in a large heavy saucepan, melt chocolate and butter over low heat. Gradually stir in the confectioners' sugar, vanilla and enough milk to reach drizzling consistency. Remove from heat; drizzle over cooled cookies.

Freeze option: Place the wrapped logs in a freezer container and freeze. To use, unwrap frozen logs and cut into slices. If necessary, let dough stand 15 minutes at room temperature before cutting. Bake as directed.

1 cookie: 106 cal., 5g fat (3g sat. fat), 11mg chol., 100mg sod., 13g carb. (7g sugars, 0 fiber), 1g pro.

MANGO FUDGE REFRIGERATOR RIBBON COOKIES

These layered ribbon cookies taste like two or three different cookies rolled into one special treat. They have a rich chocolate layer balanced by a bright orange-mango layer—a special combination.
—Jeanne Holt, Mendota Heights, MN

Prep: 30 min. + chilling
Bake: 10 min./batch + cooling
Makes: 4 dozen

TEST KITCHEN TIP

The outermost part of a citrus fruit has the most desirable flavor. Be careful not to grate too far down into the peel. The lighter-colored inner part of the peel, the pith, tastes bitter.

- 1 cup butter, softened
- 1 cup sugar
- 1 large egg, room temperature
- 2 Tbsp. 2% milk
- 1½ tsp. vanilla extract
- 3 cups all-purpose flour
- 1½ tsp. baking powder
- ½ tsp. salt
- ½ cup 60% cacao bittersweet chocolate baking chips, melted and cooled
- ⅓ cup miniature semisweet chocolate chips
- ½ cup finely chopped dried mango
- ⅓ cup finely chopped pistachios
- 2 tsp. grated orange zest

1. Cream the butter and sugar until light and fluffy, 5-7 minutes. Beat in the egg, milk and vanilla. In another bowl, whisk together flour, baking powder and salt; gradually add to the creamed mixture.

2. Divide the dough in half. Mix the melted chocolate into 1 half; stir in miniature chips. Mix mango, pistachios and orange zest into remaining half dough.

3. Line an 8x4-in. loaf pan with plastic wrap, letting ends extend over sides. Press half chocolate dough onto bottom of pan; top with half the mango dough. Repeat layers.

4. Lifting with plastic, remove dough from pan; fold the plastic over dough to wrap completely. Refrigerate the dough in pan until firm, 2 hours or overnight.

5. Preheat oven to 375°. Unwrap and cut dough crosswise into ½-in.-thick slices; cut each slice crosswise into thirds. Place 2 in. apart on ungreased baking sheets.

6. Bake until the edges are lightly browned, 10-12 minutes. Remove from pans to wire racks to cool.

1 cookie: 104 cal., 5g fat (3g sat. fat), 14mg chol., 58mg sod., 13g carb. (7g sugars, 1g fiber), 1g pro.

MANGO FUDGE
REFRIGERATOR
RIBBON COOKIES

MEXICAN CRINKLE COOKIES

MEXICAN CRINKLE COOKIES

When it's baking time, my family lobbies for these Mexican crinkle cookies. You can replace 1 ounce unsweetened chocolate with 3 tablespoons cocoa powder plus 1 tablespoon shortening, butter or oil.
—Kim Kenyon, Greenwood, MO

Prep: 25 min. + chilling • **Bake:** 10 min./batch
Makes: about 2 dozen

- ¾ cup butter, cubed
- 2 oz. unsweetened chocolate, chopped
- 1 cup packed brown sugar
- ¼ cup light corn syrup
- 1 large egg, room temperature
- 2 cups all-purpose flour
- 2 tsp. baking soda
- 1½ tsp. ground cinnamon, divided
- ¼ tsp. salt
- ½ cup confectioners' sugar

1. In a microwave, melt the butter and chocolate; stir until smooth. Beat in the brown sugar and corn syrup until blended. Beat in egg. In another bowl, whisk flour, baking soda, 1 tsp. cinnamon and salt; gradually beat into the brown sugar mixture. Refrigerate, covered, until firm, about 1 hour.
2. Preheat oven to 350°. In a shallow bowl, mix confectioners' sugar and remaining cinnamon. Shape dough into 1½-in. balls; roll in the confectioners' sugar mixture. Place 2 in. apart on greased baking sheets.
3. Bake until set and the tops are cracked, 10-12 minutes. Cool on pans 2 minutes. Remove to wire racks to finish cooling.
1 cookie: 158 cal., 7g fat (4g sat. fat), 23mg chol., 184mg sod., 22g carb. (13g sugars, 1g fiber), 2g pro.

CANNOLI WAFER SANDWICHES

My family loves to visit an Italian restaurant that has a wonderful dessert buffet. The cannoli is among our favorite choices, so I just had to come up with my own simple version. These sandwiches are best served the same day so the wafers remain crisp.
—Nichi Larson, Shawnee, KS

Prep: 35 min. + standing • **Makes:** 3½ dozen

- 1 cup whole-milk ricotta cheese
- ¼ cup confectioners' sugar
- 1 Tbsp. sugar
- ¼ tsp. vanilla extract
- 1 pkg. (12 oz.) vanilla wafers
- 12 oz. white candy coating, melted
- ½ cup miniature semisweet chocolate chips
  Additional confectioners' sugar

1. In a small bowl, mix the ricotta cheese, confectioners' sugar, sugar and vanilla until blended. Spread 1 scant tsp. filling on the bottoms of half the wafers; cover with the remaining wafers.
2. Dip each sandwich cookie halfway into candy coating; allow excess to drip off. Place on waxed paper; sprinkle with the chocolate chips. Let stand until set, about 10 minutes.
3. Serve within 2 hours or refrigerate until serving. Dust with additional confectioners' sugar just before serving.
1 sandwich cookie: 93 cal., 5g fat (3g sat. fat), 4mg chol., 38mg sod., 13g carb. (10g sugars, 0 fiber), 1g pro.

PEANUT BUTTER PRETZEL BARS

For these rich no-bake bites, pretzels are my secret. They add a salty crunch.
—Jennifer Beckman, Falls Church, VA

Prep: 15 min. + chilling • **Makes:** 4 dozen

- 1 pkg. (16 oz.) miniature pretzels
- 1½ cups butter, melted
- 1½ cups peanut butter
- 3 cups confectioners' sugar
- 2 cups semisweet chocolate chips
- 1 Tbsp. shortening

1. Line a 13x9-in. baking pan with foil, letting ends extend up sides. Set aside 1½ cups of pretzels for topping. Pulse remaining pretzels in a food processor until fine crumbs form. In a large bowl, mix the butter, peanut butter, confectioners' sugar and pretzel crumbs.
2. Press into prepared pan. In a microwave, melt chocolate chips and shortening; stir until smooth. Spread over peanut butter layer. Break reserved pretzels and sprinkle over top; press down gently. Refrigerate, covered, until set, about 1 hour. Lifting with foil, remove from pan. Cut into bars.
1 bar: 201 cal., 13g fat (6g sat. fat), 15mg chol., 233mg sod., 22g carb. (12g sugars, 1g fiber), 3g pro.

TEST KITCHEN TIP

Before putting peanut butter in a measuring cup, lightly coat the inside with water or oil. The peanut butter will slide right out without having to scrape the cup multiple times with a spatula.

PEANUT BUTTER PRETZEL BARS

APPLE-PEANUT BLONDIES

These blondies are mostly layers of apples, with a little bit of blondie mixed in, creating the perfect layered dessert. I started with a similar recipe and did a bit of tweaking to make it our family's own.
—Julie Peterson, Crofton, MD

Prep: 15 min. • **Bake:** 25 min. + cooling
Makes: 9 servings

- 1 cup packed brown sugar
- ½ cup butter, melted
- 1 large egg, room temperature
- 1 tsp. vanilla extract
- 1 cup all-purpose flour
- ½ tsp. baking powder
- ¼ tsp. baking soda
- ¼ tsp. salt
- 2 small apples (about 9 oz.), peeled and sliced
- ½ cup chopped salted peanuts

1. Preheat oven to 350°. Beat brown sugar and butter until light and fluffy, 5-7 minutes. Add egg and vanilla; beat until smooth. In a separate bowl, whisk together flour, baking powder, baking soda and salt; gradually beat into brown sugar mixture just until combined (batter will be thick).
2. Spread all but ¼ cup batter into a greased and floured 8-in. square baking dish. Layer with apple slices; dot with remaining batter. Sprinkle with chopped peanuts. Bake until the top is golden brown and center is set, 22-28 minutes. Cool on a wire rack.
1 blondie: 302 cal., 15g fat (7g sat. fat), 48mg chol., 256mg sod., 39g carb. (26g sugars, 1g fiber), 4g pro.

FROSTED WALNUT BROWNIE CUPS

Enjoy a little taste of heaven with these cute brownie cups. They are always a hit and are simple to make.
—Crystal Strick, Boyertown, PA

Prep: 30 min. • **Bake:** 20 min. + cooling
Makes: 32 brownie cups

- 2 cups semisweet chocolate chips
- 1 cup butter, cubed
- 1⅓ cups sugar
- 4 large eggs, room temperature
- 2 tsp. vanilla extract
- 1 cup all-purpose flour
- 1 cup chopped walnuts

GANACHE
- 2 cups semisweet chocolate chips
- ¾ cup heavy whipping cream

1. In a microwave, melt chocolate chips and butter; whisk until smooth. Cool slightly.
2. In a large bowl, beat sugar and eggs. Stir in vanilla and chocolate mixture. Gradually add flour; stir in walnuts. Fill paper-lined miniature muffin cups almost full.
3. Bake at 350° for 20-23 minutes or until a toothpick inserted in the center comes out clean. Cool for 5 minutes before removing from pans to wire racks to cool completely.
4. For ganache, place chocolate chips in a small bowl. In a small saucepan, bring cream just to a boil. Pour over chocolate; whisk until smooth. Cool 30 minutes or until ganache reaches a spreading consistency, stirring occasionally. Spread over brownie cups.
1 brownie cup: 353 cal., 24g fat (13g sat. fat), 49mg chol., 56mg sod., 39g carb. (32g sugars, 3g fiber), 4g pro.

FROSTED WALNUT BROWNIE CUPS

SANTA'S ELF COOKIES

These rosy-cheeked elf cookies will make a showstopping addition to your holiday cookie tray. Or set them atop cupcakes for an extra-cute treat.
—Josh Rink, Food Stylist

- -

Prep: 2 hours + standing
Bake: 10 min./batch + cooling
Makes: about 4 dozen

1¾ cups confectioners' sugar, divided
2 oz. almond paste
1¼ cups butter, softened
1 large egg, room temperature
¼ cup 2% milk
1 tsp. vanilla extract
4 cups all-purpose flour
½ tsp. salt
ROYAL ICING AND DECORATIONS
2 cups confectioners' sugar
2 Tbsp. water plus 2 tsp. water
4½ tsp. meringue powder
¼ tsp. cream of tartar
Food coloring
Black nonpareil sprinkles
Pink luster dust, optional
Edible food writing pen
Chocolate frosting of your choice

SANTA'S ELF COOKIES

1. In the bowl of a food processor fitted with the blade attachment, pulse ½ cup confectioner's sugar and almond paste until well mixed and texture resembles finely ground cornmeal. In a large bowl, cream the butter and remaining 1¼ cups confectioners' sugar until light and fluffy. Add almond paste mixture and beat until fully incorporated. Beat in egg, milk and vanilla. Combine flour and salt; gradually add to creamed mixture and mix well. Cover and refrigerate 1 hour.
2. Preheat oven to 375°. On a lightly floured surface, roll out dough to ¼-in. thickness. Cut out using a floured 3½-in. elf cookie cutter. Place 1 in. apart on parchment-lined baking sheets. Bake until cookies are light golden brown and firm, 7-8 minutes. Let stand for 2 minutes before removing to wire racks to cool.

3. For icing, in a large bowl, combine confectioners' sugar, water, meringue powder and cream of tartar; beat on low speed just until blended. Beat on high until stiff peaks form, 4-5 minutes. Divide icing into thirds. Tint 1 portion of icing with red food coloring; tint second portion with desired food coloring for face. Leave the remaining portion white.
4. Place icings into piping bags fitted with fine round tips. Pipe icing onto cookies to create clothing, hat and face. While icing is still wet, place black sprinkles to create eyes. Let the icing dry completely. If desired, dip a small brush into pink luster dust; tap off excess and dab onto cookies to create pink cheeks. Using leaf tip #67, pipe frosting to create ears. Using a small round tip, pipe icing to create nose. Using an edible pen or round tip, draw mouth. Place the chocolate frosting into a piping bag fitted with #14 star tip; pipe along top of face and rim of hat to create hair. Store in an airtight container.
1 cookie: 134 cal., 6g fat (3g sat. fat), 18mg chol., 72mg sod., 19g carb. (10g sugars, 0 fiber), 2g pro.

DID YOU KNOW?

Royal icing is a specific type of icing. What sets it apart from other frostings and glazes is that it hardens when cooled, making it an ideal choice for decorated cookies, like these elf cookies, and gingerbread houses.

The secret ingredient in royal icing is the meringue powder. This egg white substitute helps the icing achieve its glossy consistency. You can buy meringue powder online or at many grocery or craft stores.

GRAFFITI CUTOUT COOKIES

Talk about playing with your food! Edible color spray lets you create ombre and color blends unlike any other decorating technique. To re-create my ombre lines, hold a sheet of paper over desired sections as you spray to layer the color.
—Shannon Norris, Senior Food Stylist

Prep: 30 min. + freezing
Bake: 15 min. + cooling
Makes: 15 cookies

- ¼ cup butter, softened
- ½ cup sugar
- 1 large egg, room temperature
- 1 tsp. vanilla extract
- 2 cups almond flour
- ¼ tsp. salt
- ¼ tsp. baking soda
- ROYAL ICING
- 2 cups confectioners' sugar
- 2 to 6 Tbsp. water
- 5 tsp. meringue powder
  Food color spray, optional

1. In a bowl, cream butter and sugar until light and fluffy, 5-7 minutes. Beat in egg and vanilla. In another bowl, whisk almond flour, salt and baking soda; gradually beat into creamed mixture.

2. Preheat oven to 325°. Between 2 pieces of waxed paper, roll dough to ¼-in. thickness. Place on a cutting board in the freezer until firm, about 20 minutes. Remove paper; cut with 3-in. cookie cutters. Place 2 in. apart on parchment-lined baking sheets.

3. Bake until lightly browned on the edges, 12-15 minutes. Cool on baking sheets for 2 minutes. Remove cookies to wire racks to cool completely.

4. For the icing, in a large bowl, combine confectioners' sugar, 2 Tbsp. water and meringue powder; beat on low speed just until blended. Beat on high until stiff peaks form, 4-5 minutes. Add water as necessary to reach desired consistency. Keep unused icing covered at all times with a damp cloth. If necessary, beat again on high speed to restore texture.

5. Frost the cookies and let stand at room temperature several hours or until frosting is dry and firm. If desired, decorate with food color spray. Store in an airtight container.
1 cookie: 209 cal., 11g fat (3g sat. fat), 21mg chol., 103mg sod., 26g carb. (23g sugars, 2g fiber), 4g pro.

TRIPLE-CHOCOLATE CHEESECAKE BARS

What's better than a brownie crust layered with chocolate cheesecake and topped with chocolate ganache? These bars will satisfy even the biggest chocolate lovers.
—Andrea Price, Grafton, WI

Prep: 35 min. • **Bake:** 25 min. + chilling
Makes: 2½ dozen

- ¼ cup butter, cubed
- ½ cup sugar
- 3 Tbsp. baking cocoa
- ½ tsp. vanilla extract
- 1 large egg, room temperature
- ¼ cup all-purpose flour
- ⅛ tsp. baking powder
- ⅛ tsp. salt
- CHEESECAKE LAYER
- 2 pkg. (8 oz. each) cream cheese, softened
- ½ cup sugar
- 1½ tsp. vanilla extract
- ¾ cup semisweet chocolate chips, melted and cooled
- 2 large eggs, room temperature, lightly beaten
- GANACHE
- 1½ cups semisweet chocolate chips
- ½ cup heavy whipping cream
- 1 tsp. vanilla extract

1. Preheat oven to 350°. Line a 13x9-in. pan with foil, letting ends extend up sides; grease foil. In a microwave, melt butter in a large microwave-safe bowl. Stir in sugar, cocoa and vanilla. Add egg; blend well. Add the flour, baking powder and salt; stir just until combined. Spread as a thin layer in prepared pan. Bake until top appears dry, 6-8 minutes.

2. Meanwhile, in a large bowl, beat the cream cheese, sugar and vanilla until smooth. Beat in cooled chocolate chips. Add the beaten eggs; beat on low speed just until combined. Spread over brownie layer. Bake until filling is set, 25-30 minutes. Cool 10 minutes on a wire rack.

3. For ganache, place chocolate chips in a small bowl. In a saucepan, bring cream just to a boil. Pour over chocolate; let stand for 5 minutes. Stir with a whisk until smooth. Stir in vanilla extract; cool slightly, stirring occasionally. Pour over cheesecake layer; cool in pan on a wire rack 1 hour. Refrigerate at least 2 hours. Lifting with foil, remove brownies from pan. Cut into bars.
1 bar: 180 cal., 13g fat (7g sat. fat), 42mg chol., 81mg sod., 17g carb. (14g sugars, 1g fiber), 2g pro.

DID YOU KNOW?

Ganache is a French term for a smooth, velvety mixture of chocolate and cream.

KEY LIME PIE BALLS

The classic creamy filling, graham cracker crust and tart citrusy burst of lime are all mixed together in every bite of these easy rolled cookies.
—*Taste of Home* Test Kitchen

Prep: 25 min. + chilling
Makes: about 5 dozen

- 1 pkg. (8 oz.) cream cheese, softened
- 1 can (14½ oz.) sweetened condensed milk
- 3½ cups graham cracker crumbs
- 3 Tbsp. lime juice
- 2 tsp. grated lime zest
- ¼ tsp. salt
- ¼ tsp. ground cinnamon
- ½ cup confectioners' sugar

1. In a large bowl, beat the first 7 ingredients until blended. Shape into 1-in. balls. Roll cookie balls in the confectioners' sugar. Refrigerate 30 minutes or until firm.
2. Store cookies between pieces of waxed paper in an airtight container and store in the refrigerator.
1 cookie: 72 cal., 3g fat (1g sat. fat), 7mg chol., 60mg sod., 11g carb. (8g sugars, 0 fiber), 1g pro.

CHERRY-COCONUT SLICES

CHERRY-COCONUT SLICES

My mother loved to make this recipe from well-known home economist Emmie Oddie, who had a column in a Canadian farming newspaper. Oddie would test reader recipes in her own kitchen and write about them. These tasty sweets are so rich that you need only a small piece.
—Judy Olson, Whitecourt, AB

Prep: 15 min. + chilling
Cook: 5 min. + cooling • **Makes:** 32 bars

- 3 cups graham cracker crumbs
- 1½ cups miniature marshmallows
- 1 cup unsweetened finely shredded coconut
- ½ cup chopped maraschino cherries
- 1 can (14 oz.) sweetened condensed milk
- 1 tsp. maple flavoring

FROSTING
- 1 cup packed brown sugar
- ⅓ cup butter, cubed
- ¼ cup 2% milk
- 1 cup confectioners' sugar

1. In a large bowl, mix the cracker crumbs, marshmallows, coconut and cherries; stir in condensed milk and flavoring. Press into a greased 8-in. square baking pan.
2. For the frosting, in a small saucepan, combine the brown sugar, butter and milk. Bring to a boil, stirring constantly; cook and stir 3 minutes. Transfer to a small bowl; cool until lukewarm, about 15 minutes. Stir in confectioners' sugar until smooth. Spread over the crumb mixture; refrigerate until set, about 1½ hours.
3. Cut into bars. Store bars in an airtight container in the refrigerator.
1 bar: 169 cal., 6g fat (4g sat. fat), 9mg chol., 82mg sod., 28g carb. (22g sugars, 1g fiber), 2g pro.

DID YOU KNOW?

Maraschino cherries—the darling of cocktails, fluffy fruit salads and vintage desserts like these bars—can be made from any type of cherry.

SKILLET STOUT BROWNIES

These stout brownies are so rich and fudgy. I love that you need only one bowl and a skillet to make this quick dessert, so it's perfect for a busy weeknight.
—Mandy Naglich, New York, NY

- -

Prep: 30 min. • **Bake:** 25 min. + cooling
Makes: 12 servings

- 8 oz. semisweet chocolate, chopped
- 1 cup butter, cubed
- 1 cup milk stout beer
- 1 large egg, room temperature
- 2 large egg yolks, room temperature
- ¾ cup sugar
- ¼ cup packed brown sugar
- ¾ cup all-purpose flour
- ⅓ cup baking cocoa
- ½ tsp. salt
  Vanilla ice cream, optional

1. Preheat oven to 350°. Place chocolate in a large bowl. In a 10-in. cast-iron or other ovenproof skillet, combine butter and stout. Bring to a boil; reduce heat. Simmer for 10 minutes, stirring constantly. Pour over chocolate; stir with a whisk until smooth. Cool slightly. In another large bowl, beat egg, egg yolks and sugars until blended. Stir in chocolate mixture. In another bowl, mix the flour, baking cocoa and salt; gradually add to chocolate mixture, mixing well.
2. Spread into skillet. Bake until brownies are set, 25-30 minutes. Cool completely in skillet on a wire rack. If desired, serve with vanilla ice cream.

1 piece: 363 cal., 24g fat (14g sat. fat), 87mg chol., 229mg sod., 29g carb. (21g sugars, 1g fiber), 4g pro.

NO-BAKE CEREAL COOKIE BARS

We pull out all the goodies—like raisins and coconut—for these chewy bars. For more color, sprinkle the M&M's after the bars are in the pan. Then lightly press them into the cereal mixture.
—Connie Craig, Lakewood, WA

- -

Prep: 10 min. • **Cook:** 15 min. + cooling
Makes: 3 dozen

- 4½ cups Rice Krispies
- 3¼ cups quick-cooking oats
- ½ cup cornflakes
- ½ cup sweetened shredded coconut
- ½ cup butter, cubed
- 1 pkg. (16 oz.) miniature marshmallows
- ¼ cup honey
- ½ cup M&M's minis
- ¼ cup raisins

1. Grease a 15x10x1-in. pan. In a large bowl, combine the first 4 ingredients.
2. In a large saucepan, melt the butter over low heat. Add the marshmallows; stir until completely melted. Stir in the honey until blended. Pour over cereal mixture; stir until evenly coated. Cool 5 minutes.
3. Stir in M&M's minis and raisins; press into prepared pan using a greased spatula. Let stand for 30 minutes before cutting. Store bars between layers of waxed paper in an airtight container.

1 bar: 137 cal., 4g fat (3g sat. fat), 8mg chol., 58mg sod., 24g carb. (13g sugars, 1g fiber), 2g pro. **Diabetic exchanges:** 1½ starch, ½ fat.

SKILLET STOUT BROWNIES

BIG SOFT GINGER COOKIES

BIG SOFT GINGER COOKIES

These nicely spiced, soft gingerbread cookies are perfect for folks who like the flavor of ginger but don't care for crunchy gingersnaps.
—Barbara Gray, Boise, ID

- -

Prep: 20 min. • **Bake:** 10 min./batch
Makes: 2½ dozen

¾ cup butter, softened
1 cup sugar
1 large egg, room temperature
¼ cup molasses
2¼ cups all-purpose flour
2 tsp. ground ginger
1 tsp. baking soda
¾ tsp. ground cinnamon
½ tsp. ground cloves
¼ tsp. salt
Additional sugar

1. In a large bowl, cream the butter and sugar until light and fluffy, 5-7 minutes. Beat in egg and molasses. Combine flour, ginger, baking soda, cinnamon, cloves and salt. Gradually add to creamed mixture; mix well.
2. Roll into 1½-in. balls, then roll in sugar. Place 2 in. apart on ungreased baking sheets. Bake at 350° until puffy and lightly browned, 10-12 minutes. Remove to wire racks to cool.
1 cookie: 111 cal., 5g fat (3g sat. fat), 19mg chol., 98mg sod., 16g carb. (8g sugars, 0 fiber), 1g pro.

ASK SARAH

SHOULD I USE UNSALTED OR SALTED BUTTER WHEN BAKING COOKIES AND BARS?

The salt level makes a huge difference in baking. If a recipe calls for butter (neither unsalted nor salted) and salt, it's safe to assume the recipe has been precisely calibrated with unsalted butter in mind.

LEMON THYME ICEBOX COOKIES

I found this recipe at my grandmother's house, and I made it as soon as I got home. The lovely melt-in-your-mouth butter cookie is very unique. It is almost savory because of the thyme, which pairs well with the lemon.
—Catherine Adams, Westwego, LA

Prep: 15 min. + chilling
Bake: 15 min./batch + cooling
Makes: about 2 dozen

- ½ cup butter, softened
- 5 Tbsp. sugar
- 1 Tbsp. minced fresh thyme
- 1 to 2 tsp. grated lemon zest
- 1 large egg yolk, room temperature
- 1 cup all-purpose flour
- ¼ tsp. baking powder
- ¼ tsp. salt

1. Cream the butter, sugar, thyme and lemon zest until light and fluffy, 5-7 minutes. Beat in egg yolk. In another bowl, whisk the flour, baking powder and salt; gradually beat into creamed mixture.
2. Roughly shape dough into a 12-in. roll along the edge of a 12x12-in. sheet of waxed paper. Tightly roll waxed paper over dough, using the paper to mold the dough into a smooth roll. Place wrapped roll in airtight container. Refrigerate 1 hour or overnight.
3. Preheat oven to 350°. Uncover and cut dough crosswise into ½-in. slices. Place 2 in. apart on ungreased baking sheets. Bake until edges begin to brown, 12-15 minutes. Cool in pans 5 minutes. Remove to wire racks to finish cooling.
1 cookie: 65 cal., 4g fat (3g sat. fat), 18mg chol., 61mg sod., 7g carb. (3g sugars, 0 fiber), 1g pro.

S'MORES BROWNIES

My family simply adores our daughter's fudgy s'mores brownies. The cinnamon graham cracker crust and dark chocolate brownies bring our passion for s'mores to a whole new level!
—Jennifer Gilbert, Brighton, MI

Prep: 20 min. • **Bake:** 30 min.
Makes: 2 dozen

- 1½ cups graham cracker crumbs (about 10 whole crackers)
- ¼ cup sugar
- 1 tsp. ground cinnamon
- ½ cup butter, melted

BROWNIES
- 1 oz. unsweetened baking chocolate
- ½ cup butter, softened
- 1¼ cups sugar
- 3 large eggs, room temperature
- 1 tsp. vanilla extract
- 1¼ cups all-purpose flour
- ⅓ cup dark baking cocoa
- ½ tsp. baking powder
- ¼ tsp. salt
- 1 cup miniature marshmallows

TOPPING
- 1 cup miniature marshmallows
- 5 whole graham crackers, broken into bite-sized pieces

1. Preheat oven to 350°. Combine cracker crumbs, sugar and cinnamon. Stir in melted butter. Press onto bottom of an ungreased 13x9-in. baking pan. Bake 7-9 minutes or until lightly browned. Cool on a wire rack.
2. For brownies, melt unsweetened baking chocolate on high in a microwave, stirring every 30 seconds. Cool slightly. Cream the butter and sugar on medium speed until light and fluffy, 5-7 minutes. Add eggs and beat well; beat in melted chocolate and vanilla. In another bowl, whisk together the flour, baking cocoa, baking powder and salt; stir into creamed mixture. Fold in 1 cup of the miniature marshmallows.
3. Spread batter over graham cracker crust. Top with 1 cup marshmallows and broken graham crackers. Bake until center is set, 18-22 minutes (do not overbake).
1 brownie: 215 cal., 10g fat (6g sat. fat), 44mg chol., 157mg sod., 30g carb. (17g sugars, 1g fiber), 3g pro.

S'MORES BROWNIES

KEY LIME BLONDIE BARS

KEY LIME BLONDIE BARS

Here's my tropical take on a beloved treat. These Key lime bars combine the taste of the classic pie with blondie batter and cream cheese frosting. You can make a thicker crust if desired.
—Kristin LaBoon, Austin, TX

- -

Prep: 35 min. + chilling
Bake: 25 min. + cooling • **Makes:** 16 servings

- 1⅓ cups graham cracker crumbs, divided
- ⅓ cup plus 2 Tbsp. melted butter, divided
- 3 Tbsp. plus ¼ cup packed brown sugar, divided
- ⅔ cup butter, softened
- 1 cup plus 1 Tbsp. sugar, divided
- 2 large eggs, room temperature
- 1 large egg white, room temperature
- 3 Tbsp. Key lime juice
- 4½ tsp. grated Key lime zest
- 1 cup all-purpose flour
- ½ tsp. plus ⅛ tsp. salt, divided
- 1 tsp. vanilla extract
- ⅛ tsp. ground cinnamon

FROSTING

- ¼ cup butter, softened
- ¼ cup cream cheese, softened
- 4 cups confectioners' sugar
- 2 Tbsp. 2% milk
- 1 tsp. vanilla extract
Key lime slices, optional

1. Preheat oven to 350°. Line a 9-in. square baking pan with parchment, letting ends extend up sides. Combine 1 cup cracker crumbs, ⅓ cup melted butter and 3 Tbsp. brown sugar; press onto bottom of prepared pan. Bake 10 minutes. Cool on a wire rack.
2. For blondie layer, in a large bowl, cream softened butter and 1 cup sugar until light and fluffy, 5-7 minutes. Beat in eggs, egg white, and lime juice and zest. In a small bowl, mix flour and ½ tsp. salt; gradually add to creamed mixture, mixing well.
3. Spread over crust. Bake until a toothpick inserted in the center comes out clean, 25-30 minutes (do not overbake). Cool completely in pan on a wire rack.
4. For streusel, combine the remaining ⅓ cup cracker crumbs, 2 Tbsp. melted butter, ¼ cup brown sugar, 1 Tbsp. sugar and ⅛ tsp. salt, along with the vanilla and cinnamon, until crumbly. Reserve ½ cup for topping.
5. In a large bowl, combine the 5 frosting ingredients; beat until smooth. Stir in the remaining ½ cup streusel. Spread over bars. Sprinkle with reserved topping. Refrigerate at least 4 hours before cutting. Lifting with the parchment, remove from pan. Cut into bars. Store in an airtight container in the refrigerator. If desired, garnish with sliced Key limes.

1 blondie: 422 cal., 19g fat (11g sat. fat), 69mg chol., 283mg sod., 62g carb. (51g sugars, 1g fiber), 3g pro.

CINNAMON-CANDY COOKIES

I was trying to make a unique Christmas cookie inspired by my brother's love of Red Hots, so I used the candies for cinnamon flavor in these lacelike cookies.
—Wendy Rusch, Cameron, WI

- -

Prep: 20 min. + chilling
Bake: 10 min./batch + cooling
Makes: about 5 dozen

- ⅔ cup Red Hots
- 2⅓ cups all-purpose flour
- 1 cup butter, softened
- 1 cup sugar
- 1 tsp. vanilla extract

FROSTING

- 2 cups confectioners' sugar
- ½ cup butter, softened
- ½ tsp. vanilla or cinnamon extract
- ⅛ tsp. salt
- 4 to 6 Tbsp. 2% milk

1. Place Red Hots in a food processor; process until fine and powdery. Add flour; pulse to combine. In a large bowl, cream butter and sugar until light and fluffy, 5-7 minutes. Beat in vanilla. Gradually beat in flour mixture. Shape dough into two 8-in. rolls; wrap each in waxed paper. Chill until firm, about 1 hour.
2. Preheat oven to 350°. Unwrap rolls and cut into ¼-in. slices. Place 2 in. apart on ungreased baking sheets. Bake until edges are just lightly browned, 7-9 minutes. Cool on pans 2 minutes before removing to wire racks to cool completely.
3. For frosting, in a small bowl, beat the confectioners' sugar, butter, extract, salt and enough of the milk to reach desired consistency. Decorate cookies as desired.

Freeze option: Place wrapped logs in a freezer container; freeze. To use, unwrap frozen logs and cut into slices. If necessary, let the dough stand a few minutes at room temperature before cutting. Bake and decorate cookies as directed.

1 cookie: 98 cal., 5g fat (3g sat. fat), 12mg chol., 42mg sod., 14g carb. (9g sugars, 0 fiber), 1g pro.

CINNAMON-CANDY COOKIES

EASY SLICE & BAKE COOKIES

Anyone who loves a monster cookie will appreciate these large slice-and-bake treats. Since the dough is frozen, you can pull it out of the freezer and slice as many (or as few) cookies as you want to enjoy at any given time.
—Heather Chambers, Largo, FL

- -

Prep: 30 min. + freezing
Bake: 10 min./batch + cooling
Makes: about 4 dozen

- 1 cup unsalted butter, softened
- ⅓ cup Nutella
- ¾ cup sugar
- ¾ cup packed brown sugar
- 2 large eggs, room temperature
- 1 Tbsp. vanilla extract
- 2¾ cups all-purpose flour
- 1 tsp. baking soda
- 1 tsp. salt
- 1¼ cups white baking chips

1. Cream butter, Nutella and sugars until light and fluffy, 5-7 minutes. Beat in the eggs and vanilla. In another bowl, whisk flour, baking soda and salt; gradually beat into creamed mixture. Stir in chips.
2. Divide dough in half. Roughly shape each portion into a 12-in. roll along the edge of a 12x12-in. sheet of waxed paper. Tightly roll waxed paper over dough, using it to mold the dough into a smooth roll. Place wrapped rolls in airtight containers. Freeze until firm, about 1 hour.
3. Preheat oven to 375°. Unwrap and cut dough crosswise into ½-in. slices. Place 2 in. apart on ungreased baking sheets. Bake until lightly browned, 10-12 minutes. Remove from pans to wire racks to cool.
1 cookie: 123 cal., 6g fat (3g sat. fat), 19mg chol., 85mg sod., 16g carb. (10g sugars, 0 fiber), 1g pro.

M&M PRETZEL COOKIES

Kids and grown-ups alike adore these sweet and crunchy no-bake cookies. Add more candy for lovers of M&M's, or toss in a few additional pretzels for an extra-salty bite.
—Madison Allen, Destrehan, LA

- -

Prep: 20 min. + chilling • **Makes:** 6 dozen

- ½ cup butter, cubed
- 2 cups sugar
- ½ cup 2% milk
- 2 Tbsp. baking cocoa
- 1 cup creamy peanut butter
- 2 tsp. vanilla extract
- 3 cups quick-cooking oats
- 1 cup coarsely crushed pretzels
- 1 cup milk chocolate M&M's

1. In a large saucepan, combine the butter, sugar, milk and cocoa. Bring to a boil over medium heat, stirring constantly. Cook and stir 1 minute.
2. Remove from heat; stir in peanut butter and vanilla until blended. Stir in oats; let stand for 5 minutes to cool. Fold in the pretzels and M&M's. Drop mixture by tablespoonfuls onto waxed paper-lined baking sheets. Refrigerate until set.
1 cookie: 87 cal., 4g fat (2g sat. fat), 4mg chol., 46mg sod., 12g carb. (8g sugars, 1g fiber), 2g pro.

M&M PRETZEL COOKIES

CINNAMON BUN COOKIES

BUTTERSCOTCH-RUM RAISIN TREATS

I love making rum raisin rice pudding around the holidays, and the classic flavors inspired this confection. Crispy rice cereal adds crunch, but nuts could do the job, too.
—Crystal Schlueter, Northglenn, CO

Takes: 20 min. • **Makes:** about 4½ dozen

- 1 pkg. (10 to 11 oz.) butterscotch chips
- 1 pkg. (10 to 12 oz.) white baking chips
- ½ tsp. rum extract
- 3 cups Rice Krispies
- 1 cup raisins

1. Line 56 mini muffin cups with paper liners. In a large bowl, combine butterscotch and white chips. Microwave, uncovered, on high for 30 seconds; stir. Microwave in additional 30-second intervals, stirring until smooth.
2. Stir in extract, Rice Krispies and raisins. Drop by rounded tablespoonfuls into the prepared mini muffin cups. Chill until set.
Freeze option: Freeze treats in freezer containers, separating layers with waxed paper. Thaw before serving.
1 treat: 76 cal., 4g fat (3g sat. fat), 1mg chol., 21mg sod., 11g carb. (9g sugars, 0 fiber), 0 pro.

CINNAMON BUN COOKIES

I love cinnamon rolls, but working with yeast can be a little intimidating. These cookies give you the taste of a cinnamon roll in cookie form—no yeast required! They are pretty enough for special occasions.
—Erin Raatjes, New Lenox, IL

Prep: 30 min. + chilling
Bake: 10 min./batch + cooling
Makes: about 4 dozen

- 1 cup unsalted butter, softened
- ¾ cup confectioners' sugar
- ⅓ cup sugar
- 1½ tsp. grated orange zest
- ½ tsp. salt
- 1 large egg, room temperature
- 1 tsp. vanilla extract
- 2¼ cups all-purpose flour

FILLING
- 5 Tbsp. unsalted butter, softened
- ¼ cup packed brown sugar
- 1½ tsp. light corn syrup
- ½ tsp. vanilla extract
- 2 Tbsp. all-purpose flour
- 1 Tbsp. ground cinnamon
- ½ tsp. salt

GLAZE
- 1 cup confectioners' sugar
- ¼ cup light corn syrup
- 2 tsp. vanilla extract
- 1 to 2 tsp. water

1. Cream first 5 ingredients until light and fluffy, 5-7 minutes. Beat in egg and vanilla. Gradually beat in flour. On a baking sheet, roll dough between 2 sheets of waxed paper into a 12-in. square. Refrigerate 30 minutes.
2. For filling, beat butter, brown sugar, corn syrup and vanilla. Add flour, cinnamon and salt; mix well. Remove top sheet of waxed paper; spread filling over dough to within ¼ in. of edges. Using waxed paper, roll up tightly jelly-roll style, removing paper as you roll. Cover and freeze until firm, about 30 minutes.
3. Preheat oven to 375°. Uncover and cut dough crosswise into ¼-in. slices. Place slices 2 in. apart on parchment-lined baking sheets. Bake until edges are lightly browned, 10-12 minutes. Cool on pans 5 minutes. Remove to wire racks to cool completely.
4. For the glaze, mix confectioners' sugar, corn syrup, vanilla and enough water to reach desired consistency. Spread or drizzle over cookies. Let cookies stand at room temperature until set.
1 cookie: 103 cal., 5g fat (3g sat. fat), 17mg chol., 53mg sod., 13g carb. (8g sugars, 0 fiber), 1g pro.

PEANUT BUTTER PENGUINS

Could these be any more adorable? To treat your loved ones to chocolaty, peanut buttery goodness, just cover Nutter Butter cookies with chocolate and decorate! They are a lot of fun to make and even more fun to eat.
—*Taste of Home* Test Kitchen

- -

Prep: 1 hour + standing
Makes: about 2½ dozen

1¼	lbs. dark chocolate candy coating, chopped
1	pkg. (16 oz.) Nutter Butter cookies
64	candy eyes
32	bright white candy coating disks
32	orange M&M's minis
64	orange milk chocolate M&M's

Microwave candy coating; stir until smooth. Dip 1 cookie in the chocolate; allow excess to drip off. Place on waxed paper. Attach 2 candy eyes and a white coating disk for the belly. Add an M&M's mini for beak and 2 regular M&M's for feet. Repeat to dip and decorate all cookies. Let stand until set.

1 cookie: 156 cal., 8g fat (5g sat. fat), 0 chol., 57mg sod., 21g carb. (16g sugars, 1g fiber), 2g pro.

PUMPKIN PECAN WHOOPIE PIES

PUMPKIN PECAN WHOOPIE PIES

These whoopie pies are chock-full of pumpkin flavor—a perfect treat for fall! As a finishing touch, I like to roll the outside edges in mini chocolate chips or chopped nuts and dust the pies with cinnamon sugar.
—Rashanda Cobbins, Food Editor

- -

Prep: 30 min. • **Bake:** 10 min./batch + cooling
Makes: 20 whoopie pies

3¼ cups all-purpose flour
1½ cups sugar
2 tsp. baking powder
2 tsp. baking soda
1½ tsp. ground cinnamon
1 tsp. ground nutmeg
1 tsp. ground cloves
½ tsp. salt
5 large eggs, room temperature
1 can (15 oz.) pumpkin
½ cup water
½ cup canola oil
1 tsp. vanilla extract
FILLING
6 Tbsp. all-purpose flour
1 dash salt
1 cup plus 2 Tbsp. unsweetened almond milk
1½ cups shortening
3 cups confectioners' sugar
3 tsp. vanilla extract
Optional: Toasted chopped pecans, miniature semisweet chocolate chips and ground cinnamon

1. In a large bowl, combine flour, sugar, baking powder, baking soda, cinnamon, nutmeg, cloves and salt. In another bowl, whisk the eggs, pumpkin, water, oil and vanilla. Stir into the dry ingredients just until moistened.

2. Drop by 2 tablespoonfuls 2 in. apart onto parchment-lined baking sheets. Bake at 350° for 8-10 minutes. Remove to wire racks to cool.

3. For the filling, combine the flour and salt in a small saucepan. Gradually whisk in milk until smooth; bring to a boil over medium-high heat. Reduce the heat to medium; cook and stir until thickened, about 2 minutes. Refrigerate, covered, until completely cooled.

4. In another bowl, beat the shortening, confectioners' sugar and vanilla until smooth. Add chilled milk mixture; beat until light and fluffy, about 7 minutes. Spread about 3 Tbsp. filling on each bottom of half the cookies; cover with remaining cookies. Store in refrigerator. If desired, roll the filled pies in pecans or chocolate chips and sprinkle with additional cinnamon.

1 whoopie pie: 424 cal., 22g fat (5g sat. fat), 47mg chol., 277mg sod., 53g carb. (34g sugars, 1g fiber), 4g pro.

CHOCOLATE MERINGUE STARS

These light, delicate, chewy cookies sure make for merry munching. Their big chocolate flavor makes it difficult to keep the kids away from them long enough to get any on the cookie tray.
—Edna Lee, Greeley, CO

- -

Prep: 25 min. • **Bake:** 30 min./batch + cooling
Makes: about 4 dozen

- 3 large egg whites
- ¾ tsp. vanilla extract
- ¾ cup sugar
- ¼ cup baking cocoa

GLAZE
- 3 oz. semisweet chocolate, chopped
- 1 Tbsp. shortening

1. Place egg whites in a large bowl; let stand at room temperature for 30 minutes. Add vanilla; beat on medium speed until soft peaks form. Gradually add sugar, about 2 Tbsp. at a time, beating until stiff peaks form and sugar is dissolved. Gently fold in the cocoa.

2. Insert a large open star tip into a pastry bag; fill the bag half full with the meringue. Pipe stars, about 1¼ in. in diameter, or drop by rounded teaspoonfuls onto parchment-lined baking sheets.

3. Bake at 300° for 30-35 minutes or until lightly browned. Remove from paper; cool on wire racks.

4. In a microwave, melt chocolate and shortening; stir until smooth. Dip cookies halfway into glaze; allow excess to drip off. Place on waxed paper; let stand until set.

2 cookies: 40 cal., 1g fat (0 sat. fat), 0 chol., 7mg sod., 7g carb. (7g sugars, 0 fiber), 1g pro.

BUTTER PECAN ICEBOX COOKIES

BUTTER PECAN ICEBOX COOKIES

My grandmother used to bake very similar cookies. As a little girl, I always loved their flavor and was fascinated by the way she prepared them (from logs she took out of the icebox!). These are simple but delicious old-fashioned cookies. The dough logs can be stored in the freezer, then pulled out to defrost a day or two before baking time.
—Lisa Varner, El Paso, TX

- -

Prep: 15 min. + chilling
Bake: 10 min./batch + cooling
Makes: about 6½ dozen

- ½ cup butter, softened
- ½ cup shortening
- 1 cup sugar
- 1 cup packed brown sugar
- 2 large eggs
- 1 tsp. vanilla extract
- 3 cups all-purpose flour
- 1 tsp. baking soda
- ½ tsp. salt
- 1 cup finely chopped pecans

1. Cream butter, shortening and sugars until light and fluffy, 5-7 minutes. Beat in eggs and vanilla. In another bowl, whisk flour, baking soda and salt; gradually beat into creamed mixture. Stir in pecans.

2. Divide dough in half; shape each into a 10-in.-long roll. Place wrapped rolls in airtight containers. Refrigerate 8 hours or overnight.

3. Preheat oven to 350°. Uncover and cut dough crosswise into ¼-in. slices. Place 2 in. apart on ungreased baking sheets. Bake until edges begin to brown, 7-9 minutes. Remove from pans to wire racks to cool.

1 cookie: 70 cal., 4g fat (1g sat. fat), 8mg chol., 42mg sod., 9g carb. (5g sugars, 0 fiber), 1g pro.

TWO-TONE CARAMEL BROWNIES

This dessert is a mashup of two of my favorite bar recipes. A woman I worked with just after high school gave me the recipe for chocolate caramel brownies and I have an easy recipe for bars made with yellow cake mix. I wondered what they would taste like if I baked them together, so I tried it and I've been making them ever since!
—Staci Mergenthal, Verdi, MN

- -

Prep: 40 min. • **Bake:** 20 min. + cooling
Makes: 40 servings

- 1 pkg. chocolate cake mix (regular size)
- ¾ cup butter, melted
- 1 can (5 oz.) evaporated milk, divided
- 1 pkg. (11 oz.) Kraft caramel bits
- 1 cup semisweet chocolate chips
- 1 pkg. yellow cake mix (regular size)
- 1 large egg, room temperature
- ½ cup plus 1 Tbsp. butter, softened, divided
- 1 can (14 oz.) sweetened condensed milk
- 1 pkg. (11½ oz.) milk chocolate chips

1. Preheat oven to 350°. Line a 13x9-in. baking pan with parchment; grease paper. In a large bowl, beat chocolate cake mix, melted butter and ⅓ cup evaporated milk until blended; batter will be thick. Reserve ¼ cup batter for topping. Spread remaining batter into prepared pan. Bake 6 minutes.
2. Meanwhile, in a microwave, melt caramel bits and remaining ⅓ cup evaporated milk; stir until smooth. Sprinkle hot chocolate crust with semisweet chips; pour caramel mixture over top. Set aside.
3. In another large bowl, beat yellow cake mix, egg and ½ cup softened butter until combined; batter will be thick. Reserve half for topping. Crumble the remaining mixture over caramel layer. Bake 6 minutes.
4. In a microwave, melt the sweetened condensed milk, milk chocolate chips and remaining 1 Tbsp. softened butter; stir until smooth. Pour over yellow cake layer. Sprinkle with reserved yellow and chocolate cake batters. Bake until top is golden brown, 20-25 minutes. Cool completely on a wire rack. Store in an airtight container.
1 brownie: 272 cal., 13g fat (8g sat. fat), 27mg chol., 260mg sod., 38g carb. (28g sugars, 1g fiber), 3g pro.

TWO-TONE CARAMEL BROWNIES

**FUDGY LAYERED
IRISH MOCHA
BROWNIES**

CHEWY PEANUT BUTTER PAN SQUARES

With seven of us in our family, including two teenage boys, these peanut butter squares never last long! It's hard to believe how simple they are to prepare.
—Deb DeChant, Milan, OH

- -

Prep: 10 min.
Bake: 30 min.
Makes: 2 dozen

- ½ cup butter, cubed
- ½ cup creamy peanut butter
- 1½ cups sugar
- 1 cup all-purpose flour
- 2 large eggs, room temperature, lightly beaten
- 1 tsp. vanilla extract

1. In a microwave-safe bowl, melt butter and peanut butter; stir until smooth. Combine the sugar and flour; gradually add to butter mixture and mix well. Beat in eggs and vanilla.
2. Spread into a greased 13x9-in. baking pan. Bake at 350° until lightly browned and edges start to pull away from sides of pan, 28-32 minutes. Cool on a wire rack.
1 square: 139 cal., 7g fat (3g sat. fat), 28mg chol., 69mg sod., 18g carb. (13g sugars, 0 fiber), 2g pro.

TEST KITCHEN TIP
To give these peanut butter bars a fun twist, top with a chocolate frosting of your choice and sprinkle with Reese's pieces.

FUDGY LAYERED IRISH MOCHA BROWNIES

My husband and I are big fans of Irish cream, so I wanted to incorporate it into a brownie. I started with my mom's brownie recipe, then added frosting and ganache. This decadent recipe is the result, and we really enjoy them!
—Sue Gronholz, Beaver Dam, WI

- -

Prep: 35 min. • **Bake:** 25 min. + chilling
Makes: 16 servings

- ⅔ cup all-purpose flour
- ½ tsp. baking powder
- ¼ tsp. salt
- ⅓ cup butter
- 6 Tbsp. baking cocoa
- 2 Tbsp. canola oil
- ½ tsp. instant coffee granules
- 1 cup sugar
- 2 large eggs, room temperature, beaten
- 1 tsp. vanilla extract

FROSTING
- 2 cups confectioners' sugar
- ¼ cup butter, softened
- 3 Tbsp. Irish cream liqueur

GANACHE TOPPING
- 1 cup semisweet chocolate chips
- 3 Tbsp. Irish cream liqueur
- 2 Tbsp. heavy whipping cream
- ½ tsp. instant coffee granules

1. Preheat oven to 350°. Sift together flour, baking powder and salt; set aside. In a small saucepan over low heat, melt the butter. Remove from heat; stir in cocoa, oil and instant coffee granules. Cool slightly; stir in sugar and beaten eggs. Gradually add flour mixture and vanilla; mix well. Spread batter into a greased 8-in. square pan; bake until the center is set (do not overbake), about 25 minutes. Cool in pan on wire rack.
2. For the frosting, whisk together the confectioners' sugar and butter (mixture will be lumpy). Gradually whisk in the Irish cream liqueur; beat until smooth. Spread over slightly warm brownies. Refrigerate until frosting is set, about 1 hour.
3. Meanwhile, prepare ganache: Combine all ingredients and microwave on high for 1 minute; stir. Microwave 30 seconds longer; stir until smooth. Cool slightly until ganache reaches a spreading consistency. Spread over frosting. Refrigerate until set, 45-60 minutes.
1 brownie: 295 cal., 14g fat (7g sat. fat), 43mg chol., 116mg sod., 41g carb. (34g sugars, 1g fiber), 2g pro.

BROWN SUGAR POUND CAKE
PAGE 264

Cakes & Pies

A homemade cake or pie is the highlight of any gathering—whether it's a birthday, graduation or just a weeknight dinner. No matter what the occasion, rely on these wow-worthy cakes, from-scratch pies and tarts, and other nostalgic favorites when you want to whip up your best baked desserts.

FRENCH
SILK PIE

FRENCH SILK PIE

I experimented with this recipe until I came up with a version that was perfect.
—Lisa Francis, Elba, AL

- -

Prep: 40 min. • **Cook:** 10 min. + chilling
Makes: 6 servings

- 1 sheet refrigerated pie crust
- ⅔ cup sugar
- 2 large eggs, room temperature
- 2 oz. unsweetened chocolate, melted
- 1 tsp. vanilla extract
- ⅓ cup butter, softened
- ⅔ cup heavy whipping cream
- 2 tsp. confectioners' sugar
  Optional: Whipped cream and chocolate curls

1. Cut pie crust in half. Repackage and refrigerate 1 half for another use. On a lightly floured surface, roll remaining half into an 8-in. circle. Transfer to a 7-in. pie plate; flute edge.
2. Line shell with a double thickness of heavy-duty foil. Bake at 450° for 4 minutes. Remove foil; bake crust for 2 minutes or until golden brown. Cool on a wire rack.
3. In a small saucepan, combine sugar and eggs until well blended. Cook over low heat, stirring constantly, until mixture reaches 160° and coats the back of a metal spoon. Remove from the heat. Stir in chocolate and vanilla until smooth. Cool to lukewarm (90°), stirring occasionally.
4. In a small bowl, cream butter until light and fluffy, 5-7 minutes. Add the cooled chocolate mixture; beat on high speed until light and fluffy, about 5 minutes.
5. In another large bowl, beat cream until it begins to thicken. Add confectioners' sugar; beat until stiff peaks form. Fold whipped cream into the chocolate mixture.
6. Pour into cooled crust. Chill for at least 6 hours before serving. If desired, garnish with whipped cream and chocolate curls. Refrigerate leftovers.
1 piece: 450 cal., 33g fat (19g sat. fat), 139mg chol., 223mg sod., 38g carb. (24g sugars, 1g fiber), 5g pro.

LEMON RHUBARB
TUBE CAKE

LEMON RHUBARB TUBE CAKE

Try my dessert for a taste of summer. The cake's fresh lemon flavor and tart rhubarb topping are so refreshing.
—Courtney Stultz, Weir, KS

- -

Prep: 35 min. • **Bake:** 50 min. + cooling
Makes: 12 servings

- 3 medium lemons
- 1 cup butter, softened
- 2 cups sugar
- 3 large eggs, room temperature
- 3 cups all-purpose flour
- 1 tsp. baking powder
- ½ tsp. baking soda
- ½ tsp. salt
- 1 cup buttermilk
  RHUBARB TOPPING
- 1 cup sugar
- 1 cup sliced fresh or frozen rhubarb
- 1 cup halved fresh strawberries
  Confectioners' sugar, optional

1. Preheat oven to 350°. Grease and flour a 10-in. fluted tube pan. Finely grate enough zest from lemons to measure 2 Tbsp. zest. Cut lemons crosswise in half; squeeze juice from lemons to measure ¼ cup juice. Save remaining juice for another use.
2. In a large bowl, cream butter and sugar until light and fluffy, 5-7 minutes. Add 1 egg at a time, beating well after each addition. Beat in lemon juice and zest. In another bowl, whisk flour, baking powder, baking soda and salt; add to creamed mixture alternately with buttermilk, beating well after each addition.
3. Transfer batter to prepared pan. Bake until a toothpick inserted near the center comes out clean, 50-60 minutes. Cool in pan for 10 minutes before removing to a wire rack.
4. Meanwhile, for topping, combine sugar and rhubarb in a small saucepan. Bring to a boil; reduce heat. Simmer until rhubarb is almost tender, 8-10 minutes. Add halved strawberries; cook until strawberries and rhubarb are softened. Serve with cake. If desired, dust with confectioners' sugar.
1 slice with ¼ cup sauce: 481 cal., 17g fat (10g sat. fat), 88mg chol., 371mg sod., 78g carb. (53g sugars, 2g fiber), 6g pro.

DOUGHNUT HOLE CAKE

This is the easiest yet most impressive cake I have ever made! Feel free to use chocolate, lemon or strawberry cake mix in the place of red velvet.
—Robert Pickart, Chicago, IL

Prep: 15 min. • **Bake:** 35 min. + cooling
Makes: 16 servings

- 32 vanilla cake doughnut holes
- 1 pkg. red velvet cake mix (regular size)
- 1 can (16 oz.) vanilla frosting

1. Preheat oven to 350°. Place 16 doughnut holes in each of 2 greased 8-in. round baking pans. Prepare cake mix according to package directions. Pour batter over the doughnuts, dividing evenly.
2. Bake until a toothpick inserted in cake comes out clean, 35-40 minutes. Cool in pans 10 minutes before removing to a wire rack to cool completely. Spread frosting between layers and over top of cake.

1 piece: 420 cal., 20g fat (7g sat.fat), 38mg chol., 401mg sod., 57g carb. (36g sugars, 1g fiber), 4g pro.

CREAMY BISCOFF PIE

CREAMY BISCOFF PIE

I tasted Biscoff cookie butter at a grocery store one day, and it was so delicious that I decided to create a no-bake pie with it. You can also use peanut butter or another kind of spread and matching toppings.
—Katrina Adams, Mount Olive, AL

Prep: 20 min. + freezing
Makes: 2 pies (8 servings each)

- 1 pkg. (8 oz.) cream cheese, softened
- 1 cup Biscoff cookie butter spread
- ¾ cup confectioners' sugar
- 2 cartons (8 oz. each) frozen whipped topping, thawed, divided
  Two 9-in. graham cracker crusts (about 6 oz. each)
- ¼ cup caramel sundae syrup
- 4 Biscoff cookies, crushed

In a large bowl, beat the cream cheese, cookie spread and confectioners' sugar until combined. Fold in 1 carton whipped topping. Divide between crusts. Top with remaining container whipped topping. Drizzle with syrup; sprinkle with cookie crumbs. Freeze, covered, until firm, at least 4 hours.

1 piece: 367 cal., 21g fat (10g sat. fat), 14mg chol., 187mg sod., 40g carb. (31g sugars, 0 fiber), 3g pro.

TEST KITCHEN TIP
You'll find Biscoff cookie butter spread near the peanut butter at your store, or online. Biscoff cookies will be located in the cookie aisle.

PEANUT BUTTER CHOCOLATE POKE CAKE

When my family is planning a get-together, I can count on three or four people asking me if I'm bringing this cake. If you don't have a chocolate cake mix, you can use a white or yellow one—just stir in 3 tablespoons of baking cocoa.
—Fay Moreland, Wichita Falls, TX

- -

Prep: 20 min. • **Bake:** 25 min. + chilling
Makes: 20 servings

- 1 pkg. chocolate cake mix (regular size)
- 2 tsp. vanilla extract, divided
  Dash salt
- ⅔ cup creamy peanut butter
- 2 cans (14 oz. each) sweetened condensed milk
- 1 cup confectioners' sugar
  Topping: Chopped peanut butter cups, peanut butter-filled sandwich cookies or a combination of the two

1. Preheat oven to 350°. Prepare cake mix according to package directions, adding 1 tsp. vanilla and salt before mixing batter. Transfer to a greased 13x9-in. baking pan. Bake and cool completely as package directs.
2. Whisk the peanut butter and milk until blended. Using the end of a wooden spoon handle, poke holes in cake 2 in. apart. Slowly pour 2 cups peanut butter mixture over the cake, filling each hole. Refrigerate cake and remaining peanut butter mixture, covered, until cake is cold, 2-3 hours.
3. Combine remaining 1 tsp. vanilla and remaining peanut butter mixture; gradually beat in enough of the confectioners' sugar to reach a spreading consistency. Spread frosting over cake. Add toppings as desired. Refrigerate leftovers.
1 piece: 360 cal., 16g fat (4g sat. fat), 41mg chol., 312mg sod., 49g carb. (40g sugars, 1g fiber), 7g pro.

BREAD PUDDING PIE

This unique dessert is a bread pudding-pie combination. It was created by my paternal grandmother's family. They had a farm and made their own bread, which made this an economical dessert.
—Kelly Barnes, Lexington, IN

- -

Prep: 15 min. • **Bake:** 55 min. + chilling
Makes: 8 servings

     Pastry for single-crust pie
- 1 cup cubed bread
- 2 large eggs, room temperature
- 2 cups 2% milk
- ¾ cup sugar
- ½ tsp. vanilla extract
- ¼ tsp. ground nutmeg
- 2 tsp. butter

1. Preheat oven to 425°. On a floured surface, roll dough to fit a 9-in. pie plate. Trim and flute edge. Arrange the bread in bottom of pie crust. In a large bowl, whisk eggs, milk, sugar and vanilla; pour over the bread. Sprinkle with nutmeg and dot with butter. Bake 10 minutes. Reduce the oven setting to 350°.
2. Bake until a knife inserted in the center comes out clean, 45-50 minutes longer. Cover edges of pie crust with foil during the last 15 minutes to prevent overbrowning if necessary. Cool on a wire rack for 1 hour. Refrigerate the pie for at least 3 hours before serving.
1 piece: 314 cal., 15g fat (9g sat. fat), 84mg chol., 230mg sod., 39g carb. (22g sugars, 1g fiber), 6g pro.
Pastry for single-crust pie (9 in.): Combine 1¼ cups all-purpose flour and ¼ tsp. salt; cut in ½ cup cold butter until crumbly. Gradually add 3-5 Tbsp. ice water, tossing with a fork until dough holds together when pressed. Cover and refrigerate 1 hour.

PEANUT BUTTER
CHOCOLATE POKE CAKE

WINNIE'S MINI RHUBARB & STRAWBERRY PIES

BROWN SUGAR POUND CAKE

This tender pound cake is the first one I mastered. The browned butter icing tastes like pralines.
—Shawn Barto, Winter Garden, FL

Prep: 20 min. • **Bake:** 55 min. + cooling
Makes: 16 servings

- 1½ cups unsalted butter, softened
- 2¼ cups packed brown sugar
- 5 large eggs, room temperature
- 2 tsp. vanilla extract
- 3 cups all-purpose flour
- 1 tsp. baking powder
- ¼ tsp. salt
- 1 cup sour cream

GLAZE

- 3 Tbsp. unsalted butter
- ¼ cup chopped pecans
- 1 cup confectioners' sugar
- ¼ tsp. vanilla extract
  Dash salt
- 2 to 3 Tbsp. half-and-half cream

1. Preheat oven to 350°. Grease and flour a 10-in. fluted tube pan.
2. Cream butter and brown sugar until light and fluffy, 5-7 minutes. Add 1 egg at a time, beating well after each addition. Beat in the vanilla. In another bowl, whisk flour, baking powder and salt; add to creamed mixture alternately with sour cream, beating after each addition just until combined.
3. Transfer to prepared pan. Bake until a toothpick inserted near center comes out clean, 55-65 minutes. Cool cake in pan for 10 minutes before removing to a wire rack to cool completely.
4. For glaze, combine butter and pecans in a small saucepan over medium heat, stirring constantly, until butter is light golden brown, 4-5 minutes. Stir into confectioners' sugar. Add vanilla, salt and enough cream to reach a drizzling consistency. Drizzle glaze over cake, allowing some to drip down sides. Let stand until set.
1 slice: 473 cal., 25g fat (15g sat. fat), 121mg chol., 193mg sod., 57g carb. (38g sugars, 1g fiber), 5g pro.

WINNIE'S MINI RHUBARB & STRAWBERRY PIES

Every spring, we grew strawberries and rhubarb on our farm just outside Seattle. These fruity hand pies remind me of those times and of Grandma Winnie's baking.
—Shawn Carleton, San Diego, CA

Prep: 25 min. + chilling • **Bake:** 15 min.
Makes: 18 mini pies

- 3 Tbsp. quick-cooking tapioca
- 4 cups sliced fresh strawberries
- 2 cups sliced fresh rhubarb
- ¾ cup sugar
- 1 tsp. grated orange zest
- 1 tsp. vanilla extract
- ¼ tsp. salt
- ¼ tsp. ground cinnamon
- 3 drops red food coloring, optional
  Pastry for double-crust pie
  Sweetened whipped cream, optional

1. Place tapioca in a small food processor or spice grinder; process until finely ground.
2. In a large saucepan, combine the sliced strawberries, rhubarb, sugar, orange zest, vanilla, salt, cinnamon, ground tapioca and, if desired, food coloring; bring to a boil. Reduce heat; simmer, covered, until the strawberries are tender, stirring occasionally, 15-20 minutes. Transfer to a large bowl; cover and refrigerate overnight.
3. Preheat oven to 425°. On a lightly floured surface, roll half of dough to an 18-in. circle. Cut 12 circles with a 4-in. biscuit cutter, rerolling scraps as necessary; press crust onto bottom and up sides of ungreased muffin cups. Repeat with remaining dough, cutting 6 more circles. Spoon strawberry mixture into muffin cups.
4. Bake until filling is bubbly and crust is golden brown, 12-15 minutes. Cool in pan 5 minutes; remove to wire racks to cool. If desired, serve with whipped cream.
1 mini pie: 207 cal., 10g fat (6g sat. fat), 27mg chol., 171mg sod., 27g carb. (11g sugars, 1g fiber), 2g pro.

Pastry for double-crust pie (9 inches): Combine 2-½ cups all-purpose flour and ½ tsp. salt; cut in 1 cup cold butter until crumbly. Gradually add ⅓ to ⅔ cup ice water, tossing with a fork until dough holds together when pressed. Divide dough in half. Shape each into a disk; wrap in plastic wrap. Refrigerate 1 hour or overnight.

BROWN SUGAR
POUND CAKE

CHOCOLATE CHESS PIE

CHOCOLATE CHESS PIE

This is my mother's spin on classic chess pie.
—Ann Dickens, Nixa, MO

- -

Prep: 30 min. • **Cook:** 40 min. + chilling
Makes: 8 servings

- 1¼ cups all-purpose flour
- ¼ tsp. salt
- ¼ cup cold butter, cubed
- ¼ cup shortening
- 3 to 4 Tbsp. ice water

FILLING

- 2 large eggs, room temperature
- 1 cup packed brown sugar
- ½ cup sugar
- 1½ oz. unsweetened chocolate, melted and cooled
- 2 Tbsp. 2% milk
- 1 Tbsp. all-purpose flour
- 1 tsp. vanilla extract
- ½ cup butter, melted

1. Combine flour and salt; cut in butter and shortening until crumbly. Gradually add ice water, tossing with a fork until dough holds together when pressed. Shape the dough into a disk. Wrap and refrigerate for 1 hour or overnight.

2. On a floured surface, roll the dough to fit a 9-in. pie plate. Trim and flute edge. Refrigerate 30 minutes. Preheat oven to 425°. Line unpricked crust with a double thickness of foil. Fill with pie weights. Bake on a lower oven rack until light golden brown, 15-20 minutes. Remove foil and weights; bake until bottom is golden brown, 3-6 minutes. Cool on a wire rack. Reduce oven setting to 325°.

3. In a large bowl, whisk eggs, sugars, melted chocolate, milk, flour and vanilla. Gradually whisk in butter. Pour into crust. Cover edge with foil to prevent overbrowning.

4. Bake at 325° until a knife inserted in the center comes out clean, 35-40 minutes. Remove foil. Cool on a wire rack. Refrigerate, covered, for 3 hours or until chilled.

1 piece: 436 cal., 22g fat (13g sat. fat), 93mg chol., 240mg sod., 57g carb. (40g sugars, 1g fiber), 5g pro.

LEMON-BERRY ICE CREAM PIE

I love the combination of fresh strawberries and lemon curd. It's so refreshing, especially in an easy make-ahead dessert like this ice cream pie.
—Roxanne Chan, Albany, CA

Prep: 15 min. + freezing • **Makes:** 8 servings

- 1   pint strawberry ice cream, softened
- 1   graham cracker crust (9 in.)
- 1   cup lemon curd
- 2   cups frozen whipped topping, thawed
- 1   pint fresh strawberries, halved

1. Spoon ice cream into pie crust; freeze 2 hours or until firm.
2. Spread lemon curd over ice cream; top with whipped topping. Freeze, covered, 4 hours or until firm.
3. Remove from freezer 10 minutes before serving. Serve with strawberries.
1 piece: 370 cal., 13g fat (7g sat. fat), 40mg chol., 171mg sod., 58g carb. (40g sugars, 1g fiber), 2g pro.

TEST KITCHEN TIPS

When purchasing strawberries, look for brightly colored, plump and fragrant berries with the green hulls intact. Avoid any that are soft, shriveled or moldy. Wash berries before removing hulls. One pint of strawberries yields 1½ to 2 cups sliced.

YELLOW LAYER CAKE WITH CHOCOLATE BUTTERCREAM

This will become your go-to recipe for birthdays, but the tender yellow cake with flavorful chocolate buttercream is perfect for any occasion.
—*Taste of Home* Test Kitchen

Prep: 15 min. • **Bake:** 25 min. + cooling
Makes: 16 servings

- ⅔   cup butter, softened
- 1¾ cups sugar
- 2   large eggs, room temperature
- 1½ tsp. vanilla extract
- 2½ cups all-purpose flour
- 2½ tsp. baking powder
- ½   tsp. salt
- 1¼ cups 2% milk

CHOCOLATE BUTTERCREAM

- 2   cups butter, softened
- 4   cups confectioners' sugar, sifted
- ½   cup Dutch-processed cocoa, sifted
- 1½ tsp. vanilla extract
- ⅛   tsp. salt
- ⅓   cup 2% milk

1. Preheat oven to 350°. Grease and flour two 9-in. round baking pans. In a large bowl, cream butter and sugar until light and fluffy, 5-7 minutes. Add eggs, 1 at a time, beating well after each addition. Beat in vanilla. In another bowl, whisk flour, baking powder and salt; add to creamed mixture alternately with milk, beating well after each addition.
2. Transfer to prepared pans. Bake until a toothpick inserted in the center comes out clean, 25-30 minutes. Cool in pans for 10 minutes before removing to wire racks to cool completely.
3. For buttercream, in a large bowl, beat butter until creamy. Gradually beat in the confectioners' sugar and cocoa until smooth. Add vanilla and salt. Add milk; beat until light and fluffy, about 5 minutes.
4. Spread buttercream between layers and over top and sides of cake.
1 piece: 593 cal., 33g fat (21g sat. fat), 107mg chol., 432mg sod., 72g carb. (53g sugars, 4g fiber), 5g pro.

YELLOW LAYER CAKE WITH CHOCOLATE BUTTERCREAM

EASY PISTACHIO TUBE CAKE

Mixes make this light cake a breeze to bake, and a Bundt pan gets it party-ready. Go for the pistachios on top—the extra crunch is very much worth it.
—Dina Crowell, Fredericksburg, VA

- -

Prep: 15 min. • **Bake:** 35 min. + cooling
Makes: 12 servings

- 1   pkg. yellow cake mix (regular size)
- 1   pkg. (3.4 oz.) instant pistachio pudding mix
- 4   large eggs, room temperature
- 1½ cups water
- ¼   cup canola oil
- ½   tsp. almond extract
-     Confectioners' sugar
-     Finely chopped pistachios, optional

1. Preheat oven to 350°. Grease and flour a 10-in. fluted tube pan.
2. In a bowl, combine the first 6 ingredients; beat on low speed 30 seconds. Beat on medium 2 minutes. Transfer to prepared pan. Bake until a toothpick inserted near the center comes out clean, 35-40 minutes. Cool in pan 10 minutes before removing to a wire rack to cool completely.
3. Dust with confectioners' sugar. If desired, sprinkle with pistachios.
1 slice: 266 cal., 10g fat (2g sat. fat), 62mg chol., 416mg sod., 41g carb. (24g sugars, 0 fiber), 4g pro.

EASY BOURBON PECAN PIE

This pecan pie has a mellow bourbon flavor—not too strong and not too sweet. It's crunchy, chewy and easy to make.
—Nick Iverson, Denver, CO

- -

Prep: 10 min. + freezing
Bake: 1¼ hours
Makes: 10 servings

- 12 oz. toasted pecan halves, divided
- 4   large eggs, room temperature
- ½   cup packed dark brown sugar
- ¼   cup sugar
- 1   cup dark corn syrup
- 8   Tbsp. unsalted butter, melted
- ¼   cup bourbon
- 2   tsp. vanilla extract
- ¼   tsp. salt
- 1   sheet refrigerated pie crust
-     Vanilla ice cream, optional

1. In a food processor, pulse half the pecans until coarsely chopped; reserve remaining pecans. Combine eggs and sugars until well mixed. Add the next 5 ingredients and the chopped pecans.
2. Unroll crust into a 9-in. metal pie plate; flute edge. Pour filling into crust. Arrange reserved pecan halves over filling. Place filled pie in freezer for 30 minutes.
3. Preheat oven to 425°. Bake until crust is set, about 15 minutes. Reduce oven setting to 350°; continue baking until pie is puffed and set in the middle, about 1 hour (tent loosely with aluminum foil if needed to prevent overbrowning). Cool. If desired, serve with vanilla ice cream.
1 piece: 600 cal., 41g fat (11g sat. fat), 103mg chol., 221mg sod., 56g carb. (43g sugars, 3g fiber), 7g pro.

EASY BOURBON PECAN PIE

RASPBERRY MOSCOW MULE CAKE

CHOCOLATE CHEESECAKE PIE

Guests always ask for seconds of this rich but simple pie. I top it with fresh raspberries or cherry pie filling.
—Sandy Schwartz, Brooklyn, NY

Takes: 30 min. • **Makes:** 8 servings

- 1 pkg. (8 oz.) cream cheese, softened
- ¼ cup butter, softened
- ⅓ cup sugar
- 1½ tsp. vanilla extract
- 1½ cups milk chocolate chips, melted and cooled
- 1 carton (8 oz.) frozen whipped topping, thawed
- 1 graham cracker crust (9 in.) Chocolate curls, optional

In a large bowl, beat cream cheese, butter, sugar and vanilla until smooth. Beat in cooled chocolate. Fold in whipped topping. Spoon filling into crust. Refrigerate until serving. Decorate with chocolate curls as desired.

1 piece: 535 cal., 35g fat (20g sat. fat), 53mg chol., 270mg sod., 48g carb. (38g sugars, 1g fiber), 6g pro.

RASPBERRY MOSCOW MULE CAKE

This cake was inspired by my favorite cocktail—the Moscow mule. It's so moist and flavorful, and the best cake I have ever made from scratch.
—Becky Hardin, St. Peters, MO

Prep: 25 min. • **Bake:** 70 min. + cooling
Makes: 16 servings

- 1½ cups unsalted butter, softened
- 2¾ cups sugar
- 5 large eggs, room temperature
- 1 Tbsp. vanilla extract
- 3 cups cake flour
- ½ tsp. salt
- 1 cup alcoholic raspberry ginger beer or nonalcoholic plain ginger beer
- 2 cups fresh raspberries

SYRUP
- ½ cup alcoholic raspberry ginger beer or nonalcoholic plain ginger beer
- ½ cup sugar
- ¼ cup lime juice

GLAZE
- 1½ cups confectioners' sugar
- 2 to 3 Tbsp. lime juice

1. Preheat oven to 325°. Grease and flour a 10-in. fluted tube pan.
2. In a large bowl, cream the butter and sugar until light and fluffy, 5-7 minutes. Add eggs, 1 at a time, beating well after each addition. Beat in the vanilla. In another bowl, whisk cake flour and salt; add to the creamed mixture alternately with the ginger beer, beating well after each addition (mixture may appear curdled).
3. Gently fold raspberries into batter; pour into prepared pan. Bake until a toothpick inserted near the center comes out clean, 70-80 minutes. Meanwhile, for syrup, in a small saucepan, bring ginger beer, sugar and lime juice to a boil. Reduce the heat; simmer 10 minutes. Cool slightly.
4. Poke holes in warm cake using a fork or wooden skewer. Slowly spoon syrup over cake. Cool 15 minutes before removing from pan to a wire rack; cool completely. For the glaze, in a small bowl, mix the confectioners' sugar and enough lime juice to reach desired consistency; pour over cake. Let stand until set. If desired, top the cake with additional fresh raspberries.

1 slice: 488 cal., 19g fat (11g sat. fat), 104mg chol., 100mg sod., 75g carb. (53g sugars, 1g fiber), 5g pro.

COOKIE CAKE

This oversized cookie "cake" is so easy and quick, I'm tempted to make it my go-to cookie treat.
—Lisa Kaminski, Associate Digital Editor

Prep: 15 min. • **Bake:** 20 min. + cooling
Makes: 8 servings

- ¾ cup butter, softened
- ½ cup sugar
- ½ cup packed brown sugar
- 1 large egg plus 1 large egg yolk, room temperature
- 2 tsp. vanilla extract
- 2 cups all-purpose flour
- 2 tsp. cornstarch
- 1 tsp. baking soda
- ¼ tsp. salt
- 1 cup semisweet chocolate chips

FROSTING
- ½ cup butter, softened
- 4½ cups confectioners' sugar
- 1½ tsp. vanilla extract
- 5 to 6 Tbsp. 2% milk
  Optional: Food coloring and sprinkles

1. Preheat oven to 350°. Line the bottom of a 9-in. springform pan with parchment. In a large bowl, cream butter and sugars until light and fluffy, 5-7 minutes. Beat in egg, egg yolk and vanilla. In another bowl, whisk flour, cornstarch, baking soda and salt; gradually beat into creamed mixture. Stir in chips. Press onto the bottom of prepared pan.
2. Bake until golden brown, 20-25 minutes. Cool on a wire rack 10 minutes. Loosen sides from pan with a knife; cool completely. Remove rim from pan. Carefully remove cookie cake from bottom pan; transfer to serving platter.
3. In a large bowl, beat softened butter, confectioners' sugar, vanilla and enough milk to reach piping consistency. If desired, beat in food coloring. Pipe around edge of cookie cake. If desired, garnish with sprinkles.
1 piece: 861 cal., 37g fat (23g sat. fat), 123mg chol., 482mg sod., 132g carb. (104g sugars, 2g fiber), 6g pro.

FLUFFY KEY LIME PIE

FLUFFY KEY LIME PIE

For a taste of paradise, try this light and creamy tropical confection. It's low in fat, sugar and fuss. Dessert doesn't get any better than that!
—Frances VanFossan, Warren, MI

Prep: 20 min. + chilling • **Makes:** 8 servings

- ¼ cup boiling water
- 1 pkg. (0.3 oz.) sugar-free lime gelatin
- 2 cartons (6 oz. each) Key lime yogurt
- 1 carton (8 oz.) frozen fat-free whipped topping, thawed
- 1 reduced-fat graham cracker crust (8 in.)

1. In a large bowl, add boiling water to the gelatin; stir 2 minutes to completely dissolve. Whisk in yogurt. Fold in whipped topping. Pour into crust.
2. Refrigerate, covered, until set, about 2 hours.
1 piece: 194 cal., 3g fat (1g sat. fat), 2mg chol., 159mg sod., 33g carb. (18g sugars, 0 fiber), 3g pro. **Diabetic exchanges:** 2 starch, ½ fat.

ASK SARAH

WHAT EXTRA GARNISHES CAN I ADD TO THIS NO-BAKE KEY LIME PIE?

After its 2-hour stint in the fridge, this pie is ready for a finishing touch or two. For extra tropical flair, sprinkle toasted coconut over the top to give the pie crunch and extra color. If you have fresh Key limes, garnish with a few slices and some stemmed maraschino cherries. And don't forgot everyone's favorite finishing touch—whipped cream!

OLIVE OIL CAKE

A good olive oil cake isn't overly sweet, so it can be more than just a dessert. Try it as a breakfast treat or an afternoon snack.
—Lisa Kaminski, Associate Digital Editor

- -

Prep: 15 min. • **Bake:** 45 min. + cooling
Makes: 16 servings

- 3   large eggs, room temperature
- 1½ cups sugar
- ¾   cup extra virgin olive oil
- ¾   cup ground almonds
- ½   cup 2% milk
- 4   tsp. grated orange zest
- 1   tsp. vanilla extract
- 1¾ cups all-purpose flour
- 2   tsp. baking powder
- ½   tsp. salt
- ¾   cup confectioners' sugar
- 2   to 3 Tbsp. orange juice
       Sliced almonds, toasted, optional

1. Preheat oven to 350°. Grease and flour a 10-in. fluted tube pan. In a large bowl, beat eggs on high speed 3 minutes. Gradually add sugar, beating until thick and lemon-colored. Gradually beat in olive oil. Beat in ground almonds, milk, orange zest and vanilla.
2. In another bowl, whisk flour, baking powder and salt; fold into egg mixture. Transfer batter to prepared pan, spreading evenly. Bake until a toothpick inserted near the center comes out clean, 45-50 minutes. Cool in pan 15 minutes before removing to a wire rack to cool completely.
3. For the icing, in a small bowl, whisk the confectioners' sugar and enough orange juice to reach a drizzling consistency. Drizzle over cake. If desired, sprinkle with sliced toasted almonds.
1 slice: 279 cal., 14g fat (2g sat. fat), 35mg chol., 152mg sod., 37g carb. (25g sugars, 1g fiber), 4g pro.

EASY PEANUT BUTTER & PRETZEL PIE

EASY PEANUT BUTTER & PRETZEL PIE

Crispy, salty pretzel crust is just begging for a creamy no-bake peanut butter filling and a layer of chocolate ganache.
—Gina Nistico, Denver, CO

- -

Prep: 10 min. • **Bake:** 15 min. + chilling
Makes: 8 servings

- 2¾ cups crushed pretzel sticks
- 1   cup sugar, divided
- ¾   cup butter, melted
- 1   envelope unflavored gelatin
- ¼   cup cold water
- 1   cup creamy peanut butter
- ¼   cup butter, softened
- 2   oz. cream cheese, softened
- ¾   cup heavy whipping cream, divided
- ½   cup milk chocolate chips
       Additional crushed pretzel sticks, optional

1. Preheat oven to 350°. Combine crushed pretzels and ⅓ cup sugar with melted butter. Using the bottom of a glass, press onto bottom and up the sides of a greased 9-in. deep-dish pie plate. Bake 12-15 minutes or until set. Cool completely on a wire rack.
2. Meanwhile, sprinkle gelatin over cold water; let stand 5 minutes. Beat peanut butter, softened butter, cream cheese and remaining sugar until smooth. Gradually beat in ½ cup cream. Microwave gelatin on high until melted, about 10 seconds; stir into peanut butter mixture. Transfer to crust.
3. Microwave milk chocolate chips and remaining cream on high; stir until smooth. Cool slightly. Spread chocolate mixture over peanut butter mixture. If desired, top with additional crushed pretzels. Refrigerate, covered, until set, about 3 hours.
1 piece: 750 cal., 54g fat (26g sat. fat), 96mg chol., 738mg sod., 60g carb. (36g sugars, 3g fiber), 13g pro.

PLUM UPSIDE-DOWN CAKE

The delicate flavor of plums is a pleasing change of pace in this upside-down cake.
—Bobbie Talbott, Veneta, OR

- -

Prep: 15 min. • **Bake:** 40 min.
Makes: 10 servings

⅓ cup butter
½ cup packed brown sugar
1¾ to 2 lbs. medium plums,
   pitted and halved
2 large eggs, room temperature
⅔ cup sugar
1 cup all-purpose flour
1 tsp. baking powder
¼ tsp. salt
⅓ cup hot water
½ tsp. lemon extract
   Whipped cream, optional

1. Melt the butter in a 10-in. cast-iron or other ovenproof skillet. Sprinkle brown sugar over butter. Arrange the plum halves, cut side down, in a single layer over the sugar; set aside.
2. In a large bowl, beat the eggs until thick and lemon-colored; gradually beat in sugar. Combine the flour, baking powder and salt; add to egg mixture and mix well. Blend water and lemon extract; beat into batter. Pour over plums.
3. Bake at 350° until a toothpick inserted in the center comes out clean, 40-45 minutes. Immediately invert onto a serving plate. Serve warm, with whipped cream if desired.
1 piece: 245 cal., 7g fat (4g sat. fat), 53mg chol., 173mg sod., 43g carb. (32g sugars, 1g fiber), 3g pro.

FRESH RASPBERRY ICEBOX CAKE

Layered icebox cakes are so fun because they look impressive but couldn't be easier. Fresh raspberries make this one extra special. If you can find them at your grocer, use Anna's Ginger Thins with scalloped edges. Regular gingersnaps are fine, too.
—Elisabeth Larsen, Pleasant Grove, UT

- -

Prep: 25 min. + chilling • **Makes:** 12 servings

1 carton (8 oz.) mascarpone cheese
3 cups cold heavy whipping cream
2 Tbsp. sugar
2 Tbsp. grated lemon zest
   (about 2 lemons)
2 pkg. (5¼ oz. each) thin
   ginger cookies
5 cups fresh raspberries
   (about 20 oz.), divided

1. Stir mascarpone cheese; let stand at room temperature 30 minutes. Meanwhile, beat cream until it begins to thicken. Add sugar; beat until soft peaks form. Reserve ½ cup thickened cream; cover and refrigerate. Add lemon zest and mascarpone to remaining whipped cream; beat until stiff peaks form, 30-60 seconds.
2. On a serving plate, spread ½ cup of the cream mixture in a 7-in.-diameter circle. Arrange 6 cookies in a circle on top of the cream, placing a seventh cookie in the center. Gently fold 4 cups of raspberries into the remaining cream mixture. Spoon about 1 cup raspberry cream mixture over the cookies. Repeat layers 6 times, ending with cookies (there will be 8 cookie layers in all). Spread reserved whipped cream over the cookies; top with remaining raspberries. Refrigerate, covered, overnight.
1 piece: 421 cal., 35g fat (21g sat. fat), 91mg chol., 132mg sod., 25g carb. (13g sugars, 3g fiber), 4g pro.

PLUM UPSIDE-DOWN CAKE

EASY LEMON PIE

BLUEBERRIES & CREAM COFFEE CAKE

Growing up, my boys enjoyed this blueberry coffee cake as a Saturday morning tradition. It's also my go-to recipe for all of our holiday parties because it's perfect for brunch or dessert. It's easy to make and so delicious.
—Susan Ober, Franconia, NH

Prep: 20 min. • **Bake:** 55 min. + cooling
Makes: 12 servings

- 1 cup butter, softened
- 2 cups sugar
- 2 large eggs, room temperature
- 1 tsp. vanilla extract
- 1¾ cups all-purpose flour
- 1 tsp. baking powder
- ¼ tsp. salt
- 1 cup sour cream
- 1 cup fresh or frozen unsweetened blueberries
- ½ cup packed brown sugar
- ½ cup chopped pecans, optional
- 1 tsp. ground cinnamon
- 1 Tbsp. confectioners' sugar

1. In a large bowl, cream butter and sugar until light and fluffy, 5-7 minutes. Add eggs, 1 at a time, beating well after each addition. Beat in vanilla. Combine the flour, baking powder and salt; add to the creamed mixture alternately with sour cream, beating well after each addition. Fold in blueberries.
2. Spoon half of batter into a greased and floured 10-in. fluted tube pan. In a small bowl, combine the brown sugar, pecans if desired, and cinnamon. Sprinkle half over the batter. Top with the remaining batter; sprinkle with the remaining brown sugar mixture. Cut through batter with a knife to swirl the brown sugar mixture.
3. Bake at 350° until a toothpick inserted near center comes out clean, 55-60 minutes. Cool 10 minutes before removing from pan to a wire rack to cool completely. Just before serving, dust with confectioners' sugar.
1 slice: 428 cal., 20g fat (12g sat. fat), 76mg chol., 233mg sod., 60g carb. (45g sugars, 1g fiber), 4g pro.

EASY LEMON PIE

I've had this one-bowl lemon pie recipe for years. It's my twist on chocolate French silk pie, and it's easy to make with refrigerated pie pastry.
—Glenna Tooman, Boise, ID

Prep: 15 min. • **Bake:** 40 min. + chilling
Makes: 8 servings

- 1 sheet refrigerated pie crust
- ½ cup sugar
- 2 Tbsp. all-purpose flour
- 4 large eggs, room temperature
- 1 cup light corn syrup
- 1 tsp. grated lemon zest
- ⅓ cup lemon juice
- 2 Tbsp. butter, melted
- **WHIPPED CREAM**
- 1 cup heavy whipping cream
- 2 Tbsp. confectioners' sugar

1. Preheat oven to 350°. Unroll crust into a 9-in. pie plate; flute edge. Refrigerate while preparing filling.
2. In a bowl, mix the sugar and flour until blended. Whisk in eggs, corn syrup, lemon zest, lemon juice and melted butter until blended. Pour into crust.
3. Bake the pie on a lower oven rack until the filling is golden brown and thickened, 40-45 minutes; cover the edge loosely with foil during the last 15 minutes if needed to prevent overbrowning. Remove foil; cool for 1 hour on a wire rack. Refrigerate, covered, 2 hours or until cold.
4. For whipped cream, in a bowl, beat cream until it begins to thicken. Add confectioners' sugar; beat until soft peaks form. Serve pie with whipped cream.
1 piece: 475 cal., 23g fat (13g sat. fat), 147mg chol., 197mg sod., 65g carb. (50g sugars, 0 fiber), 5g pro.

BLUEBERRIES &
CREAM COFFEE CAKE

TASTE OF HOME
TEST
KITCHEN
RECIPE OF THE YEAR

CHOCOLATE-PEANUT BUTTER DUMP CAKE

I am a huge fan of the chocolate-peanut butter combination. I'm also a fan of easy recipes, including dump cakes. On occasion, I've omitted the peanut butter chips from this recipe and used 1½ cups semisweet chocolate chips with delicious results.
—Lisa Varner, El Paso, TX

- -

Prep: 15 min. • **Bake:** 20 min. + cooling
Makes: 15 servings

  1 **pkg. (3.9 oz.) instant chocolate pudding mix**
1¾ **cups 2% milk**
  1 **pkg. chocolate cake mix or devil's food cake mix (regular size)**
  6 **pkg. (1½ oz. each) peanut butter cups, chopped**
 ¾ **cup peanut butter chips**
 ¾ **cup semisweet chocolate chips**
 ½ **cup chopped unsalted peanuts**
    Optional: Vanilla ice cream or sweetened whipped cream

1. Preheat oven to 350°. Grease a 13x9-in. baking pan. In a large bowl, combine the pudding mix and milk until blended. Stir in cake mix (batter will be thick). Fold in the peanut butter cups, peanut butter chips and chocolate chips. Spread into prepared pan. Sprinkle with peanuts.

2. Bake until a toothpick inserted in the center comes out with moist crumbs, 20-25 minutes. Cool completely in pan on a wire rack. Serve with ice cream or whipped cream if desired.

1 piece: 349 cal., 14g fat (6g sat. fat), 3mg chol., 373mg sod., 51g carb. (33g sugars, 3g fiber), 7g pro.

CHOCOLATE-PEANUT BUTTER DUMP CAKE

PATCHWORK QUILT CAKE

This cake has a great homemade flavor. The buttery frosting adds a burst of vanilla.
—Aria Thornton, Milwaukee, WI

- -

Prep: 55 min. • **Bake:** 40 min. + cooling
Makes: 15 servings

⅔ cup butter, softened
1¾ cups sugar
1 Tbsp. vanilla extract
2 large eggs, room temperature
2½ cups all-purpose flour
2½ tsp. baking powder
½ tsp. salt
1¼ cups 2% milk
FROSTING
1 cup butter, softened
3 cups confectioners' sugar
4 tsp. vanilla extract
3 to 4 Tbsp. heavy whipping cream
Assorted fresh berries

1. Preheat oven to 350°. Grease a 13x9-in. baking dish.
2. Cream the butter and sugar until light and fluffy, 5-7 minutes. Add vanilla and eggs, 1 at at time, beating well. In another bowl, whisk together flour, baking powder and salt; beat into creamed mixture alternately with milk. Transfer to prepared dish.
3. Bake until a toothpick inserted in center comes out clean, 40-45 minutes. Place on a wire rack; cool completely.
4. For frosting, beat butter until creamy; gradually beat in confectioners' sugar until smooth and light in color, about 3 minutes. Beat in vanilla and 3 Tbsp. cream until light and fluffy, about 2 minutes; thin frosting with additional cream if desired. Spread over cake. Before serving, top with berries in a patchwork quilt pattern.
1 piece: 477 cal., 23g fat (14g sat. fat), 84mg chol., 342mg sod., 65g carb. (48g sugars, 1g fiber), 4g pro.

DOUBLE BUTTERSCOTCH COCONUT CAKE

DOUBLE BUTTERSCOTCH COCONUT CAKE

I got this recipe for coconut cake from a co-worker years ago, then I changed it up a bit by adding a family favorite: butterscotch. It's easy to throw together and makes a perfect accompaniment to coffee or tea.
—Marina Castle Kelley, Canyon Country, CA

- -

Prep: 20 min. • **Bake:** 40 min. + cooling
Makes: 16 servings

1 pkg. yellow cake mix (regular size)
1 pkg. (3.4 oz.) instant butterscotch pudding mix
4 large eggs, room temperature
1 cup canned coconut milk
¼ cup canola oil
1 cup sweetened shredded coconut
½ cup butterscotch chips
GLAZE
½ cup butterscotch chips
2 Tbsp. heavy whipping cream
⅓ cup sweetened shredded coconut, toasted

1. Preheat oven to 350°. Grease and flour a 10-in. fluted tube pan.
2. In a large bowl, combine the cake mix, pudding mix, eggs, coconut milk and canola oil; beat on low speed 30 seconds. Beat on medium speed for 2 minutes. Stir in the coconut and butterscotch chips. Transfer to prepared pan.
3. Bake until a toothpick inserted near center comes out clean, 40-45 minutes. Cool in pan 10 minutes before removing to a wire rack to cool completely. For glaze, in a microwave, melt butterscotch chips and cream; stir until smooth. Drizzle over the cake; sprinkle with toasted coconut.
1 slice: 327 cal., 15g fat (10g sat. fat), 49mg chol., 359mg sod., 42g carb. (30g sugars, 1g fiber), 4g pro.

"This Bundt cake takes minutes to whip together and has a solid—not too sweet—butterscotch flavor."
—MARGARET KNOEBEL, CULINARY ASSISTANT

DOUBLE-CRUST RHUBARB PIE

Old-fashioned and delicious, rhubarb pie is springtime comfort food. The first time I made this pie was when my husband and I started dating. He loved it, and I've made it many times since. I recommend placing a baking sheet under this pie while it bakes, as the filling sometimes runs over.
—Lavonn Bormuth, Westerville, OH

Prep: 20 min. • **Bake:** 45 min.
Makes: 8 servings

- 1 cup sugar
- 3 Tbsp. all-purpose flour
- ½ tsp. ground cinnamon
- 2 large eggs, lightly beaten, room temperature
- 4 cups chopped fresh rhubarb or frozen rhubarb
  Pastry for double-crust pie
- 1 Tbsp. butter

1. In a large bowl, combine sugar, flour and cinnamon. Add eggs; whisk until smooth. Gently stir in rhubarb. Line a 9-in. pie plate with crust; add filling. Dot with butter.
2. Roll out remaining dough to fit top of pie; place over filling. Trim, seal and flute edge. Cut slits in top.
3. Bake at 400° until crust is golden brown and filling is bubbly, 45-50 minutes. Cool on a wire rack. Store in the refrigerator.
1 piece: 392 cal., 17g fat (7g sat. fat), 67mg chol., 233mg sod., 56g carb. (28g sugars, 1g fiber), 4g pro.
Pastry for double-crust pie (9 inches):
Combine 2-½ cups all-purpose flour and ½ tsp. salt; cut in 1 cup cold butter until crumbly. Gradually add ⅓ to ⅔ cup ice water, tossing with a fork until dough holds together when pressed. Divide dough in half. Shape each into a disk; wrap in plastic wrap. Refrigerate 1 hour or overnight.

EASY STRAWBERRY LEMONADE FREEZER PIE

EASY STRAWBERRY LEMONADE FREEZER PIE

Three simple ingredients mixed together and spread into a graham crust make magic while your freezer does the the work. Make this pie ahead and freeze it overnight or even longer. Feel free to vary the fruit.
—Debbie Glasscock, Conway, AR

Prep: 15 min. + freezing • **Makes:** 8 servings

- 1 container (23.2 oz.) frozen sweetened sliced strawberries, thawed (2½ cups thawed)
- 1 pkg. (3.4 oz.) instant lemon pudding mix
- 1 carton (8 oz.) frozen whipped topping, thawed
- 1 graham cracker crust (9 in.)
  Optional: Additional whipped topping and fresh strawberries

1. In a large bowl, combine the strawberries (with juices) and pudding mix; let stand until slightly thickened, about 5 minutes. Fold in the whipped topping. Spread into graham cracker crust.
2. Freeze at least 8 hours or overnight. Let stand 5-10 minutes before serving. If desired, serve with additional whipped topping and fresh strawberries.
1 piece: 306 cal., 10g fat (6g sat. fat), 0 chol., 273mg sod., 51g carb. (45g sugars, 2g fiber), 1g pro.

CONFETTI BIRTHDAY CAKE

Here's a moist and fluffy vanilla cake with lots of sprinkles and a whipped vanilla buttercream. It's almost impossible not to feel happy when you see the fun pop of rainbow confetti!
—Courtney Rich, Highland, UT

- -

Prep: 30 min. • **Bake:** 35 min. + cooling
Makes: 16 servings

- 1 cup unsalted butter, room temperature
- ⅓ cup vegetable oil
- 1¾ cups sugar
- 3 large eggs, room temperature
- 3 large egg whites, room temperature
- 1 Tbsp. vanilla extract
- 3 cups cake flour
- 2 tsp. baking powder
- 1 tsp. salt
- 1 cup buttermilk, room temperature
- ¼ cup rainbow sprinkles

BUTTERCREAM
- 1½ cups unsalted butter, softened
- 4½ cups confectioners' sugar, sifted
- 3 Tbsp. heavy whipping cream

- 2 tsp. clear vanilla extract
  Soft pink paste food coloring

1. Preheat oven to 325°. Grease a 13x9-in. baking dish. In a large bowl, cream butter, oil and sugar until light and fluffy, 5-7 minutes. Add eggs, then egg whites, 1 at a time, beating well after each addition. Beat in vanilla. In another bowl, whisk flour, baking powder and salt; add to creamed mixture alternately with buttermilk, beating well after each addition. Fold in sprinkles.
2. Transfer to prepared pan. Bake until a toothpick inserted in center comes out clean, 35-40 minutes. Cool completely on a wire rack.
3. For buttercream, in a large bowl, beat butter until creamy. Gradually beat in the confectioners' sugar until smooth. Add cream, vanilla and food coloring. Beat until light and fluffy, 5-7 minutes. Frost top of cake with frosting, and, if desired, top with additional sprinkles.
1 piece: 823 cal., 47g fat (26g sat. fat), 138mg chol., 279mg sod., 97g carb. (75g sugars, 0 fiber), 6g pro.

EASY GRASSHOPPER ICE CREAM PIE

This quick pie is such an ego booster! My family gives me compliments the entire time they're eating it. A big hit at work potlucks, too, it's good to the last crumb.
—Kim Murphy, Albia, IA

- -

Prep: 15 min. + freezing • **Makes:** 8 servings

- 4 cups mint chocolate chip ice cream, softened
- 1 chocolate crumb crust (8 in.)
- 5 Oreo cookies, chopped
- ⅓ cup chocolate-covered peppermint candies
  Chocolate hard-shell ice cream topping

Spread ice cream into crust. Sprinkle with cookies and candies; drizzle with ice cream topping. Freeze until firm. Remove from the freezer 15 minutes before serving.
Note: This recipe was tested with Junior Mints chocolate-covered peppermint candies.
1 piece: 374 cal., 19g fat (9g sat. fat), 25g chol., 182g sod., 47g carb. (35g sugar, 1g fiber), 4g pro.

CONFETTI BIRTHDAY CAKE

COCONUT PINEAPPLE UPSIDE-DOWN CAKE

This recipe is one of my favorites! The tropical flavors remind me of being on vacation with my family in the Caribbean. It brings back so many fun memories.
—Stephanie Pichelli, Toronto, ON

- -

Prep: 30 min. • **Bake:** 55 min. + cooling
Makes: 12 servings

- 1 **can (20 oz.) unsweetened sliced pineapple, drained**
- ¾ **cup unsalted butter, softened**
- ¼ **cup coconut oil**
- 1½ **cups sugar**
- 2 **large egg yolks, room temperature**
- 1 **tsp. coconut extract**
- 3 **cups cake flour**
- 3 **tsp. baking powder**
- ½ **tsp. salt**
- 1 **can (13.66 oz.) coconut milk**
- 6 **large egg whites, room temperature**
- ⅛ **tsp. cream of tartar**
  Toasted sweetened shredded coconut, optional

1. Preheat oven to 350°. Arrange pineapple in a single layer in a well seasoned 12-in. cast-iron or other ovenproof skillet.
2. In a large bowl, cream butter, coconut oil and sugar 5-7 minutes or until light and fluffy. Add egg yolks, 1 at a time, beating well after each addition. Beat in coconut extract. In another bowl, whisk the flour, baking powder and salt; add to creamed mixture alternately with coconut milk, beating well after each addition.
3. With clean beaters, beat egg whites and cream of tartar on high speed just until stiff but not dry. Fold a fourth of the whites into batter, then fold in remaining whites. Gently spread over pineapple. Bake cake until a toothpick inserted in center comes out clean, 55-60 minutes. Cool 10 minutes before inverting onto a serving plate. Serve warm, with toasted coconut if desired.
1 piece: 458 cal., 22g fat (17g sat. fat), 61mg chol., 262mg sod., 59g carb. (31g sugars, 1g fiber), 6g pro.

COCONUT PINEAPPLE UPSIDE-DOWN CAKE

WHITE CHOCOLATE CAST-IRON TART

This dessert is worth every calorie. If you aren't a fan of citrus, leave out the orange flavoring and the white chocolate will really shine through.
—Phoebe Saad, Framingham, MA

Prep: 45 min. + chilling
Bake: 15 min. + cooling • **Makes:** 12 servings

- ½ cup coarsely crushed almond biscotti (about 4 whole cookies)
- ½ cup coarsely crushed amaretti cookies (about 16 cookies)
- 2 Tbsp. sugar
- 6 Tbsp. unsalted butter, melted

FILLING

- ½ cup sugar, divided
- 3 Tbsp. all-purpose flour
- 1 cup 2% milk
- 3 large eggs, separated
- 14 oz. white baking chocolate, finely chopped
- 2 Tbsp. unsalted butter, cubed
- ½ tsp. orange extract
- ¼ tsp. plus dash salt, divided

1. Preheat oven to 375°. Place biscotti, amaretti cookies and sugar in a food processor; pulse until coarsely ground. Add butter; pulse until combined. Press mixture firmly into bottom of a 9-in. cast-iron or other ovenproof skillet. Bake until lightly browned, 12-15 minutes. Cool on a wire rack. In a heavy saucepan, mix ¼ cup sugar and flour. Whisk in the milk. Cook and stir over medium heat until thickened and bubbly. Reduce heat to low; cook and stir 2 minutes longer. Remove from heat. In a small bowl, whisk a small amount of hot mixture into egg yolks; return all to pan, whisking constantly. Bring mixture to a gentle boil; cook and stir 2 minutes. Remove from heat. Stir in white chocolate, butter, orange extract and ¼ tsp. salt until chocolate is melted.

2. Preheat oven to 350°. For meringue, in a large bowl, beat egg whites with remaining dash salt on medium speed until foamy.

Gradually add remaining ¼ cup sugar, 1 Tbsp. at a time, beating on high after each addition until sugar is dissolved. Continue beating until soft glossy peaks form.

3. Carefully transfer hot filling to crust. Spread meringue evenly over filling, sealing to edge of crust. Bake until meringue is golden brown, 12-15 minutes. Cool 1 hour on a wire rack. Refrigerate at least 6 hours before serving.

1 piece: 352 cal., 20g fat (13g sat. fat), 73mg chol., 119mg sod., 41g carb. (38g sugars, 0 fiber), 6g pro.

TEST KITCHEN TIP

It's important to clean your cast-iron skillet shortly after use, but be sure the skillet is cool to the touch before submerging it in cold water or the skillet might crack. Don't let the skillet soak too long, as it could begin to rust.

ORANGE CHOCOLATE MOUSSE MIRROR CAKE

A shiny, mirrorlike orange glaze covers a chocolate mousse cake to create a delicious show-stopping dessert your guests will be talking about for weeks to come.
—Matthew Hass, Ellison Bay, WI

- -

Prep: 45 min. + freezing • **Makes:** 16 servings

- 2 **cups crushed Oreo cookies (about 20 cookies)**
- 1 **tsp. grated orange zest**
- ¼ **cup butter, melted**

FILLING
- 1 **envelope unflavored gelatin**
- 6 **Tbsp. orange juice**
- 8 **oz. semisweet chocolate, chopped**
- 2½ **cups heavy whipping cream, divided**
- 3 **pkg. (8 oz. each) cream cheese, softened**
- ¾ **cup sugar**
- ¼ **cup dark baking cocoa**
- 1 **Tbsp. grated orange zest**

GLAZE
- 1 **envelope unflavored gelatin**
- ½ **cup plus 1 tsp. water, divided**
- ¾ **cup sugar**
- ⅓ **cup sweetened condensed milk**
- 1 **cup white baking chips**
  Orange paste food coloring

1. Mix crushed cookies, orange zest and butter; press onto bottom of a greased 9-in. springform pan. Set aside.

2. In a small saucepan, sprinkle gelatin over orange juice; let stand 1 minute. Stir over low heat until gelatin is dissolved. Set aside.

3. For filling, melt chocolate with ½ cup cream in microwave; stir until smooth. Cool slightly; stir in dissolved gelatin. In a large bowl, beat cream cheese, sugar and cocoa until smooth. Gradually add the chocolate mixture and orange zest; mix well.

4. In another bowl, beat remaining cream until stiff peaks form. Gently fold into the cream cheese mixture. Spoon over crust. Refrigerate, covered, until set, about 4 hours. Freeze, covered, overnight.

5. For glaze, sprinkle gelatin over ¼ cup water in a small bowl; set aside (mixture will solidify). Meanwhile, in a small saucepan, combine sugar, milk and remaining water. Bring to a simmer over medium heat, stirring occasionally. Remove from heat. Stir in the gelatin mixture until dissolved. Add baking chips; stir with a whisk until melted. Stir in food coloring; mix well. Cool glaze, stirring occasionally, until it reaches 90°, about 40 minutes.

6. Place cake on an inverted 9-in. pie plate in a foil-lined 15x10x1-in. pan. Remove the sides of the springform. Pour cooled glaze over frozen cake, allowing excess to drip off. Let glaze set 15 minutes before removing drips from bottom edge of cake. Refrigerate 2 hours before serving.

1 piece: 610 cal., 43g fat (25g sat. fat), 97mg chol., 244mg sod., 47g carb. (40g sugars, 1g fiber), 7g pro.

TEST KITCHEN TIP

Make sure your cream cheese is at room temperature to avoid any lumps in the filling. If you're having trouble getting the cream cheese smooth, try passing it through a fine mesh strainer before adding the chocolate mixture and orange zest.

ORANGE CHOCOLATE MOUSSE MIRROR CAKE

CITRUS CRANBERRY PIE

CITRUS CRANBERRY PIE

To showcase the pure beauty of bright-red cranberries, we came up with this lattice-topped pie. A dollop of orange cream complements the slightly tart flavor.
—*Taste of Home* Test Kitchen

- -

Prep: 30 min. • • **Bake:** 50 min. + cooling
Makes: 8 servings

3½ cups fresh or frozen cranberries
1 cup sugar
2 tsp. grated lemon zest
1 tsp. grated orange zest
1 small navel orange, peeled, sectioned and chopped
2 Tbsp. butter, melted
2 Tbsp. all-purpose flour
¼ tsp. salt

Pastry for double-crust pie
1 large egg, lightly beaten
Additional sugar

ORANGE CREAM
1 cup heavy whipping cream
1 Tbsp. sugar
2 tsp. grated orange zest
½ tsp. orange extract, optional

1. Preheat oven to 450°. Toss together first 8 ingredients.

2. On a lightly floured surface, roll 1 half of dough to a ⅛-in.-thick circle; transfer to a 9-in. pie plate. Trim crust even with rim. Add the filling.

3. Roll remaining dough to a ⅛-in.-thick circle; cut into strips. Arrange over filling in a lattice pattern. Trim and seal strips to edge of bottom crust; flute edge. Brush lattice with egg; sprinkle with additional sugar.

4. Bake 10 minutes. Reduce oven setting to 350°; bake 40-45 minutes or until golden brown, covering edge with foil if crust is getting too dark. Cool completely on a wire rack; refrigerate until serving.

5. Meanwhile, beat whipping cream until it begins to thicken. Add remaining ingredients; beat until soft peaks form. Refrigerate until serving. Serve with pie.

1 piece: 515 cal., 29g fat (15g sat. fat), 85mg chol., 323mg sod., 62g carb. (33g sugars, 2g fiber), 4g pro.

Pastry for double-crust pie (9 inches):
Combine 2-½ cups all-purpose flour and ½ tsp. salt; cut in 1 cup cold butter until crumbly. Gradually add ⅓ to ⅔ cup ice water, tossing with a fork until dough holds together when pressed. Divide dough in half. Shape each into a disk; wrap in plastic wrap. Refrigerate 1 hour or overnight.

POUTINE CAKE

Recently my daughter was talking about her favorite food, poutine. I was inspired and created a homemade poutine-inspired cake for her 19th birthday. She was thrilled!
—Donna Zacharias, Carrot River, SK

- -

Prep: 1 hour • **Bake:** 30 min. + cooling
Makes: 16 servings

- 3 cups all-purpose flour
- 2 cups sugar
- ⅔ cup baking cocoa
- 2 tsp. baking soda
- 2 tsp. baking powder
- 1 tsp. salt
- 2 large eggs, room temperature
- ⅔ cup canola oil
- 2 tsp. vanilla extract
- 2 cups boiling water

BUTTERCREAM
- 1 cup unsalted butter, softened
- 1 tsp. 2% milk
- 1 tsp. vanilla extract
- ⅛ tsp. salt
- 3½ cups confectioners' sugar

ASSEMBLY
- 12 crisp ladyfinger cookies
- 8 oz. white candy coating, melted
- 2 cups butterscotch-caramel ice cream topping

1. Preheat oven to 350°. Line bottoms of 2 greased 8-in. round baking pans with parchment; grease parchment.
2. In a large bowl, whisk flour, sugar, baking cocoa, baking soda, baking powder and salt. In another bowl, whisk eggs, oil and vanilla; stir into flour mixture. Stir in boiling water; batter will be thin.
3. Transfer to prepared pans. Bake until a toothpick inserted in center comes out clean, 30-35 minutes. Cool in pans for 10 minutes before removing to wire racks; remove paper. Cool completely.
4. For frosting, in a large bowl, beat butter until creamy. Beat in milk, vanilla and salt. Gradually beat in confectioners' sugar until smooth. Spread the frosting between cake layers and over top and sides of cake. Using cookies, decorate cake as desired to look like french-fried potatoes. Drop the candy coating by tablespoonfuls to resemble cheese curds. Drizzle with the ice cream topping to resemble gravy.
1 piece: 719 cal., 28g fat (13g sat. fat), 65mg chol., 475mg sod., 114g carb. (81g sugars, 1g fiber), 6g pro.

LIME-RASPBERRY PIE WITH COCONUT CREAM

In my many family trips to Florida, I've had Key lime pie from many restaurants, and each one is different. I wanted to create my own spin on the pie to make it my signature dessert. Whipped egg whites in the filling make it mousselike, sweet raspberries balance the tart filling, and coconut and cashews amp up the tropical flavor. Garnish with fresh raspberries and toasted shredded coconut if you'd like.
—Elise Easterling, Chapel Hill, NC

- -

Prep: 50 min. • **Bake:** 25 min. + chilling
Makes: 12 servings

- 3 large egg whites
- 18 whole graham crackers, crushed (about 2½ cups)
- ½ cup packed brown sugar
- ½ cup unsalted cashews, finely chopped
- ¾ cup butter, melted
- 2 cans (14 oz. each) sweetened condensed milk
- ¾ cup Key lime juice
- 6 large egg yolks
- ¼ cup sugar

TOPPINGS
- 1 can (13.66 oz.) coconut milk
- 1 cup heavy whipping cream
- ½ cup confectioners' sugar
- ½ cup seedless raspberry jam
  Optional: Fresh raspberries and toasted flaked coconut

1. Place egg whites in a small bowl; let stand at room temperature 30 minutes. Preheat oven to 350°.
2. In a large bowl, mix crushed crackers, brown sugar and cashews; stir in melted butter. Press onto bottom and 2 in. up sides of a greased 9-in. springform pan.
3. In a large bowl, mix condensed milk, lime juice and egg yolks until blended. With clean beaters, beat egg whites on medium speed until soft peaks form. Gradually add sugar, 1 Tbsp. at a time, beating on high after each addition until sugar is dissolved. Continue beating until stiff peaks form. Fold into milk mixture; pour into crust.
4. Bake 25-30 minutes or until filling is set. Cool 4 hours on a wire rack. Refrigerate 6 hours or overnight, covering when cold.
5. Spoon the cream layer from top of the coconut milk into a large bowl (discard remaining liquid). Add whipping cream and confectioners' sugar to bowl; beat until stiff peaks form.
6. Spread jam over pie. Dollop coconut cream over pie or serve on the side. If desired, top with raspberries and coconut.
1 piece: 678 cal., 34g fat (20g sat. fat), 168mg chol., 349mg sod., 86g carb. (69g sugars, 1g fiber), 11g pro.

LIME-RASPBERRY PIE
WITH COCONUT CREAM

STRAWBERRY BUTTERMILK
SKILLET SHORTCAKE
PAGE 302

Desserts

There's always room for dessert! Whether you need a homemade tart for an upcoming potluck, a velvety cheesecake to contribute to a dinner party or a no-fuss sweet to surprise the family, you're sure to find the perfect grand finale among these easy yet impressive specialties.

PRETTY
PEACH TART

PRETTY PEACH TART

When ripe peaches finally arrive at local fruit stands, this is the first recipe I reach for. The tart is true perfection—a delightful way to celebrate spring's arrival. You can make the tart with other varieties of fruit, too.
—Lorraine Caland, Shuniah, ON

- -

Prep: 30 min. • **Bake:** 40 min. + cooling
Makes: 8 servings

¼ cup butter, softened
3 Tbsp. sugar
¼ tsp. ground nutmeg
1 cup all-purpose flour
FILLING
2 lbs. peaches (about 7 medium), peeled and sliced
⅓ cup sugar
2 Tbsp. all-purpose flour
¼ tsp. ground cinnamon
⅛ tsp. almond extract
¼ cup sliced almonds
   Whipped cream, optional

1. Preheat oven to 375°. Cream the butter, sugar and nutmeg until light and fluffy, 5-7 minutes. Beat in the flour until blended (mixture will be dry). Press the dough firmly onto bottom and up sides of an ungreased 9-in. fluted tart pan with removable bottom.
2. Place on a baking sheet. Bake on a middle oven rack until the crust is lightly browned, 10-12 minutes. Cool on a wire rack.
3. In a large bowl, toss peaches with sugar, flour, cinnamon and extract; add to crust. Sprinkle with almonds.
4. Bake tart on a lower oven rack until the crust is golden brown and the peaches are tender, 40-45 minutes. Cool on a wire rack. If desired, serve with whipped cream.
1 piece: 222 cal., 8g fat (4g sat. fat), 15mg chol., 46mg sod., 36g carb. (21g sugars, 3g fiber), 4g pro.

OREO CUPCAKES WITH COOKIES & CREAM FROSTING

OREO CUPCAKES WITH COOKIES & CREAM FROSTING

No one will be able to resist these Oreo cupcakes. If you want to pipe the frosting, be sure to thoroughly crush the Oreos.
—*Taste of Home* Test Kitchen

- -

Prep: 20 min. • **Bake:** 20 min. + cooling
Makes: 2 dozen

⅔ cup butter, softened
1¾ cups sugar
2 large eggs, room temperature
1½ tsp. vanilla extract
2½ cups all-purpose flour
2½ tsp. baking powder
½ tsp. salt
1¼ cups 2% milk
2 cups coarsely crushed Oreo cookies
FROSTING
1 cup butter, softened
3 cups confectioners' sugar
2 Tbsp. 2% milk
1 tsp. vanilla extract
1½ cups finely crushed Oreo cookie crumbs

Optional: Additional Oreo cookie crumbs and mini Oreo cookies

1. Preheat oven to 350°. Line 24 muffin cups with paper liners.
2. In a large bowl, cream butter and sugar until light and fluffy, 5-7 minutes. Add eggs, 1 at a time, beating well after each addition. Beat in vanilla. In another bowl, whisk flour, baking powder and salt; add to the creamed mixture alternately with milk, beating well after each addition. Fold in crushed cookies.
3. Fill prepared cups three-fourths full. Bake 20-22 minutes or until a toothpick inserted in the center comes out clean. Cool in pans 10 minutes before removing to wire racks to cool completely.
4. In a large bowl, combine the butter, confectioners' sugar, milk and vanilla; beat until smooth. Fold in cookie crumbs. Pipe or spread frosting over cupcakes. If desired, sprinkle with additional cookie crumbs and garnish with mini Oreo cookies.
1 cupcake: 411 cal., 19g fat (10g sat. fat), 51mg chol., 346mg sod., 58g carb. (40g sugars, 2g fiber), 4g pro.

PEACH
CREAM PUFFS

PEACH CREAM PUFFS

On a sizzling day, we crave something light, airy and cool. Nothing says summer like cream puffs stuffed with peaches and whipped cream.
—Angela Benedict, Dunbar, WV

- -

Prep: 55 min. + cooling
Bake: 25 min. + cooling
Makes: 16 servings

- 1   **cup water**
- ½ **cup butter, cubed**
- ⅛ **tsp. salt**
- 1   **cup all-purpose flour**
- 4   **large eggs, room temperature**

FILLING

- 4   **medium peaches, peeled and cubed (about 3 cups)**
- ½ **cup sugar**
- ½ **cup water**
- ½ **cup peach schnapps liqueur or peach nectar**
- ½ **tsp. ground cinnamon**
- ¼ **tsp. ground nutmeg**

WHIPPED CREAM

- 2   **cups heavy whipping cream**
- ½ **cup confectioners' sugar**
- 3   **Tbsp. peach schnapps liqueur, optional**
       Additional confectioners' sugar

1. Preheat oven to 400°. In a large saucepan, bring water, butter and salt to a rolling boil. Add flour all at once and beat until blended. Cook over medium heat, stirring vigorously until mixture pulls away from sides of pan and forms a ball. Transfer dough to a large bowl; let stand 5 minutes.

2. Add the eggs, 1 at a time, beating well after each addition until smooth. Continue beating until mixture is smooth and shiny.

3. Cut a ½-in. hole in tip of a pastry bag. Transfer dough to bag; pipe sixteen 2-in. mounds 3 in. apart onto parchment-lined baking sheets.

4. Bake on a low oven rack 25-30 minutes or until puffed, firm and golden brown. Pierce side of each puff with a knife to allow steam to escape. Cool completely on wire racks.

5. Meanwhile, in a large saucepan, combine filling ingredients; bring to a boil, stirring occasionally. Reduce the heat; simmer, uncovered, 25-30 minutes or until the mixture is slightly thickened and peaches are tender. Cool completely.

6. In a bowl, beat cream until it begins to thicken. Add confectioners' sugar and, if desired, peach schnapps; beat until soft peaks form.

7. Cut top third off each cream puff. Pull out and discard the soft dough from inside tops and bottoms.

8. To serve, spoon 2 Tbsp. whipped cream into each bottom; top with 2 Tbsp. filling and 2 Tbsp. additional whipped cream. Replace the tops. Dust with additional confectioners' sugar.

1 cream puff with ¼ cup whipped cream and 2 Tbsp. filling: 256 cal., 18g fat (11g sat. fat), 103mg chol., 94mg sod., 21g carb. (14g sugars, 1g fiber), 3g pro.

BLUEBERRY RHUBARB COUNTRY TART

When rhubarb comes in, mix it with blueberries for a rustic and bubbly tart. Offer it to a friend with a warm cup of tea.
—Jeanne Ambrose, Milwaukee, WI

Prep: 15 min. • **Bake:** 40 min.
Makes: 8 servings

> **Dough for single-crust pie**
> ¾ cup sugar
> ¼ cup all-purpose flour
> 4 cups chopped fresh or frozen rhubarb, thawed
> 1 cup fresh or frozen blueberries, thawed
> 2 Tbsp. 2% milk
> 1 Tbsp. coarse sugar

1. Preheat oven to 400°. On a lightly floured surface, roll the dough into a 14-in. circle. Transfer to a parchment-lined baking sheet.
2. In a large bowl, mix sugar and flour. Add rhubarb and blueberries; toss to coat. Spoon filling over crust to within 2 in. of edge. Fold crust edge over filling, pleating as you go and leaving a 4-in. opening in the center. Brush folded crust with milk; sprinkle with coarse sugar. Bake 40-45 minutes or until crust is golden. Transfer to a wire rack to cool.
1 piece: 290 cal., 12g fat (7g sat. fat), 30mg chol., 159mg sod., 44g carb. (23g sugars, 2g fiber), 3g pro.
Dough for single-crust pie: Combine 1¼ cups all-purpose flour and ¼ tsp. salt; cut in ½ cup cold butter until crumbly. Gradually add 3-5 Tbsp. ice water, tossing with a fork until dough holds together when pressed. Cover and refrigerate 1 hour.

BLUEBERRY RHUBARB
COUNTRY TART

LEMON COCONUT STREUSEL ICE CREAM CAKE

Here's a cool treat my family loves anytime, but we find it especially refreshing on a hot summer day. The sweet cream of coconut and the tart lemon juice make a delicious combo, and the streusel adds a nice crunch. You can use any crunchy sugar, lemon or coconut cookie in place of the shortbreads, as long as each cookie is about 2 inches.
—Janet Gill, Canton, OH

Prep: 30 min. + freezing • **Makes:** 16 servings

> 1 pkg. (11.2 oz.) shortbread cookies
> ½ cup sweetened shredded coconut, toasted
> ¼ cup macadamia nuts, coarsely chopped and toasted
> 1 tsp. grated lemon zest
> 1 can (15 oz.) cream of coconut
> ½ cup lemon juice
> 1½ qt. vanilla ice cream, softened
> 1 carton (8 oz.) frozen whipped topping, thawed, divided
>   Optional: Fresh blueberries, raspberries and strawberries

1. Reserve 10 cookies for decoration. Crush remaining cookies; transfer to a bowl. Stir in coconut, macadamia nuts and lemon zest. Reserve 2 Tbsp. crumb mixture for topping. In a large bowl, whisk the cream of coconut and lemon juice until combined. Stir in the softened ice cream until smooth. Fold in 1 cup whipped topping.
2. Sprinkle 1 cup crumb mixture onto the bottom of a greased 9-in. springform pan. Top with half the ice cream mixture. Layer with remaining 1 cup crumbs and ice cream mixture. Place the reserved whole cookies around edge of pan. Top with remaining 2½ cups whipped topping; sprinkle with reserved 2 Tbsp. crumb mixture. Freeze, covered, until firm, at least 8 hours or overnight. If desired, serve with berries.
1 piece: 384 cal., 21g fat (13g sat. fat), 29mg chol., 149mg sod., 45g carb. (35g sugars, 1g fiber), 4g pro.

PUMPKIN PIE TARTLETS WITH MAPLE PECAN CRUST

I came up with this recipe after discovering I had multiple food sensitivities that were affecting my health. Learning to eat healthier has dramatically improved my health. I knew it was important that I could still participate in family holidays and events where food was being served, so I began developing recipes that would be safe for me, but that others would enjoy, too. These mini pumpkin pie tarts are so delicious, you would never suspect that they're free of gluten, egg and dairy!
—Chantale Michaud, Guelph, ON

- -

Prep: 45 min. + cooling
Bake: 35 min+ cooling • **Makes:** 1½ dozen

- 2 cups old-fashioned oats
- 4 cups chopped pecans
- ½ cup maple syrup
- 2 tsp. ground cinnamon
- 1 tsp. sea salt
- 1 tsp. vanilla extract
- ¼ tsp. ground cloves

FILLING
- ½ cup maple syrup
- 3 Tbsp. cornstarch
- 2¼ cups canned pumpkin or homemade pumpkin puree
- ¼ cup cream of coconut, warmed
- 2 tsp. vanilla extract
- 2 tsp. ground cinnamon
- ½ tsp. sea salt
- ½ tsp. ground nutmeg
- ¼ tsp. ground ginger
- ¼ tsp. ground cloves

TOPPING
- ½ cup chopped pecans
- 2 tsp. maple syrup
  Dash sea salt

1. Preheat oven to 350°. Process oats in a food processor until a fine powder forms. Add pecans; pulse until nuts are chopped. Add next 5 ingredients; pulse until mixture is moistened. Remove from processor.
2. Fill 18 greased muffin cups with ⅓ cup oat mixture each. Using a wet 1 Tbsp. measure, press mixture onto bottom and up sides of muffin cups. Bake until lightly browned, about 10 minutes. Cool on a wire rack.
3. For filling, whisk together maple syrup and cornstarch. In another bowl, mix the remaining filling ingredients and add maple syrup mixture. Spoon about 3 Tbsp. into each crust.
4. Combine topping ingredients; spoon about 1 tsp. onto each tartlet. Bake until dark golden and set, 35-40 minutes. Cool 10 minutes before removing tartlets to a wire rack; cool 1 hour. If desired, refrigerate before serving.
1 tartlet: 302 cal., 21g fat (2g sat. fat), 0 chol., 173mg sod., 28g carb. (16g sugars, 5g fiber), 4g pro.

UPSIDE-DOWN PEAR PANCAKE

There's a pear tree in my yard that inspires me to bake with its fragrant fruit. This upside-down pancake works best with a firm pear, not one that is fully ripe.
—Helen Nelander, Boulder Creek, CA

- -

Takes: 30 min. • **Makes:** 2 servings

- ½ cup all-purpose flour
- ½ tsp. baking powder
- 1 large egg, room temperature
- ¼ cup 2% milk
- 1 Tbsp. butter
- 1 tsp. sugar
- 1 medium pear, peeled and thinly sliced lengthwise
  Confectioners' sugar

1. Preheat the oven to 375°. In a large bowl, whisk flour and baking powder. In a separate bowl, whisk the egg and milk until blended. Add to the dry ingredients, stirring just until combined.
2. Meanwhile, in a small ovenproof skillet, melt butter over medium-low heat. Sprinkle with sugar. Add pear slices in a single layer; cook 5 minutes. Spread prepared batter over pears. Cover and cook until top is set, about 5 minutes.
3. Transfer pan to oven; bake until edges are lightly brown, 8-10 minutes. Invert onto a serving plate. Sprinkle with confectioners' sugar. Serve warm.
½ pancake: 274 cal., 9g fat (5g sat. fat), 111mg chol., 197mg sod., 41g carb. (12g sugars, 4g fiber), 8g pro. **Diabetic exchanges:** 2 starch, 1½ fat, 1 medium-fat meat, ½ fruit.

**DUTCH OVEN CHERRY
CHOCOLATE DUMP CAKE**

ASK SARAH

SHOULD I INSPECT MY DUTCH OVEN BEFORE I BAKE IN IT?

Yes! Before you put it in the oven, check the inside for chips and cracks. Be sure to clean off any burnt-on bits inside the pan, too, as they can add an unsavory flavor to baked goods. Finally, check that the lid is oven-safe. Some less expensive models have plastic handles, which can melt at high oven temperatures.

DUTCH OVEN CHERRY CHOCOLATE DUMP CAKE

Looking for a super quick dessert that will make people think you spent all day in the kitchen? This easy dessert will wow your guests. Feel free to use your favorite pie filling in place of cherry.
—Rashanda Cobbins, Food Editor

Prep: 5 min. • **Bake:** 35 min.
Makes: 8 servings

   1   **can (21 oz.) cherry pie filling**
   1   **can (12 oz.) evaporated milk**
   1   **pkg. chocolate cake mix
        (regular size)**
  ⅓   **cup sliced almonds**
  ¾   **cup butter, melted
        Vanilla ice cream, optional**

Preheat oven to 350°. Line 4-qt. Dutch oven with parchment; lightly spray with cooking spray. Combine pie filling and evaporated milk; spread filling mixture into bottom of Dutch oven. Sprinkle with the cake mix (unprepared) and almonds; drizzle with butter. Bake, covered, until cake springs back when touched, 35-40 minutes. If desired, serve with ice cream.
1 cup: 515 cal., 24g fat (15g sat. fat), 61mg chol., 605mg sod., 68g carb. (44g sugars, 3g fiber), 7g pro.

RED, WHITE & BLUE BERRY TRIFLE

This luscious trifle tastes best if you make it the day before serving. I always keep extra blueberries and raspberries on hand to garnish the top.
—Kaia McShane, Munster, IN

- -

Prep: 20 min. + chilling • **Makes:** 12 servings

- 1 **can (14 oz.) sweetened condensed milk**
- 1½ **cups 2% milk**
- 2 **pkg. (3.4 oz. each) instant lemon pudding mix**
- ½ **cup sour cream**
- 2 **cups fresh blueberries**
- 2 **cups fresh raspberries**
- 1 **Tbsp. lemon juice**
- 1 **loaf (16 oz.) frozen pound cake, thawed and cubed**
- 1 **container (8 oz.) frozen whipped topping, thawed Optional: Additional blueberries and raspberries**

1. In a large bowl, whisk condensed milk, 2% milk and pudding mix 2 minutes. Fold in the sour cream. In another bowl, toss the blueberries and raspberries with lemon juice.
2. In a greased 9-in. springform pan, layer half each of the following: pound cake cubes, berry mixture and pudding mixture. Repeat layers. Refrigerate, covered, at least 2 hours before serving.
3. To serve, remove the rim from the pan. Serve with whipped topping and, if desired, additional berries.
1 piece: 418 cal., 15g fat (10g sat. fat), 74mg chol., 397mg sod., 65g carb. (48g sugars, 2g fiber), 7g pro.

QUICK & EASY
BAKLAVA SQUARES

QUICK & EASY BAKLAVA SQUARES

I love baklava but rarely indulge because it takes so much time to make. Then a friend gave me this simple recipe. I've made it for family, friends and co-workers—they can't get enough! I am always asked to bring these squares to special gatherings and parties, and I even give them as gifts during the holidays.
—Paula Marchesi, Lenhartsville, PA

- -

Prep: 20 min. • **Bake:** 25 min. + cooling
Makes: 2 dozen

- 1 **lb. (4 cups) chopped walnuts**
- 1½ **tsp. ground cinnamon**
- 1 **pkg. (16 oz., 14x9-in. sheets) frozen phyllo dough, thawed**
- 1 **cup butter, melted**
- 1 **cup honey**

1. Preheat oven to 350°. Coat a 13x9-in. baking dish with cooking spray. Combine walnuts and cinnamon.
2. Unroll phyllo dough. Layer 2 sheets of phyllo in prepared pan; brush with butter. Repeat with 6 more sheets of the phyllo, brushing every other 1 with butter. (Keep the remaining phyllo covered with a damp towel to prevent it from drying out.)
3. Sprinkle ½ cup nut mixture in the pan; drizzle with 2 Tbsp. honey. Add 2 more phyllo sheets, brushing with the butter; sprinkle another ½ cup nut mixture and 2 Tbsp. honey over phyllo. Repeat layers 6 times. Top with remaining phyllo sheets, brushing every other 1 with butter.
4. Using a sharp knife, score the surface to make 24 squares. Bake until golden brown and crisp, 25-30 minutes. Cool on a wire rack 1 hour before serving.
1 piece: 294 cal., 21g fat (6g sat. fat), 20mg chol., 145mg sod., 26g carb. (13g sugars, 2g fiber), 5g pro.

EASY LEMON BERRY TARTLETS

These cute, fruity, flaky tartlets filled with raspberries and topped with lemon-tinged cream cheese are a sweet ending to any weeknight meal. They are elegant yet come together quickly and easily.
—Elizabeth Dehart, West Jordan, UT

Takes: 15 min. • **Makes:** 15 tartlets

- ⅔ **cup frozen unsweetened raspberries, thawed and drained**
- 1 **tsp. confectioners' sugar**
- 1 **pkg. (1.9 oz.) frozen miniature phyllo tart shells**
- 4 **oz. reduced-fat cream cheese**
- 2 **Tbsp. lemon curd**
  Fresh raspberries, optional

1. In a small bowl, combine the thawed raspberries and the confectioners' sugar; mash with a fork. Spoon into tart shells.
2. In another small bowl, combine cream cheese and lemon curd. Pipe or spoon over filling. Top with fresh raspberries if desired.
1 tartlet: 51 cal., 3g fat (1g sat. fat), 7mg chol., 43mg sod., 5g carb. (2g sugars, 0 fiber), 1g pro. **Diabetic exchanges:** ½ starch, ½ fat.

WINTER WISHES TRIFLE

I created this light, fluffy trifle for a dear friend who was looking for a stunning dessert. This recipe hit the mark.
—Susan Stetzel, Gainesville, NY

Prep: 20 min. + chilling • **Makes:** 12 servings

- 1 **prepared angel food cake (8 to 10 oz.)**
- 4 **oz. white baking chocolate**
- 4 **cups heavy whipping cream, divided**
- ½ **tsp. peppermint extract**
- 12 **peppermint candies, crushed**

1. Place mixer beaters in a large metal bowl; refrigerate 30 minutes. Cut or tear cake into bite-sized pieces; set aside.
2. Break the white chocolate into smaller pieces; microwave at 70% power, stirring after 45 seconds. Microwave until melted, about 30 seconds more. Stir until smooth.

Let stand 5 minutes; stir ¼ cup heavy cream into white chocolate until smooth.
3. In the chilled bowl, beat remaining heavy cream until soft peaks form. Gently fold two-thirds of whipped cream into white chocolate. Stir extract into remaining whipped cream.
4. In a trifle bowl, layer cake and white chocolate mixture, repeating layers. Top with peppermint-flavored whipped cream. Refrigerate, covered, until serving. Sprinkle with crushed candies.
1 serving: 392 cal., 32g fat (20g sat. fat), 90mg chol., 173mg sod., 25g carb. (12g sugars, 0 fiber), 4g pro.

TEST KITCHEN TIP
If you want a touch of color, add a couple of drops of red food coloring to the whipped cream.

WINTER WISHES TRIFLE

UPSIDE-DOWN
PUMPKIN
PECAN TARTS

PEACH MELBA TRIFLE

This dream of a dessert tastes extra good on a busy day because you can make it ahead of time. If you don't have fresh peaches handy, use canned peaches.
—Christina Moore, Casar, NC

- -

Prep: 20 min. + chilling • **Makes:** 12 servings

- 2 pkg. (12 oz. each) frozen unsweetened raspberries, thawed
- 1 Tbsp. cornstarch
- 1½ cups fat-free peach yogurt
- ⅛ tsp. almond extract
- 1 carton (8 oz.) frozen reduced-fat whipped topping, thawed
- 2 prepared angel food cakes (8 to 10 oz. each), cut into 1-in. cubes (about 8 cups)
- 4 small peaches, peeled and sliced (about 2 cups)

1. In a large saucepan, mix the raspberries and cornstarch until blended. Bring to a boil; cook and stir 1-2 minutes or until thickened. Strain seeds; cover and refrigerate.
2. In a large bowl, mix yogurt and extract; fold in the whipped topping. In a 4-qt. bowl, layer half each of the cake cubes, yogurt mixture and peaches. Repeat the layers. Refrigerate, covered, at least 3 hours before serving. Serve with raspberry sauce.
⅔ cup: 201 cal., 3g fat (2g sat. fat), 1mg chol., 298mg sod., 41g carb. (10g sugars, 3g fiber), 4g pro.

UPSIDE-DOWN
PUMPKIN PECAN TARTS

These flaky treats with a creamy filling are a fantastic twist on pumpkin pie and can be prepared a day before they are needed.
—Darlene Buerger, Peoria, AZ

- -

Prep: 45 min. • **Bake:** 45 min. + cooling
Makes: 12 servings

- 1¼ cups melted butter, divided
- ⅓ cup packed brown sugar
- ¼ cup maple syrup
- ½ cup chopped pecans
- 12 oz. cream cheese, softened
- ½ cup sugar
- 1 tsp. vanilla extract
- 2 large eggs, room temperature
- ¾ cup canned pumpkin
- 2 Tbsp. all-purpose flour
- 2 tsp. pumpkin pie spice
- 36 sheets phyllo dough (14x9-in. size)
   Optional: Whipped cream and additional pumpkin pie spice

1. Preheat the oven to 325°. In a bowl, combine ¼ cup melted butter, brown sugar and maple syrup. Divide between 12 greased jumbo muffin cups. Sprinkle with pecans; set aside.

2. In a large bowl, beat cream cheese, sugar and vanilla until smooth. Add eggs, 1 at a time, until blended. Remove 1 cup for filling. Stir in the pumpkin, flour and pie spice to remaining cream cheese mixture; set aside.
3. Place 1 sheet of phyllo dough on a work surface; brush with melted butter. Layer with 5 additional phyllo sheets, brushing each layer. (Keep remaining phyllo covered with a damp towel to prevent it from drying out.) Cut sheets into a 9x7-in. rectangle. Carefully press the stack into a prepared muffin cup. Repeat with remaining phyllo.
4. Spoon 1 heaping Tbsp. plain cream cheese mixture into each phyllo cup. Top with 3 Tbsp. pumpkin mixture. Pinch corners of phyllo together and twist to seal; brush with remaining butter. Bake until golden brown, 45-50 minutes. Cool 5 minutes before inverting onto wire racks to cool completely. If desired, serve with whipped cream and sprinkle with additional pumpkin pie spice.
1 tart: 487 cal., 34g fat (18g sat. fat), 111mg chol., 392mg sod., 42g carb. (22g sugars, 2g fiber), 7g pro.

SLOW-COOKER
PEACH COBBLER

SLOW-COOKER PEACH COBBLER

Unlike most cobblers, the "topping" of this simple dessert is on the bottom. Placing the batter underneath the peaches helps it cook through evenly in the slow cooker.
—*Taste of Home* Test Kitchen

- -

Prep: 15 min. • **Cook:** 2 hours
Makes: 8 servings

- 1¼ cups all-purpose flour, divided
- 2 Tbsp. sugar
- 1 tsp. baking powder
- ¼ tsp. ground cinnamon
- ⅛ tsp. salt
- 1 large egg, room temperature
- ¼ cup 2% milk, warmed
- 2 Tbsp. butter, melted
- 6 cups sliced peeled fresh peaches (about 6 large)
- 2 Tbsp. brown sugar
- 1 Tbsp. lemon juice
- 1 Tbsp. vanilla extract
  Vanilla ice cream, optional

1. Whisk together 1 cup flour, sugar, baking powder, cinnamon and salt. In another bowl, whisk together egg, milk and butter; add to dry ingredients, stirring just until moistened (batter will be thick). Spread onto bottom of a greased 5-qt. slow cooker.
2. Combine peaches, the remaining ¼ cup flour, brown sugar, lemon juice and vanilla; spoon over batter. Cook, covered, on high until peach mixture is bubbly, 1¾-2 hours. If desired, serve with vanilla ice cream.
1 serving: 198 cal., 6g fat (3g sat. fat), 35mg chol., 145mg sod., 33g carb. (17g sugars, 2g fiber), 4g pro.

CARAMEL APPLE STRUDEL

CARAMEL APPLE STRUDEL

My father, who was born and raised in Vienna, Austria, would tell us stories about how his mother covered all of the kitchen counters with dough whenever she made apple strudel. This recipe is a modern, delicious way to carry on part of my family's heritage.
—Sarah Haengel, Bowie, MD

- -

Prep: 35 min. + cooling • **Bake:** 25 min
Makes: 8 servings

- 5 medium apples, peeled and chopped (5 cups)
- ¾ cup apple cider or juice
- ¼ cup sugar
- ½ tsp. ground cinnamon
- ¼ tsp. ground allspice
- ¼ tsp. ground cloves
- 1 frozen puff pastry sheet, thawed
- ¼ cup fat-free caramel ice cream topping
- 1 large egg
- 1 Tbsp. water
- 1 Tbsp. coarse sugar
  Optional: Sweetened whipped cream and additional caramel ice cream topping

1. Preheat the oven to 375°. In a large saucepan, combine the first 6 ingredients. Bring to a boil. Reduce the heat; simmer, uncovered, 15-20 minutes or until the apples are tender, stirring occasionally. Cool completely.
2. Unfold puff pastry onto a large sheet of parchment; roll into a 16x12-in. rectangle. Transfer parchment and pastry to a baking sheet, placing a short side of the rectangle facing you. Using a slotted spoon, arrange apples on bottom half of pastry to within 1 in. of edges. Drizzle the apples with the caramel topping. Roll up jelly-roll style, starting with the bottom side. Pinch seams to seal, and tuck ends under.
3. In a small bowl, whisk egg with water; brush over pastry. Sprinkle with coarse sugar. Cut slits in top. Bake 25-30 minutes or until golden brown. If desired, serve with whipped cream and additional caramel topping.
1 slice: 270 cal., 9g fat (2g sat. fat), 26mg chol., 140mg sod., 46g carb. (24g sugars, 4g fiber), 3g pro.

YOGURT-RICOTTA CHEESECAKE

I love Italian ricotta cheesecakes, but they have too much sugar for me. I made a light version, and my family could not tell the difference! I serve mine with sugar-free strawberry ice cream topping and fresh strawberries.
—Diane Shipley, Mentor, OH

Prep: 35 min. • **Bake:** 1 hour 20 min. + chilling
Makes: 16 servings

- 2 pkg. (8 oz. each) reduced-fat cream cheese
- 2 cups reduced-fat ricotta cheese
  Sugar substitute blend (made with sucralose) equivalent to 1½ cups sugar
- 2 cups vanilla yogurt
- ½ cup butter, melted
- ¼ cup cornstarch
- 3 Tbsp. all-purpose flour
- 2 Tbsp. lemon juice
- 1 tsp. vanilla extract
- 4 large eggs, room temperature, lightly beaten
  Halved fresh strawberries, optional

1. Preheat oven to 325°. In a large bowl, beat cream cheese, ricotta and sugar blend until smooth. Beat in yogurt, butter, cornstarch, flour, lemon juice and vanilla. Add eggs; beat on low speed just until blended. Pour into a greased 9-in. springform pan. Place pan on a baking sheet.
2. Bake 80-85 minutes, until center is almost set. Cool on wire rack for 10 minutes. Loosen sides from pan with a knife. Cool for 1 hour longer. Refrigerate cheesecake overnight, covering when completely cooled.
3. Remove rim from pan. If desired, serve cheesecake with strawberries.
1 piece: 246 cal., 15g fat (9g sat. fat), 91mg chol., 231mg sod., 19g carb. (16g sugars, 0 fiber), 9g pro.

GRILLED FRUIT PHYLLO TART

GRILLED FRUIT PHYLLO TART

This tart was a hit at my friend's baby shower. It reminds me of a fruit salad my mother used to make with cream cheese and whipped topping. Everyone loves the flaky crust and bright colors.
—Laura McAllister, Morganton, NC

Prep: 30 min. • **Grill:** 10 min.
Makes: 12 servings

- 3 Tbsp. butter, melted
- 4 tsp. canola oil
- 8 sheets phyllo dough (14x9-in. size)
- 1 large lemon
- 3 medium peaches, peeled and halved
- 2 cups large fresh strawberries, stems removed
- 4 slices fresh pineapple (½ in. thick)
- ⅓ cup packed brown sugar
- ½ tsp. salt
- ½ cup heavy whipping cream
- 1 pkg. (8 oz.) cream cheese, softened
- ⅓ cup confectioners' sugar
- 2 Tbsp. chopped fresh mint

1. Preheat oven to 400°. In a small bowl, mix the butter and oil. Brush a 15x10x1-in. baking pan with some of the butter mixture. Place 1 sheet of phyllo dough into the prepared pan; brush with the butter mixture. Layer with 7 additional phyllo sheets, brushing each layer. (Keep the remaining phyllo covered with a damp towel to prevent it from drying out.) Bake 5-7 minutes or until golden brown (phyllo will puff up during baking). Cool completely.
2. Finely grate enough zest from lemon to measure 1 Tbsp. Cut lemon crosswise in half; squeeze out juice. In a large bowl, toss peaches, strawberries, pineapple, brown sugar, salt, lemon zest and juice. Remove strawberries; thread fruit onto 3 metal or soaked wooden skewers.
3. Place fruit on oiled grill rack. Grill, covered, over medium heat until fruit is tender, turning once, 8-10 minutes for pineapple slices and peaches, 4-5 minutes for strawberries. Remove and set aside.
4. In a small bowl, beat the cream until soft peaks form. In another bowl, beat the cream cheese and confectioners' sugar until smooth. Fold in whipped cream. Spread over phyllo crust. Slice grilled fruit; arrange over filling. Sprinkle with mint; cut into pieces.
1 piece: 233 cal., 15g fat (8g sat. fat), 38mg chol., 216mg sod., 24g carb. (18g sugars, 2g fiber), 3g pro.

CHERRY FUDGE TRUFFLE COCONUT CHEESECAKE

Cherries and chocolate come together in this dazzling coconut cheesecake. It's a real showstopper any time of year!
—Jeanne Holt, Mendota Heights, MN

Prep: 40 min. • **Bake:** 1 hour 20 min. + chilling
Makes: 16 servings

1⅔ cups crushed Oreo cookies
    (about 17 cookies)
⅔ cup sweetened
    shredded coconut, toasted
¼ cup butter, melted

FILLING

4 pkg. (8 oz. each) cream cheese,
    softened, divided
1 cup sugar
¾ cup cream of coconut
1 tsp. coconut extract
3 large eggs, room temperature,
    lightly beaten
¼ cup chopped maraschino cherries
1 cup 60% cacao bittersweet
    chocolate baking chips,
    melted and cooled
⅓ cup cherry preserves,
    finely chopped

TOPPING

½ cup 60% cacao bittersweet
    chocolate baking chips,
    melted and cooled
1 cup sweetened whipped cream
⅓ cup sweetened
    shredded coconut, toasted
16 maraschino cherries with
    stems, patted dry

1. Preheat oven to 375°. Place a greased 10-in. springform pan on a double thickness of heavy-duty foil (about 18 in. square). Wrap foil securely around the pan. Place on a baking sheet.
2. In a small bowl, mix crushed cookies and coconut; stir in butter. Press onto bottom and ½ in. up sides of prepared pan. Bake 10 minutes. Cool on a wire rack. Reduce oven setting to 325°.
3. In a large bowl, beat 3 packages cream cheese and sugar until smooth. Beat in cream of coconut and extract. Add eggs; beat on low speed just until blended. Stir in chopped cherries. Pour 3 cups batter into crust. In another bowl, beat remaining 8 ounces cream cheese until smooth. Beat in cooled chocolate and cherry preserves. Drop by tablespoonfuls over the coconut batter. Carefully spoon remaining coconut batter over top. Place springform pan in a larger baking pan; add 1 in. hot water to larger pan.
4. Bake until the center is just set and top appears dull, 80-85 minutes. Remove the springform pan from the water bath. Cool the cheesecake on a wire rack 10 minutes. Loosen sides from pan with a knife; remove foil. Cool 1 hour longer. Once completely cool, cover and refrigerate overnight.
5. Remove rim from pan. Top cheesecake with chocolate, whipped cream, toasted coconut and cherries.

1 piece: 545 cal., 37g fat (22g sat. fat), 108mg chol., 290mg sod., 52g carb. (44g sugars, 2g fiber), 6g pro.

CHERRY FUDGE TRUFFLE COCONUT CHEESECAKE

PEANUT BUTTER & JELLY ICE CREAM

STRAWBERRY BUTTERMILK SKILLET SHORTCAKE

This scratch-made buttermilk shortcake is a family favorite. It's become tradition for my grandmother to make it every summer.
—Claudia Lamascolo, Melbourne, FL

Prep: 25 min. • **Bake:** 50 min.
Makes: 10 servings

- 10 Tbsp. shortening
- ¼ cup butter, softened
- 1 cup sugar
- 2 large eggs, room temperature
- 2½ cups all-purpose flour
- 3 tsp. baking powder
- ½ tsp. salt
- ⅔ cup buttermilk
STREUSEL TOPPING
- ⅔ cup all-purpose flour
- ½ cup sugar
- 1 tsp. ground cinnamon
- ¼ tsp. ground allspice
- ½ cup butter, softened
- 2 cups sliced fresh strawberries
  Whipped cream

1. Preheat oven to 350°. In a large bowl, cream shortening, butter and sugar until light and fluffy, 5-7 minutes. Add eggs, 1 at a time, beating well after each addition. In another bowl, whisk flour, baking powder and salt; add to creamed mixture alternately with the buttermilk, beating well after each addition. Transfer to a 12-in. cast-iron or other ovenproof skillet.
2. For streusel topping, in a small bowl, mix the flour, sugar, cinnamon and allspice; cut in the butter until crumbly. Sprinkle over batter. Top with the strawberries. Bake 50-60 minutes or until center is puffed and edges are golden brown. Serve warm with whipped cream.
1 piece: 526 cal., 27g fat (12g sat. fat), 74mg chol., 418mg sod., 64g carb. (33g sugars, 2g fiber), 6g pro.

PEANUT BUTTER & JELLY ICE CREAM

What could be better than peanut butter and jelly ice cream? You'll love the sweet-salty combination. Use your favorite flavor of jelly and switch to crunchy peanut butter if you like extra texture.
—*Taste of Home* Test Kitchen

Prep: 30 min. + freezing
Makes: 10 servings (1¼ qt.)

- 1½ cups whole milk
- ⅔ cup packed brown sugar
- ½ tsp. salt
- 1 large egg, lightly beaten
- ⅔ cup creamy peanut butter
- 2 cups heavy whipping cream
- 2 tsp. vanilla extract
- ½ cup grape jelly or strawberry jelly

1. In a large heavy saucepan, heat the milk, brown sugar and salt until bubbles form around sides of pan. Whisk a small amount of hot mixture into the egg. Return all to the pan, whisking constantly.
2. Cook and stir over low heat until mixture is thickened and coats the back of a spoon. Remove from heat; whisk in peanut butter. Quickly transfer to a bowl; place in ice water and stir for 2 minutes. Stir in cream and vanilla. Press waxed paper onto surface of custard. Refrigerate for several hours or overnight.
3. Fill the cylinder of ice cream freezer two-thirds full; freeze according to the manufacturer's directions.
4. When ice cream is frozen, spoon into a freezer container, layering with jelly; freeze for 2-4 hours before serving.
½ cup: 393 cal., 28g fat (14g sat. fat), 77mg chol., 231mg sod., 32g carb. (29g sugars, 1g fiber), 7g pro.

STRAWBERRY BUTTERMILK
SKILLET SHORTCAKE

TASTE OF HOME
TEST
KITCHEN
RECIPE OF THE YEAR
★★★★★

NO-BAKE CHOCOLATE CHIP CANNOLI CHEESECAKE

I make this cheesecake in the summer for a flavorful and refreshing treat. I love the added bonus of not having to turn on the oven in hot weather.
—Kristen Heigl, Staten Island, NY

Prep: 25 min. + chilling • **Makes:** 8 servings

1 pkg. (4 oz.) cannoli shells
½ cup sugar
½ cup graham cracker crumbs
⅓ cup butter, melted

FILLING

2 pkg. (8 oz. each) cream cheese, softened
1 cup confectioners' sugar
½ tsp. grated orange zest
¼ tsp. ground cinnamon
¾ cup part-skim ricotta cheese
1 tsp. vanilla extract
½ tsp. rum extract
½ cup miniature semisweet chocolate chips
Chopped pistachios, optional

1. Pulse the cannoli shells in a food processor until coarse crumbs form. Add sugar, cracker crumbs and melted butter; pulse just until combined. Press onto bottom and up sides of a greased 9-in. pie plate. Refrigerate until firm, about 1 hour.

2. Beat the first 4 filling ingredients until blended. Beat in ricotta cheese and extracts. Stir in chocolate chips. Spread into crust.

3. Refrigerate, covered, until set, about 4 hours. If desired, top with pistachios.

1 piece: 548 cal., 36g fat (20g sat. fat), 88mg chol., 292mg sod., 51g carb. (38g sugars, 1g fiber), 8g pro.

TEST KITCHEN TIP

Pistachios are classic in cannoli, but if you don't have them, you can still add crunch by topping the pie with additional crumbled cannoli shells.

NO-BAKE CHOCOLATE CHIP CANNOLI CHEESECAKE

BERRY, LEMON & DOUGHNUT HOLE TRIFLE

I was able to whip up this quick, yet impressive dessert, in only a few minutes after my son called and said he was bringing home his college roommates. It's been a family favorite ever since.
—Ellen Riley, Murfreesboro, TN

Takes: 25 min. • **Makes:** 10 servings

- 2 cups cold 2% milk
- 1 pkg. (3.4 oz.) instant lemon pudding mix
- 1 carton (8 oz.) frozen whipped topping, thawed and divided
- 16 to 32 plain doughnut holes
- 3 cups fresh strawberries, halved
- 2 cups fresh blueberries

1. Whisk milk and pudding mix for 2 minutes. Let stand for 2 minutes or until soft-set. Fold in 2½ cups whipped topping; set aside.
2. Place half the doughnut holes in a 3-qt. trifle bowl; spread half the pudding mixture over the top. Top pudding with half the strawberries and blueberries. Repeat layers. Top with remaining whipped topping. Chill until serving.
1 cup: 250 cal., 11g fat (7g sat. fat), 6mg chol., 250mg sod., 33g carb. (24g sugars, 2g fiber), 3g pro.

MINT CHOCOLATE CHEESECAKE

I created this mint chocolate cheesecake for our high school's annual fundraiser. We learned it brought a hefty price and was one of the first desserts to go! If desired, you can stir the cookie pieces into the batter instead of adding them in a layer. Keep the pieces fairly small, because otherwise they have a tendency to rise to the top.
—Sue Gronholz, Beaver Dam, WI

Prep: 20 min. • **Bake:** 1¼ hours + chilling
Makes: 16 servings

MINT CHOCOLATE
CHEESECAKE

- 1 cup Oreo cookie crumbs
- 3 Tbsp. sugar
- 2 Tbsp. butter, melted

FILLING
- 4 pkg. (8 oz. each) cream cheese, softened
- 1 cup sugar
- 1 cup white baking chips, melted and cooled
- 6 Tbsp. creme de menthe
- ¼ cup all-purpose flour
- 2 Tbsp. creme de cacao
- ½ tsp. peppermint extract
- 4 large eggs, room temperature, lightly beaten
- 1 cup coarsely crushed Oreo cookies (about 10 cookies)

GANACHE
- ¾ cup semisweet chocolate chips
- 6 Tbsp. heavy whipping cream

1. Preheat oven to 325°. Place a greased 9-in. springform pan on a double thickness of heavy-duty foil (about 18 in. square). Wrap foil securely around pan. In a small bowl, mix cookie crumbs and sugar; stir in butter. Press onto bottom of prepared pan.
2. In a large bowl, beat cream cheese and sugar until smooth. Beat in the cooled chips, creme de menthe, flour, creme de cacao and extract. Add the eggs; beat on low speed just until blended. Pour half the batter over crust; sprinkle with crushed Oreos. Carefully spoon remaining batter over top. Place springform pan in a larger baking pan; add 1 in. hot water to larger pan.
3. Bake until the center is just set and the top appears dull, 75-80 minutes. Remove the springform pan from water bath. Cool the cheesecake on a wire rack 10 minutes. Loosen sides from the pan with a knife; remove foil. Cool 1 hour longer. Refrigerate overnight, covering when completely cooled.
4. Remove rim from pan. Place chocolate chips in a bowl. In a saucepan, bring cream just to a boil. Pour over chocolate; stir with a whisk until smooth. Spread over cheesecake.
1 piece: 518 cal., 33g fat (18g sat. fat), 116mg chol., 296mg sod., 46g carb. (38g sugars, 1g fiber), 7g pro.

STRAWBERRY BLISS

STRAWBERRY BLISS

You'll love this homemade puff pastry crust topped with a soft-set pudding layer that has a hint of strawberry flavor. This dessert needs to chill for at least an hour, so it's a fabulous make-ahead dish.
—Candace Richter, Stevens Point, WI

- -

Prep: 30 min. • **Bake:** 20 min. + chilling
Makes: 12 servings

- 1 cup water
- ½ cup butter, cubed
- 1 cup all-purpose flour
- 4 large eggs, room temperature
- 1 pkg. (8 oz.) cream cheese, softened
- ½ cup sugar
- 5 Tbsp. seedless strawberry jam
- 3 cups cold whole milk
- 1 pkg. (5.1 oz.) instant vanilla pudding mix
- ½ cup heavy whipping cream
- 3 cups quartered fresh strawberries

1. Preheat oven to 400°. In a large saucepan, bring water and butter to a rolling boil. Add flour all at once and beat until blended. Cook over medium heat, stirring vigorously until mixture pulls away from sides of pan and forms a ball. Remove from heat; let stand 5 minutes.
2. Add 1 egg at a time, beating well after each addition. Continue beating until the mixture is smooth and shiny.
3. Spread into a greased 15x10x1-in. baking pan. Bake 20-25 minutes or until puffed and golden brown (surface will be uneven). Cool completely in pan on a wire rack.
4. In a large bowl, beat cream cheese, sugar and jam until smooth. Beat in the milk and pudding mix until smooth. In a small bowl, beat cream until stiff peaks form; fold into the pudding mixture. Spread over crust. Refrigerate at least 1 hour.
5. Just before serving, top the dessert with quartered strawberries.
1 piece: 377 cal., 22g fat (13g sat. fat), 131mg chol., 332mg sod., 40g carb. (27g sugars, 1g fiber), 7g pro.

CHOCOLATE & FRUIT TRIFLE

This pretty dessert layered with devil's food cake, a creamy pudding mixture, red berries and green kiwi is perfect for the holidays. I make it in a clear glass trifle bowl.
—Angie Dierikx, State Center, IA

- -

Prep: 20 min. + chilling
Bake: 20 min. + cooling
Makes: 16 servings

- 1 pkg. devil's food cake mix (regular size)
- 1 can (14 oz.) sweetened condensed milk
- 1 cup cold water
- 1 pkg. (3.4 oz.) instant vanilla pudding mix
- 2 cups heavy whipping cream, whipped
- 2 Tbsp. orange juice
- 2 cups fresh strawberries, chopped
- 2 cups fresh raspberries
- 2 kiwifruit, peeled and chopped

1. Prepare cake batter according to package directions; pour into a greased 15x10x1-in. baking pan. Bake at 350° for 20 minutes or until a toothpick inserted in the center comes out clean. Cool completely on a wire rack. Crumble enough cake to measure 8 cups; set aside. (Save remaining cake for another use.)
2. In a large bowl, whisk the milk, water and pudding mix for 2 minutes. Let stand for 2 minutes or until soft-set. Fold in the whipped cream.
3. To assemble, spread 2½ cups pudding mixture in a 4-qt. glass bowl. Top with half the crumbled cake; sprinkle with 1 Tbsp. orange juice. Arrange half the berries and kiwi over cake.
4. Repeat pudding and cake layers; sprinkle with remaining orange juice. Top trifle with the remaining pudding mixture. Spoon the remaining fruit around edge of bowl. Cover and refrigerate until serving.
1 cup: 419 cal., 22g fat (10g sat. fat), 77mg chol., 362mg sod., 51g carb. (35g sugars, 2g fiber), 6g pro.

FIGGY APPLE BRIE TART

Our family gatherings often included baked Brie. I transformed it into a dessert that's savory and sweet. It makes a wonderful appetizer, too.
—Kristie Schley, Severna Park, MD

- -

Prep: 25 min. • **Bake:** 15 min.
Makes: 8 servings

- 3 Tbsp. butter, softened
- ¾ cup sugar
- 2 large apples
- 1 cup dried figs, halved
- ½ lb. Brie cheese, rind removed, sliced
- 1 sheet refrigerated pie crust

1. Preheat oven to 425°. Spread butter over bottom of a 10-in. ovenproof skillet; sprinkle evenly with sugar.
2. Peel, quarter and core apples; arrange in a circular pattern over sugar, rounded side down. Place figs around apples. Place skillet over medium heat; cook until the sugar is caramelized and apples have softened slightly, 10-12 minutes. Remove from heat; top with cheese.
3. Unroll the crust; place over the apples, tucking under edges. Place the skillet in oven on an upper rack; bake until crust is golden brown, 15-18 minutes. Let cool in skillet 5 minutes. Carefully invert onto a serving plate; serve warm.
1 piece: 394 cal., 19g fat (11g sat. fat), 45mg chol., 315mg sod., 50g carb. (33g sugars, 2g fiber), 8g pro.

PEANUTTY CREAM-FILLED PASTRY SHELLS

These delicious desserts say indulgent and decadent, but couldn't be any easier to make. Make them ahead for that weekend party coming up; they're perfect for guests.
—Teri Rasey, Cadillac, MI

- -

Prep: 15 min. + freezing • **Bake:** 20 min.
Makes: 12 servings

- 2 pkg. (10 oz. each) frozen puff pastry shells
- 1 pkg. (8 oz.) cream cheese, softened
- 1 cup creamy peanut butter
- 1 can (14 oz.) sweetened condensed milk
- 1 tsp. lemon juice
- 1½ cups whipped topping
   Chocolate hard-shell ice cream topping
- ¼ cup chopped unsalted peanuts

1. Bake puff pastry shells according to package directions. Cool completely. Meanwhile, in a large bowl, beat cream cheese until light and fluffy. Add peanut butter, milk and lemon juice. Fold in the whipped topping.

2. Place shells on waxed paper-lined baking sheet. Remove tops; save for another use. Pour 1 tsp. hard-shell topping into each pastry shell. Mound ⅓ cup cream cheese mixture over topping. Drizzle with an additional 1 tsp. topping; sprinkle with peanuts. Freeze 30 minutes or until firm.

3. Let stand at room temperature for 5 minutes before serving.

1 serving: 601 cal., 42g fat (16g sat. fat), 32mg chol., 436mg sod., 47g carb. (28g sugars, 3g fiber), 15g pro.

SKILLET CARAMEL APRICOT GRUNT

SKILLET CARAMEL APRICOT GRUNT

Here's an old-fashioned pantry dessert made with items you can easily keep on hand. Mix up a second batch of the dry ingredients for the dumplings to save a few minutes the next time you prepare it.
—Shannon Norris, Senior Food Stylist

- -

Prep: 20 min. + standing • **Bake:** 20 min.
Makes: 8 servings

- 2 cans (15¼ oz. each) apricot halves, undrained
- 2 tsp. quick-cooking tapioca
- ⅓ cup packed brown sugar
- 1 Tbsp. butter
- 1 Tbsp. lemon juice

DUMPLINGS
- 1½ cups all-purpose flour
- ½ cup sugar
- 2 tsp. baking powder
- 2 Tbsp. cold butter
- ½ cup whole milk

TOPPING
- ¼ cup packed brown sugar
- 1 Tbsp. water
   Half-and-half cream, optional

1. In a large saucepan, combine apricots and tapioca; let stand for 15 minutes. Add the brown sugar, butter and lemon juice. Cook and stir until mixture comes to a full boil. Reduce heat to low; keep warm.

2. For dumplings, in a large bowl, combine the flour, sugar and baking powder; cut in butter until crumbly. Add milk; mix just until combined. Pour warm fruit mixture into an ungreased 9- or 10-in. cast-iron skillet. Drop the batter in 6 mounds onto fruit mixture.

3. Bake, uncovered, at 425° until a toothpick inserted into a dumpling comes out clean, about 15 minutes. Stir together the brown sugar and water; microwave until sugar is dissolved, stirring frequently, 30 seconds. Spoon over dumplings; bake 5 minutes longer. Serve with cream if desired.

1 serving: 336 cal., 5g fat (3g sat. fat), 13mg chol., 170mg sod., 71g carb. (51g sugars, 2g fiber), 4g pro.

CHOCOLATE & CARDAMOM COCONUT TART

This holiday-worthy tart with a cardamom-scented crust is my nod to our family's Scandinavian heritage. The filling is rich in all the right ways, with chocolate, coconut and cranberries.
—Carole Holt, Mendota Heights, MN

- -

Prep: 20 min. + chilling
Bake: 50 min. + cooling • **Makes:** 16 servings

1⅓ **cups butter, softened**
1⅓ **cups sugar**
2 **tsp. grated orange zest**
1 **large egg, room temperature**
2⅔ **cups all-purpose flour**
¾ **tsp. ground cardamom**
¾ **cup pistachios**
½ **cup fresh cranberries**
¾ **cup sweetened shredded coconut**
⅓ **cup plus ½ cup 60% cacao bittersweet chocolate baking chips, divided**
⅔ **cup sweetened condensed milk**
½ **cup white baking chips**
   Coarsely shredded orange zest, optional

1. Preheat oven to 325°. Cream butter, sugar and orange zest until light and fluffy, 5-7 minutes. Beat in egg. Add the flour and cardamom, mixing well. Divide dough in half. Cover and refrigerate for 30 minutes.
2. Meanwhile, pulse pistachios in a food processor until finely chopped; remove. Repeat with fresh cranberries. For filling, in a small bowl combine the chopped cranberries, coconut, ⅓ cup bittersweet chocolate chips, milk and ⅓ cup chopped pistachios.
3. Press half the dough onto bottom and ¼ in. up sides of a greased 9-in. springform pan. Spread cranberry mixture over dough. Between sheets of waxed paper, roll the remaining dough into a 9-in. circle. Remove top sheet of paper. Gently flip dough and place over pistachio filling; remove remaining paper. Press dough around edge to seal. Place pan on a 15x10-in. rimmed baking pan.

4. Bake until golden brown, 50-60 minutes. Cool in pan 15 minutes. Loosen sides from pan with a knife; cool completely. Remove rim from pan. Microwave the white baking chips on high until melted, stirring every 30 seconds; remove. Repeat with the remaining ½ cup bittersweet chips. Drizzle tart with white and bittersweet melted chocolate. Sprinkle with remaining ⅓ cup chopped pistachios and, if desired, orange zest.

Freeze option: Cover and freeze unbaked tart. To use, remove from freezer 30 minutes before baking (do not thaw). Preheat oven to 325°. Place tart on a baking sheet; cover loosely with foil. Bake as directed, increasing time as necessary. Cool and top as directed.
1 piece: 449 cal., 25g fat (15g sat. fat), 58mg chol., 185mg sod., 53g carb. (34g sugars, 2g fiber), 6g pro.

CHOCOLATE & CARDAMOM
COCONUT TART

CHOCOLATE PECAN PAVLOVA TORTE

This will definitely capture your taste buds! This recipe is one of my family's favorites—especially at the holidays. Although it may take a little longer to make and assemble, it is truly worth the work. It's a rich-tasting, light dessert that everyone will enjoy. I usually use pecans, but you can substitute walnuts, hazelnuts or other nuts.
—Nancy Preussner, Delhi, IA

- -

Prep: 25 min. • **Bake:** 45 min. + cooling
Makes: 8 servings

- 4 large egg whites, room temperature
- 1 tsp. vanilla extract
- ¼ tsp. cream of tartar
- 1⅔ cups sugar, divided
- 2 Tbsp. baking cocoa
- 1 cup ground pecans
- 4 oz. cream cheese, softened
- 2 Tbsp. butter, softened
- 1 cup heavy whipping cream
- 3 Tbsp. coffee liqueur
- ½ cup hot fudge ice cream topping, divided
- ¼ cup coarsely chopped pecans

1. Place the egg whites in a large bowl. Line a baking sheet with parchment. Trace two 8-in. circles 1 in. apart on the parchment; invert parchment.

2. Preheat oven to 300°. Add vanilla and cream of tartar to egg whites; beat on medium speed until foamy. Sift 1⅓ cups sugar and cocoa together twice. Gradually add sugar mixture, 1 Tbsp. at a time, beating on high after each addition until sugar is dissolved. Continue beating until stiff glossy peaks form. Gently fold in ground pecans. Spread evenly over circles on prepared pan.

3. Bake until meringue is set and dry, 45-55 minutes. Turn off oven (do not open oven door); leave meringues in oven 1 hour. Remove from oven; cool completely on baking sheet. Carefully remove 1 meringue to a serving plate.

4. In a large bowl, beat the cream cheese, butter and remaining ⅓ cup sugar until smooth. In a small bowl, beat cream until soft peaks form; fold into cream cheese mixture. Stir in the liqueur.

5. Spread ⅓ cup fudge ice cream topping over the meringue. Top with half the cream cheese filling. Layer with remaining meringue and remaining filling. Sprinkle with chopped pecans. Warm remaining fudge ice cream topping; drizzle over top. Refrigerate at least 2 hours before serving.

1 piece: 553 cal., 33g fat (13g sat. fat), 56mg chol., 129mg sod., 61g carb. (55g sugars, 2g fiber), 6g pro.

CHOCOLATE PECAN
PAVLOVA TORTE

MINIATURE NAPOLEONS

It can be a challenge to come up with an elegant sweet that works well for a cocktail party. These marvelous, bite-sized desserts are easy to enjoy while mingling.
—*Taste of Home* Test Kitchen

- -

Prep: 30 min. + chilling
Bake: 10 min. + freezing • **Makes:** 4½ dozen

6	Tbsp. sugar
2	Tbsp. cornstarch
¼	tsp. salt
1	cup 2% milk
1	large egg yolk, beaten
2	Tbsp. butter, divided
½	tsp. vanilla extract
1	sheet frozen puff pastry, thawed
½	cup heavy whipping cream
2	oz. semisweet chocolate, chopped

1. In a small saucepan, combine the sugar, cornstarch and salt. Stir in the milk until smooth. Cook and stir over medium heat until thickened and bubbly. Reduce heat; cook and stir 1 minute longer.
2. Remove from the heat. Stir a small amount of hot mixture into egg yolk; return all to the pan, stirring constantly. Bring to a gentle boil; cook and stir 1 minute longer. Remove from the heat. Stir in 1 Tbsp. butter and vanilla. Cool to room temperature without stirring. Refrigerate until chilled.
3. Unfold puff pastry; place on an ungreased baking sheet. Prick dough thoroughly with a fork. Bake according to package directions. Remove to a wire rack to cool.
4. In a small bowl, beat the cream until stiff peaks form. Fold into custard. Use a fork to split pastry in half horizontally. Spread filling over the bottom half; replace top. Cover and freeze for 4 hours or until firm.
5. Cut pastry into 1½x1-in. rectangles. In a microwave, melt chocolate and remaining butter; stir until smooth. Drizzle over the pastries. Freeze until serving.
1 serving: 49 cal., 3g fat (1g sat. fat), 8mg chol., 32mg sod., 5g carb. (2g sugars, 0 fiber), 1g pro. **Diabetic exchanges:** ½ starch, ½ fat.

CINNAMON TWIRL ROLY-POLY

My whole house smells incredible when this cake is in the oven. Change it up with other extracts—maple is heavenly.
—Holly Balzer-Harz, Malone, NY

Prep: 40 min. + chilling
Bake: 10 min. + cooling • **Makes:** 12 servings

- 3 **large eggs, room temperature**
- ¾ **cup sugar**
- ⅓ **cup water**
- 1 **tsp. vanilla extract**
- 1 **cup all-purpose flour**
- 1½ **tsp. baking powder**
  Dash salt
- 6 **Tbsp. butter, softened**
- ½ **cup packed brown sugar**
- 2 **tsp. ground cinnamon**

FILLING
- 4 **oz. cream cheese, softened**
- ¼ **cup butter, softened**
- 1 **cup confectioners' sugar**
- ½ **tsp. ground cinnamon**
- 1 **to 2 tsp. half-and-half cream or whole milk**
- ¼ **cup finely chopped walnuts, optional**

GLAZE
- ¼ **cup butter**
- 1½ **cups confectioners' sugar**
- 1 **tsp. vanilla extract**
- 2 **to 3 Tbsp. half-and-half cream or whole milk**
- ¼ **cup chopped walnuts, optional**

CINNAMON TWIRL ROLY-POLY

1. Preheat oven to 375°. Line bottom and sides of a greased 15x10x1-in. baking pan with parchment; grease parchment.

2. Beat eggs on high speed until thick and pale, about 5 minutes. Gradually beat in sugar until well mixed. Reduce speed to low; beat in water and vanilla. In another bowl, whisk together the flour, baking powder and salt; add to egg mixture, mixing just until combined.

3. Transfer batter to prepared pan. Bake until cake springs back when lightly touched, 10-12 minutes. Cool 5 minutes. Invert onto a kitchen towel dusted with confectioners' sugar. Gently peel off parchment. Roll up cake in the towel jelly-roll style, starting with a short side. Cool completely on a wire rack.

4. Meanwhile, beat butter, brown sugar and cinnamon until creamy. Unroll cake; spread brown sugar mixture over cake to within ½ in. of edges.

5. For filling, beat cream cheese and butter until creamy. Beat in confectioners' sugar and cinnamon; gradually add cream until mixture reaches a spreadable consistency. Spread filling over brown sugar mixture. If desired, sprinkle with walnuts. Roll up again, without towel; trim ends if needed. Place on a platter, seam side down.

6. For glaze, heat butter in a small saucepan over medium-low heat until foamy and golden, 6-8 minutes. Remove from heat. Stir in confectioners' sugar and vanilla, then add cream 1 Tbsp. at a time, stirring well, until mixture reaches a pourable consistency. Slowly pour glaze over top of cake, allowing some to flow over sides. If desired, top with chopped walnuts. Refrigerate, covered, at least 2 hours before serving.

1 slice: 396 cal., 18g fat (11g sat. fat), 93mg chol., 341mg sod., 56g carb. (47g sugars, 1g fiber), 4g pro.

PINEAPPLE UPSIDE-DOWN MUFFIN CAKES

A friend submitted this recipe to a cookbook our school district was compiling. The first time I made them, the whole family declared the recipe a winner. Delicious and light to boot, they remain favorites to this day.
—Joan Hallford, North Richland Hills, TX

- -

Prep: 25 min. • **Bake:** 15 min.
Makes: 1 dozen

- ⅓ cup packed brown sugar or 3 Tbsp. brown sugar substitute blend
- 2 Tbsp. butter, melted
- 3 canned pineapple slices

CAKES

- ⅓ cup butter, softened
- ½ cup sugar
- 1 large egg, room temperature
- ½ tsp. vanilla extract
- 1 cup all-purpose flour
- 1 tsp. baking powder
- ¼ tsp. baking soda
- ¼ tsp. salt
- ½ cup fat-free lemon or vanilla Greek yogurt
- ¼ cup fat-free milk

1. Preheat oven to 350°. Coat 12 muffin cups with cooking spray. Mix brown sugar and melted butter; divide among prepared cups. Quarter each pineapple slice; place 1 piece in each cup.
2. For cakes, cream butter and sugar until light and fluffy, 3-5 minutes; beat in egg and vanilla. In another bowl, whisk together flour, baking powder, baking soda and salt; add to creamed mixture alternately with yogurt and milk, beating well after each addition.
3. Fill prepared cups two-thirds full. Bake until a toothpick inserted in center comes out clean, 12-15 minutes. Cool in pan for 2 minutes; invert onto a serving plate. Serve warm or at room temperature.
1 muffin cake: 177 cal., 8g fat (5g sat. fat), 34mg chol., 178mg sod., 25g carb. (17g sugars, 0 fiber), 3g pro. **Diabetic exchanges:** 1½ starch, 1½ fat.

PEANUT BUTTER CUP NAPOLEONS

Top layers of puff pastry and peanut butter ice cream with a warm, sweet drizzle the whole family will love! It's a terrific last-minute dessert. Or make them a day in advance and pop them in the freezer.
—Jeanne Holt, Mendota Heights, MN

- -

Prep: 10 min. • **Bake:** 15 min. + cooling
Makes: 4 servings

- 1 sheet frozen puff pastry, thawed
- 2 cups peanut butter ice cream with peanut butter cup pieces, softened
- ¾ cup butterscotch-caramel ice cream topping
- 3 Tbsp. creamy peanut butter
- ¼ cup chopped chocolate-covered peanuts

1. Preheat oven to 400°. Unfold the puff pastry. Cut into eight 4½x2¼-in. rectangles. Place on a greased baking sheet. Bake until golden brown, 12-15 minutes. Cool completely on a wire rack.
2. Scoop ½ cup ice cream onto each of 4 pastries. Top with remaining pastries. Freeze until serving.
3. Combine ice cream topping and peanut butter in a small microwave-safe bowl. Cover and cook on high 30-45 seconds or until warmed. Drizzle over napoleons and sprinkle with peanuts.
1 serving: 994 cal., 54g fat (21g sat. fat), 78mg chol., 507mg sod., 112g carb. (56g sugars, 8g fiber), 18g pro.

PINEAPPLE UPSIDE-DOWN MUFFIN CAKES

**SUGAR PLUM
PHYLLO KRINGLE**

RASPBERRY SWIRL CHEESECAKE PIE

I use jam made from plentiful wild raspberries on our farm to give this pretty dessert its marbled effect. While the cheesecake refrigerates overnight, its flavors blend beautifully.
—Sandy McKenzie, Braham, MN

- -

Prep: 20 min. • **Bake:** 25 min. + chilling
Makes: 8 servings

    Pastry for single-crust pie
2 **pkg. (8 oz. each) cream cheese, softened**
½ **cup sugar**
½ **tsp. vanilla extract**
2 **large eggs, room temperature**
3 **Tbsp. raspberry jam**

1. On a floured surface, roll dough to fit 9-in. pie plate. Trim and flute edges. Line unpricked crust with a double thickness of heavy-duty foil. Bake at 450° for 5 minutes; remove foil. Bake 5 minutes longer. Remove from the oven; reduce heat to 350°.
2. In a bowl, beat cream cheese, sugar and vanilla until smooth. Add eggs, beating on low speed just until combined. Pour into pastry shell. Stir jam; drizzle over the filling. Cut through filling with a knife to swirl the jam. Bake for 25-30 minutes or until center is almost set. Cool on a wire rack for 1 hour. Refrigerate overnight. Let stand at room temperature for 30 minutes before slicing.
1 piece: 305 cal., 18g fat (10g sat. fat), 89mg chol., 200mg sod., 31g carb. (18g sugars, 0 fiber), 5g pro.
Dough for single-crust pie: Combine 1¼ cups all-purpose flour and ¼ tsp. salt; cut in ½ cup cold butter until crumbly. Gradually add 3-5 Tbsp. ice water, tossing with a fork until dough holds together when pressed. Cover and refrigerate 1 hour.

SUGAR PLUM PHYLLO KRINGLE

Thanks to store-bought phyllo dough, this pastry is easier to make than it looks. Serve it not only for dessert with a scoop of ice cream, but also for breakfast and brunch.
—Johnna Johnson, Scottsdale, AZ

- -

Prep: 30 min. • **Bake:** 20 min. + cooling
Makes: 6 servings

¾ **cup chopped dried apricots**
½ **cup dried cherries**
⅓ **cup water**
¼ **cup sugar**
¼ **cup raisins**
¾ **cup chopped walnuts**
1 **Tbsp. lemon juice**
1 **pkg. (8 oz.) cream cheese, softened**
12 **sheets (14x9 in. each) phyllo dough**
    Butter-flavored cooking spray
    Confectioners' sugar

1. Preheat oven to 375°. In a large saucepan, bring apricots, cherries, water, sugar and raisins to a boil. Reduce heat; simmer, uncovered, until liquid is thickened, about 6-8 minutes. Stir in walnuts and lemon juice. Remove from heat; cool completely.
2. In a small bowl, beat cream cheese until smooth. Place 1 sheet of phyllo dough on a work surface; spritz with cooking spray. Layer with remaining phyllo, spritzing each layer. Spread cream cheese over phyllo to within 2 in. of edges; top with dried fruit mixture. Fold in edges; roll up, starting with a long side.
3. Place in a parchment-lined 15x10x1-in. baking pan, seam side down. Spritz top with cooking spray. Bake until golden brown, 20-25 minutes. Cool on a wire rack. Sprinkle with confectioners' sugar.
1 slice: 446 cal., 25g fat (9g sat. fat), 38mg chol., 224mg sod., 52g carb. (31g sugars, 3g fiber), 7g pro.

RASPBERRY SWIRL
CHEESECAKE PIE

Recipe Index